The Graves Are Not Yet Full

THE GRAVES ARE NOT YET FULL

Race, Tribe and Power in the Heart of Africa

BILL BERKELEY

A New Republic Book

BASIC
BOOKS

A Member of the Perseus Books Group

Published by Basic Books,
A Member of the Perseus Books Group

Maps by Patti Isaacs.
Photo research by Alison Morley.

A Cataloging-in-Publication record for this book is available from the Library of Congress.
ISBN 0-465-00641-8

Design by Jane Raese
First edition

01   02   03   04 / 10   9   8   7   6   5   4   3   2   1

For Mary Jane

"You is sharks, sartin; but if you gobern de shark in you,

why den you be angel; for all angel is not'ing more

dan de shark well goberned."

  —Herman Melville, *Moby Dick*

"For the liberation of a people more is needed

than an economic policy, more than industry:

if a people is to become free, it needs pride and willpower,

defiance, hate, hate and once again hate."

  —Adolf Hitler, 1923

"You have missed some of the enemies.

You must go back there and finish them off.

The graves are not yet full!"

—Radio-Télévision Libre des Mille Collines, Kigali, Rwanda, 1994

CONTENTS

Prologue: A Farmer   1

Introduction   5

1   The Rebel   21

2   The Assistant Secretary   63

3   "A Voice of Good Sense and Good Will"   103

4   The Collaborator   143

5   Three Ph.D.s and a New Kind of African Leader   195

6   The Defendant   245

Acknowledgments   285
Bibliography   287
Index   295

PROLOGUE: A FARMER

"I KILLED BECAUSE I WAS FORCED TO," said that man in the dirty white shirt, his face knotted with anxiety, eyes averted. "I either had to do it or I would die myself. Many were killed for refusing to kill."

His name was François-Xavier Sibomana, forty-seven years old and balding. He had thin wrists and knobby, callused fingers. He was talking about the murder of his brother-in-law, Isaac Kimonyo.

"I did not kill him single-handedly," he explained. "We would converge on a person. We killed a number of people, but jointly." In his own village they killed nine people, he said. He used a machete; others used clubs. "I knew some of them personally. They were neighbors."

But his own brother-in-law?

"He did not deserve to die. He was an old man."

François rubbed his hands on his worn gray cotton trousers, crudely repaired with black stitches at the crotch. He brushed the ground with his blue canvas sneakers, with no laces, no socks. "We killed him in his house," he continued. "He was dragged from the bedroom and killed in the sitting room. Emmanuel struck him first. He was the leader of the militia. I could not do it myself. For me, I stood by and watched. There was nothing I could do."

Nothing he could do?

"I made no effort to stop the killers because we were led by the leader of the militia," François insisted. "So nobody would dare to ask to spare the man."

François Sibomana had spent most of his life cultivating sorghum and sweet potatoes on the steep mountain slopes of Kibungo Prefecture in eastern Rwanda. He said he had never killed before. He had a wife and eight children, though he didn't know where they were. He was now in captivity—an admitted member of the *Interahamwe* militia, "those who attack together," the Hutu death squads that had stabbed, clubbed and hacked to death up to a half million Rwandans, mostly ethnic Tutsis, in the weeks just prior to our meeting.

"Everybody had to join," François told me. "It was the thing to do."

We were sitting in a vacant lot in a rubble-strewn, rebel-held town called Kabuga, on the outskirts of Kigali, the Rwandan capital. It was June 1994. Rwanda's genocide was still unfolding in the south. Hundreds of dazed survivors of the massacres, some of them wrapped in gauze that barely concealed their hideous machete wounds, loitered amid the wreckage of their lives in the looted and gutted ruins nearby.

From a crackling transistor radio behind me I could hear Radio-Télévision Libre des Mille Collines (A Thousand Hills Free Radio-Television), the state-allied broadcasting arm. "Defend your rights and rise up!" a voice on the radio was singing. There were drums and guitars in the background. A popular crooner named Simon Bikindi was beseeching his fellow Hutus—the *bene sebahinzi*, the sons of cultivators—to carry on the slaughter without delay. "Defend your rights and rise up against those who want to oppress you!" The drumming and strumming had an oddly intimate effect. Bikindi was singing in riddles, addressing *mbira abumva*, "those who can understand." His voice was soft, gently cadenced, almost lyrical. He was warning his listeners of the malign intentions of the *bene sebatunzi*, the sons of pastoralists—the Tutsis. "The Tutsi are ferocious beasts, the most vicious hyenas, more cunning than the rhino," he cooed. "The Tutsi *inyenzi*"—cockroaches—"are bloodthirsty murderers. They dissect their victims, extracting vital organs, the heart, liver and stomach."

In the days leading up to my meeting with François, I had visited a plain brick church by a dirt road south of Kigali that was filled waist-high with about two hundred putrid, maggot-riddled, freshly slaughtered corpses. Later I met a wide-eyed eleven-year-old girl named Umulisa, dressed in a threadbare blue and red sweater, with smudged cheeks and a luminous smile. Umulisa had laughed at me hysterically, irrepressibly, rather than tell me in her own words about the day two weeks earlier when she fled from her home as the militia arrived, then returned an hour later and discovered her mother and father, brothers and sisters, aunts and uncles in a heap of severed heads and arms and legs on the floor of her living room.

The previous evening, in an abandoned store less than a block from the lot in which François and I were talking, I had met a middle-aged gentleman named Isadore, who had survived with his wife and children but lost twenty immediate relatives. Isadore had stared at me with tired, quizzical eyes. "I was very much surprised," he said. "Looking at my neighbors, I thought they were friends. I was very much surprised that they were among the people who came to try to kill us."

As I sat now with François in that vacant lot in Kabuga, the old familiar questions were running through my mind, from another part of the world, a half century earlier: How was such a horror possible? How could ordinary men like this one—a farmer, middle-aged, the father of eight—participate in a monstrous crime? What malignant blend of bigotry and fear, coercion or cowardice, history, politics, poverty and ignorance, envy, opportunism, unquestioning obedience, peer pressure perhaps—what brought out the shark in this man?

I looked into François' eyes. He seemed bewildered by my questions. All he said was this: "The message from the top was passed down to the local village chiefs, the *conseillers*. The *conseillers* had lists of Tutsis who should be killed. They simply organized their constituents."

He kicked a pebble and stared into the middle distance.

"The leaders of the party and the leaders of the militia rounded up all the men in the village. We were told that we had a mission. We were given a list of people to kill. If we met someone on the list, they would be killed."

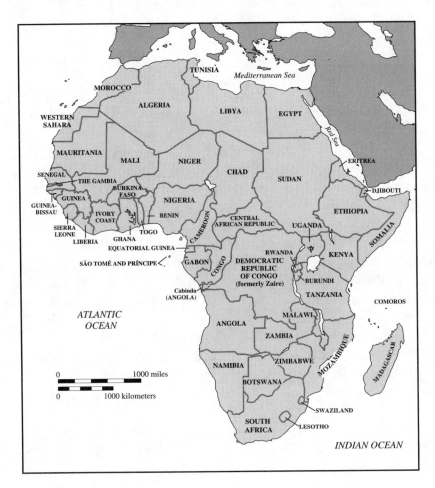

Africa

INTRODUCTION

THIS IS A BOOK ABOUT EVIL. Its setting is Africa. The characters are mostly African, with an American narrator and Americans in supporting roles. The time is the last decade of the twentieth century, post–Cold War. But the questions are timeless and universal: How do evil people operate? What accounts for their power? Why do people follow?

I first went out to Africa in 1983 as a wide-eyed freelance newspaper correspondent drawn to the great emancipation drama then unfolding in South Africa. I had fancied myself a budding specialist on race relations when, fresh out of college a few years earlier, I had gone to work for newspapers in Alabama and Georgia. But I was born too late to witness the wrenching traumas of the civil rights era. I had studied history in college, and as a journalist I wanted to watch history in the making. I was also the sort of person who, while shopping for fitted bedsheets in a Kmart in suburban Atlanta, felt myself suffocating, yearning to explore some of the grittier precincts of the globe. The struggle to bring down apartheid was my kind of story: a stirring crusade against manifest evil, the infamous system of racial tyranny helpfully delineated in black and white.

As is often the case in Africa, things didn't work out the way I had planned them. Visa problems kept me out of South Africa for a time, and so I wound up taking the slow road down the continent from Cairo: trains, buses, boats, trucks, taxis packed so tightly that my arms and legs fell asleep. There is a joke among expatriates in Sudan that once you have drunk from the White Nile, you're infected for life. In spite of myself, I had to agree. There was something about Africa that got into my blood and stayed there.

Partly it was the magnitude of the dramas sweeping the continent. Africa is a part of the world, I discovered, where multiple eras of history are taking place simultaneously: biblical plagues and famines, genocide, slavery, revolution, emancipation, nation building. In Sudan, I learned, a civil war had begun the year I was born and lasted until I was in high school. Half a million southern Sudanese had died. This was ten times as many casualties as Americans suffered during roughly the same period in Vietnam, out of a population one tenth the size. I considered myself reasonably well informed, with as good an education as money can buy. Yet I had never heard of this war.

In February 1983 I bounced and lurched for three days on top of a coffee truck that broke down eleven times between Costi and Juba, the heart of what had been Sudan's war zone. In a mud-walled town called Malakal, I was told that Sudan's war might start all over again, and a few months later it did. The latest round of war has lasted seventeen years and so far has claimed another 2 million lives—the greatest number of civilian casualties in any conflict since World War II. And it has featured devastating famine, locust plagues and AIDS, slavery, genocide, ethnic cleansing, warlordism, feudalism, capitalism, communism, terrorism, military dictatorships, Cold War intrigue, radical Islam—even five chaotic years of multiparty democracy.

Mostly, though, what gripped me in Sudan and across much of the rest of the continent was the people I was meeting. From afar, the Africans who appear in news photographs and on our television screens come across as an undifferentiated mass of pathetic victims. Up close, the personalities I was encountering were as vivid and alive as any I had ever met. The awesome struggles of their lives, the extreme, all-consuming dramas in which they were entwined, seemed to draw out human qualities that were unusually stark, larger than life.

Those whom I came to admire most displayed not just the stoicism for which Africans are justly renowned, but bravery, idealism, generosity of spirit, a capacity for forgiveness, outrageous humor. I worked for a time as an investigative reporter for a human rights organization in the mid-1980s. I found myself working alongside African journalists who routinely risked arrest and beatings, or worse, while they hunted and pecked on clattering manual typewriters under ceiling fans, amid the din of electric generators, speaking the truth to power. There were doctors and nurses tending to mine victims in grimy, fly-ridden wards without the benefit of basic medicines or even running water. There were priests and lawyers diligently documenting the latest summary killings, beatings and gang rapes. And there were the witnesses and survivors themselves, recounting unimaginable horrors with austere dignity.

Then there were the bad guys. Up close, there was little evidence that Africa's villains were any more venal than scoundrels elsewhere in the world through the ages. On the contrary, from the boy "fighters" looting toys and sweets in Monrovia to the dim-witted careerists in the old South African Police, there was more than a little evidence for Hannah Arendt's notion of the banality of evil. Yet there seemed to be something about the arenas in which they were operating that rendered their calculations and miscalculations hugely destructive. There was something about Africa that seemed to bring out the worst in people—or at least, in the Darwinian sense, to select for the worst among them.

America's awareness of Africa focuses overwhelmingly on the victims. I found I was interested mostly in the perpetrators: the "Big Men" and their acolytes, the warlords and militiamen, smugglers and con artists, gangsters and spies. I wanted to meet as many of these people as I could: the cast of characters at the top, especially, whose interests and machinations and evasions of responsibility might help explain the suffering of so many below. They became the main targets of my reporting, and they are the primary subjects of this book.

In 1997, at the height of the war that brought down Mobutu Sese Seko in Zaire, *The New Republic* published a special issue devoted to Africa. The cover featured a striking black-and-white photograph of ragged refugees in flight, and an ominous headline across the top in appropriately grim, gray letters: "AFRICA IS DYING." The headline captured the conventional American conception of Africa as a unitary landscape of unremitting despair. But this and other attempts at apocalyptic concision hardly squared with my experience of a continent churning with passion and rage. Most Africans I encountered, far from passively succumbing to their fate, were struggling mightily, and ingeniously, to survive. Others, for reasons of their own, were killing, raping, torturing and looting. On the ground, at least, Africa felt less like a terminal ward than a seething, writhing, operatic drama charged with intrigue, dominated by larger-than-life characters trapped in Macbethian logic, compelled to shed ever greater quantities of blood merely to survive.

"A black and incomprehensible frenzy"

My first newspaper dispatch from Africa appeared in May 1983 in the *Atlanta Journal-Constitution*. It was an account of a massacre in Uganda. This was in the final stages of Uganda's descent into huge-scale mass slaughter—the work of Idi Amin, and of the less notorious but no less wanton Milton Obote. Possibly a million Ugandans were murdered in two decades of sheer terror. The massacre I reported on was a lurid affair in which seventy men, women and children were hacked to pieces in the region north of Kampala known as the Luwero Triangle. Between 1980 and 1986, a quarter of Luwero's children were orphaned by Obote's notorious Uganda National Liberation Army. For my readers back in Georgia, I explained the massacre with a cursory paragraph summarizing what I called "complex tribal, religious and political divisions that have crippled the country since independence from Britain in 1962."

I had no idea what I meant by "tribal," or what "tribalism" had to do with politics, or what politics had to do with religion, or why any of this had become violently problematic since the demise of British colonial rule. For that matter, I knew next to nothing about the mechanics of British colonial rule.

For me, and no doubt for most of my readers, this latest massacre in Uganda fit the familiar image of Africa as a "heart of darkness," a primitive world where the law of the jungle obtains, as if the jungle were unique to Africa or inherent in its people. "Unspeakable," "mysterious," "a black and incomprehensible frenzy"—these were the words Joseph Conrad himself used to evoke the image of black Africa in a white man's mind, an image of what he called "an implacable force brooding over an inscrutable intention."

Many Americans still imagine that Africa's seemingly chronic carnage flows from some mysterious, exotic savagery. Much of American media coverage of Africa conveys an impression of "age-old hatreds." Not a few books and articles I carried in my rucksack on that first trip down the continent fed the perception that Africans are different, possessed of an inherent, unknowable impulse toward violence. David Lamb's survey, *The Africans*, had just been published that spring. An admirable book in many ways, it nevertheless reinforced this notion of the Africans as a breed apart. Lamb wrote: "Below the paper-thin veneer of civilization in Africa lurks a savagery that waits like a caged lion for an opportunity to spring."

One might have hoped we civilized white folks had long since learned as much about ourselves. Hitler killed 6 million Jews. Stalin killed 20 million Soviets. Japanese imperial troops machine-gunned, bayoneted, raped and beheaded some 300,000 Chinese civilians in just six weeks in the Rape of Nanking.

The worst genocide in recorded African history was perpetrated not by Africans but by the Belgians, in what came to be known as the Belgian Congo—Europe's richest colony in Africa and the actual setting for Conrad's *Heart of Darkness*. Between 1885 and 1912 King Leopold's private army, composed primarily of African conscripts led by European officers, shot, starved, and worked to death between 5 million and 10 million native inhabitants.

More than a decade after *The Africans* was published, two more widely read books by American journalists, one black, one white, echoed Lamb's theme of inscrutable otherness. Keith B. Richburg, a correspondent for the *Washington Post*, reflected on the slaughter he witnessed in Rwanda in *Out of Africa: A Black Man Confronts Africa*. Richburg described young killers "carrying clubs and machetes and Panga knives and smashing their neighbors' skulls and chopping off their limbs," and he concluded: "Fully evolved human beings in the 20th Century don't do things like that."

Robert D. Kaplan, in an influential article in *The Atlantic Monthly*, "The Coming Anarchy," wrote that "in places where the Western enlightenment has not penetrated and where there has always been mass poverty, people find liberation in violence. . . . Physical aggression is part of being human. Only when people attain a certain economic, educational and cultural standard is this trait tranquilized." In his subsequent book, *The Ends of the Earth: A Journey at the Dawn of the New Century*, Kaplan speculated that Liberia's civil war was a product of "new-age primitivism" born of "superstitions" that supposedly flourish in tropical rain forests.

This book is intended in part as a pointed rebuttal to that sort of nonsense. In a decade of reporting from East, West, Central and Southern Africa, in which I traveled some 25,000 miles through two dozen countries, seeking answers from Africans—soldiers and priests, politicians, scholars, diplomats, lawyers, doctors and nurses, journalists, anthropologists, civil servants, market women, street children, money changers, bartenders, truck drivers and all manner of victims and perpetrators high and low, left and right, black and white, rich and poor—I found no evidence of "new age primitivism" or "superstitions" that could explain mass murder.

The key actors who appear in this book are sophisticated, highly intelligent, and well educated. Many have graduate degrees from elite universities in England, France, and the United States, and several have Ph.D.s. A conspicuous feature of Africa's seemingly primitive conflicts is the central role played by intellectuals in fomenting them. The killers themselves, like François Sibomana of Rwanda, may be illiterate, dressed in rags and rubber flip-flops. Their leaders, when I met them, were notably suave, clean-shaven, smartly dressed, with soft hands and sensible shoes. Charles Taylor, the Liberian "rebel," wore shiny black Oxfords. So did South Africa's Zulu "chief," Mangosuthu Gatsha Buthelezi. His co-conspirator, General Pieter Hendrik "Tienie" Groenewald, former chief of South African Military Intelligence in Pretoria, wore light-gray soft leather Hush Puppies. Jac Buchner, one of apartheid's most notorious covert operatives, wore Topsiders and blue kneesocks, his golfing attire. Chester Crocker, President Reagan's assistant secretary of state for African affairs, wore brown suede wingtips.

It took a few more years and more than a few massacres, but by the time I met François Sibomana in 1994, I had come to understand that the forces that drove men like him to barbarism are no more peculiar to Africa—and no less evil—than the forces that drove fascism a half century earlier are to Europe.

The ultimate question I put to François—"How is such a horror possible?"—is no more readily answered in Central Africa than it has been in Central Europe. Yet in Africa as in Europe there are elements that can be understood. This thing called "tribalism" is barbarous, it is evil, but it is not exotic. In each of the conflicts I came to know best in the decade after that first massacre in Uganda in 1983, I found a constellation of factors and events and personalities that obeyed a recognizable logic. These catastrophes are not as senseless as they seem. They are not inevitable products of primordial, immutable hatreds. There is method in the madness.

"Kinship corporations"

But what do I mean by evil? The individuals encountered here are not all evil people. What they have in common is not the depth of their venality as individuals but the extent to which, collectively, they personify some of the roots and requirements of large-scale mass slaughter. Each in his own way is a creature of evil, and each has magnified the potential for evil in the arena in which he has operated. Each embodies a history, a culture, a symbiosis of interests, calculations, and assumptions which, taken together, add up to a catalog of essential elements that can transform latent evil into reality. And each has been a survivor, a well-adapted creature of a malignant environment.

This is a book about the methods of tyranny. Its central argument is that ethnic conflict in Africa is a product of tyranny. By "product" I mean in both an immediate sense—it is a tactic that tyrants use to divide and rule—as well as in a deeper, historical sense: ethnic conflict is a legacy of tyranny.

The countries examined here—Liberia, Congo-Zaire, South Africa, Sudan, Uganda and Rwanda—are diverse in many ways, but they have this much in common: all have at least a century-long history of racial or ethnically based tyranny. Belgian and British colonial rule, apartheid in South Africa, Arab domination in Sudan, and the oligarchy of the Americo-Liberians, descendants of freed American slaves—all were race-based tyrannies, and all relied upon institutionalized mechanisms of coercion and co-optation that were inherently divisive.

Ethnically based militias, ethnically skewed education systems, arbitrary justice, and, above all, "indirect rule"—the widespread colonial practice of dominating a majority by investing power and privilege in a favored minority—had a way of outlasting the tyrannies they were designed to preserve. They seeped into the social and political fabric of society, and into the minds of its inhabitants. They rendered these countries especially vulnerable to the divisive tactics of those just cynical and reckless enough to exploit this vulnerability for their own ends.

This interplay between the man and the moment, the reckless individual and his combustible environment, the one shaping the other and vice versa in a fusion that yields huge-scale mass murder—this is what I mean by evil.

There is a widespread assumption that "tribalism" is an indelible remnant of traditional, precolonial Africa, reflecting ancient, atavistic enmities. The opposite is the case. What we think of as tribalism in Africa is a relatively modern phenomenon that evolved in response to outside interventions rather than in spite of them.

The Nigerian historian Peter Ekeh has argued that the spread and reinforcement of "kinship ties and manipulations"—what we think of today as "tribalism"—became a dominant mode of political life in Africa in the major slaving years, in the eighteenth century or earlier, when the existing states either failed to defend citizens from violence and enslavement or collaborated with the slave traders. Tribalism was a form of self-defense. Slave-trading African states became dependent for their viability on external sources, whether to export captives for enslavement or to import the firearms that slaving raids (or defense against them) required. As these slaving states became increasingly predatory, Ekeh concluded, "Kinship systems were strengthened and elaborated as a means of providing protection against the dangers of the violence created by the slave trade."

The very term "tribe" came into general use in the colonial era. The term was associated with stereotypes of Africans as primitive brutes. For evolutionist anthropologists in their nineteenth-century heyday, "tribal" society conjured up an early stage of human development with minimal state organization, class structure, literacy or other features of "civilized" societies.

But the gathering of Africans into identifiable "tribes" was also a convenient administrative tool. Particularly under British administration, in countries like Uganda, Kenya and South Africa, administrative subdivisions were built upon this image of "tribal" blocks. Tribalism solved the colonial dilemma of how to dominate and exploit vast numbers of indigenous inhabitants with a limited number of colonial agents, by mobilizing groups on the basis of linguistic and cultural similarities that formerly had been irrelevant.

Ethnic consciousness has grown since the demise of colonial rule, along with uneven development and individual and group competition within the borders left behind by the colonial powers. In just the same way as "kinship corporations" were strengthened as a means of protection against a predatory state during the slave trade, the predatory nature of postcolonial or "neocolonial" states provoked self-defense by means of kinship ties and their bureaucratic equivalents, and with this, a corresponding subversion of the state by smuggling and related kinds of economic crime. The deadly conflicts examined here all occurred in situations of acute economic competition and deep poverty, where the state was perceived as representing the interests of a single dominant group.

There is nothing "primitive" or irrational about this. The eminent British historian Richard Sandbrook, in his seminal work, *The Politics of Africa's Economic Stagnation*, put it this way: "Ethnic consciousness, we must affirm, is neither irrational nor ephemeral. From the perspective of ordinary people, ethnicity appears no less sensible a basis for political mobilization than class. Ethnic mobilization, after all, is just a means to an end, a way of forging a coalition to pursue scarce material benefits."

Not least among these benefits, he might have added, is security. For among the most important legacies of a century of colonial tyranny was the absence of legitimate institutions of law and accountability. Justice was in the eye of the colonial power, and served its interests. Police powers were all but completely unchecked. The coercive arms of authority—police and army, secret police—were often ethnically based, and they tended to outlast the tyrannies they were created to defend.

It should also be stressed here that although "tribalism"—what the Kenyan scholar Michael Chege has called "neo-fascist ethnic extremism"—is widespread in parts of Africa today, my own experience across the continent has taught me that Africans in ever greater numbers favor ethnic and racial tolerance, the rule of law, and the sanctity of individual rights. Hate mongering in Africa, no less than elsewhere in the world, is an acquired skill.

"Kill the slave through the slave"

Africa in the decade since the end of the Cold War has been in thrall to embattled tyrannies. Some of its worst tyrants have been rendered especially vulnerable—and therefore especially dangerous—for reasons of history and circumstance much akin to those in the Balkans, Afghanistan, and parts of the former Soviet Union. In all of these regions the divisive potential of ethnicity has been magnified amid the shifting ground between tyranny and anarchy.

Many suppose that tyranny and anarchy are at opposite ends of a linear spectrum. But often they are side by side on what might better be described as a circle: the one is a product of the other, and vice versa. The law of the jungle does obtain in parts of Africa, but the jungle is inhabited by men. Anarchy is a vacuum that brings out the worst in men and selects for the worst among them. The pursuit of power is a life-and-death struggle. Those who excel distinguish themselves through nothing more exotic than boundless cunning and ruthlessness. The most successful of all become tyrants, and the anarchy in which they thrive is called tyranny.

Even the most rigidly institutionalized tyrannies—Rwanda was one, South Africa another—rely above all on the total absence of lawful accountability for the criminal abuse of power. They harness the forces of anarchy to their own ends, the forces of lawlessness and terror, murder and rape, arson and theft. For them, anarchy is an instrument of tyranny.

In South Africa, where "black-on-black" violence killed 20,000 between 1985 and 1994 and nearly derailed the transition to majority rule, they called it "informal repression." The Afrikaner police who fueled the fighting called it the *"kleur teen kleur beginsel"*—the "color-against-color principle."

In Sudan, where northern Arabs through the ages have dominated the state and decimated the south by pitting one black African tribe against another, they say *"Aktul al-abid bil abid"*—"Kill the slave through the slave."

It is a phenomenon that runs like poison through all of Africa's seemingly senseless wars: Big Men using little men, cynically maneuvering for power and booty while thousands perish. Harnessing proxies, arming ethnically based militias, cultivating warlords, propagating hate and fear, preying on ignorance, manufacturing rumors and myths, stacking the police and army with ethnic kinsmen, demonizing dissidents as traitors to the tribe, or faith, or *"volk"*—these are the tactics of the crafty despot with his back against the wall.

Call it "tribalism," call it "nationalism," call it "fundamentalism"—the role of political leaders in fomenting civil conflicts has been the paramount human rights issue of the post–Cold War era. Africa is merely that part of the world where it has been most destructive by far.

Inflamed ethnic passions are not the cause of political conflict, but its consequence. In a lawless world, ethnicity is a badge of legitimacy and protection—and justice. It is the bond by which men high and low adhere to a vigilante code. Lesser men like François Sibomana may appear to be acting on mindless, "primitive" impulse; in fact, they are making rational calculations of their own self-interest—not least, survival. The depth of their preexisting prejudices may explain the potency of the symbols their leaders choose to exploit, but it is the logic of their lawless environment that transforms those prejudices into terror.

Ethnic conflict in Africa is a form of organized crime. The "culture" driving Africa's conflicts is akin to that of the Sicilian Mafia, or of the Crips and Bloods in Los Angeles, with the same imperatives of blood and family that bind such gangs together. Africa's warring factions are best understood not as "tribes" but as racketeering enterprises, their leaders calculating strategy after the time-honored logic of Don Vito Corleone.

It is the stakes in Africa that are different—multiplied exponentially in circumstances where the state itself is a gang and the law doesn't exist. It is as if men like Vito Corleone seized control of not just "turf" on the margins of society, but of the state itself and all of its organs: police and army, secret police, the courts, the central bank, the civil service, the press, TV and radio.

A widespread misconception of the post–Cold War era is that ethnic conflict is a by-product of "failed states." Rwanda represented the opposite: a state—albeit criminal—that was all too successful in mobilizing along rigidly hierarchical lines from the top down, from the head of state and his ruling clique down to the last village mayor, making possible the slaughter, mostly with clubs and machetes, of hundreds of thousands in barely three months.

"The message from the top was passed down," François Sibomana told me. Indeed, it is by now well established that Rwanda's catastrophe was "more than a simple tribal meltdown," as *Time* magazine put it. All too often, however, the calculated quality of Rwanda's genocide is cited to distinguish it from other, presumably spontaneous African slaughters. But there is no such thing as a "simple tribal meltdown." There were elements in Rwanda that distinguished it from other African calamities, but calculation was not among them. Nor was the depth of evil. All of Africa's conflicts are orchestrated from on high. They are all products of calculated evil.

"The enemy of my enemy is my friend"

"I killed nobody," François Sibomana was telling me now. It was March 1998. Four years after our first encounter in Kabuga, I had returned to Rwanda and tracked François down in the huge Nsimda Prison in his native Kibungo Prefecture. The middle-aged father of eight, who in June 1994 had told me he was "forced to kill" his brother-in-law, was one of 125,000 accused *génocidaires* languishing in densely crowded, stench-filled, disease-ridden jails across Rwanda.

He looked fitter than he had four years earlier, dressed now in the standard prison-issue pink cotton tunic and shorts, with white rubber flip-flops. And like nearly all of the accused in custody four years after the slaughter, François now denied participating in genocide.

Had he not, after all, killed his brother-in-law? I asked.

"It's not true," he replied. "That's not what happened. I did not tell you that."

In fact, he had told me that and I believed him. I don't believe his denial. But who is to know, and how? François said he had yet to be charged, had never seen a lawyer, and knew of no plans for a trial. The Rwandan government, for its part, was estimating that at its current rate, genocide trials would be completed in four hundred years.

This is, finally, a book about justice. There are many challenges for Africans to surmount if they can ever hope to reverse the multiple afflictions besetting their continent. Most of them are beyond the scope of this book. But none is more important than justice, and none will amount to much at all in the absence of justice. By that I mean, among other things, justice in its most basic sense: accountability to law for criminal acts—not least those committed by the Big Men on high. This is not a policy prescription from afar. It is what Africans themselves across a broad spectrum routinely risk their lives and livelihoods for.

A common illusion of the post–Cold War era is that the superpower rivalry suppressed traditional ethnic rivalries that have since resurfaced with a vengeance. In fact, all too often the opposite has been the case. The superpowers did precious little to suppress ethnic conflicts and much to spawn them—by elevating, financing, and arming tyrants who would one day exploit ethnicity as a means of clinging to power. Buffeted by history's changing winds, bereft of their superpower backing, one by one the embattled creatures of the old world order have struggled to survive in the new by playing the ethnic card.

Until the end of the Cold War the United States paid scant heed to the rule of law in Africa. Understandably perhaps, given the global competition with communism, we threw in our lot with the meanest of the meanest, embracing the logic that "the enemy of our enemy is our friend." We rationalized our choice of clients with patronizing references to the "standards of Africa." But those were the standards of gangsters and tyrants throughout history. We neglected a basic lesson taught by all of Africa's wars: bigotry is fueled by injustice, and injustice causes conflict.

Americans tend to think of Africa's wars as remote from our history and irrelevant to our interests. In fact, the United States is deeply implicated in all of the tyrannies examined here. And it was not just Cold War zealots who armed and financed, apologized, rationalized or looked the other way. Private American interests ponied up essential capital. Firestone, for example, operated the world's largest rubber plantation in Liberia for nearly a century. At the time of Burundi's genocide in 1972, when a Tutsi-dominated army murdered between 100,000 and 200,000 Hutus, Folgers, the American coffee giant, accounted for 65 percent of Burundi's foreign exchange earnings. Cold Warriors and industrialists were abetted for years by the quiet collusion of many liberals and African Americans, who for reasons of their own refrained from pointing the finger at black African tyrants.

The Clinton administration was justly condemned for turning a blind eye as Rwanda descended into genocide. But President Clinton's belatedly acknowledged brush-off of Rwanda was consistent with a century-long involvement with Africa by Americans left and right, black and white, characterized less by mere neglect than by active complicity in tyranny. We were the enablers.

This book is not a comprehensive survey of an entire continent in chaos. Not all the news in Africa is bad, and much of it is hopeful. Even the bad news has long since moved beyond this book's central preoccupations. In the spring of 2000, the entire continent did seem to be spiraling into chaos. A broad swath of interconnected, mutually reinforcing conflicts extended all the way from the Horn of Africa in the northeast down to Namibia in the southwest. Sierra Leone was the crisis of the moment, as rebels infamous for chopping off the limbs of civilians, led by the notorious warlord and diamond smuggler Foday Sankoh—Charles Taylor's protégé—took hostage a hapless contingent of U.N. peacekeepers and besieged the capital, Freetown. Congo, formerly Zaire, was being torn asunder by a veritable kaleidoscope of outside predators and proxies. The erstwhile rebel Laurent Kabila, who had succeeded in ousting Mobutu Sese Seko after a seven-month war in 1997, was now fighting against his former allies, Uganda and Rwanda, and they in turn were fighting each other. The U.N. estimated that 1.7 million Congolese had died in just two years of war and related famine and disease.

In the Horn of Africa, meanwhile, Ethiopia and Eritrea, former allies, were reigniting a horrendous border conflict that featured trench warfare reminiscent of World War I. All but forgotten in the rush of depressing news were the old perennials, Sudan and Angola, where the decades of war and pillaging carry on with no end in sight.

I watched these events from afar, from the home office of the *New York Times* in midtown Manhattan, where by then I was writing editorials. But the patterns of conflict were familiar. These latest examples merely reinforced the lessons I had begun to learn as far back as that first massacre in Uganda in 1983, and which I had sought to examine systematically in a series of magazine assignments for *The Atlantic Monthly*, beginning in Liberia in 1992. Those lessons, rather than the latest breaking news, are my subject here.

My aim is to illuminate ethnic conflict generally, using African examples. I point the finger at tyranny not so much to condemn as to describe, to scrutinize, to break it down into its component parts and see how they work. Justice here is not only an answer to tyranny but a window on it; I qualify not as a prosecutor but as a witness.

A word about numbers. Nearly 2 million dead in Sudan, as many as 800,000 killed in Rwanda, 150,000 in Liberia—numbers like these defy comprehension, and they may make a figure like 20,000 killed in South Africa look like, well, a "peaceful" transition to majority rule. Yet the number killed in South Africa's embattled province of KwaZulu-Natal *since* the historic 1994 election exceeds the total number killed in thirty years of sectarian violence in Northern Ireland; it's more than the number of Palestinians killed in the entire seven-year *Intifada* against Israeli occupation. The value we attach to numbers is often arbitrary. The element of race has a way of coloring our judgement. Virtually all of those casualties in KwaZulu-Natal were black. Yet they were, as we shall see, most assuredly produced by the tactics and legacies of white tyranny—the most recognizably evil of any of the tyrannies examined here.

The bad guys in this book are black and white, and shades in between. So are the good guys. These stories are a measure of how much Africans have in common with the rest of humankind, not how much they differ. The Kenyan scholar Michael Chege, long since exiled from his homeland, put it this way: "Today there is genuine cultural diversity in the gallery of twentieth-century demonology, the late arrival of black fascism providing the ultimate testimony that political sin, as with all other kinds of sin and virtue, truly knows no color."

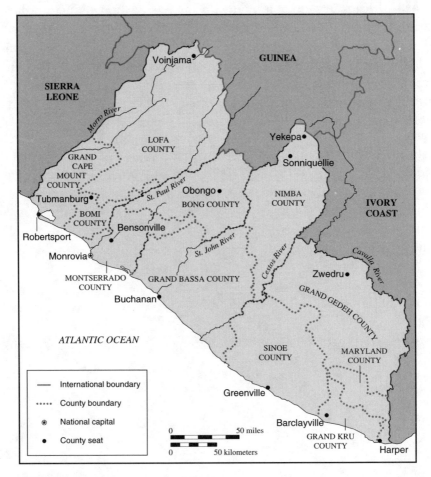

Liberia

1

THE REBEL

On a Saturday morning in June 1992, the Liberian port of Buchanan sweltered in the dense tropical humidity of West Africa's rainy season. Four small boys ambled up a muddy and pothole-ridden sidewalk and entered a tea stall on the city's main street. They looked to be scarcely older than ten. Dressed in baggy jeans and grimy T-shirts, not much taller than the loaded Soviet-era Kalashnikov assault rifles they cradled in their arms, the boys shuffled heavily in big brown military boots that on them resembled the outsized paws on a puppy.

"How the day?" one of them muttered.

A shudder ran down my spine. The bullets were bigger than his fingers. The boy brushed by the stool where I was sitting and approached the woman who owned the stall. He lifted his fingers to his mouth. The owner dutifully fetched some bananas and buttered some rolls. The boys shuffled out into the street—no word of thanks, no suggestion of payment—savoring their breakfast as they walked.

It was six years since I had last visited Liberia, a country founded by freed American slaves and for a century and a half America's closest ally in Africa. In 1986 I had written some unkind words about the country's mercurial tyrant, Samuel K. Doe, and his confederates, and Doe had flattered me with a personal rebuke. "Lies, lies, lies, bias and misinformation," the president said of my work, and he banned its distribution in Liberia. The chief of Doe's personal militia, a notorious butcher named Charles Julu, whom I had singled out for his particularly egregious conduct, had let it be known that he could not guarantee my safety if I chose to return. A friend of mine, Gabriel Williams, one of Liberia's many fearless journalists, had apprised me

21

of these developments in a letter from Monrovia, signing off, "Keep fit and keep well, don't come to Liberia now."

So I had watched from afar as the country descended from repression into slaughter—from tyranny into lethal anarchy. On Christmas Eve, 1989, a band of insurgents invaded Liberia from neighboring Ivory Coast. Within months, in a spiraling conflagration that had long been feared, tens of thousands of Liberians were murdered, half the population was scattered into exile, and much of the country was bombed and looted into ruins. The much-loathed Doe was captured by a rebel gang and tortured to death. Charles Julu fled into exile.

Now, two years later, Liberia was in thrall to armed children and teenagers, to a mind-numbing array of con artists, embezzlers, and murderers, and to ghosts from its peculiar past.

The boys in Buchanan were soldiers in the National Patriotic Front of Liberia (NPFL), the rebel force that had launched the war against Doe, and that at this moment of attenuated stalemate controlled 95 percent of the country outside Monrovia, the capital. They were among several hundred scruffy, edgy, blank-expressioned members of the "Small Boys Unit" attached to the personal security force of Charles Taylor, the rebel leader. They were not paid, but neither were they hungry. They got what they wanted with their guns.

"Many of these boys are orphans of the war," Taylor told me when we met the following day. "Some of them saw their mothers wrapped in blankets, tied up, poured with kerosene, and burned alive." The rebel leader paused reflectively, then explained, "We keep them armed as a means of keeping them out of trouble. It's a means of control."

Charles McArthur Taylor is an Americo-Liberian, a descendent of the freed American slaves who founded Liberia in 1847. Buchanan, like Monrovia fifty miles up the coast, was named after an American president. For 133 years Americans acquiesced in and profited from the exclusionary rule of the Americo-Liberians. For decades Americans trained and equipped the armed forces that would violently seize power in 1980. In the last years of the Cold War, the Reagan administration contributed a half billion dollars in aid that helped soldiers of Samuel Doe's ethnic Krahn militias bludgeon their rivals into submission. With abuses mounting and alarm bells sounding, American officials were memorably obfuscatory. When Taylor's war finally came, in 1990, four U.S. Navy ships carrying two thousand marines floated off the coast as the slaughter intensified, evacuating Americans, but declining to intervene.

Before Taylor's war few Americans could locate Liberia on a map of the seven continents. Once the fighting started, Liberia briefly captured our imagination as Hell on Earth, an especially lurid example of apparently senseless slaughter. Taylor against Doe, Gio against Krahn—the images that flickered across our TV screens were as inscrutable as they were chilling and bizarre. Sadistic teenage killers with names like "General Fuck Me Quick" and "Babykiller" raped, shot and beheaded at roadside checkpoints decorated with human heads and entrails. Fighters fortified by amphetamines, marijuana and palm wine sashayed irresistibly for photographers, decked out in looted wedding gowns and women's wigs and shower caps, or in novelty-store fright masks. Some sported fetishes they believed made them impervious to bullets. Accounts of cannibalism were commonplace, and apparently credible. Taylor's fighters, among others, were said to eat the hearts and genitals of their slain enemies to enhance their "power."

The fact that so many of Taylor's fighters were children added an especially surreal element. One British newspaper carried a photograph of uniformed peacekeeping troops trying to lure Taylor's fighters out of the bush by offering them sweets and toys. Another featured a picture of a Taylor confederate looting a large teddy bear from a Monrovia shop.

Liberia's fifteen minutes of infamy seemed to spring full-blown out of the most sensational Western images of Darkest Africa. But Taylor's war, like Rwanda's genocide in 1994, was not as senseless as it seemed. In Liberia, no less than in Rwanda, there was method to the madness.

Charles Taylor comes as close as anyone in this volume to being outright evil—or "wicked," as Liberians say. Race war was his method. By "race war" I mean not a war between whites and blacks but rather between groups distinguished by ethnicity, in which their ethnicity is a calculated instrument of mobilization. In this case it was a war between groups distinct not just from each other but from the man who set them against each other. It was Taylor's signature insight that someone else's will to mass slaughter, that of the aggrieved Gio people toward Samuel Doe's tiny minority Krahn, could be harnessed to his own will to power. "Kill the Krahn!" became his battle cry.

As many as 150,000 Liberians were murdered in the seven years between 1989 and 1997 out of Liberia's prewar population of 2.5 million, and 25,000 women and girls were raped, as Taylor made one disastrous miscalculation after another, survived to fight another day, and finally prevailed.

Like so many of the Big Men examined here, Taylor early on proved adept at turning a stalemated war into a lucrative business enterprise. He became the prototypical gangland impresario thriving in a lawless market. And like all of the others, Taylor is both a molder of his environment and a reflection of it. He is quintessentially a creature of Liberia's sinister history who became its master by exploiting and magnifying its most "wicked" features.

The story of Taylor's conquest of Liberia includes many of the threads in the larger pattern of evil that has consumed so much of the African continent in the decade since the end of the Cold War: the historical legacies of tyranny, the links between tyranny and anarchy, and those between ethnicity and organized crime. Not least, the swaggering, twisted orphans of Taylor's Small Boys Unit exemplified a time-honored method employed by racial tyrannies across Africa through the ages, from Monrovia to Khartoum to Johannesburg: let the natives do the dirty work, not least in war.

"Peace is our answer"

"There was no other way to get power from Samuel Doe than to resort to arms," Taylor was telling me now. "He killed people. He maimed people. He beheaded people. He raped students. He had wrecked the country. Nothing short of arms would have removed him from power."

The rebel leader and I were sitting in leather-upholstered chairs in the plush, carpeted, air-conditioned living room of his "official residence" in Buchanan. A satellite dish sprouted from the roof, and a big screen TV dominated a corner of the room. The scene was as cool and comfortable as any home in suburban America. By the standards of wartime Liberia, this trim, whitewashed villa was a veritable palace.

Buchanan, like Monrovia, is a quaintly seedy seaside port with salty air drifting in from the Atlantic Ocean and blending with the pungent emissions of teeming tin-roof slums on the city's periphery. Even before the war, loiterers and beggars patrolled the streets. The beach was lined with mounds of garbage. Open sewers bred rats and mosquitoes.

I had spent the previous night in Buchanan's only functioning hotel, a dingy, roach-infested bungalow with candles for light and buckets for bathing. The night before that, Taylor's fighters, drunk and stoned, had set me up in what they presumed to be the choicest accommodation in town, the grimy, one-room hovel of a teenage prostitute named Irene. Her bedroom walls were decorated with extremely lewd pornographic magazine photos. Irene spoke no English. She stared at me uncomprehendingly when it became clear that I was in Buchanan to consort not with her but with "President Taylor," as the rebel leader had come to be known in the territories under his control.

Taylor was born in 1948 in a small Americo-Liberian settlement outside Monrovia called Arthington. He was the third of fifteen children born to a former servant girl and a rural Baptist schoolteacher and circuit judge. Like most children of the Americo-Liberian elite, he was sent to the United States to college after graduating from high school; he received a degree in economics from Bentley College in Boston, then did graduate work at New Hampshire College. Taylor spent nine years in the states, becoming an outspoken leader of the expatriate Liberian students movement and a vocal opponent of President William Tolbert's inept regime.

After Doe's coup in 1980, Taylor returned home, and, through his wife's family connections to one of Doe's co-conspirators, a charismatic soldier named Thomas Quiwonkpa, he succeeded in ingratiating himself with the new junta. The People's Redemption Council, made up as it was primarily of illiterate conscripts, was in dire need of capable managerial talent. Taylor shrewdly emerged as director of the obscure General Services Agency, the government's main procurement office. There he soon managed to amass a personal fortune by cleverly centralizing government procurement in his own hands and taking commissions on each contract he arranged. He also served, briefly, as deputy minister of commerce.

In 1983 Taylor was accused of embezzling $900,000 from the purchasing agency he headed by negotiating bogus contracts with his own front company in New Jersey. Whether the charge was true or not is difficult to know. It may well have been politically motivated, for it was around that same time that Taylor's brother-in-law and military patron, Thomas Quiwonkpa, was falling out with Doe. In any case Taylor fled to the United States, and the following year he was arrested by U.S. marshals in Somerville, Massachusetts. He spent sixteen months in jail while his lawyers fought his extradition. He finally escaped from the Plymouth House of Corrections by paying guards $50,000 in bribes. He would pass through Mexico, Spain and France before returning to West Africa in late 1985 or 1986 and surviving two more stretches in jail for vaguely defined transgressions in Ghana and Sierra Leone, repairing to Libya for training in guerrilla warfare, and finally emerging in his present incarnation as rebel leader, racketeer and aspiring head-of-state.

Taylor comes across as an intelligent man, suave and urbane, articulate and smooth as butter. He has an oval face and a close-cropped beard and slits for eyes. His skin is several shades lighter than that of most indigenous Liberians—evidence of his Americo-Liberian roots. He has the disarming Americo-Liberian habit of calling friend and stranger alike "my dear," as in, "The danger in this, my dear, is that we are involved in guerrilla warfare."

Taylor speaks with a pretty close approximation of an American accent, as distinguished from the thick Liberian creole spoken by most Liberians. He speaks in a silken baritone, in measured, cadenced sentences that convey a thoughtful temperament. The words tumble out of him in a rolling, reassuring, sermonlike delivery. He says things like "I have always shown respect for other views and values, and I've always shown respect for the rule of law."

For our encounter Taylor exchanged his battle fatigues for a pressed white cotton shirt, navy pinstripe slacks, and black Oxfords. He said he enjoys Handel and Bach—"not Beethoven"—and that his favorite singer is Mahalia Jackson. (I would later discover that these were personal touches he shared with nearly every foreign journalist he met). A bevy of obsequious aides were gathered around us, and a crew from Taylor's fledgling TV station was deployed to record the great man's interview with this presumably distinguished American correspondent.

"War is not our answer," Taylor purred. "Peace is our answer." On the other hand, he added, "I cannot be held responsible for the anger of my people. Here is my projection: I can see the people being very violent."

From his rebel domain Taylor loomed over Liberia as a larger-than-life, infinitely potent political personality, an object of obsession for friend and foe alike. I heard him described as flamboyant, a womanizer, a con artist, a gangster, an "emasculator"—and also as shrewd, bold, magnetic. "He is a superb negotiator," said one diplomat; "a deft political operator," added another.

"He is much slicker than Doe," I was told in Buchanan; "that's what makes him dangerous."

No one doubted that Taylor is a figure of immense cunning and ruthlessness, and monumental recklessness, who would stop at nothing—not mass murder, not gang rape, not even the wholesale ruination of his country—in pursuit of power and the loot that goes with it.

At the time of my visit with Taylor, Liberia's war was in a lull. The country was split in two, with two governments, two economies, three currencies, at least four armed factions, and some twenty thousand armed "fighters" hustling for survival without pay—and with much blood on their hands for which they would rather not be held accountable. Rival militias were proliferating. Profiteers were milking the stalemate and stripping mines and forests. More than 700,000 refugees languished in limbo in neighboring countries. There were forces at play and interests at stake that suggested to many Liberians that renewed military conflict was likely. And they were right.

Three months after my visit, Taylor launched an assault on Monrovia code-named "Operation Octopus." Attacking the capital from three sides, his drug-addled fighters bombarded residential neighborhoods, looted, raped and pillaged on an awesome scale, and murdered several thousand civilians. Taylor failed to take the city, however, and he was finally driven out by West African peacekeepers. He licked his wounds and bided his time.

"A mad, horrified people"

"We have been angry a long time," said Blamo Nelson, cochairman of SELF, the home-grown relief organization that was overseeing the distribution of food in besieged Monrovia at the time of my visit. Nelson's mother had starved to death during Taylor's war. "We all wear masks," he told me. "Behind those masks is a mad, horrified people."

Charles Taylor's war was not a purely "tribal" affair. Taylor's rebels sought to eliminate not just Doe's ethnic Krahn but also people of means, people who wore fine clothes or lived in decent houses. The fighters assumed that people of means had collaborated with Doe. The Krahn suffered disproportionately not just because they were

Krahn but because their leaders had appropriated an inequitable and oppressive system and exaggerated its worst features.

It was the Americo-Liberians who built that system. Ultimately the Krahn, traditionally one of Liberia's poorest ethnic groups, took the fall for 133 years of simmering hatred born of envy. It is a sinister irony that Charles Taylor and many who bankrolled his war against that system are themselves Americo-Liberians.

Evidence of Liberia's American roots are pervasive all along the coast, from Robertsport to Maryland County. Quaint echoes of the antebellum South can be found amid the crumbling, mildewy streets. The freed slaves built tin-roof houses on the model of their former masters' dwellings, with pillared porches, gabled roofs and dormer windows, and they still stand, albeit unsteadily. Liberia's contemporary culture abounds with touches of inner-city Washington or Detroit. Taylor's radio station, KISS-FM, broadcasts up-tempo soul music, played by disk jockeys with names like Marcus Brown, "the guy with the glide who will put a smile in your slide." The cinemas show films like *Mean Mother*, featuring a protagonist who was "mean and wild, smashing the man and the mob for his woman."

Liberia's flag is a replica of the American Stars and Stripes, with a single star. The constitution—alas, for its neglect—was drafted by a Harvard law professor. The people have names like Sawyer, Cooper, Johnson and Richardson. They wear secondhand American jeans shipped in bales and sold wholesale to sidewalk hawkers. The police wear the discarded summer uniforms of the New York City police. The soldiers wear U.S. Army fatigues and helmets, with M-16's slung over their soldiers. Baptist churchgoers sing "Nearer Thy God to Thee." The protesters, when they can get away with it, sing "We Shall Overcome" and "Where Have All the Flowers Gone?"

Liberia was founded in 1821, the brainchild of the American Colonization Society, whose members were white Americans with a mix of motives, some philanthropic, others nakedly racist. Not a few of them feared the black "horror" likely to ensue with the coming of emancipation; they sought to establish a mechanism for ridding the United States of slavery's progeny. The small number of ex-slaves who took up the society's offer of free passage and returned to Africa likewise had a mix of motives: some were missionaries, some were entrepreneurs, some merely despaired of any hope for a better life in the United States. Their small settlement on the Atlantic coast of Africa was secured by a blend of bribery, deception and coercion. The first deed of settlement was secured, at gunpoint, in return for three hundred dollars' worth of muskets, beads, tobacco, gunpowder, clothing, mirrors, food and rum, from a chief named "King Peter", who reportedly came only later to understand the full implications of the term "sale."

The first freed American slaves arrived in 1822, but white governors ruled the settlement on behalf of the Colonization Society until 1847, when Liberia was handed over to the settlers—the Americo-Liberians—and proclaimed Africa's first independent republic. The new country's motto, "The love of liberty brought us here," survives to this day. But the years of settler rule were characterized by severe exploitation of the indigenous inhabitants, who still constitute more than 97 percent of Liberia's 2.5 million population. Half the country's national income was enjoyed by less than five percent of the population. The ruling True Whig party, composed entirely of Americo-Liberians, maintained a kind of feudal oligarchy, monopolizing political power. While the settlers along the coast developed an elaborate lifestyle reminiscent of the antebellum South, complete with top hats and morning coats and a Society of Masons, the indigenous peasants eked out a meager, brutish existence on the thin edge of survival. Exploitation reached a nadir in the 1920s, when high government officials were implicated in a flourishing international slave trade and domestic forced labor.

Among those linked to forced labor was the Firestone rubber company, which operated the world's largest rubber plantation in Liberia. After World War I, which spurred the growth of the automobile industry in the United States, Firestone secured a ninety-nine-year lease for a million acres in Liberia. The Americo-Liberian elite was experiencing acute economic difficulties and hoped through the Firestone presence to solidify its position by strengthening its ties to American capital. Firestone in turn ensured its own stable source of rubber by becoming deeply enmeshed in the political and economic culture of the Americo-Liberians. The company provided spacious homes for government officials. It retained True Whig leaders on the company payroll. By 1950 Firestone alone was responsible for a quarter of Liberia's tax revenues.

Graft and repression peaked during the prolonged regime of President William V. S. Tubman, who ruled from 1944 to 1971. Tubman is said to have appropriated more money for ceremonial bands than for public health; he devoted more than 1 percent of the national budget to the upkeep of his presidential yacht. Tubman created a personal cult based on an elaborate network of kinship and patronage, personal loyalty, the manipulation and co-optation of tribal chiefs—and force. He built an extensive secret police network and laid the groundwork for much of what was to come under Doe: a personal autocracy based on weak institutions and contempt for law.

But Tubman established himself as a reliable ally of the United States in the early stages of the Cold War, and this won him both financial and military support. It was during Tubman's rule that the United States built the Voice of America relay station for broadcasts throughout Africa and the Omega navigation tower for shipping up and down the Atlantic Coast. The American embassy in Monrovia became the main transfer point for intelligence gathered in Africa. U.S. military planes were granted landing and refueling rights on twenty-four hours' notice at Roberts Field, outside Monrovia, which had been built by Americans as a staging ground during World War II. Liberia cast a key vote in the United Nations in support of the creation of Israel.

Tubman's successor, William Tolbert, did try to liberalize the political machinery, but his reforms merely heightened expectations that could not be satisfied. One memorable confrontation in Monrovia, on April 14, 1979, almost exactly a year before Doe's coup, highlighted the wide gap between the ruling elite and the indigenous masses. At a time of intensifying hardship for most Liberians and increasingly ostentatious displays of wealth by the elite, Tolbert announced an increase in the price of rice, the Liberian staple. When it became apparent that Tolbert and members of his family stood to benefit personally from the price increases, residents of a seething Monrovia slum known as West Point rose up in a series of street demonstrations. Tolbert ordered the police to open fire on the unarmed demonstrators. More than forty were killed. The "rice riots," as they came to be remembered, created a groundswell of ill will from which Tolbert never recovered.

Unfortunately, the agent of change was the army. Originally called the Frontier Force, Liberia's army was created in 1907 as a means of securing the country's borders against French and British colonial encroachment. President William Howard Taft sent the first U.S. training officers to help out in 1912. The army assumed two essential responsibilities: tax collection—one might say "taxation without representation"—and suppression of dissent. The army fought twenty-three brutal wars against indigenous uprisings, and the United States intervened directly in nine of them. By 1951 the United States had established a permanent mission in Liberia to train its army. Many top officers were sent to America for training. Samuel Doe was trained by the Green Berets.

The enlisted ranks were mainly illiterate peasants, school dropouts and street toughs. In the hinterland areas under their control, they were kings—unpaid but able to plunder what they needed, from cattle and rice to women and girls. It was a West African version of Haiti's *Tonton Macoutes*.

The Armed Forces of Liberia (AFL), as it came to be called, was a malignant organism in the body politic, inherently opportunistic, unlikely to be a source of progressive change. In retrospect it's clear that the institution of the army was a microcosm for what ailed Liberia. A gang culture flourished. Violence was rampant. Ties of blood and ethnicity were paramount. The construction of ethnic patronage systems by rival soldiers would become one of the most important causes of Liberia's subsequent collapse.

On April 12, 1980, Samuel Doe, then an unknown semiliterate master sergeant, and a band of sixteen collaborators—the youngest was sixteen years old—stormed the Executive Mansion in Monrovia, captured President Tolbert in his pajamas and disemboweled him. Two weeks later, in an unforgettable public spectacle that haunts Liberia to this day, thirteen members of Tolbert's cabinet were tied to telephone poles on the beach and mowed down by a drunken firing squad. There followed weeks of bloodletting in which hundreds were killed.

Nevertheless, Doe's coup was widely applauded at first. There was dancing in the streets of Monrovia. Casting himself as the liberator of the indigenous masses, Doe promised an end to the corrupt and oppressive domination of the Americo-Liberian elite and a more equitable distribution of the nation's wealth. He also pledged to return the country to civilian rule in five years. But he soon proved to be a lawless and brutal tyrant.

Master Sergeant Doe and his comrades styled themselves the "People's Redemption Council" (PRC), and they lost no time in consolidating their control. Within a matter of days after the coup, the PRC suspended the constitution and declared martial law. Political activity was banned. Military rule evolved into a byzantine pattern of plotting and intrigue, alleged conspiracies, and executions by firing squad. In his first five years in power Doe executed more than fifty rivals, real and imagined, after secret trials. Scores of civilians were detained without trial for violating the ban on political activity. Informal charges ranged from plotting coups to "discussing Sgt. Doe's level of education." Doe, for his part, adapted to the perquisites of power in a manner familiar to leaders across the continent, expanding from the scrawny sergeant in battle fatigues to a blowfish-fat, self-proclaimed doctor in a three-piece suit.

"When the coup took place in 1980, it was an exact reflection of the kind of army that the system had produced," said Commany Wesseh, a onetime student activist who spent a decade in exile during Doe's regime. "Arrest on mere suspicion, strip people naked, parade people naked through the streets, kill people on the beach after summary trials—the same acts that were carried out against my own father and others prior to 1980 were carried out against their creators. Doe was the embodiment of everything that had happened before. The difference with Doe was a difference in scale, not quality. If Tolbert did it twice, Doe did it a thousand times."

"Some rapes"

Patrick Seyon, president of the University of Liberia, likewise emphasized the continuity from one regime to the next. "Those who found themselves in power after 1980 went along with the world that had been set in place by the freed American slaves," Seyon told me. "No one saw that there was something systemic in the level of inequality that existed. They followed right in line."

Dr. Seyon is a gentle, soft-spoken scholar with a wry wit and wispy white goatee. In 1981, when he was forty-three and vice president of the university, he was jailed for two weeks on suspicion of plotting to overthrow Doe's year-old government. He told me he received fifty lashes twice a day for eight consecutive days. Flogging has long been the most common form of summary punishment in Liberia. This, too, was a legacy of the old Americo-Liberian regime, under which common criminals were subjected to what was known as "breakfast and dinner," twenty-five lashes in the morning and twenty-five lashes in the evening.

"There were two of them, two soldiers," Dr. Seyon recalled. "One of them used a fan belt from an army truck, doubled up. The other used a strip from a rubber tire. The rubber portion of the thing was removed, so that the fiber, the nylon, was exposed. First they put water on your back. Then they sprinkle sand on your back so that when the piece of rubber was used, you get traction. The sensation you got was as if your skin was being pulled off your back."

The campus of the University of Liberia is a modest collection of tan and red cement-block buildings directly across the street from the Executive Mansion, on the edge of downtown Monrovia. It has been a focal point of conflict for years. In the 1970s it was the scene of protest against the regime of President Tolbert. In the 1980s the campus was roiled by protest and repression under Doe. In 1982 Doe issued an infamous edict, Decree 2A, banning all academic activities that "directly or indirectly impinge, interfere with or cast aspersion upon the activities, programs or policies of the People's Redemption Council." Faculty members and student leaders were repeatedly detained and harassed under martial law.

On August 22, 1984, in an event that left an indelible impression on a generation of Liberians, uniformed troops of Doe's personal militia, the Executive Mansion Guard, opened fire on unarmed student demonstrators. They killed a still-unknown number of students. Doe's justice minister at the time, Jenkins Scott, acknowledged there had also been "some rapes" on the campus of both students and staff, but the episode was never investigated, and no one was ever prosecuted.

In October 1985 Doe brazenly stole an election that was to have ushered in civilian rule. There were piles of burning ballots. The Special Election Commission appointed to verify the vote was abruptly replaced with a new panel stacked with Doe partisans. Opposition parties had been banned, criticism outlawed, newspapers closed, opposition leaders detained and beaten.

Doe by then was well on his way toward bankrupting the country. In a decade in power Doe and his cronies are estimated to have stolen about $300 million—equal to half of the anemic gross domestic product for their final year at the till. Doe himself stashed $5.7 million in a London branch of the notoriously corrupt, now liquidated Bank of Credit and Commerce International (BCCI). He had turned Liberia's distinctive American panache—the U.S. dollar remains legal tender—into a lucrative money-laundering racket. At a time when Liberia's legitimate economy was contracting almost by half, the number of banks in Monrovia rose from six to fourteen.

Liberia has always been a poor country. By the mid-eighties only one in four Liberians had access to safe running water—and only 6 percent in the rural areas, where most of the prewar population lived. Barely one in four adults could read or write, and only one in five school-age children finished elementary school. Infant mortality was ten times the American average. Life expectancy was fifty-two years.

Doe, for his part, had largely disappeared from public view by the time I arrived in 1986. Unpolished, inarticulate, consumed with the intrigue of barracks politics, Doe never went in for the kind of personality cult promoted by the likes of Mobutu in Zaire. His activities were usually not reported. His methods and motives were largely unknown to the general public. "This fellow," as he was called in hushed conversations with a mixture of fear and derision, had had little success in dealing with his country's mounting woes. The populist fervor that had greeted his sudden rise to power in 1980 was a distant memory.

My own first impression of Samuel Doe's Liberia: On the day I arrived in Monrovia, in March 1986, I discovered I needed a new wallet. For more than a century the U.S. dollar had been the only currency in Liberia. After Doe seized power, corruption and mismanagement began outpacing the government's ability to meet its payroll. So Doe started minting "Doe dollars," heavy, octagonal coins that were officially valued on a par with the U.S. greenback. U.S. notes were soon trading at a premium on the black market, and Doe dollars fell to a third of the official rate. Inflation soared, one awkward result being that it was necessary to carry huge quantities of these coins around just to make petty purchases. The coins were too ungainly to carry in my pocket, or in my wallet. The solution was a heavily reinforced leather pouch, the kind of thing one associates with currency transactions in the Middle Ages. I duly obtained one of these pouches from a roadside vendor almost as soon as I emerged, pockets bulging, from changing traveler's checks in the largest bank in Monrovia, the Chase Manhattan Bank.

I had been sent to Monrovia to investigate an event that would prove to be the catalyst for Charles Taylor's war five years later. On November 12, 1985, barely a month after the stolen election, Taylor's mentor, the erstwhile fellow putschist of Doe's named Thomas Quiwonkpa, attempted a coup. The coup nearly succeeded, and Doe finally put it down with horrific violence, killing hundreds of presumed supporters of Quiwonkpa—mostly members of the Gio and Mano ethnic groups from the remote border region of Nimba County.

The "November 12 business," as it came to be called, established an unprecedented new level of brutality and yielded a critical mass of enduring hatred for Doe—particularly among the Gio and Mano. This was the ethnic division that Charles Taylor would exploit for his own ends five years later. It was from Nimba County that Taylor launched his rebellion in 1990; he would call it "a continuation of November 12."

"The November 12 business"

All of Africa's ethnic conflicts start at the top and spread downward. People hungry for power use violence as a means of achieving it. They use ethnicity to mobilize constituencies—above all, the militias they need to vanquish their foes and protect themselves.

Ultimately what happened in Liberia was that a personal rivalry developed between two of the putschists from 1980: Samuel Doe, the coup leader, and Thomas Quiwonkpa, perhaps his most popular co-conspirator. Their personal rivalry translated into tension in the ranks between their respective ethnic constituencies, Doe's Krahn and Quiwonkpa's Gio and Mano. After Quiwonkpa's failed coup in 1985, the struggle ramified outward from the army into society at large, as Doe's forces purged Gio and Mano from the armed forces and then punished Gio and Mano civilians, killing on a massive scale as a form of collective punishment. As late as 1997, all the nominal heads of the militias, including Charles Taylor, were former associates of Samuel Doe.

Liberia's descent into all-out war was, among other things, a vivid refutation of the most widely accepted explanation for Africa's ethnic wars: arbitrary borders. Africa's borders were drawn up by the European colonial powers in Berlin in 1884, with no consideration for its multiple ethnic groupings. Some tribes were split apart, others were roped together, supposedly creating inevitable friction over state power and scarce resources. Many assume that Africa's tribes are inherently hostile toward one another, incapable of peaceable coexistence or negotiated resolution of conflict. It isn't true. Most African tribes live side by side without conflict.

The border between Liberia and Ivory Coast is a typically arbitrary border—the river that forms the border was nothing more than a dry creek when I was there. It slices directly through both the Krahn and the Gio territories. On the Liberian side of the border, the Krahn and the Gio descended in 1990 into a genocidal civil war. Yet on the Ivorian side, the Krahn and the Gio have lived peaceably side by side for as long as anyone can remember, and more than 100,000 refugees from Liberia's war settled peaceably among them after Taylor's invasion. I visited Danané on the Ivorian side in 1992, and I was able to interview Krahn and Gio refugees from Liberia, living in communities less than an hour from each other along a dirt road. From their competing versions of the war I was able to learn a great deal about the epic events of the previous decade that had led these two groups into a fight to the death on one side of the creek, even as their brethren on the other side continued living in harmony.

There were in fact no violent ethnic divisions among indigenous groups in Liberia before 1980, when the country was dominated by the Americo-Liberians. Liberia's sixteen distinct ethnic groups speak different dialects and practice different social and spiritual customs, but in their scattered domains across the overwhelmingly rural country, they frequently intermarried, traded with each other, and for the most part coexisted peaceably. After the 1980 coup, however, with indigenous Liberians exercising power for the first time, relations between Samuel Doe's Krahn group and almost all others became increasingly strained. This may have been inevitable to some extent, but Doe's erratic and increasingly violent method of personal rule inflamed the problem.

Before Doe took power Liberia's Krahn had been an obscure community comprising barely four percent of the population. For years it had been maligned by other larger groups, who considered the Krahn to be backward and uncivilized. After 1980, members of a tiny faction, or clan, within the Krahn community, most of them from Doe's own home village of Tuzon in Grand Gedeh County, began to emerge with what appeared to be a disproportionate share of the fruits of indigenous rule. The perception of special treatment may have exceeded reality, but there was no question that the Krahn were disproportionately represented where it counted: in the leadership of the armed forces. In addition to Doe, the commander in chief, Krahn soldiers headed all the most important uniformed divisions within the army, including the vital Executive Mansion Guard, military intelligence, and all three mobile infantry battalions. The chief of staff of the army was Krahn. So, too, was the governor of the National Bank. In the manifold upheavals of Doe's decade-long rule, Krahn soldiers had responded to repeated protests, alleged assassination plots and failed coups by murdering, raping and pillaging on a huge scale.

Thomas Quiwonkpa was a Gio man from Nimba County. His coup attempt was widely popular. "The entire nation was jubilating," Isaac Bantu, the BBC stringer in Monrovia, told me, recalling the early-morning hours of November 12, when it appeared Quiwonkpa had succeeded in toppling Doe. "Hundreds of civilians were killed right in the streets when the tide turned."

After Quiwonkpa's coup failed, Gios and the linguistically related Manos were the main targets of reprisals. Krahn soldiers loyal to Doe herded hundreds of Gios and Manos onto the grounds of the Executive Mansion and the Barclay Training Center military barracks, stripped them naked, and killed them. Eye-witness accounts of what occurred in these two locations disclosed bloodcurdling brutality. Quiwonkpa himself was captured three days after the coup attempt, pummeled beyond recognition in front of many witnesses, and finally castrated and dismembered. His genitals were paraded before the public and then consumed by hysterical Krahn soldiers in accordance with a Krahn ritual that had long since been repudiated by most other groups in Liberia.

Evidence of ritual violence in Liberia, including widespread reports of cannibalism, would feature prominently in accounts of the war Taylor launched five years later. There was often a suggestion that ritual elements like cannibalism cast Liberia's violence in a fundamentally different light from that of more, shall we say, conventional violence. There was in fact a long history of ritual violence in Liberia. It was associated with the already brutally violent currency of power dating back to the Americo-Liberians. Political leaders of all stripes over the years sought to buttress their power by linking it with the occult traditions of rural "bush-spirits." Taylor himself was reported, probably accurately, to have drank the blood of sacrificial victims.

The British scholar Stephen Ellis, who has probed into the role of ritual elements in Liberia's violence, noted the importance of manhood initiation rites in the Poro and Sende secret societies, still common in the rural areas of northern and western Liberia, in which "rituals of death" are enacted in a "theatre of terror." The acquisition of power is associated with ritual sacrifice and the eating of human flesh and blood, represented symbolically by animal sacrifice and the ritual scarifying of an initiate, symbolizing his spiritual death and resurrection. It is not surprising that in a society suffused with extreme violence, in which the competition for political power has degenerated into a life-and-death struggle prosecuted by very young men and boys who have been radically dehumanized, these symbolic representations have sometimes been enacted literally.

"The observation that there is a 'cultic' element to violence of this type does not imply that the militias fight primarily as a form of ritual behavior," Ellis has written. "Clearly the prime motive is to gain wealth and power through violence, with the cultic aspects being a means of spreading terror and also of psychologically strengthening fighters, using a lexicon of symbols which is widely understood."

My own view is that ritual elements in Liberia's carnage, troubling as they are, could scarcely be more troubling than the scale of the violence itself. Who is to say that cannibalism is any worse than mass murder, or gang rape, or fifty lashes a day for eight days with a fan belt?

In any case, President Doe never publicly responded to reports of this extreme behavior by his subordinates. No one was ever disciplined or prosecuted. On the contrary, it was reported that Doe personally congratulated the two young soldiers who murdered Quiwonkpa even as hundreds of civilians lingered nearby, viewing Quiwonkpa's dismembered body. There could have been no more fitting expression of Doe's absolute contempt for law save that of the jungle—that is to say, anarchy.

"I saw truckloads of bodies"

In March 1986, four months after the failed coup, I boarded a jam-packed minivan taxi and made my way up to Nimba County, several hours northeast of Monrovia along the border with Ivory Coast. Nimba is home of the Gio, Thomas Quiwonkpa's people. It was rumored in the aftermath of Quiwonkpa's failed coup that thousands of Gios and the linguistically related Manos had been slaughtered there and buried in mass graves. Not a word of this had made it into the Western press. I wanted to know what had happened.

The trip carried me directly into the ethnically charged environment that Charles Taylor would deftly exploit five years later. It yielded an indelible lesson in the dynamics of ethnic conflict, and in the link between tyranny and anarchy.

My guide in Nimba was Isaac Bantu, a journalist who was then the Liberia stringer for the BBC. Bantu was among the most prominent Liberian reporters who over the years had risked arrest, beatings and even murder, carrying on a tradition of fearless journalism with roots in America's own First Amendment. Many Liberian journalists have been educated in the United States and inspired by its constitutional freedoms. It is a paradox of Liberian history that while one dictatorial regime after another enjoyed the most cynical American backing during the Cold War, many Liberians were inspired by the most enlightened of American values.

Bantu, who was then thirty-three, is a stocky, bearded, gregarious man with a broad smile and ready laugh that masks a drive and intensity typical of so many Liberian journalists I came to know. He was a popular figure across much of the country because of his remarkably candid dispatches for the BBC's *Focus on Africa* news program, broadcast from London on a shortwave band each afternoon.

Bantu was not a dispassionate observer. He was a democrat living under a military dictatorship. He was also a Gio man from Nimba, and his own personal experience was emblematic of the wrenching ordeal of the Gios under Doe.

In the aftermath of the November 12 coup attempt, Bantu was one of the scores of prominent opposition figures, activists and journalists who were detained without charge in horrific conditions. Some two dozen armed, uniformed soldiers surrounded his house and beat him with rifle butts as they took him into custody. The soldiers threw rocks though his windows, then set the house on fire before leaving.

Bantu was taken to the headquarters of Military Intelligence, known as G-2. The building was a dilapidated wood-frame structure with peeling green clapboard sides and a rusting corrugated roof. Bantu was held in the G-2 headquarters for nine days.

"For the first seven days, I ate nothing, drank nothing," he told me. "I had malaria, a running stomach, a backache from the beatings."

As elsewhere in Africa, conditions in detention in Liberia have always been abysmal: gross overcrowding, poor ventilation, primitive sanitation facilities, including open sewers and stagnant water in which swarms of mosquitoes thrive in West Africa's tropical humidity. Malaria is endemic. Detainees are fortunate if their relatives can smuggle in money with which to bribe the guards to bring them mosquito repellent and malaria pills. Former detainees describe grim bouts with ringworm, typhoid and amebic dysentery, the latter transmitted by use of communal chamber pots. Blankets and mattresses are infested with lice. Access to medical care is extremely limited. "This is all part of the punishment," a former prison doctor told Bantu and me. "There is not a drop of medicine in these places," he said. Meals, served once a day, consist of the so-called "black diet"—half-cooked rice mixed in palm oil, occasionally supplemented by pigs-feet soup.

Bantu was held with several dozen others in a room too small for everyone to sit down simultaneously. A single screenless window was left wide open, permitting mosquitoes to feast on the detainees. There were no blankets with which to fight off the chills. Detainees were permitted to urinate in beer bottles. Bantu was finally transferred after nine days to the Central Prison. He walked free after fifty-five days. He was never charged, nor even interrogated.

During his first week in custody in the G-2 headquarters, Bantu at least was permitted to sit on a porch on the roof of the building during the day. From there he was able to watch Doe's troops mop up and consolidated their hold on the capital. "I saw truckloads of bodies," he told me.

"These people are bad"

Bantu was an ideal guide to Nimba County—a popular Gio hero who shared their rage against Doe. We were greeted with open arms at every door we knocked on. Stories were candidly told—albeit in hushed tones, under conditions of anonymity.

The focus of reprisals in Nimba County was a remote mining town near the Guinean border called Yekepa. This was the domain of Charles Julu, Doe's close associate who would later issue the death threat against me that kept me out of the country for five years. According to the many witnesses and survivors Bantu and I spoke to,

Julu ordered more than a dozen summary executions in Yekepa, perhaps many more. Julu was a Krahnman and chief of "Joint Security" in
Nimba, in charge of all the overlapping police and military security
forces in the region. He was also director of security for a multinational mining concern, the Liberian-American Swedish Minerals
Company (LAMCO), the largest employer in Yekepa. Yekepa is basically LAMCO's company town.[1]

As director of LAMCO's private security force, the Plant Protection
Force (PPF), Julu exercised authority over a unit of about two hundred uniformed security officers and patrolmen, most of whom were
armed with pistols and batons. The connection between Julu's private
and military roles was deliberately blurred, residents of the area told
us. "He's the boss man for this area as far as security," said one. "That's
all we know."

Julu was an outsider in Nimba County, a Krahnman surrounded by
Gios. He became a focal point for simmering rage against Doe. On
the morning of November 12, Julu went into hiding. After the tide
turned and Doe regained control of the capital, Julu mobilized his
PPF officers and a detachment of army soldiers, and embarked on a
spree of brutality and terror. He detained dozens of Gio civilians at
the LAMCO headquarters in Yekepa and ordered PPF officers to flog
them. He also engaged marked LAMCO trucks and vans to transport
an undetermined number of Gio soldiers and civilians up to the
Nimba mountain range above Yekepa, where they were executed.

Some of the victims were presumed supporters of the coup attempt;
others apparently were Julu's own personal rivals. Some had been implicated in an earlier coup attempt, in 1983, in which Julu's son was
killed. One of these was a man named Lewis Dokie, the brother of
Sammy Dokie, who would become one of Charles Taylor's earliest co-
conspirators. Lewis Dokie was flogged to death by Julu.

Bantu and I pieced together these details from interviews we
furtively conducted in the backyard of a simple cinder-block house on
the outskirts of the LAMCO company compound. A dozen sullen
men were gathered around us, summoned by a friend of Bantu's to

---

[1]The Bethlehem Steel Company had owned 25 percent of LAMCO until only the year before, when the giant American company sold its interest to Doe's government in an agreement
whereby Bethlehem Steel pledged to buy 2 million tons of iron ore annually through 1987.

share their experience of those events. We spoke in hushed tones on the condition that no names be used. A lookout covered the front of the house.

"Remember," one of them recalled, "when people heard about the coup in Monrovia? Oh my God, the people bombarded this town just like a damn picnic. People were going from home to home, shouting, singing, dancing. Julu was in hiding. But then Doe came over the radio."

One by one they described being rounded up by Julu's men, being stripped, beaten, flogged, and left to nurse their wounds for days without benefit of clean water. A few had witnessed executions.

"I was trying to see what was going on down there," one of them told us. "Julu was there. D.K. [a popular Gio politician] stepped out of the truck and approached Julu with his arms out like this. Before he could even say 'Julu,' bang! bang! bang! bang! bang! bang! They killed him in cold blood. They shot him in the leg. They shot him in the heart. They shot him in the head."

The man began crying as he spoke. "Can you imagine that?" he asked. He was sobbing uncontrollably now. "He was my friend. They just killed him." He paused to collect himself. Then he shook his head and whispered, "He's a wicked guy, that Julu."

Years later, what sticks in my memory about these conversations is the boiling rage these men conveyed. There was no talk about "the standards of Africa." There was no sense of an exotic context in which a different set of expectations applied.

"You have no rights in Liberia," one of Bantu's friends muttered. "Whenever you are accused of being an enemy of the government, whether it is proven or not, you have no rights. Your rights as a human being are denied completely. The treatment you receive is worse even than the pet in your house can receive." When I asked this man if he had considered bringing legal action against the government, he laughed. "There is no legal remedy," he said. "Nobody will listen. Why even waste your time? The government is always right. The government can do no wrong."

I recall as well how clearly these embittered men foresaw the nightmare that awaited Liberia. The prospect of massive reprisals against the Krahn in the event that Doe was violently removed from power was anticipated by all sides. "The general feeling now," a diplomat had told me, "is that if there is another coup, the Krahn will be totally wiped out."

The observation was better made by Liberians themselves. A Gio scholar from Nimba County, Alfred Kulah, who was detained for two weeks and flogged by Krahn soldiers in Yekepa, told me, "I'm afraid that if they allow this man [Doe] to be killed, it will be recorded in history that there was once a tribe called Krahn in Liberia."

A Gio businessman in Yekepa, who was detained for eleven days after November 12 and whose back, five months later, was still crisscrossed with the dark scars he sustained from flogging by Krahn soldiers, summed up a view I heard over and over again in Nimba: "Constitutional change—that is what we are trying to do. But the authorities don't believe such change will be in their favor. They will try, for their own survival, to keep themselves in power, because they are afraid they will be made to pay for their wrongdoing. And they are right, I'm afraid. It's going to be a cycle of violence. A cycle of recriminations. Because people all over want revenge."

A farmer sought to explain to me the emotions he felt after being detained and flogged at a roadblock on the day after the coup attempt. "Just imagine," he said. "They strip you. They put you down on the ground. They put a gun on your neck. And then they whip you. For nothing. Just because you are not Krahn." The man shook his head and looked me in the eye. "Yes there will be revenge. These people are bad. The Krahn are too bad."

"We know that something will happen to us"

A week after my trip to Nimba, I visited Grand Gedeh, President Doe's home region. Grand Gedeh is a remote, densely forested region on the border with Ivory Coast. I made this trip without Bantu, needless to say. As a Gio man identified with radio reports critical of Doe, he would be as good as dead the moment he arrived.

It didn't take me long to discover that the Krahn themselves were aware of their precarious position. The Krahn coexist throughout Grand Gedeh with several other ethnic groupings in a patchwork of scattered rural thatch-roof and mud-hut villages. After the failed November 12 coup, Krahn soldiers, many of them acting on their own authority, apprehended scores of Grebos, Gios and Manos, stripped them naked, beat them with rattans and rifle butts, and detained them for days or weeks. In one especially brutal public spectacle, six secondary school students who were seen celebrating Quiwonkpa's coup were gathered up by Doe's Executive Mansion Guard, acting with a posse of the students' classmates and teachers. The students were paraded through town, hacked with machetes in front of their peers, and carried out of town and buried in a mass grave.

The tension was still palpable when I visited Grand Gedeh four months afterward. People looked over their shoulders as they spoke. A Krahn man declined to be interviewed in the presence of a Grebo driver, expressing his fear—"I cannot talk to you here"—in a written note he passed to me furtively underneath the table in his own kitchen. One afternoon while I was there, a rumor of unrest in Monrovia passed though Zle Town, the county seat, causing panic in the marketplace. Merchants abruptly shuttered their shops and the market-women fled into the bush. Schools were let out and the students ran home. "Everyone knows that anything can happen," I was told.

A Krahn farmer in Zle Town told me, "We are in fact living in fear. We know that when power changes hands, everyone will suffer. Whatever happens, the way Africans carry out politics, they will not make an exception for us. What I think is that, if there is an eventuality, if you know what I mean, there will have to be revenge. The situation in the country is very grave. We know that something will happen to us. We know that nothing lasts forever. We've got the feeling that something is in the making. When that thing explodes, then God have mercy on all of us."

When this man spoke of "the way Africans carry out politics," he was right. Africans carry out politics the way peoples the world over throughout history have carried out politics in the absence of legitimate law. With no chance of lawful accountability for criminal acts, people take the law into their own hands. Where justice is impossible, vigilantism follows. The ultimate legacy of Samuel Doe's tyranny was a litany of unsolved, unaccounted-for crimes begging for justice—in a word, anarchy. These were the jungle conditions that Charles Taylor would cynically exploit in his quest for power. Taylor understood that in the absence of individual accountability for political crimes, groups could be blamed—"Kill the Krahn!"

One of my earliest Liberian friends, Tiawan Gongloe, a Columbia-educated lawyer, himself a Gio man who lost many relatives in Taylor's war, put it this way: "The Krahn are not inherently wicked. It was the quality of leadership they received that made them wicked. Doe made them wicked by putting them in a position where their very survival depended on his survival in power."

"I am a strong believer in human rights"

At the end of my visit in 1986, I called on Doe's justice minister, Jenkins Z. B. Scott. Scott had emerged as the de facto spokesman for the government in place of the inarticulate Doe. In the pantheon of Liberia's villains, Justice Minister Scott came to personify contempt for the law under Doe. It was Scott who, after the August 22, 1994, attack on student demonstrators at the University of Liberia, famously confirmed at a Washington press conference that there were "some rapes," but that, alas, none of the perpetrators could be identified—and no investigation was planned.

Liberia's Justice Ministry is a peeling, tilting, two-story edifice on a side street in downtown Monrovia. As elsewhere in the capital even then, telephone service was erratic and appointments needed to be arranged in person. When I presented myself at the front door of the Justice Ministry one weekday morning and asked for an interview with the minister, a uniformed policeman took my business card and told me to take a seat in the waiting room. Ten minutes later, I was guided upstairs and ushered into the office of the minister.

Jenkins Scott turned out to be a glib, vain, ingratiating man with a shiny bald pate and dramatic muttonchop sideburns. He wore a navy-blue short-sleeved safari suit and a matching blue and white polka-dot ascot. He apparently had nothing better to do that day than meet with an investigative reporter on assignment for an American human rights organization; indeed, he seemed to relish the challenge I represented. He eagerly gestured for me to take a seat on a plush, crimson velour sofa. Then he held forth for three hours on the subject of human rights in Doe's Liberia.

I began by asking Scott about the November 12 business. What about all those reports of summary executions? Scott assured me that he too was concerned about these reports. Had he ordered an investigation? I asked. Indeed he had, Scott said, but none had been undertaken. "There are limitations on manpower." I told him about the evidence I had compiled of mass killings, gang rape, detentions without trial and flogging. The justice minister sighed. "Really, I do not know," he finally said. "I hope it didn't happen, but who do you ask? No eyewitnesses have come to me."

Scott characterized the abuses after the coup attempt as unrepresentative, the consequence of an extraordinary upheaval over which the government had no control. "People talk about human rights and ignore the circumstances in which human rights abuses occur. For example, I was arrested during the coup. I was stripped, beaten. One of my eyes was badly beaten. I was handcuffed. It took three months for my hands to heal, and one of my hands still hurts."

Nevertheless, Scott assured me, he harbored no bitterness toward those who beat him. "It was the circumstances," he explained. "There were no orders to abuse human rights from Quiwonkpa. Likewise, there were no orders to abuse human rights from Doe. The man who beat me is still at large, but I'm not going to pursue him. He did that on that day because that was the thing to do. It was the circumstances. But under normal circumstances, he would not have done it."

The justice minister was warming to his subject now. "When you have an uprising, the law tends to break down," he said. "The problem is that complaints are made to people like you rather than to people like me. Since I have been the minister of justice, no one has come to me and said, 'Minister, this officer beat me.' "

I suggested that perhaps more people would come to him if they were confident that he respected their rights as much as I did. "I am a strong believer in human rights," the justice minister protested. "The idea is a good one. And I'm not excusing the abuses. I will not say there have not been human rights abuses. But it is not government policy. Under the circumstances, it looks like human nature. The human instinct, or the animal instinct, tends to come out."

The minister gave an illustration. "What would you do if a man raped your wife?" he asked. Before I had a chance to respond, he answered for me. "Chances are you would shoot him."

What about due process? I asked.

"Due process is foreign to Africa," the justice minister replied. "That is the Western type of culture. There must be an educational process. Human rights is not the sole responsibility of the government. It is the responsibility of the society at large."

The justice minister leaned forward and looked me in eye professorially. "The law of the frontier still rules to some extent," he explained.[2]

"What was done to us must be done to them"

Even those who predicted all-out civil war scarcely imagined the depths to which Liberia would descend in 1990. Charles Taylor's rebellion began in Nimba County with barely 150 insurgents. In less than a year it consumed not just Doe but many thousands of civilians in an orgy of killing and destruction. More than a million Liberians—half the population—abandoned their homes. Much of the country was bombed, burned and looted into ruins.

Taylor's war was widely popular when it began. Everyone wanted to get rid of Doe. But Taylor's method was to exploit the genocidal rage of the Gio and the Mano against Doe's Krahn, to inflame their lust for revenge through mass murder. In a word, his method was anarchy.

He began with mostly Gio exiles from Nimba, men like Sammy Dokie, who by 1992 had become chief of Taylor's fledgling leather-jacketed secret police. Dokie had been in exile for six years after twice failing to topple Doe. Two of his brothers had been murdered.

---

[2]In 1990, Jenkins Scott fled Liberia when Monrovia came under siege by Taylor's rebels. But he made sure to sort out his financial affairs before taking flight. Together with Emmanuel Shaw, Doe's equally nefarious finance minister (more recently appointed "ambassador extraordinaire" by Taylor), Scott hatched a swan-song scam that underlined the depths of chicanery commonplace among Doe's top aides up until the bitter end. Scott and Shaw, while serving as ministers in Doe's cabinet, had set up a front company with a monopoly over the sale of petroleum products in Liberia. The arrangement netted millions in profits for the two of them. Scott and Shaw fled the country in May 1990—but not before preparing official documents purporting to bind the government to pay $27 million in debts to their own company. In fact the debts, though they bore the official signatures of the justice and finance ministers, were fictitious.

Having set the plan in motion, Shaw and Scott packed their bags and flew to London, where they persuaded a British court to order a worldwide injunction freezing Liberian government assets up to $27 million until their company obtained full payment. Scott then proceeded to federal court in New York and obtained a similar injunction that effectively deprived Liberia of all its assets in the United States. This was at a time when tens of thousands of Liberians were starving in the war-torn country that Shaw and Scott had left behind. Not until nearly a year later was Liberia's interim government able to get the injunction lifted by demonstrating "blatant, massive and enduring fraud."

"We all came back with that revengeful attitude," Sammy Dokie told me in Buchanan, "that what was done to us must be done to them to pay the Krahn back. So we fought a very bitter war."

With Dokie and his confederates on board, Taylor sought international backing for an armed rebellion. The Cold War was coming to an end, but the United States still appeared to be standing behind Doe. So Taylor turned to Libya.

The Libyan strongman, Muammar Qaddafi, had been seeking a foothold in sub-Saharan Africa for years, in Chad, Sudan, and Nigeria, among other countries. After Doe seized power in Liberia, Qaddafi briefly flirted with the new junta, offering a variety of bribes and blandishments that have since been cited by American policy-makers as a major justification for generous U.S. financial backing for Doe. For instance, toward the end of Doe's first year in power, around Christmas 1980, Doe's cash-strapped government threatened to seek a bailout directly from Qaddafi; the American assistant secretary of state at the time, Richard Moose, reportedly flew into Monrovia on a chartered plane and delivered $10 million in cash. Doe soon blew off Qaddafi.

A decade later, Qaddafi, ever keen to stick it to the Americans, was cultivating all manner of "revolutionaries" across West Africa. Charles Taylor made his way to Tripoli, and soon he arranged for a small band of Liberians—Sammy Dokie among them—to receive military training in Libya. On Christmas Eve, 1989, they attacked across the Liberia border in Nimba County.

Taylor early on proved adept at using the radio as a means of bolstering his stature and mobilizing support, in this case the BBC. In radio interviews Taylor made what many Liberians recognized as a naked appeal to ethnic animosity. He declared his rebellion "a continuation" of the famous failed coup of November 12, 1985. His message was lost on no one—least of all on Doe.

Predictably, Doe responded with a ruthless counterinsurgency campaign—led by Charles Julu. Julu, on the strength of his performance in Nimba in 1985, had been promoted to head Doe's personal militia, the Executive Mansion Guard. Under Julu's command, Doe's troops, almost entirely Krahn, hastened to Nimba to confront Taylor's invasion, killing with abandon, raping, looting and burning villages, driving tens of thousands of Gios and Manos into the bush. Doe also dispatched Krahn death squads in Monrovia to round up prominent opposition figures, who were beheaded, their remains left to rot on the street.

The result was exactly what Taylor might have hoped for. Gios and Manos by the thousands rushed to join up with Taylor's forces. And he welcomed them. "As the NPFL came in," Taylor told me, "We didn't even have to act. People came to us and said, 'Give me a gun. How can I kill the man who killed my mother?' "

Orphans bent on revenge, illiterate teenage peasants and school dropouts seizing the main chance, unemployed street toughs known as "grunah boys" (grown-up boys), and others merely driven by fear, hunger, peer pressure—Taylor armed them all. He sent them into battle with a minimum of training. He even opened up the jails as he passed through towns and armed the inmates. "Kill the Krahn!" they chanted. Within months, a force of 150 trained insurgents snowballed into a marauding gang of thousands, barely trained but heavily armed, seeking liberty, vengeance and booty. Taylor fought tyranny with anarchy, fire with fire.

No one really knows how many people died. The best guess is that between 150,000 and 200,000 were killed in six years. What a visitor gradually realizes is that virtually everyone lost a relative. In 1992 I took a poll of the staff at the El Meson Hotel in Monrovia. Harrison, the laundry man, had a brother killed in crossfire between the AFL and the NPFL; his father died of sickness and starvation. Saybah, the chambermaid, lost two brothers and her father to the AFL. Boakai, the maintenance man, who managed to produce hot running water in my room on my last weekend, lost a first cousin in an NPFL ambush—"They wanted his car and he refused to give it to him, so they shot him dead," he told me—and his brother-in-law died of cholera. Wleh Nypen, the security guard, lost his brother, a rebel fighter, in a clash with the West African peacekeepers; his mother died of cholera. Rebecca, the lovely receptionist, lost a cousin to starvation. Joseph, her weekend replacement, lost a brother and sister, her sister's husband who was Krahn, and their three children—all killed by Taylor's men; the grown-ups were shot, he said, and the children had their throats slit. "The people Taylor has are not educated," Joseph explained. "Taylor has brainwashed them."

Doe's home county, Grand Gedeh, was "cleansed"—to borrow a word not yet coined, as it was to be later in the Balkans. More than

100,000 Krahn refugees fled into neighboring Ivory Coast, telling stories of wanton slaughter. The first of three major battles for Monrovia, in the summer and fall of 1990, degenerated into chaos. Water stopped running. Electricity was cut off. Food ran out. Civilians scavenged for grass and weeds. NPFL rebels, high on marijuana and weirdly decked out in women's wigs and dresses looted from stores—"We fight to loot" was their motto—shot people who "smelled" Krahn. Krahn soldiers committed epic massacres, at one point killing 600 Gio refugees holed up in a Lutheran church. As civilians fled, soldiers and rebels alike looted with abandon: homes, stores, offices, government ministries, hospitals, embassies, churches—and banks. Nearly 50 million Liberian dollars in cash disappeared, one-fifth of all the money in circulation. After Doe was finally captured and killed, surviving Krahn soldiers set about burning the city down—"No Doe, no Monrovia" was *their* motto.

"I'm sad about the lives"

When I met Taylor in Buchanan, I asked him if it had not been a reckless war. "Quite the opposite," he replied, his deep silken voice a model of calm assurance. "Doe had sufficiently antagonized the country with a reign of terror. It must be recorded, it took me two active years of preparation. I knew that unless it was controlled, there would have been a bloodbath."

But there *was* a bloodbath, I noted.

Taylor scarcely blinked. "I must say with a high degree of sincerity, they did not go after the Krahn as they would have without the training that we provided."

Whatever "training" Taylor provided the original 150 insurgents, none was given to the thousands of vengeance-seeking, booty-hunting, pot-smoking boys and teenagers who made up the bulk of his marauding militia. Moreover, Taylor's "high degree of sincerity" not withstanding, going after the Krahn was the very key to attracting support for his rebellion.

"It was an uprising," Taylor insisted. "The people took up arms and uprooted the system. Given the opportunity, the people will be able to put in a system that no military will ever be able to put out."

There was an Orwellian quality to this last pronouncement. For of course what Taylor was really trying to do was put a military force in power—his own ragtag gang of thieves and murderers—that no peo-ple will ever be able to put out. "I'm happy that we had this opportu-nity," Taylor concluded. "I'm sad about the lives, but now we can use this opportunity to build a new country."

As I sat in his air-conditioned living room, surrounded by Taylor's fawning aides and sycophantic journalists, and by his heavily armed gang of twisted children, nothing was more clear to me than that this man was anything but "sad about the lives" it might cost to achieve his goal. Unbridled terror was the very essence of his game. Even as we spoke, it subsequently developed, Taylor was plotting "Operation Oc-topus," the unsuccessful siege of Monrovia in October 1992 that left three thousand civilians dead and the capital in ruins.

I asked Taylor about accountability for war crimes. He had, after all, cited Doe's crimes as justification for his war. Hadn't Doe's failure to hold anyone accountable for the escalating crimes of his regime con-tributed to the cycle of violence into which Taylor had so eagerly thrown himself?

"I cannot be held responsible for the anger of the people," Taylor replied. "The whole problem is like the chicken and the egg. Which came first? We cannot go back and constitute blame. There are too many skeletons in the closet to begin to apportion blame. Forget blame."

"Where's the money?"

Doe, for his part, was killed not by Taylor but instead by members of a break-away rebel faction led by Brigadier General Prince Y. Johnson, a former Taylor ally who managed to beat him to the capital. Johnson by all accounts was an alcoholic psychopath, renowned for personally executing friends and foes alike in fits of pique. He had been Thomas Quiwonkpa's aide-de-camp. In September 1990, Johnson's gang am-bushed Doe in Monrovia. They took him back to their base. There they conducted a frenzied, boozy interrogation that was recorded on videotape. The hour-long video is readily available in Monrovia. It is a lurid document. Doe sits on the ground, naked and flabby, with his legs stretched out before him, bloodied from a gunshot wound. His elbows are bound tightly together behind his back in what is known as the *tabey* position. A swarm of sweaty, glassy-eyed rebels circle the un-fortunate despot, shouting and hooting in derision.

"What? What?" Doe says repeatedly, straining to hear the questions above the din.

"What did you do with the Liberian peoples' money?" Johnson demands, cracking open yet another can of Budweiser.

"Prince, gentlemen, we are all one," Doe pleads.

"Cut off his ears!" cries Johnson, and the troops set upon the howling prisoner with knives.

"Where's the money?" Johnson persists.

"I'm in a lot of pain," Doe replies, wincing, gasping, increasingly incoherent. "If you save my life I'll do anything," he moans.

He is said to have "died of his wounds."

"The business of war"

On that steamy weekend in Buchanan, the city's port was alive with a bustling commerce that was difficult to square with the tribulations of a nation reeling from war. Huge cranes loaded ton after ton of timber onto a French-chartered freighter called *The Optimist*. Italian, German and Lebanese ships took on iron ore freshly mined and transported by rail from the rich mines in Nimba County. Dock workers sported T-shirts with slogans like "Charles in Charge" and "Chuckie Did It." A billboard declared: "For Peace and Stability, Choose Taylor."

Buchanan at the time was the commercial heart of "Greater Liberia," the area controlled by Charles Taylor and his collaborators. It was a vivid example of a phenomenon central to all of Africa's conflicts: the business of war.

Taylor's NPFL evolved early on into a lucrative money-making enterprise. Foreign shareholders—mostly French, Italian, German, Lebanese, some Americans and, increasingly, Russians—paid Taylor millions in "taxes" for the right to exploit Liberia's timber, rubber, iron ore, gold and diamond reserves. Access to foreign exchange played a vital role in the financing of Taylor's NPFL and the arming of his fighters, allowing him to conquer areas with easily exploitable resources. Throughout the war Taylor maintained personal bank accounts worth millions of dollars in Ivory Coast, Burkina Faso and Switzerland, and he spent millions more on arms.

From the outset of the war Taylor exploited foreign business anxieties about access to their sites in Liberia. He turned to foreign mining firms for cash and military aid. According to William Reno, an American scholar who has probed deeply into Taylor's business activities, a British firm, African Mining Consortium, Ltd., paid Taylor $10 million a month for permission to ship stockpiled ore on an existing railroad that ran through Taylor-controlled territory. A French-owned company, Sollac, also purchased stockpiled ore from Taylor.

Indeed, Reno found, Taylor was especially adept at attracting French corporate attention and exploiting French government interest in his campaign after the West African peacekeeping force known as ECOMOG entered Liberia in August 1990. ECOMOG was dominated by English-speaking Nigeria and enjoyed the financial and diplomatic support of the United States. In a pattern that would become familiar in French-speaking Zaire and later Rwanda, France was ever on the alert for allies in Africa who were prepared to subvert what France viewed as the expansion of Anglophone interests in traditional French zones of influence.

Jean-Christophe Mitterrand, the former French president's son and the director of the official *cellule africaine* in the president's office, whose influence would appear later on in Zaire and Rwanda, was an early backer of Taylor's enterprise. France became Taylor's main customer for timber products; indeed, Taylor-held Liberia became France's third-largest supplier of tropical timber in 1991—in the depths of the war when half the population was displaced and most of the rest was depending on international famine relief to survive. Taylor used neighboring Ivory Coast, France's closest regional ally, as a base to attract logging firms to his areas. Another neighboring state with close ties to France, Burkina Faso, served as a conduit for arms shipments to Taylor.

The country was basically consumed by organized crime. The U.N. estimated in 1994 that there were some sixty thousand Liberians under arms, of whom no more than a handful had received any form of formal military training. As we have seen, most of the fighters were not soldiers but armed civilians, often teenagers and boys. Militia gangs based themselves wherever there were exploitable resources, especially in diamond-producing areas, or where villagers were still producing crops, or where humanitarian convoys could be looted. There emerged a mosaic of militia zones of control, in which civilians enjoyed a degree of protection but had to pay tribute in kind to the local warlord. The militias defended these positions against all rivals while raiding the territory of rival militias, looting, pillaging, and commandeering slave labor, including women and girls as sex slaves.

The militias rarely confronted each other head-on; instead they preyed on civilians. Survivors described the pattern: a militia would surround a village and bribe someone to inform them of which villagers had possessions worth looting. The militia would then attack, instilling maximum fear with a few acts of exemplary violence—a beheading, say. Then they would assemble the villagers and read out the names of those whom they knew had goods worth looting.

Gang rape was commonplace. Women and girls were often kidnapped and "kept" as sex slaves; others were threatened with death until their husbands or fathers put up ransom. Men and boys, too, were sometimes abducted to serve as porters. Survivors of this regime told tales of gratuitous torture: relentless beatings and branding with heated axes.

Taylor's fighters, including the children, operated checkpoints and roadblocks where they could extort a better living than they were ever likely to make without guns. At the same time, Taylor's senior commanders preyed on their soldiers, taking a cut of the booty. A mode of production evolved in which the main aim was enrichment through looting, and wealth was sucked upward within the militias' rudimentary hierarchies, from fighters to their officers.

In Taylor's "Greater Liberia," the people with guns were the law. Taylor allowed his top commanders to run sectors of the countryside as personal fiefdoms. Taylor's brother, Nelson, netted $10 million in three months from gold and diamond mining in his own corner of southwest Liberia. "It's legitimate," Nelson Taylor assured me when I met him in a waiting room teeming with courtiers and supplicants at "President" Taylor's Executive Mansion in Gbarnga, the tin-roof town north of Monrovia that Taylor called his capital for much of the war.

By the end of the war Taylor was alienated from France but allied with the military regime of Sani Abacha in Nigeria. Commanders of ECOMOG, which was mostly Nigerian, went into business for themselves, stripping the country of railroad stock, mining equipment, public utilities—and selling them abroad. They made lucrative deals with former Doe allies like Roosevelt Johnson, the leader of a Krahn-dominated militia known as Ulimo-Johnson, and George Boley, who led yet another Krahn-dominated militia reassuringly titled the Liberian Peace Council.

In January 1996 fighting broke out along Liberia's eastern border with Sierra Leone, between ECOMOG and "Ulimo-J"—Roosevelt Johnson's gang. A rotation of local ECOMOG commanders had removed an officer who was collaborating with Johnson in local mining operations. The new ECOMOG commander refused to go along with the old arrangement and tried to disarm Johnson's soldiers. Johnson found this unacceptable. His soldiers duly attacked ECOMOG, killing sixty troops. Thus began a high-stakes struggle for control of the region's diamonds, which several months later would extend to Monrovia and consume the lives of as many as three thousand in yet another spasm of seemingly senseless carnage.

"When Taylor came into Liberia, he had imbibed the mafia culture," Boima Fahnbullah, a former university professor in Monrovia, told me. "Killing without compunction, terror, reduce the mind to a slave, oppose it and you are dead—it became a way of life."

Fahnbullah had served briefly under Doe as education minister before resigning in disgust. "This was a war not for liberation and dignity," he told me, "but for Taylor to grab more of Liberia's millions than he was able to do before he fled the country in 1984. He [Taylor] had the pretext, the unpopularity of the Doe regime, and the cannon fodder—the Gio and the Mano who had been victimized by years of repression under the Doe regime. Here was an ideal marriage of convenience: an unscrupulous and venal rascal with an eye on wealth and an aggrieved people hungry for revenge. This was a recipe for disaster and the Liberian people have been the victims."

"The man is a cornered rat"

If it was mostly Gios and Manos who fought Taylor's war, it is mostly Americo-Liberians like Taylor—light-skinned men and women with familiar Americo-Liberian names like Cooper, DeShields, Eastman, Richardson, and Dennis—who would come to enjoy its fruits. They lived through much of the war in Gbarnga in a compound of villas built by USAID and abandoned during the war. Taylor and his friends simply appropriated the compound, fixed it up and moved in. They gathered nightly on their screened-in porches, turned on their stereos and VCRs, and sipped chilled German wine while unpaid Gio fighters in jeans and flip-flops guarded the compound.

In mid-war Taylor abruptly obtained a new middle name: "Ghankay," which means "warrior" in the indigenous Gola language. He was seeking to highlight his servant mother's Gola ancestry and to downplay his Americo-Liberian roots. For Taylor had a problem. He used the Gio and was beholden to them for his power, not to mention his survival, but he is not of them. Throughout the war there were multiple attempts on his life. It was also widely noted that a half dozen prominent Gio politicians—men who might be seen as having a more legitimate claim to Gio leadership than Taylor—were murdered under mysterious circumstances. Among them was Jackson Doe, the man who had actually won the stolen election in 1985. Taylor of course denied any role in these murders, but few Liberians doubt that he was behind them. In the many rounds of peace negotiations, Taylor insisted on provisions that would allow him to maintain 150 of his own body guards even if the NPFL was disarmed. "The man is a cornered rat," I was told.

In our interview in Buchanan, I asked Taylor about the Krahn and the Gio. What was it that brought them into conflict? Taylor responded with a line that would become familiar to me as I moved from country to country in my travels.

"I do not think I can say accurately who is responsible," he began. "We do have evidence of two previous tribal wars between the Gios and the Krahn. The first was won in most part by the Krahn. The second was won by the Gio. This was seventy or eighty years ago. As a result slaves were taken for Nimba. In Nimba today you have people who are partly Krahn. They are descendants of Krahn slaves. It is believed that Doe, realizing this and being committed to his tribe, tried to avenge this earlier loss. This was the business, the insensitivity of Doe, the lack of understanding, that led to the slaughtering of the Gio."

This was rubbish. No amount of bloodshed "seventy or eighty years ago" could explain the current carnage. But Taylor was articulating a view of "age-old" tribal conflict that had the benefit of obscuring his own role in exploiting and magnifying more recent antagonisms.

Would that Taylor were as candid as his erstwhile ally, Sammy Dokie. It was Dokie, whose brother Lewis had been flogged to death by Charles Julu, who frankly acknowledged to me that he and other Gio confederates were motivated to join Taylor by "that revengeful attitude."

Dokie and I had spoken on that Saturday morning in Buchanan, the day before my interview with Taylor. He had taken over one of the large, airy wood-frame houses built by Americo-Liberians on the model of the antebellum South. At the time he was Taylor's "interior minister"—that is, chief of the secret police. Jeans-clad, gun-toting guards milled around us as we spoke. Dokie, like Jenkins Scott, seemed to have all the time in the world for me, and we talked for almost three hours. Dokie was short and stocky, potbellied, with thick-rimmed glasses and a day-old stubble. He wore a T-shirt and Adidas soccer shorts, and rubber flip-flops.

I had asked Dokie about posters I'd seen around Buchanan urging Liberians to "Forget the past." How could people be expected to forget about the past when so many crimes were unaccounted for, and so many criminals were still at large, running amok?

"Forget about the past," Dokie replied. "That's the solution because what has happened since 1980 and Samuel Doe took power up to the present has been people revenging for what has happened in the past."

Then what about prosecuting people for war crimes? I asked. Wouldn't that be a way of arresting this cycle of revenge?

"I'm very practical in my thinking," Dokie replied. "It would be impossible to talk about prosecuting those crimes of 1985 without prosecuting certain crimes during the civil war. And if the possibility exists to carry out prosecutions of the crimes of 1985 and crimes during the war, we will end up going from year to year just prosecuting because there have been numerous crimes against innocent Liberian citizens. And a lot of the doers are at large in other countries."

I asked Dokie if he and Taylor had intended to start a race war. "Definitely," he replied matter-of-factly. "I was a practical man in thinking. After reading about the atrocities committed by Krahn soldiers against Gios and Manos, I knew that one day there would be a racial war, if nothing was done to heal the wounds of those who were victimized. But I regret that it all ever happened."

So then Dokie had regrets?

"I cannot say there are no regrets," he replied. "There was no alternative. There is regret because I am a human. But I do not think that we who are the architects can be held responsible because every Liberian knew it was inevitable that one day such a war would exist."

"A nation of laws and not of men"

In July 1997 Charles Taylor was elected president of Liberia, in balloting that was judged to have been free and fair. Most Liberians, it seemed, preferred to give Taylor what he wanted rather than risk another round of bloodshed.

"I will not be a wicked president," he solemnly vowed.

Six months later, the charred remains of Sammy Dokie and his wife and daughter were discovered, decapitated with their eyes gouged out, in a ravine in rural Bong County. The chief of Taylor's presidential bodyguard quickly emerged as the primary suspect. For Dokie's murder adhered to an unmistakable logic. It was the logic of inexorable "wickedness," which Taylor had done so much to exploit and from which at this late date even he could not escape.

Dokie and two other top figures in the NPFL, Tom Woewiyu and Laveli Supuwood, had split with Taylor in July 1994. Woewiyu, a great big gregarious man who had been Taylor's defense minister when I met him in Buchanan in 1992, told reporters at the time of the split that "to help end the war Taylor must be arrested and killed like a snake." He said Taylor was a "deranged and confused person who does not know what he is doing." Sammy Dokie, for his part, denounced Taylor that same month as an "enemy" of the Liberian people and accused him of "atrocities."

Taylor charged his former confederates with mutiny. He asserted that Dokie was engaged in a "vicious plot" to "wage war on Liberia by attacking NPFL positions around the borders of Guinea and the Ivory Coast." He also accused his three former lieutenants of "embarking on a campaign of lies, deception, betrayal and connivance to discredit, impugn and in fact destroy the NPFL." The charge was not far from the truth. For the three former Taylor allies had duly joined a "coalition of forces" that included nearly all of myriad militias aligned against Taylor.

Some sense of the tone of the split between Taylor and Dokie—and the stakes—could be gleaned from an incident in August 1994, when Taylor's chief of staff, General Nixon Gaye, was fatally wounded in a shootout with members of his own battalion. Gaye, who was twenty-five years old, had been one of Taylor's most trusted associates. After Gaye's death Taylor told reporters that Gaye had been plotting a mutiny with Sammy Dokie and was trying to persuade his men to join him. The men refused, and an exchange of gunfire ensued. The wounded Gaye was brought to Taylor's headquarters, where, Taylor said, he "bled to death" during an interrogation. "We did not torture him," Taylor assured reporters. "I would have hoped he would still have been around to have told more than we got out of him. But it would have ended up in execution anyway. If he had not died during his interrogation, I would have ordered his execution by midday today."

Dokie and his two fellow defectors were among Taylor's earliest targets during the April 1996 conflagration in Monrovia. They were narrowly saved from assassination when a truck from ECOMOG's Guinean contingent spirited them off to the relative safety of the nearest Guinean command post. Minutes later, Dokie's official residence (at the time, he was deputy speaker of the Interim Legislative Assembly) was flattened by rockets from NPFL men led by Joe Tate, the police director.

On Saturday, November 29, 1997, Dokie was arrested in downtown Gbarnga, still the functioning capital of Taylor's government, along with his wife, his cousin and a body guard, while they were in route to a wedding in Nimba County. They subsequently disappeared. The local police who made the arrests told witnesses they were acting on orders of Taylor's personal body guard, Benjamin Yeaten, director of the Special Security Service (SSS), the presidential security unit.

For six days Taylor's government denied knowledge of Dokie's arrest and ordered a massive search. But after lawyers for the Dokie family secured a writ of *habeas corpus* from the high court, the government announced the discovery of the charred and mutilated bodies of Dokie and his family.

Liberians recalled Taylor's threats to "deal with" Dokie. At the time Taylor said his enemies would not be able to hide from him "even in the womb." Dokie had been one of Taylor's closest associates during the early stages of the war. "He knew all the secrets," I was told. "He knew more about Taylor's history than anyone."

Moreover, it was not lost on Liberians that Dokie was but the latest in a long line of prominent Gio leaders to be murdered, going back as far as Jackson Doe. As a Gio man Dokie was a natural rival for leadership of the very group Taylor had exploited in his drive for power. He had to be eliminated. Thus, in the murder of an erstwhile rebel comrade by the plainclothes forces of Taylor's brand-new police state, did anarchy come full circle in a fledgling tyranny.

A day after Dokie's murder was announced, President Taylor, returning from a state visit to Nigeria, where he had met with "my friend and brother" General Sani Abacha, the Nigerian dictator, addressed the nation. Since learning the "sad news" of Dokie's demise, Taylor said, "I have been groaning in agony, lost for expression, and perplexed at how this tragedy could befall the Liberian nation, especially at this time when we had begun to enjoy the fruits of our successful transition to peace, stability and reconciliation."

Taylor ordered the police to leave "no stone unturned." He said "an enormous crime has been committed not only against the Dokie family and the families of the other victims, but against the entire Liberian nation, which if not appropriately addressed, could erode the very fiber of our national heritage. We invite all peace-loving Liberians to join us in categorically condemning this cold-blooded and barbaric act, and we assure you that the law will definitely take its course.

"This incident, my fellow citizens," Taylor concluded, "is viewed by this administration with the gravest of concerns in that it has the propensity to cast a dark shadow over our nation, and create fear and panic, and the erosion of confidence in our ability to protect the lives and properties of our citizens. It is in this light that we have called for swift justice to take its course, so that our country can continue to remain a nation of laws and not of men."

Benjamin Yeaten was granted a brief "leave of absence" from the SSS but was never charged; he returned to work a month later. Five SSS men were identified as suspects in Dokie's murder and two were charged, tried—and acquitted in two days. No one was ever convicted.

So "swift justice" had taken its course, and Liberia had come full circle. It was a country without law, dominated by a single survivor. Fittingly, President Taylor's new "legal adviser" was another survivor, none other than Doe's old justice minister, Jenkins Scott. There was in fact no justice in Liberia, nor could there be. Its president would appear to be a war criminal. Taylor's skill in promoting lethal anarchy succeeded in toppling Samuel Doe's tyranny; now he presided over a tyranny of his own. The cost: as many as 150,000 lives, 25,000 rapes, a nation in ruins.

2

THE ASSISTANT SECRETARY

THE HEARING ROOM of the United States Senate Committee on Foreign Relations is an imposing, cherry-paneled chamber on the fourth floor of the Everett Dirksen Office Building on Washington's Capitol Hill. Big brass neoclassical lanterns illuminate the press and spectators' gallery. A carved Senate seal adorns the wall behind the senators on their elevated semicircular tier. In the waning stages of the Cold War, in the mid-1980s, the acrimonious foreign policy controversies of the Reagan era—Nicaragua and El Salvador, Star Wars, democracy in the Philippines, the Iran-*contra* affair—were debated in this hall in klieg-lit solemnity.

The august atmospherics of Capitol Hill might have seemed far removed from the dilapidated towns and cities of tropical West Africa and the crude machinations of Samuel K. Doe and his ilk. But these debates and the interests at stake would play a vitally important role not just in Liberia's descent into mass slaughter but in that of a half dozen other African countries as well in the wake of the Cold War era. They represent an essential backdrop to any serious examination of Africa's proliferating wars.

On December 10, 1985, members of the Senate committee's Subcommittee on Africa leaned forward in their leather-upholstered chairs. Assistant Secretary of State Chester A. Crocker, the Reagan administration's top policy-maker on Africa, was breaking his months-long silence on the troubling news of events roiling Liberia, America's closest black African ally. It had been two months since Samuel Doe stole the election that was to have ushered in civilian rule, and a month since the November 12 business, Thomas Quiwonkpa's failed coup attempt and its murderous aftermath.

"It's time that the U.S. stopped playing Uncle Sucker to this dictator," Senator John Kerry, Democrat of Massachusetts, had declared.

"Why should the U.S. contribute ninety million dollars a year to what is clearly an unstable and unpopular regime," Senator Nancy Kassebaum of Kansas, the subcommittee's Republican chairman, wanted to know.

Crocker was a lean, bespectacled forty-four-year-old scholar-turned-diplomat with wavy, balding hair and a neatly trimmed salt-and-pepper mustache. He spoke in a softly ingratiating voice that belied a formidable ego and a barely concealed contempt for those whom he considered ill-informed—that is to say, those with views opposed to his own. He made little effort to hide his disdain for Congress. In turn, he was widely scorned on Capitol Hill. "He has kind of a Kissinger-like view of the Hill," a congressional staffer told the *New York Times*. "He seems to view Congress as an obstacle to conducting foreign policy." Crocker, said the *Times*, was "widely regarded as arrogant by members and aides."

It was not just Congress that had a problem with Crocker. All across Africa, Crocker was the public face of an American administration widely viewed as arrogant, insensitive, even racist. By the time he arrived on Capitol Hill to talk about Liberia, Crocker had long since established himself as a lightning rod for controversy as the architect of "constructive engagement" with apartheid-ruled South Africa. "Constructive engagement" was the diplomatic term of art for a strategy that emphasized "quiet diplomacy" and close regional ties with Pretoria—including military and intelligence ties—rather than sanctions or outspoken criticism of its racist system. From the racially polarized perspective of war-ravaged southern Africa, "constructive engagement" was widely seen as a euphemism for coddling the devil.

The controversies buffeting Crocker's constructive engagement with South Africa were amply chronicled. Hardly noticed at the time or since was that constructive engagement was the premise of U.S. policy not just toward white tyranny in South Africa but also toward "friendly" black tyrannies all across the continent, from Liberia and Zaire to Sudan and Somalia.

Crocker began his testimony with an overview of the close ties between the United States and Liberia. "As you know," he told the senators, "the United States and Liberia have a history of long, friendly and special relations. Our country was closely involved in the founding of Liberia. Many Liberians have family ties and educational and other cultural connections in America. Nearly five thousand Americans live in Liberia. U.S. investment there approaches half a billion dollars. We have important regional communications facilities in Liberia, including the Voice of America transmission station which sends our country's message through radio to people in cities and villages all over Africa and parts of the Middle East and Southeast Asia. Liberia has been a reliable ally in war and a good friend in peace, at the United Nations and elsewhere. We want to maintain our friendly, mutually beneficial relations with the Liberian Government and people. For all of these reasons, we have taken special interest in Liberia's efforts to put itself on a course of stability, national reconciliation, democracy, and economic growth following the overthrow of the previous government in 1980."

The United States, the senators knew, had embraced Samuel Doe after his 1980 coup. It contributed nearly $500 million in economic and military aid in the first five years of Doe's regime—a third of Liberia's operating budget. President Reagan invited Doe to the White House—though he embarrassed his guest by introducing him to the press as "Chairman Moe." There was a concern that the young soldier and his populist backers might tilt toward Libya and even Moscow. There was also an "implicit bargain," as one American diplomat told me at the time, "that the military would let go if its needs were looked after." Indeed, the United States contributed $250,000 to the election process in 1985.

But the military had not let go. Now the question was, what was the Reagan administration going to do about it?

Crocker told the committee that the administration agreed with some of the "criticisms" of the election campaign and its outcome, including the banning of the two most popular parties and the infamous "Decree 88A," which outlawed criticism of the authorities and, he conceded, "could inhibit open debate." He noted that the "vote was counted behind closed doors without the presence of opposition party representatives."

Yet, despite what he called "these shortcomings," Crocker praised the election for what he called "noteworthy positive aspects." He said the participation of four parties and coverage of the election by four newspapers and three radio stations constituted "rare achievements in Africa and elsewhere in the Third World where one-party elections covered by a single party newspaper are too often the norm." He noted the large turnout and the general perception that, despite some irregularities, "election day went off very well."

The assistant secretary's bottom line: "There is now the beginning, however imperfect, of a democratic experience that Liberia and its friends can use as a benchmark for future elections—one on which they want to build."

Crocker wasn't finished. "The prospects for national reconciliation were brightened," he said, "by Doe's claim that he won only a narrow, fifty-one percent election victory—virtually unheard of in the rest of Africa where incumbent rulers normally claim victories of ninety-five to one hundred percent. In claiming only fifty-one percent of the vote, Doe publicly acknowledged that a large segment of society—49 percent—supported other points of view and leadership than his own."

Assistant Secretary Crocker turned his attention to the November 12 coup attempt and its homicidal aftermath. The violence was "truly awful," he acknowledged, though "not on a scale known in some other African countries." Which other African countries he didn't say. He did note that the coup attempt had engendered serious ethnic divisions. Yet in doing so he managed to obscure both the scale of the abuses and who ultimately was responsible. Crocker left the impression that both sides—supporters of Doe and supporters of Quiwonkpa—were more or less equally responsible.

"The retribution by both sides during and after the coup attempt is bound to have left painful scars and to have made more difficult the task of national reconciliation," he said. "Moreover, the November coup attempt and its aftermath opened Liberia to the prospect of the kind of tribal, ideological and violent politics that bedevil the rest of the continent and that have not been part of Liberia's political history."

Crocker went to some lengths to disassociate Doe himself from the abuses of his soldiers. "Doe appealed on television for an end to retribution, ordered his armed forces not to molest civilians, and the minister of justice"—Jenkins Scott, he of "some rapes" fame—"publicly declared that those disobeying Doe's appeal would be prosecuted," he said. Crocker did not indicate when Doe made this appeal: it was ten days after the coup attempt and nearly a week after the worst abuses occurred on the grounds of the Executive Mansion itself. Nor did he inform his listeners that none of those who carried out the reprisals were in fact prosecuted or disciplined. He made no mention of the government's continuing failure to investigate these abuses, and he made no call for such an investigation. In short, Crocker made no attempt to hold Doe personally responsible for the violence of his subordinates.

Crocker was not a fool. Even as he papered over events already past, his prognosis of the future looks prescient with the benefit of hindsight. "The requirements for stability are more complicated and more urgent," he told the House Subcommittee on African Affairs a month later, "and the responsibility for keeping Liberia from going down the road to protracted tribal and ideological violence rests on more shoulders than before—government's, opposition leaders, and Liberia's true friends abroad."

Just who Liberia's "true friends" might be was left unsaid. But Crocker made clear his own continuing fealty toward Doe, based on a determination that Doe remained firmly in control of the armed forces. In his view, Doe possessed the military might, if not the popular support, to remain in power for the foreseeable future, limiting U.S. options.

"In the short run," Crocker testified, "President Doe's government seems to have the power to govern. A key lesson of the November coup attempt is that the military units that counted . . . were loyal and effective. . . . Everyone should know that an attempt to overthrow by force the present Liberian government is likely to be bloody and horrendous."

Bloody and horrendous it turned out to be. At the time, however, the Reagan administration was standing by its man, urging Doe to work out some sort of "accommodation" with his adversaries. "We intend to go forward with our policy of trying to work with President Doe's government to try to make the promise of Liberia's Second Republic succeed," Crocker concluded. "We believe there is reason to keep trying."

"War criminal!"

Chester Crocker was assistant secretary of state for eight years—the longest-serving assistant secretary of state in American history. He achieved considerable notoriety for his controversial diplomacy with South Africa, but his engagement with Samuel Doe in Liberia is less well known. Crocker's Senate testimony was scarcely noted beyond that Senate hearing room. It was not reported in the *New York Times* or any other major publication; it did not make the evening news. For that matter, Crocker made no mention of it in his own memoirs. For Crocker, Liberia was a drop in the bucket.

For Liberians, on the other hand, Crocker very nearly *was* the bucket. Fifteen years after he told Congress about "noteworthy positive aspects" of a brazenly stolen election, his name lives on in infamy.

Crocker's Senate testimony was broadcast in Liberia over the BBC and the Voice of America, and it was extensively reprinted in the country's embattled independent press. Liberians were stunned and appalled. The American's observations bore no relation to what they themselves saw. Not one of the scores of Liberians I interviewed in 1986 described the election in even remotely similar terms. Across a broad spectrum of the Liberian citizenry—excepting Doe's small band of allies—the only issue of consequence was the obvious fraud of the outcome.

"War criminal!" a student at the University of Liberia shouted at me in 1992, when I mentioned Crocker's name. Students all around me nodded approvingly. "He *is* a war criminal!" another shouted.

I wondered whether they were right. It was certainly no exaggeration to say that U.S. influence in Liberia was profound, if not decisive. By rationalizing violent repression and papering over the results of a stolen election, Crocker gave Doe a critical infusion of legitimacy at a critical time. As important, Crocker's words conveyed the implicit message that the United States was prepared to back up those words with deeds should anyone seek to challenge Doe. The United States never publicly called for an investigation of Doe's crimes at any time in his decade-long regime, and no such investigation was undertaken. On the contrary, Crocker's words sent an unmistakable signal to Liberians all across the spectrum, including Doe himself: that as far as the United States was concerned, Doe and his confederates could quite literally get away with mass murder.

No tyrant can survive for long without the backing of an outside power. Even the most cunning and ruthless need at least the illusion of protection and legitimacy, not to mention lucre. During his time as assistant secretary of state, Crocker bestowed all of these not just on

Doe but on Mobutu of Zaire, Jaafar Nimeiry in Sudan, Mohammed Siad Barre of Somalia, and, through "constructive engagement," to the generals and their loyal chiefs in South Africa, at precisely the time when they were sewing the seeds of mass slaughter in their countries. As a source of cash and comfort, Crocker was indispensable to tyrannies that would one day play the ethnic card with ruinous results.

More than a decade after Crocker left office, many Liberians would still gladly see Crocker tried as a war criminal. In Washington, however, he enjoys the august status of an elder statesman. In addition to holding a teaching position at Georgetown University, Crocker is chairman of the congressionally funded bipartisan U.S. Institute of Peace. He thus shares at least this much in common with the other, more notorious characters in this volume: a total lack of accountability to the African people over whose lives he wielded enormous power.

Yet Crocker was hardly the first American to promote American interests in Africa heedless of the interests of Africans themselves. His calculations and machinations and evasions of responsibility were consistent with those of Democratic and Republic administrations alike over the decades. Whatever his motives may have been, he was the duly appointed servant of a legitimate, elected government. What he also was, like the other Big Men in this volume, was a survivor, an especially able creature of his own peculiar environment, namely Cold War Washington.

Crocker's coddling of Samuel Doe was a case study in the ruinous consequences of the Cold War at its least-known fringes—what might better be called "destructive engagement." He personified the arrogance of unaccountable power and the calamity of Cold War intrigue in marginal nations across the Third World, from Guatemala to Afghanistan to the Philippines. The interests he was charged with protecting may or may not have been legitimate. But in Africa Crocker's standards and methods—and his country's—were of a piece with those of his African counterparts: the enemy of my enemy is my friend; let the little people do the dirty work, not least in war.

"Things were better than they might have been"

Chester Arthur Crocker is a direct descendent of the twenty-first president of the United States, Chester Arthur. He was born in New York City in 1941 and graduated from Ohio State University in 1963. He received his master's degree and a doctorate from Johns Hopkins University's School of Advanced International Studies. In 1969 he joined the faculty of American University in Washington, D.C., as a lecturer in African government and politics. A year later, before he was thirty, he was hired by Alexander M. Haig Jr., then deputy assistant to President Richard Nixon for national security affairs. He would be the African affairs expert on the National Security Council under Henry Kissinger. He developed a reputation as a disciplined, chain-smoking worker and a skilled bureaucratic infighter who imbibed Kissinger's hard-boiled, bipolar realpolitik along with his contempt for those too lame-brained or limp-wristed to go along with it.

Crocker served three years under Haig and Kissinger, then moved back to academia. He joined the faculty at Georgetown, serving as director of African studies at Georgetown's Center for Strategic and International Studies from January 1976 until 1981. He also served as a consultant to the Central Intelligence Agency during this period. When his former mentor, Al Haig, was installed as secretary of state in the new Reagan administration, he brought Crocker aboard as assistant secretary of state for African affairs. Crocker was just thirty-nine.

"Nice to meet you," Crocker said with a smile as he shook my hand and ushered me into his office at Georgetown's Center for Strategic and International Studies. It was February 1997, eight years after he left the State Department and returned to Georgetown. Crocker's modest office was a typical scholar's domain, small and book-lined. A window behind his desk looked out over the neo-Gothic towers and leafy courtyards of the Georgetown campus. It was a far cry from the immense, oak-paneled office he'd once occupied at the State Department—and even farther from the bombed-out ruins of Monrovia.

Crocker gestured toward a bookshelf filled with copies of his 1992 memoir, *High Noon in Southern Africa: Making Peace in a Rough Neighborhood*, and offered me one. I told him I'd already read it with the greatest interest. I noted a framed, signed photograph on another shelf of Crocker briefing President Reagan in the Oval Office. Did he miss those days? I asked. "Not at all," he replied with a laugh.

During his eight-year tenure as assistant secretary of state, Crocker irritated a lot of people, at both ends of the ideological spectrum. The American right considered him dangerously moderate and repeatedly sabotaged him. Liberals thought he was an apologist for white-ruled

South Africa. The South African government, for its part, humiliated him more than once by slipping out of pledges it had made. In the corridors of the United Nations, meanwhile, African diplomats recounted an anecdote about the time he once told a senior black African official who requested American support that the United States was not engaged in "toilet training."

That trademark streak of personal arrogance made him easy to loathe. He had a habit of putting people down, denigrating the intelligence and motives of those with whom he disagreed—and, by inference, highlighting his own superior mind. It was a trait he projected even before joining the Reagan administration, in copious writings for scholarly journals and Op-Ed pages. In a seminal article he wrote for *Foreign Affairs* in 1980 entitled "South Africa: a Strategy for Change," which first brought him to the attention of the Reagan campaign staff, Crocker began a pitch for the need to "engage credibly" with South Africa this way: "The problem is that the land of apartheid operates as a magnet for one-dimensional minds. How do we overcome the disturbing tendency to treat this troubled land as a political fire sale to be ransacked for confirmation of previously held convictions?" It was pithy, provocative stuff.

But what Crocker was really trying to say was that *his* mind, to be distinguished from others dealing with his subject, was multidimensional: more subtle, more open, better informed. "The beginning of wisdom," he went on in *Foreign Affairs*, "is to recognize that Americans need to do their homework and become less gullible in responding to the dissonant babble of voices from South Africa." It was an opening salvo that would set the tone for his eight tumultuous years in office.

I was prepared for an acrimonious exchange as I settled into my seat in Crocker's Georgetown office and opened my notebook. Crocker had indicated over the telephone that he was familiar with some of my writing, so I assumed that he had pegged me as yet another gullible, one-dimensional mind. To my surprise, however, after a few tense opening gambits I found I rather liked the man. We didn't see eye to eye on much, but it soon became apparent that we shared at least one thing in common: a passion for Africa. This is a rare idiosyncrasy in Washington, and a certain kind of chemistry tends to kick in between two people who share an eccentric preoccupation. For a moment it almost felt like bonding.

"Ah, the joys of having troubled clients," Crocker mused world-wearily at one point, waxing nostalgic about what he called the "singles-bar dating game ambiance of the Cold War." He had a sense of humor, it turned out, and he expressed himself in earthy, colorful language. When I asked him for a thumbnail sketch of Samuel Doe, for example, he gave me this: "A reasonably smart primary school–educated kid is what he was. He had enough intuition and initiative to emerge at the top of that bunch. But he was someone who was way, way, way, way beyond his pay-grade."

Any colorful anecdotes from his own meetings with the man? I asked. "My main color reflection," Crocker replied, more tellingly than he intended, "was that this guy was terrified. In terms of self-image in dealing with a senior American, he was terrified of Big Brother, not knowing how to conduct himself."

From this and other comments, it became clear that, as much as we shared a common obsession with Africa, our experience of the continent was entirely different. Crocker's, it appeared, was mostly that of a "senior American" engaging with elites at the highest levels of power, far removed from the crowded shantytowns and dusty rural villages—not to mention killing fields—where the destructive consequences of abusive power are most keenly felt. Most of my experience of the continent was at street level, in public taxis and jam-packed buses, at fleabag hotels, tin-roof cafés and seedy bars, among the victims and survivors and oppositionists, for whom the machinations of those on high, Crocker included, were distant and forbidding, not to say infuriating.

What was striking about Crocker's perspective on events we had both witnessed was his vast remove from the awesome traumas I'd observed among people on the ground. Quick-witted he undoubtedly was, but his attachment of value to different variables in the equation seemed arbitrary, and utterly at odds with the value attached to the same variables by people on the ground—for example, his attribution of significant value to "noteworthy positive aspects" in a blatantly stolen election.

Crocker's great remove from ground-level experience was strikingly apparent in his memoir as well. Throughout his intimate, sometimes engrossing narrative of high-stakes diplomatic intrigue in southern Africa among powerful men in suits and ties, the carnage of war scarcely registers. The cities and villages blasted into ruins, the trudging hordes of brutalized refugees, the hundreds of thousands killed and raped and maimed by mines—a sentence here, a statistic there is all we get. The word "torture" doesn't appear.

In Crocker's memoir, Liberia appears in exactly one sentence, along with Kenya and Zaire, in a roster of "troubled friends" who, Crocker says without a hint of irony, "had a reasonable expectation that we would be interested in their problems and prepared to be helpful." There is no suggestion that the United States could be anything other than "interested in their problems and prepared to be helpful"; no hint that the United States might actually have compounded those problems by arming, financing and legitimizing tyrannical regimes in all three countries. His "friends" are the Big Men at the top; for him, no less than for them, at appears, the little people scarcely exist.

"The Doe experience was obviously tough," Crocker was telling me now. "It was hard work. We told him, if he wanted American support he was going to have to conduct himself within certain parameters. We were all over him, but it was pretty obvious that he was dealing with one set of Liberians at night and another set during the day. He had ultimately to focus on the guys he saw at night. He was terrified of the different forces being brought to bear in barracks politics."

I asked Crocker to outline the various alternatives he had considered. "Should we have taken a different course of action?" he asked rhetorically. "You either abandon Doe or you don't. You can't be half pregnant. We had very difficult debates in Washington in 1981 and 1982 as to whether or not there was a heroic option. That is, to take over the place. We had three options. One, recolonize. Two, to work with that guy. Three, to abandon Liberia. If you abandon Doe, you invite chaos. Just to have walked away from Doe would probably have led to what happened in the nineties." I pointed out that not walking away from Doe *did* in fact lead to what happened in the early nineties. Crocker replied, "Things were better than they might have been."

Better than they might have been. Where had I heard that before? Jenkins Scott and Charles Taylor—they, too, had disavowed any responsibility for the chaos they helped cause by saying, as Taylor put it "with a high degree of sincerity," that "there *would* have been a bloodbath" were it not for the "training" he provided.

"The Cold War happened"

Crocker wrote a letter to the *New York Times* in 1986 in which he asserted that "the Liberian government pledged to return to civilian rule within five years" and that "the pledge has been fulfilled." The letter conceded that the election "had serious shortcomings, particularly in the vote counting." The letter added, "But in a part of the world where the norm is single-party rule, Liberia has universal franchise, a multi-party legislature, independent newspapers and radio stations, and a constitution specifying civil rights and defining limits on government power. Are we comparing Liberia with New England or with most of the rest of the world?"

When I reminded Crocker of the letter, he stood by it. "You have to look at the context," he said. "You cannot hold transitional, struggling countries that are disorderly, that do not have a tradition of democracy or the rule of law—you have to have some feel for the context."

So then how would he describe the context?

"We wanted to keep the chair full," Crocker explained. "We wanted to preempt other options. If I had gone upstairs to the president and the secretary of state and said, 'I think what we need to do is drop Mr. Doe,' I would have been met with a puzzled expression. They would have asked, 'What are you going to do to replace him with, Mr. Secretary?' These are the kinds of questions you have to ask."

Crocker was growing irritated with my questions. He looked at me and shook his head, as if I were one of his students who just didn't get it.

"A sense of history is missing from this discussion," he finally said. "We are talking about a time when we were damned certain that we were not going to let Liberia fall into a hostile influence. Above all you weren't going to have an empty chair. We counted twenty-five countries where the Libyans were trying to get in there. So there was the Libyan factor, competitive Islam. It's a destabilizing game."

I had been pressing Crocker on the collapse of the rule of law in Liberia. Did he not see the danger? "Your question implies that the only thing we were worried about was implanting the rule of law," he replied. "Global relations, client relations were damned important things."

Finally, we were getting to the meat of the matter. Crocker, at last, was telling it like it is. "I would never in a million years tell you I was seeking what was in the best interests of Liberia," he said. "I was protecting the interests of Washington. The taxpayers paid me to protect the interests of the United States, and rightly so. Ronald Reagan didn't get hired to hand Liberia over to Muammar Qaddafi. And we had some business interests there that were not insignificant."

It was a moment of welcome candor, though I was unable to get Crocker to acknowledge any gap between his calculation of America's Cold War interests and Liberian interests on the ground. Nor would he concede that his analysis of Liberia's deteriorating situation was in any way tailored to fit Washington's agenda. He insisted that his take on events in Liberia was sound, even when viewed with the benefit of hindsight.

"It would be wrong to say, this all happened because of the Cold War," Crocker concluded with some vehemence. "The Cold War happened. It was a success from the point of view of the West. It is wrong to imply that there was nothing legitimate about our conduct. I don't feel that I have anything to explain."

"Call a spade a spade"

The roots of Chester Crocker's engagement with Samuel Doe could be traced back to the Carter administration. Jimmy Carter had sustained the long-standing U.S. relationship with the Americo-Liberians, and he signaled his enthusiasm for William R. Tolbert by actually visiting Monrovia in 1977—he was the first and, until Bill Clinton, only American president to set foot in sub-Saharan Africa. "We were paying more attention to Tolbert's Baptist roots than to the manner in which his government was run," a longtime State Department Africa hand told me.

After Doe's coup in 1980, Carter embraced the new military junta at a time of near chaos, in hopes of staving off a debilitating struggle for power. Carter's Africa experts had been caught off guard by the coup. But after a policy review Carter approved an aid package intended "to exercise influence on the course of events," Richard Moose, Crocker's immediate predecessor as assistant secretary of state, told Congress in August 1980. He characterized Doe's coup as a reaction to the "corruption of the Tolbert government" and "the general indifference of the ruling elite to the plight of the people at large."

Doe was not a fool. He had been trained by the Green Berets, and he knew which side his bread was buttered on. Even after President

Reagan's "Chairman Moe" gaffe, in 1982, the humbled Liberian embraced the new Reagan administration's "hot-button" concerns. Before meeting with Reagan, Doe had closed the Libyan mission in Monrovia, as Reagan had done in Washington. He ordered reductions in the size of the Soviet embassy staff. Doe also agreed to modify the mutual defense treaty, granting staging rights on twenty-four hours' notice at Liberia's sea and airports for the U.S. Rapid Deployment Force. A year after meeting Reagan, Doe followed Mobutu's lead and established diplomatic relations with Israel, breaking away from the Arab-led boycott adopted by most of the rest of Africa after the 1973 Arab-Israeli war.

Behind the scenes, meanwhile, Doe was allowing his tiny country to be drawn into the covert machinations of Reagan's free-wheeling CIA director, William Casey. This was essential. Doe's link with Casey fit a pattern that, as we shall see, extended across much of the continent. It forms an indispensable if little-known backdrop to the downward spiral into conflict of so many of our closest allies a decade later. It also fills in some of that all-important "context" that Crocker wanted me to understand.

The journalist Bob Woodward, in his book *Veil*, reported that Casey had selected Doe as one of twelve heads of state from around the world to receive support from a special security assistance program. Doe thus joined a rogues gallery of warlords and despots on three continents that included Pakistan's president Mohammed Zia, the Philippines' president Ferdinand Marcos, Lebanon's president Amin Gemayal and the president of El Salvador, José Napoléon Duarte.

Doe was a valued player in a years-long covert American effort to bring down Libya's Qaddafi. By the time Doe called on the White House in August 1982, Casey had established Liberia as a key operational staging ground for a special CIA task force seeking to undermine Qaddafi. The task force was directed by the same small group of officials who carried out the arms-for-hostages operation that would later become the Iran-*contra* scandal: National Security Adviser John M. Poindexter, Lt. Col. Oliver North and William P. Clark, who was then deputy secretary of state. Indeed, the Reagan Doctrine, and Oliver North's Iran-*contra* crew, operated as a hidden hand behind four of the six tyrannies that precipitated the conflicts examined in this book: those in Liberia, Zaire, Sudan, and South Africa.

For Doe and the other chosen leaders, the program provided extraordinary protection, and in return, for the CIA, it provided otherwise unobtainable intelligence and access. Unknown to almost everyone else involved in making decisions about Liberia in Washington, this program gave the CIA and the White House a huge stake in keeping Doe's regime in place.

"We were prepared to use every lever against Tripoli, and Monrovia had an important part," an intelligence official told the journalist Reed Kramer of *Africa News*.

Casey's covert campaign against Qaddafi came to naught, but it was just one of the Reagan administration's covert operations in which Liberia proved useful. Monrovia's Roberts Field played a key support role as a transit point (along with Mobutu's Zaire) for the CIA's airlift of military supplies to Jonas Savimbi's UNITA (National Union for the Total Independence of Angola) insurgency in Angola.

Congress, for its part, did take a dimmer view of developments in Doe's Liberia. "The key question," Rep. Howard Wolpe, a Democrat from Michigan who chaired the House Subcommittee on Africa, said after Crocker's testimony, "is whether the government is legitimate in the eyes of the people and whether it can be sustained over time." He concluded prophetically, "I don't see it happening. I think there will be continuing unrest and turmoil in that country unless steps are taken to permit fair and free elections. For the U.S. to be closely identified with the Doe regime would be foolish."

Both the Senate and the House passed resolutions in 1986 denouncing the stolen election and calling for a suspension of security assistance. But the resolutions were nonbinding, and the Reagan administration took no action in response to them. Congress finally cut off the spigot of aid in 1986, partly because of human rights concerns, partly because of budgetary restraints. But Liberia was soon eclipsed on the congressional agenda by the question of sanctions against South Africa.

Years later, Howard Wolpe could still work himself into a lather over Crocker's 1985 election smokescreen. "The intellectual dishonesty of pretending that there was a free and fair election—that was what was really outrageous," he told me. "There was a disconnect. There is no question about the intellectual dishonesty of that calculation."

Wolpe had been a scholar of African affairs before he went to Washington. He clashed repeatedly with Crocker for eight years as Africa subcommittee chairman. When I asked Wolpe about Crocker's argument to me about the legitimacy of protecting American interests in the Cold War, Wolpe replied, "I have no quarrel with that. But every time America stood up for dictators, we actually did very little to advance American interests. We stood up for regimes that were inherently unstable. We were complicit in their crimes. We fed instability on the entire continent."

Then what was the alternative? I asked.

"Tell the truth," Wolpe replied. "We ought to have avoided identification with leaders who did such violence to our ideals. We should have been prepared to engage, but only on the premise of a credible democratic process. I think we had more leverage than we were prepared to utilize. This 'engagement or walk away' analysis—it's a false dichotomy. We ended up creating self-fulfilling prophesies. Mobutu especially. We were always told that there was no alternative to Mobutu. In the end we ensured there was nothing left behind."

I was reminded of what another Liberian journalist, Kenneth Best, editor of the *Daily Observer*, had told me back in 1986. I had asked Best what the United States should do about Doe. Best had been jailed three times in the previous four years and his paper had been banned during the election campaign and its offices fire-bombed.

"Call a spade a spade," Best had told me. "That is all we want America to do."

"The Buchanon strain of American foreign policy"

Chester Crocker was not the first American apologist for tyranny, nor was the Reagan administration the first to subordinate American ideals to geopolitical calculation. For four decades U.S. policy toward Africa was driven almost entirely by our competition with the Soviet Union. Africans scarcely existed except as strategic pawns in the great global game. Democratic and Republican administrations alike defined their options as narrowly as Crocker did with me: they seldom gave priority to initiatives that did not serve U.S. strategic interests. They often overlooked, excused, rationalized—and bankrolled—wanton repression, injustice, corruption and economic mismanagement by unelected leaders who were willing to oppose Moscow. The result was a legacy fundamentally at odds with American values—and heedless of African lives.

Samuel Doe was but one of several African tyrants who were armed, financed and legitimized by Washington, with corrosive consequences for their countrymen. Mobutu of Zaire, Mohammed Siad Barre of Somalia, Jaafar Nimeiry of Sudan—all, like Doe, cunningly exploited the East/West divide even as they magnified ethnic and clan divisions within their own societies.

It was no accident that Liberia, Zaire, and Somalia all collapsed in conflict with the end of the Cold War. Like war-ravaged, clan-ridden, crime-plagued Afghanistan, these four ruined nations embodied what Karl Meyer, an editorial writer for the *New York Times*, once called the "Buchanon strain of American foreign policy." He was referring not to Patrick Buchanan but to Tom and Daisy Buchanon, F. Scott Fitzgerald's careless couple in *The Great Gatsby*, who "smashed things up and then retreated back into their money . . . and let other people clean up the mess they had made."

"For upwards of four decades," Meyer wrote, "the United States fought overtly and covertly against Communists and their clients around the globe, often arming anomalous partners in the name of freedom. When the Cold War ended, America declared victory and pleaded new priorities, leaving the mess in Asia, Africa and Central America for others to deal with."

In the decade following World War II, the Truman and Eisenhower administrations were concerned with ensuring that Western Europe became a bulwark against Soviet expansion. They abandoned the role of the United States, articulated by President Roosevelt, as a critic of colonial rule. American officials worried about alienating allies in London, Paris and Lisbon. They also feared that abrupt decolonization of Africa might lead to chaos, creating opportunities for Communist penetration. The Eisenhower administration played almost no role in the great decolonization debates of the 1950s—taking a pass that alienated a generation of independence leaders who were that much more receptive to the anti-Western rhetoric coming out of Moscow.

The collapse of European domination of the continent, beginning in the late 1950s, coincided with the Soviet leader Nikita Khrushchev's energetic efforts to expand Soviet influence in the Third World. In 1955 the Soviet Union began supplying Egypt's president

Gamal Abdel Nasser with arms via Czechoslovakia. Suddenly Africa was an open field for superpower competition.

Vice President Richard Nixon, in a report to President Eisenhower following a visit to Africa in 1957, predicted that "the course of [Africa's] development . . . could well prove to be the decisive factor in the conflict between the forces of freedom and international Communism."

It was the Kennedy administration that helped to elevate Mobutu Sese Seko to power in what became Zaire. That was in the early sixties, at a moment of rapid decolonization across Africa and intense competition between each of the superpowers to prevent the other from filling a feared vacuum of power. Over the course of Mobutu's subsequent three decades of predatory rule, two more Democrats, President Johnson (in 1967) and President Carter (in 1977 and 1978), authorized military interventions to help Mobutu survive armed insurrections.

Republicans, for their part, would toss the more memorable rhetorical bouquets at Africa's most notorious despot. In 1976, Henry Kissinger, during a stop in Kinshasa, cooed about "the respect and affection that lie at the heart of the relationship between" the United States and Zaire; he assured Mobutu that "the United States will stand by its friends." It was President Reagan, in a felicitous phrase undoubtedly screened if not crafted by his assistant secretary of state for African Affairs, Chester Crocker, who called Mobutu "a voice of good sense and goodwill." President Bush called Mobutu "one of our most valued friends [on] the entire continent of Africa." By then the United States had ponied up $1 billion for Mobutu's predatory regime.

The collapse of Portuguese colonial rule in 1974 ushered in a new period of intense U.S. engagement in southern Africa. A civil war broke out in Angola that quickly drew both superpowers into its maw. With the Soviet Union and its Cuban allies backing one side, the United States rushed in to shore up two others, including the UNITA movement led by the brutally opportunistic warlord turned "freedom fighter" Jonas Savimbi. Secretary of State Kissinger, explaining the Ford administration's intervention in Angola, made no attempt to hide his priorities: "America's modest direct strategic and economic interests in Angola are not the central issue," Kissinger said. "The question is whether America still maintains the resolve to act responsibly as a great power." Should America's allies begin to question America's resolve to defend them, Kissinger argued, "we are likely to find a massive shift in the foreign policies of many countries and a fundamental threat over a period of time to the security of the United States."

The triumph in Angola of the Soviet Union's ally, the Movimento Popular de Libertação de Angola (MPLA), put Africa firmly back on the geopolitical map. With startling speed, both superpowers intervened in conflicts across the continent. U.S. policy-makers, reeling from the American defeat in Vietnam, worried that Soviet advances might snowball. In his final year as secretary of state, Kissinger sought to preempt Soviet gains in southern Africa by becoming deeply involved in negotiations to end white rule in Rhodesia and Namibia.

The United States was more active in Africa in the Carter and early Reagan administrations than at any time in its history. The Soviets had gained a foothold in Angola and Ethiopia. Even those in Washington who might have been more responsive to regional realities—that is, to the needs and hopes of the Africans themselves—defended their policies in geopolitical terms. Cyrus Vance, President Carter's secretary of state, wrote in his memoirs, "The critical question was what politically and militarily feasible strategies would most effectively counter Soviet actions while advancing our overall interests."

After the revolution in Iran in 1979, President Carter enunciated the so-called Carter Doctrine, which committed the United States to use military means to defend its interests in the oil-rich Persian Gulf. This greatly increased the strategic importance of Kenya, Somalia and Sudan, which could serve as way stations for troops and supplies headed for the Gulf. Dramatic increases in aid soon followed, with resulting political dividends for the countries' respective despots, Daniel arap Moi of Kenya, Mohammed Siad Barre of Somalia, and Jaafar Nimeiry of Sudan.

In the 1980s, with the Soviet Union in decline, the Reagan administration sought to reverse the gains Moscow had made in the 1970s. The so-called Reagan Doctrine called for covert military aid for "freedom fighters," guerrilla movements fighting against Soviet-backed clients. In Africa that meant covert military assistance to Savimbi's UNITA movement in Angola.

None of this is to suggest that U.S. interests in the Cold War were illegitimate, nor that alternative policies were obvious; they seldom were. "The Cold War happened," Crocker told me, and sure enough, it did. "Global relations, client relations were damned important things," he stressed, and indeed they were. "It was a success from the point of view of the West," he added, and rightly, thankfully, so. From the point of view of Liberia, alas, it was anything but. When the Cold War ended, the United States had no further use for Liberia. Soon enough it, too, like Afghanistan, was discovered to be infected with Ancient Hatreds, all the more contagious for the inadequacy of our own shameless denials of responsibility.

"We were ordered to cease and desist"

"I do not accept that the United States was in any way responsible for what happened here," the U.S. ambassador, Peter DeVos, who served through the early years of Liberia's war, told me. "It was a Liberian show. To attribute this to the U.S is beyond the pale. It's a myth, folklore." It was June 1992. We were speaking in the ambassador's office at the embassy in Monrovia. "I think there is a natural assumption among the Liberians that whenever there is something bad, it is not their fault but America's fault," DeVos said. He conceded that the United States looms large in Liberian history, but he added, "I think it's an excuse. Liberians seek legitimacy for their own mistakes by attributing them to outsiders."

Ambassador DeVos was articulating a widespread consensus among American diplomats who have worked in Liberia over the years: virtually zero remorse. By the time Liberia's war escalated, it may well have been too late for the United States to intervene. It is difficult to see how U.S. Marines could have waded ashore in Monrovia without being sucked into a quagmire. Certainly there was no domestic support for risking American lives in an obscure country that most Americans couldn't find on a map. Unfortunately, there is no constituency for Liberia in Washington.

When the war began in December 1989, the Cold War was winding down, eliminating what little self-interest the United States might have had in directly intervening—save for repeated vain attempts to persuade Doe to bail out. Nearly all of America's major assets had been destroyed in the war: the CIA listening post, the VOA broadcasting tower, Roberts Field. Firestone has been taken over by a Japanese consortium.

One American who has expressed regret about Liberia was Crocker's successor, Herman Cohen, assistant secretary of state for African affairs in the Bush administration. Without singling out

Crocker, Cohen has frankly acknowledged the long history of collusion and neglect that has characterized our relationship with Liberia, up to and including his own watch.

"Liberia was a special case," he told me in an interview in 1997. "We had a special influence there that we had nowhere else in Africa. The Liberians really looked toward us for guidance, education, et cetera. It was like family to them. After the 1980 coup, we made a mistake. We were seduced by something very interesting. The Americo-Liberians had been in power for a century. Now suddenly the country people were in power. The Carter people got caught up in that. They were seduced by the idea of majority rule. And there was a certain guilt feeling that we had acquiesced in a century of Americo-Liberian power. All of a sudden, there was 'majority rule.' The mistake we made was to fail to guide the new people in the right direction. Instead we just accepted it for what it was, a bunch of incompetents who ended up doing what they could, taking everything for their own ethnic group. At the time, coups were common in Africa."

Cohen conceded that Crocker's acquiescence in the stolen election of 1985 was, as he put it, a "big mistake. . . . The Reagan administration didn't like the idea of dumping a head of state without knowing what would have happened. But we know that country well. We could have found alternatives." Like what? I asked. Cohen declined to be more specific, but he added, "My feeling always was, Liberia is a special case. We could have really brought about change. We were coddling Doe too much. We should have treated Liberia like the French treated their colonies. We could have and didn't. But that's twenty–twenty hindsight."

In January 1990, when Samuel Doe dispatched Charles Julu to Nimba County to combat Charles Taylor's invasion, two American military officers were dispatched to advise Julu on "restoring and maintaining discipline" among the troops. Given Julu's well-established record of murderous brutality, this was a laughable proposition on its face, and it did little good. But that would be the extent of U.S. force deployed to stanch the bloodshed. After that, four U.S. Navy ships carrying 2,000 marines were dispatched—to evacuate Americans.

"We deployed a large marine amphibious force near Liberia to evacuate U.S. citizens, an operation accomplished with great efficiency," Cohen has said. "A modest intervention at that point to end the fighting in Monrovia could have avoided the prolonged conflict."

Why didn't it happen? The decision to deploy the four-ship task force was made on May 31, 1990, by the deputies committee, chaired by Robert Gates, the deputy national security adviser. Participants in the meeting told Reed Kramer of *Africa News* that they always envisioned the move as precautionary. "Gates worried that if we sent the marines ashore, desperate Liberians would rush the embassy and CNN would be there showing the grisly sight." As it was, the escalating carnage in Monrovia that summer received little attention in the United States, and there was scarcely a peep of public pressure on President Bush to intervene. Throughout 1990, Assistant Secretary Cohen never once spoke directly to President Bush about the Liberian crisis, an indication of how low a priority it was in post–Cold War Washington. Whatever hope Liberians may have had of a U.S. military intervention vanished altogether when Saddam Hussein of Iraq invaded Kuwait in August 1990.

In late August 1990, ECOMOG, the multinational West African peacekeeping force led by Nigeria, was dispatched to Liberia and managed to separate the combatants. By then, however, the country's dismemberment was far advanced and the divisions along ethnic lines were cemented in blood. The ECOMOG initiative represented the first time that a regional body had intervened to arrest a civil conflict in its own region, and at the time it was widely hailed as an "African solution to Africa's problems." There is little doubt that the West African intervention in Liberia saved many lives that year—at considerable cost to its impoverished member states. But ECOMOG units were unable to establish a lasting peace, and before long they themselves were implicated in criminal activity.

The U.S. ambassador in 1990 was James Bishop, a career diplomat and longtime Africa hand who, like Cohen, has expressed remorse about the failure of the United States to intervene that year—though not for the policies that preceded it. "I had a very difficult relationship with Doe," Bishop recalled. "When I visited Doe in the evenings, he was doing his homework. He had teachers. He was underlining in his notebooks. So he was capable of self-improvement."

Bishop sought to draw a distinction between Doe and some of Africa's more notorious leaders. "He was not Idi Amin," he told me. "He was a more complex character than that. He was not running a state that was the scene of barbaric behavior. People weren't being tortured. They weren't disappearing. Doe's human rights behavior was typical of that part of the world."

Human rights abuses of one kind or another do occur in many countries in West Africa, as they have in most parts of the world, but comparisons of scale and severity almost always obscure more than they illuminate. In Doe's Liberia, it's true, people weren't being tortured—they were being flogged. They weren't disappearing—they were being raped, beaten, shot and publicly dismembered. Whether that was barbaric behavior in the eyes of an American, it certainly was in the eyes of most Liberians, who were appalled by the conduct of Doe's soldiers. But Bishop's assessment was characteristic of all too many of his colleagues, from Crocker on down.

Bishop was clearly bitter, however, about the events of 1990, and the Bush administration's failure to intervene more forcefully to stop the conflict. "The White House got cold feet," he recalled. "We were told to butt out in the late spring of 1990. We were ordered to cease and desist."

Bishop was at the center of one particularly unfortunate intervention that had the unintended consequence of enabling a large number of Doe's top henchmen to flee Liberia and take up residence in the United States. Some of these men were closely linked with the brutality of Doe's regime; others were merely implicated in the immense corruption that bankrupted the country. The most notorious of these was none other than Charles Julu.

The story of Julu's flight to America appears to be one of good intentions gone awry. At the height of Taylor's siege of Monrovia in June 1990, Doe was barricaded in the Executive Mansion as rebels closed in on Monrovia. In an atmosphere of escalating carnage, the capital was clogged with half a million refugees from vicious fighting in the countryside. Bands of drunken Krahn soldiers, sensing defeat, roamed the streets, looting, robbing and shooting suspected dissidents from other ethnic groups. Food was running out, and an epidemic of cholera was feared.

In these dire circumstances, officials in the U.S. embassy tried to induce Doe to quit the country. This was the so-called "Marcos option"—a prearranged helicopter flight into exile like the one arranged by the Reagan administration for Ferdinand Marcos of the Philippines in 1986. But Doe refused to budge. There were suspicions that he was being held hostage by his fellow Krahn, who had good reason to fear that they would be dead meat once Doe was gone. So a strategy was devised to peel away Doe's support. Ambassador Bishop told me that U.S. visas were issued to Julu and other senior Krahn officers. "The thought was that if we could facilitate their departure, the Executive Mansion Guard would collapse around Doe, and that would reduce the likelihood of a full-scale battle in Monrovia with a huge loss of life. Unfortunately, it didn't work."

Indeed it did not. Doe held out for two more months until he was finally captured by Prince Johnson's rebel gang and tortured to death. The battle for Monrovia raged on, killing thousands in an orgy of looting, arson and revenge. In one indelible episode, Krahn soldiers massacred six hundred men, women and children holed up in a Lutheran church.

Meanwhile, Doe's surviving allies were making their way to the United States. Julu wound up settling in Worcester, Massachusetts, where his wife and grown children had a home. From there he became active in Liberian exile politics, helping to organize what became the Krahn-based ULIMO (United Liberation Movement of Liberia for Democracy) insurgency that invaded Liberia from Sierra Leone in 1992. Julu himself embarked on a quixotic coup attempt in 1994 in which he succeeded in taking control of the Executive Mansion for a few hours before ECOMOG troops managed to capture him. Julu was paraded half naked through the streets of Monrovia as hundreds jeered and threatened to lynch him. He was finally jailed, tried and convicted of treason, only to be sprung from jail by his fellow Krahn in April 1996 in the fighting that convulsed the capital that spring.

"A trend which we think is a good one"

In 1987 Chester Crocker had written a letter to the New York–based Lawyers Committee for Human Rights taking issue with the committee's bleak assessment of conditions in Liberia. "We believe there is movement in a positive direction," Crocker wrote. "If you take a moving picture, it shows a trend which we think is a good one. If you take a snapshot, then in that snapshot you can see problems. Problems are not absent, but the situation has improved."

Looking back after seven years of war, it is easy to see how wrong Crocker was. But even at the time it was hard to fathom this notion of a "moving picture" that failed to account for the importance of justice. What moviegoer would be fooled by "movement in a positive direction" in a film in which there was a grisly murder in the opening scene, and everyone knows who did it, yet after an hour there has been no investigation, no arrest and the principal suspect remains defiantly at large? Sooner or later, the audience knows, there's going to be hell to pay.

Crocker's moving-picture analogy seemed premised on a people willing to settle for a stolen election and shrug off innumerable brutalities. One had to wonder whether he could have imagined such a picture if the people in it were white. Over the years I have sometimes wondered whether not just Crocker's acquiescence in black tyranny but that of administrations before and since was born of cynicism or racism. It would be unfair to single out Crocker, for I have been inclined to believe that in Washington generally there was more than a little of both, and that the two reinforced each other. There was Cold War calculation, to be sure, but there was also an unconscious, deep-seated set of racial attitudes, a belief that Africans are incapable of governing themselves. This made it easier for the United States to intervene according to its own interests.

It wasn't just Cold War ideologues and it wasn't just whites who projected the complexities of race in America and our own convoluted racial attitudes onto Africa. There was an inadvertent collusion of those on the right and the left, including, for their own reasons, many African Americans, that eclipsed black African tyranny as a source of Africa's problems—the eclipse being one dimension of the "darkness" we associate with Africa.

In his memoir Crocker wrote that Africa's low profile in the United States allowed him, for a time at least, "the luxury of conducting foreign policy on its merits." This is an unashamedly elitist view of foreign policy making—the notion that men in pinstripe suits are best able to address the problems of the world unencumbered by the hoi polloi. But it is true that, for better or worse, U.S. policy toward Africa has been virtually immune from meaningful public scrutiny.

The "darkness" we associate with Africa is at least in part a reflection of our own blind spot: when it comes to Africa, Americans really are in the dark. From the earliest references in both scholarly and popular literature, the dominant image of the continent has been "darkest Africa"—a mysterious and chaotic place inhabited by backward peoples with inscrutable minds. Even the eminent sage George F. Kennan reflected this stilted view in an article about South Africa in *Foreign Affairs* in 1971: "The real state of mind of the South African native remains, so far as many of us can see, a book with seven seals."

The press bears a measure of responsibility for this attitude. There is a school of thought that the overwhelming emphasis on bad news creates an unrepresentative image of Africa. There may be some truth in this. My own view is that a more serious, and sinister, problem is not the quantity of bad news but the quality. Television can broadcast powerful images of war and suffering that make viewers care, but it rarely provides a context that helps them to evaluate what they are seeing. Even the most sophisticated newspapers and magazines in the United States too often convey a superficial picture of Africa's myriad problems. Centuries of history are summarized in a paragraph. Complex political conflicts are characterized as "tribal." The responsibility of individual political leaders is scarcely noted, if at all. The awful symptoms of conflict all but completely crowd out their causes. The degree to which Americans may or may not have compounded the problem by aiding and abetting bad leaders is rarely noted.

There have been exceptions over the years, and I believe there has been some improvement over the past decade. But in general, Americans who rely on the American press for an understanding of Africa can be forgiven for imagining that Africa's problems defy rational explication.

The Clinton administration was justly criticized for blocking an effective U.N. response to Rwanda's genocide, and Clinton belatedly admitted dropping the ball. But who can blame him? At the time there was no public pressure for Clinton to act—few indignant editorials, no marches on the State Department, no congressional outcry. The staff officer for Africa on the National Security Council during that period told me he received exactly one telephone call during the genocide urging a stronger U.S. response.

"Guilt"

The free hand of policy elites is also partly due to the absence of a powerful, cohesive domestic constituency concerned with Africa's problems. Crocker underscored this point in his memoir, when he turned his discussion to a rare exception to the rule: the debate over sanctions against South Africa in the mid-1980s: "By the end of 1985 the free hand we had previously enjoyed became an object of nostalgia. Suddenly, we found ourselves ensnared in the polarization, hypocrisy, and purely political logic that flourished just outside our doors in Washington. Africa would become the ultimate 'freebie' in American foreign policy. Remote from the American experience, Africa was the stuff of legends and stereotypes: it was the last remaining land of white hats and black hats, a Manichean playground for underemployed Western activists on the right and the left. Where else was there such a pure play on racism or anti-communism? Where else was there so little need for knowledge, experience, or self-discipline? Since our tangible strategic and economic interests in Africa were so modest, there was literally no penalty when politicians were caught playing with matches. There was no one to hold participants accountable if they made matters worse in the name of 'doing something' about the region's many evils."

Apart from the cheap shot about "underemployed" activists, whoever they might have been, Crocker has a point. The irony is that he himself exemplified the all but complete absence of accountability for those who "made matters worse" in Africa—until, that is, the deficiencies of constructive engagement became so flagrant that the messy machinery of democracy finally kicked into gear and put a stop to it.

Crocker's unhappy encounter with accountability was prompted in large part by TransAfrica, a Washington-based organization set up in the 1980s to ensure that black Americans have a voice in foreign policy debates. Led by Randall Robinson, an energetic and articulate lawyer-activist, TransAfrica quickly won the support of black political elites, including the Congressional Black Caucus. Most Americans had never heard of TransAfrica until he organized a protest against apartheid—and against Crocker's policy of constructive engagement—outside the South African embassy in Washington in 1984. That protest sparked a wave of demonstrations across the country. TransAfrica's activism was a catalyst for the public outcry and congressional outrage that led to the Comprehensive Anti-Apartheid Act of 1986. It also earned Robinson recognition as an authoritative representative of African American attitudes toward Africa.

But TransAfrica was mostly missing in action when it came to the rest of the continent. There is no record of TransAfrica's raising any protest against Samuel Doe's tyranny in Liberia, or against Mobutu of

Zaire, or Siad Barre of Somalia, or Nimieri of Sudan. Not until after the demise of apartheid in 1994 did Robinson turn his focus to the problem of black tyranny, first in Haiti and then in Nigeria. Black Africans for years sought in vain to enlist the support of enlightened Westerners in their struggles against black tyranny; the silence for the most part was deafening.

The exiled Kenyan scholar Michael Chege, writing about the role of African intellectuals in stoking ethnic divisions, described what he called a "specious dichotomy" between right and left in the West. "At one extreme," Chege wrote, "committed Africa bashers present all black intellectuals as incompetent—willful and irresponsible partisans in the self-destructive chaos sweeping the continent. At the other extreme, represented by uncritical Western admirers of mythical Africa and the self-styled 'Afrocentrist' school, African elites appear as innocent victims of colonialism and Western racism, a group not sinning but sinned against."

One thing that set Chester Crocker apart among Africa hands and elevated him to the position of assistant secretary of state at the age of thirty-nine was that he was one of the very few conservative scholars specializing in African affairs. In the late 1960s and early '70s the political center among Africanists moved sharply to the left. A growing number of academics embraced "dependency theory"—a theory of underdevelopment that blamed Western "neocolonialism" for the disappointing performance of independent Africa.

Among African Americans, meanwhile, there has been great sensitivity about publicly criticizing the black leadership of independent black countries. There has been a sense, rightly or wrongly, that a measure of their self-esteem as a black race in America is somehow tied to the success or failure of independent black governments running their own shows. The tragedy in this is that blacks are *not* running their own shows—the shows are being run by tyrants.

There have been exceptions over the years. Congressman Ron Dellums of California, for one, fought relentlessly to curtail U.S. support for Mobutu. But by and large the tendency has been to judge black African leaders almost entirely by the color of their skin rather than the content of their character.

Political correctness plays a part. Even at this late date there is a sense in some circles that pointing the finger at black Africans, even black African tyrants, will feed racist stereotypes. I asked Herman Cohen how he explained the U.S. failure in Liberia. He made no attempt to justify it, but emphasized the broader history in which decisions on Liberia were made. "In Africa," he said, "we were accepting military coups. We were accepting rigged elections. This was our over-all Africa policy."

But why?

"When I look back on it now, I see two reasons. One was the Cold War. The over-all policy was not to be too tough on countries that supported our foreign policy. Doe wasn't stupid. He made a serious effort to support our policy. There couldn't have been a better friend of the U.S. than General Doe. Mobutu was a close second. But this was a worldwide policy. We were accepting dictatorships in Pakistan, in Central America. We also accepted stupid economic policies."

But there was more to it than Cold War calculation, he said.

"The other was guilt, stemming from our own civil rights movement. We let the Africans get away with a lot. It was guilt over civil rights and colonialism. The African American community would pressure us. The idea was, we will not tell Africans what to do because of what we did to them in the past. There was a symbiotic linkup to civil rights."

It is one of the many tragedies of Africa that its tyrants over the decades have found refuge in the tormented, defensive, guilt-ridden pathology of America's unresolved history of racism.

"Moral hygiene"

Crocker called his memoir *High Noon in Southern Africa: Making Peace in a Rough Neighborhood*. Casting himself in a role fit for Gary Cooper, he called it "the record of an American diplomatic strategy which helped us win the Cold War in the Third World."

The memoir is an intriguing account of the nearly decade-long negotiation that led to Namibian independence in 1989. It is, Crocker wrote, "the story of how Southern Africa's own thirty years' war was finally ended, setting the stage for the recent, dramatic turn away from apartheid and one party dictatorship and toward democracy and political reconciliation in this vast region." He described himself as "an American public servant who was able to see a strategy through from conceptualization and implementation to the actual realization of a goal—in this case, a southern Africa peace settlement." He had a chance, he wrote, "to put some good, logical ideas into action." But, he noted with his signature edge, "sensible ideas do not always appeal to wishful thinkers."

Crocker wasted no time in establishing his opinion of his critics. Noting in his introduction that his policies became "ensnared in a nasty, partisan test of wills," he asserted, "Our concepts—so self-evidently consistent with responsible U.S. internationalism and activist diplomacy—became the target of bumper sticker posturing." Recalling the widespread criticism of "constructive engagement" as "all carrot but no stick," Crocker lamented that America's domestic debate over his policies "overwhelmed rational discourse. "These caricatures of U.S. policy bore no resemblance to my self-evidently centrist and idealistic conception."

Backing up his own self-evident role as an exemplar of idealism and rational discourse, Crocker cited a former ambassador to Pretoria, Edward Perkins, who described southern Africa as "a sort of 'political vending machine' into which we insert our coins to receive moral hygiene or instant ideological gratification." The reference to Perkins would stick in the craw of Liberians, who remember when Perkins, an African American, served as ambassador to Liberia prior to his assignment in Pretoria. He was America's man in Monrovia during the critical events of 1985, and he was widely viewed as an apologist for Doe.

When I was in Monrovia in March 1986, I paid a call on Perkins at the embassy. A stiffly formal diplomat, taciturn to a fault, Perkins had agreed to be interviewed "on background" only—meaning that I was not to quote him. Yet even under that cloak of anonymity he had precious little to offer beyond blandly hopeful pronouncements about Doe's supposed willingness to do the right thing. Perkins had nothing to say about Doe's crimes and dismissed my observation that the population was in a boiling rage. He also brushed aside my suggestion that perhaps some sort of investigation of the November 12 business might be in order. He assured me that he had good access to Doe and his top associates, and that he had been counseling Doe, behind closed doors, to "mix with the people" more. He expressed earnest optimism that Doe seemed to be getting the message. I scribbled in my notebook, "This man is living on another planet."

Six years later, I asked Charles Taylor about Ambassador Perkins. He remembered the man well, and his evaluation was interesting. "I think Ambassador Perkins did a whole lot of harm," Taylor said. "He's one of those black American people who came here thinking he understands the African people. And on the basis of that he conducted a stupid and misguided policy. He thought the problem was between the Americo-Liberians and the indigenous people. But the problem in Liberia has always been between those that had and those that did not. It was just garbage that it was one group against another."

Of course, Taylor is no one to judge. And in truth, Perkins was probably little more than a loyal career diplomat carrying out policies fashioned by his superiors in Washington. He had little room for independent maneuver and showed no instinct for seizing it. The fact that he was black may or may not have made any difference in his thinking about Liberia, but it would be his defining qualification on another controversial front. For Perkins was the man of the hour when Crocker's "constructive engagement" with South Africa came under fire. At the height of the sanctions debate in the summer of 1986, with the Reagan administration facing accusations of racism for coddling Pretoria, Perkins, as an African American, was the perfect antidote. He was duly reassigned to Pretoria. His close identification with Samuel Doe was scarcely noted even by the administration's critics, for what clearly mattered was not *who* Perkins was but *what* he was.

Perkins was thus uniquely suited to make his cynical observation about the "political vending machine" of southern Africa, since he was himself the "coin" Crocker inserted into the region as a source of moral hygiene.

"Logical necessity"

Crocker's policy of "constructive engagement" in South Africa is worth recalling because it coincided with the origins of "black-on-black" violence in that country in the mid-1980s, which we will examine in detail below. The policy aimed to influence South Africa with the carrot of closer ties between the United States and the white minority government in Pretoria rather than with the stick of economic sanctions. During the 1980 presidential campaign, Crocker had chaired Ronald Reagan's Africa Working Group. After the election he attracted the attention of Reagan's transition team with that article in *Foreign Affairs*, "South Africa: Strategy for Change," in which he lambasted the Carter administration for its open hostility toward Pretoria. Crocker, like Reagan, professed abhorrence for apartheid, but he argued that Carter's confrontational approach had only made the Pretoria government dig in its heals. "Effective coercive influence is a rare commodity in foreign policy," he wrote.

In the event, Crocker's brand of quiet diplomacy turned out to be anything but quiet, and not just ineffective but counterproductive. After he took office, Crocker had argued in a confidential memo that South Africa would be more pliant because the Reagan administration had "unprecedented credibility" with Pretoria. The South African government, he wrote, "knows we are the best they can expect."

In a speech in Hawaii in August 1981, Crocker announced that the Reagan administration was seeking closer ties with South Africa not because it found apartheid any less abhorrent than the Carter administration had but rather to try to influence its government and at the same time preserve American interests. "In South Africa, the region's dominant country," he declared, "it is not our task to choose between black and white."

Over the next two years, the Reagan administration eased controls on exports to South Africa, beefed up its diplomatic mission there, approved visas for South African intellectuals and military leaders, and defended South African interests in the United Nations.

Then in 1983 the South African government proposed a scheme to include Indians and people of mixed race in parliament—but not blacks. The plan was widely viewed by black South Africans as a textbook case of divide-and-rule, and it was the catalyst for the township uprising that swept across South Africa in the mid-1980s. Nevertheless the Reagan administration applauded the plan as a "step in the right direction."

South Africa responded to such gestures with a crackdown on the black majority, beginning in 1984, which not only discredited the whole policy of constructive engagement but also led to the imposition of economic sanctions that Crocker had tried so desperately to avoid. South Africa's Bishop Desmond Tutu, winner of the Nobel

Peace Prize, condemned Crocker's policy as "immoral, evil, and totally un-Christian."

Meanwhile, beyond its borders South Africa was staging commando raids and arming proxy insurgencies, with devastating results. Crocker and his colleagues did condemn cross-border raids and finally, after commando attacks on Angola and Botswana, withdrew the U.S. ambassador to Pretoria for several months. Yet Pretoria clearly felt little fear that waging covert war against its neighbors would bring serious recriminations from Washington.

And who could blame them? For even as Crocker was denouncing destabilization, he was riding a wave of congressional pressure to resume U.S. military support for Jonas Savimbi's UNITA guerrilla movement in Angola. Both the Reagan administration and Congress saw aid to UNITA as a way of sticking it to Cuba and the Soviet Union, and pressuring them to withdraw from Angola. But the policy also advanced South Africa's interests in the region. Savimbi was Pretoria's client. There was no way to aid him without going through South Africa. So the United States was "engaged" in a military alliance with South Africa in its war against its black-ruled neighbors. It is a truism that in war, the only issue is whose side you're on. From the perspective of black Africans living in a region consumed by war, Washington was on the side of white South Africa. It was a scandalous alliance that no amount to rhetoric about Washington's "abhorrence" of apartheid could allay.

For me as an American living in southern Africa at the time, it was impossible to refute the widespread impression among black Africans that my country was collaborating substantially with the apartheid system in its most pernicious and destructive tactics aimed at perpetuating white rule. Crocker himself, in his memoir, described the Mozambican guerrilla army RENAMO (Resistercia Nacional Moçambicana) as "an African Khmer Rouge." Crocker was clearly well aware of RENAMO's dependency on South African Military Intelligence—he called it "the hottest property in General Westhuizen's inventory"—a reference to General Pieter Van der Westhuizen, who was chief of Military Intelligence in the early 1980s. Yet Crocker and his colleagues still claimed to oppose apartheid even as they entered into a military alliance with the same forces backing this "African

Khmer Rouge." Congress finally enacted stringent sanctions over Reagan's veto, an unprecedented foreign policy rebuke of a president, in the fall of 1986.

By that time, even Crocker had grown frustrated with Pretoria's intransigence. He began to openly criticize the apartheid regime. In January 1986 he toured Duduza, one of South Africa's black townships especially hard hit by police and army repression. Two months later, in testimony before the House of Representatives, he became the first Reagan administration official to allude to the African National Congress as "freedom fighters" and for the first time called openly for black-majority rule. In another speech, in July 1986, he denounced South Africa for what he called its "scorched earth policy."

Constructive engagement was based on what Crocker called "the logical necessity for regional peacemaking to *precede* basic internal change in South Africa." Even at the time, however, it was clear that constructive engagement suffered from some of the same flaws as Crocker's none-too-silent diplomacy with Samuel Doe. Chief among them was the flawed premise that an embattled tyranny was genuinely capable of reforming itself, and committed to doing so. Just as in Liberia, the policy actually exacerbated the situation inside South Africa and throughout the region by indulging the white regime's divide-and-rule tactics—leading that regime, its internal and external victims and much of the rest of the world to believe that, whatever the rhetoric coming from Washington, American prestige was on the side of apartheid.

After eight tumultuous years in office, Crocker had little to show for his "nimble diplomacy" other than the Namibian peace accord. The agreement that emerged in December 1988 ended twenty-two years of fighting between South Africa and Namibian rebels and converted Crocker's "triple play": both Cuba and South Africa withdrew their forces from Angola in 1989, and Namibia achieved its independence in early 1990.

Crocker's account of this achievement was a little Orwellian. What he characterized as an eight-year process of doggedly persistent peacemaking through restraint and—his favorite word—"logic" was the very same period when, as the Reagan administration mutely averted its eyes, hard-line militarists in South Africa were pursuing ruinous proxy wars in Angola and Mozambique, killing, detaining and torturing as many as 10,000 domestic opponents, and, as we shall see, hatching the "Third Force" conspiracy in KwaZulu-Natal. The "thirty years' war" Crocker resolved in Namibia claimed between 10,000 and 20,000 lives. The casualties in Angola and Mozambique were counted in the hundreds of thousands in this period. The fighting in KwaZulu would claim more than 20,000.

Moreover, Crocker's memoir suggested that when the climate finally ripened for a settlement within the framework of "linkage" (tying Namibian independence to Cuban withdrawal from Angola) seven years behind the optimistic schedule of Crocker's original scenario, the weight of explanation should fall on his own inspired diplomacy. But really, the turning point in Namibia came as the Soviet leader Mikhail Gorbachev consolidated his grip on power and began to withdraw Soviet support for wars of liberation in the Third World.

In any case, the peace in Angola turned out to be fleeting. Nearly a decade after Crocker's vaunted peace agreement, the Cubans and Russians were long since gone from Angola, but Jonas Savimbi—our horse in that contest—was still fighting for a share of power, which he could not achieve in successive peace accords and disputed elections. By 1999, half a million Angolans had been killed and a million made homeless by three decades of fighting with no end in sight.

"*Iran*-contra *in microcosm*"

There was a subtext to "constructive engagement" that helps explain its ultimate meaning. It is of a piece with the U.S. role in Liberia and Zaire. Crocker himself highlighted this little-known saga as a means of absolving himself of responsibility for the obvious failures of his policy.

In his memoir Crocker placed considerable blame for the difficulties he encountered on President Reagan himself, for what he called "the insensitivity that would be the sad hallmark of his sporadic personal involvement on South Africa." In fact, Crocker was scathing in his account of a notorious speech Reagan made in July 1986, in which the President spoke of "a friendly nation like South Africa." "One wondered," Crocker wrote, "what conclusions leaders of various races in Southern Africa were expected to draw from this strange terminology."

Crocker went on to conclude: "Sadly, Reagan failed to convey a sense of outrage on racial issues. His comments regretting the violence and the killings were linked to the argument that much of it was blacks killing blacks, a point which implied that the problem was 'tribal.'. . . When pressed on whether he would ever 'go beyond friendly persuasion,' Reagan fell into the trap of saying that Botha himself was trying to eliminate apartheid. While there was a kernel of reality in Reagan's arguments, the President tended to discredit his case by sounding so much like the government from which he was so reluctant to distance himself."

Sad but true, and these comments suggest that Crocker understood even at the time that the policy with which he was so closely identified was problematical. But here, intriguingly, Crocker had a story to tell.

Crocker calls it "Iran-*contra* in microcosm." It is a tale of "subversion occurring in our own ranks," whereby right-wingers in the Defense Department and the CIA were briefing the South African ambassador, Herbert Beukes, about secret negotiating strategies, distributing a "special estimate" on the ANC around Washington despite opposition to its contents by most of the intelligence community.

The intimacy between William Casey's CIA and South African Military Intelligence is by now well documented. It represented a hidden thread linking the Reagan administration's otherwise baffling engagement with Pretoria to Mobutu's Zaire and Samuel Doe's Liberia. Duane ("Dewey") Clarridge, a close Casey confederate who served as Latin America Division chief in the early 1980s and was a key figure in the Iran-*contra* affair, wrote in his memoirs of giving briefings in 1982–83 to General Van der Westhuizen, chief of South African Military Intelligence, "on his visits to Langley." This was the same General Van der Westhuizen whom Crocker deplored for sponsoring an "African Khmer Rouge" in Mozambique.

Clarridge described these meetings in terms that make it clear he regarded the South African as a confederate in the anti-Communist cause—no more and no less. The two discussed the logistics of funneling support to Savimbi and his "UNITA freedom fighters against the Marxist government in Angola and its Cuban supporters. . . . We had information to share with them as well," Clarridge recalled enthusiastically, noting that Savimbi's UNITA troops were facing some of the same Cuban paramilitary personnel whom U.S. troops had captured on the island of Grenada the previous October and repatriated to Cuba. "The names of these Cubans might be useful to the South Africans and Savimbi in inducing defections from among them," Clarridge wrote.

Some of these briefings covered the *contra* war in Nicaragua. Clarridge reported that he traveled to Pretoria in 1983, initially with the aim of soliciting South Africa's help as an alternative source of supply of arms for the *contras*. But he said Casey and he finally agreed not to discuss South African support for the *contras*. "Political realities"—namely, congressional opposition to apartheid—"dictated that the Agency not ask for South Africa's help in Central America and not accept it if offered."

There was no suggestion in Clarridge's account that either Casey or he shared Congress's aversion to apartheid; it simply wasn't an issue with them. Crocker himself described Van der Westhuizen as "Casey's friend." Little wonder that among the military and security chiefs who dominated South Africa throughout the 1980s, Crocker's vaunted "constructive engagement" was understood for what it was: little more than a gloss for an ongoing military alliance between two Cold War allies. President Reagan's "insensitivity" may have rendered the gloss ineffective, but Reagan's "doctrine" was the driving force behind it.

In my own interviews with apartheid's securocrats, they never failed to remind me of what they took pains to describe as their close relations with "you guys," as one put it. "It's a brotherhood," General Jac Buchner, the notorious covert operative and torturer who was at the heart of the "black-on-black" violence in South Africa, told me wistfully. "We in the police of the various offices overseas—everybody knew you. Our training came mostly from you guys, and the Brits."

Crocker wrote in his memoir that after Congress effectively torpedoed constructive engagement, a colleague urged him to resign swiftly. "My resignation could be seen as an act of protest at the sheer incoherence within the administration as well as the terminal sanctimoniousness sweeping the land. It would be a chance to blow the whistle against the hijacking of U.S. policy in broad daylight, splitting our party, damaging the President, and handing the sanctioneers a needless victory. It would also afford me the freedom to state that constructive engagement was the only wise course, even if P. W. Botha and Ronald Reagan were not, perhaps, the ideal leaders to make it work. I dreamt of jackals tearing at a carcass left by lions on the African veldt."

But, he concluded, "my resignation would have gratified too many of the wrong people."

"We have a tremendous amount of influence"

In May 1997, the *New York Times* carried a report from Washington examining the U.S. response to an escalating civil war in Zaire that would soon bring down Mobutu. A growing concern was that the leader of the rebel alliance sweeping across the country, Laurent Kabila, was showing signs of becoming a ruthless warlord in command of a marauding army with a tendency to massacre civilians. The *Times* called on the former assistant secretary of state Chester A. Crocker, by now a sage elder statesman at Georgetown and chairman of the U.S. Institute for Peace, for comment. What could the United States do about Kabila? the *Times* wanted to know.

"The point," Crocker replied, "is that we and our friends control the keys to the clubs and the treasuries that Kabila will need to tap if he is going to rebuild the country—the World Bank, the International Monetary Fund, our development funds and those of the Europeans. So we have a tremendous amount of influence if we choose to use it, with the French and neighboring countries. But we had opportunities early in the 1990s and we did nothing to move Mobutu. We've had opportunities since October 1996, but we talked a lot and did absolutely nothing to back up our words. Kabila naturally concluded that he had a blank check, so it's important that we condition any support to his sharing power with other people."

Would that Crocker were as candid about the "tremendous amount of influence" he himself wielded when he controlled the keys to the club and admitted Doe, Mobutu and the rest, who naturally concluded that they had a blank check.

Was Crocker, finally, a war criminal? Many Liberians—and Zairians and Angolans and black South Africans—would have gladly seen him tried as one. But of course Africans had no say in the matter. Crocker wasn't accountable to them. In any case, maybe Crocker was not so much a war criminal as the kind of figure many war criminals depend on: an articulate front man, capable of putting an intellectual gloss on otherwise crude power politics. And he was assuredly a careerist, willing to mask his own ambition and the compromises it required in the rhetoric of a larger legitimating cause. His cause was the global struggle against communism. It was a legitimate cause. But it is difficult to avoid the conclusion that for Crocker, no less than for the Big Men across Africa with whom he consorted, the little people didn't exist. In any case, in fairness, if front man is what he was, he fronted not just for Doe and Mobutu and the rest—but for us.

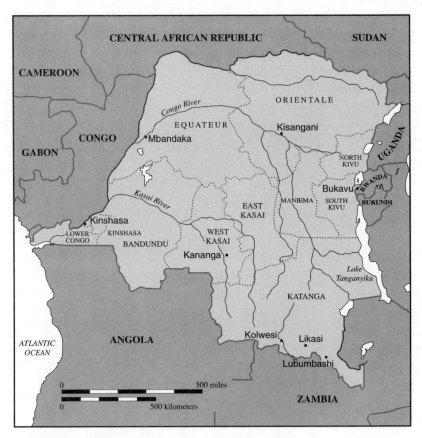

Democratic Republic of the Congo (formerly Zaire)

3

"A VOICE OF GOOD SENSE AND GOOD WILL"

"Vous êtes espion!" cried the vice governor, his voice filled with menace, eyes alight with triumph. "You are spy!" he repeated in fractured English. He rose from his desk and strutted around to where I sat in mounting alarm, sweating profusely, feeling nauseated, my skin turning green, stomach churning.

"*Voilà! Voilà!*" he screamed, towering over me now, jabbing a meaty finger in my face. His huge barrel chest puffed up inside a billowing, weirdly incongruous purple silk tunic with yellow buttons and the monogrammed logo "M.P.R."—Mobutu Sese Seko's Mouvement Populaire de la Révolution on his breast.

"*Espion! Espion! Vous êtes espion!*"

It was April 7, 1993, around 10 P.M. We were entering the fourth hour of questioning in a dingy, humid, bare-walled interrogation room at the headquarters of the Garde Civile, Mobutu's elite security police, in Lubumbashi, the capital of Shaba Province in southern Zaire. What had seemed like an unpleasant but probably benign little adventure was starting to look downright dangerous. A worst-case scenario, which I had sometimes imagined in my travels across Africa but never come close to confronting, now looked entirely possible.

I knew many Africans, of course, from Liberia to Sudan to South Africa, who had endured the nightmare of incommunicado interrogation by agents of a lawless state. I had heard them describe to me not just beatings, torture and rape, but also fear, the unthinkable terror of knowing that *anything can happen*—and *has* happened to innumerable others. I had sometimes imagined how I might respond in such a situation. Would I be brave? Might I capitulate? In my imagination I had sometimes fancied myself a tough enough customer to face down the most brutish interrogator, maybe even shame him into staying his hand.

But this was real, and I was scared. I was also tired, hungry, thirsty and desperately in need of a toilet. The physical manifestation of fear was something I hadn't expected. It seemed to be completely beyond any power of will or courage or discipline to control. The nausea swelled inside me. The sweat poured out from head to toe.

No one in the room could fail to see what was happening to me, least of all the vice governor, who looked down at me with obvious relish, and the half dozen beaming SNIP agents hovering around us. SNIP was the acronym for Service Nationale d'Intelligence et de Protection, Mobutu's secret police.

"Are you okay?" asked my wife, Mary Jane.

She had been sitting beside me throughout this ordeal, a model of composure—solid as a rock. I said I was fine. Her expression made clear that I looked anything but.

Mary Jane was twenty-nine years old at the time. She had accompanied me to Zaire on an assignment for *The Atlantic Monthly*, working as my photographer and French interpreter. She was also—though the Zairians didn't know this—a staff employee of Human Rights Watch, the New York–based monitoring group. And she was the reason for my mounting alarm. I was beginning to contemplate the very real possibility that our captors would separate us, as any half-competent interrogator would. It was a measure of their ineptitude that they hadn't already done so. But they held all the cards. And in my tired and fearful mind I was calculating the likelihood that they would finally take Mary Jane away to some other dingy room on the premises, and do with her what they might. *And there was nothing I could do to stop them.*

I pretended I spoke not a word of French, rendering me useless to them in her absence.

She went along with their presumption that, as a woman, she was too dumb and insubstantial to recall any names or details of the reporting we'd been doing.

"With all due respect, I am not at liberty to give you those names," I repeated. "I would very much appreciate it if you allowed me to contact the U.S. consulate."

Mary Jane and I had been detained shortly after noon in Kolwezi, a mining town about ten hours away by dirt road on the back of a jam-packed passenger truck—which is how we had gotten there the day before—or, alternatively, a forty-five-minute flight in a twelve-seat Jetstream aircraft owned by Gécamines, the state-owned mining giant—which is how we had returned, in custody, to Lubumbashi earlier that evening. We had gone to Kolwezi to investigate a campaign of state-sponsored ethnic cleansing, as it would now be called. Gangs of ethnic Katangese, the majority group in Shaba (previously called Katanga Province), were attacking minority Kasaians, routing them from their jobs and homes by the tens of thousands. Hundreds of displaced Kasaians were dying each day from hunger and disease.

SNIP agents in jeans and wraparound sunglasses had apprehended us at the entrance to the vast Gécamines mining compound in Kolwezi. They said they were acting on orders from the governor of Shaba, Gabriel Kyungu wa Kumwanza. Governor Kyungu was Mobutu's appointed representative in the region. He was also, by all accounts, the principal instigator of the violence.

The agents had bundled us into their car and taken us to the home of Kolwezi's mayor, P. Anschaire Moji a Kapasu. He informed us that Governor Kyungu had been displeased to learn that two *wazungu*—white people—were at large in Kolwezi, claiming to be journalists, "reporting without authorization," as he put it. We were to be dispatched to the airstrip and flown back to Lubumbashi for a meeting with the governor.

The meeting never happened. Instead, we were taken to the Garde Civile. For three hours we were interrogated by a team of cartoonishly bumbling midlevel SNIP agents. They believed we were spies plotting with local dissidents. They pawed endlessly through our passports, seeking in vain for some telltale piece of incriminating evidence. They were led by a crudely self-important thug named Bob, all glower and chest-thumping bluster, who endeavored as best he could to intimidate us by yelling and pounding on the desktop.

"Tell us the truth!" Bob shouted. "Who put you in touch with *Maître* Kanyama?"

Maître Kanyama Mbayabu had been our guide in Kolwezi. A suave and erudite lawyer in his thirties, with a wife and two children, Kanyama was a municipal judge and a leader of Kolwezi's fledgling human rights movement. He was also Kasaian. Kanyama had introduced us to leaders of the Kasaian community in Kolwezi. He set up interviews with survivors and witnesses of the violence. He had taken us to dinner the previous night with some of his activist friends. He had escorted us on our ill-fated tour of the Gécamines mining compound, and he had been arrested with us. He was flown with us in custody to Lubumbashi.

"*Courage,*" Kanyama's wife had whispered to Mary Jane as we left her behind on Kolwezi's airfield landing strip.

On the plane, Kanyama had sat right in front of me. I had stared out the window at the vast, lush expanse of the Congo River basin stretching out beneath us. I was sanguine about our situation; doubtful after years of innocuous scrapes across the continent that serious harm would befall us. In fact, I was grateful for a free flight back to Lubumbashi, on a corporate jet no less, which obviated the need for another ten hours on the back of that dust-caked, jam-packed truck. And there was the prospect of an enviably contentious encounter with Governor Kyungu.

In midflight, however, I had noticed that Kanyama was drenched in sweat, the beads literally dripping from his chin. Clearly he, if not yet I, was aware of the trouble we might be in.

Upon our arrival at the Garde Civile, Kanyama was immediately separated from us. Now he was being interrogated somewhere else on the premises—we didn't know where. Mary Jane and I both thought we heard what sounded like cries from another part of the building, but we couldn't be sure. Our imaginations were running in overdrive.

Kanyama's uncertain fate was no small part of my building anxiety. I had traveled around Africa enough to know that foreigners—that is to say, white folks, *wazungu*—enjoy protections that Africans themselves don't enjoy. Even a Kalashnikov-waving checkpoint shake-down artist in jeans and rubber flip-flops can make the elementary calculation that if something happens to a *mzungu*—in Swahili, "*wa*" is plural, "*m*" is singular—word will get back to the powers that be, diplomats will demand an accounting, and heads might have to roll. Whereas if something happens to one of the natives—even someone like Kanyama, a lawyer with foreign friends—no one will ever hear about it. It's unjust, it's unfair, but there it is. "White man's *juju,*" they sometimes call it, a form of diplomatic immunity from the culture of impunity.

At the Garde Civile in Lubumbashi, Mary Jane and I sat in metal-frame chairs in front of a battered wooden desk with no phone, no lamp, and no papers of any kind. A single light bulb hung overhead. The walls were bare, save for a waist-high border of grime and splotches of stain. A boombox sat on the floor in the corner. Bob took his seat at the desk in front of us. His SNIP buddies loitered with studied nonchalance.

At issue was whether we would provide the names of the Zairians with whom we had spoken. Mary Jane and I both knew that if we gave up those names, those who had assisted us would very likely be rounded up one by one, interrogated, and possibly shot. These people had helped us to document serious crimes by state agents and their proxies: murder, arson, theft. They had cooperated with us on the condition of utmost confidentiality. We were not prepared to put their lives in jeopardy.

"With all due respect," I repeated, hoping to conceal the fact that I felt anything but for these gentlemen. "I'm terribly sorry, but we are not at liberty to divulge those names. The people we spoke with did not authorize us to reveal their names. However, I would very much appreciate it if you allowed me to contact the consulate."

"You will give us those names," Bob countered.

We had no way of knowing how important those names were to Bob or anyone else. Nor could we know what Kanyama was telling his confederates, under what duress we could only imagine. We were at an impasse.

And there was the problem of the consulate. I had learned years ago in Liberia, where I was arrested under similar circumstances in 1986, that there is a huge difference between being detained incommunicado and being detained with the knowledge that people "out there" know where you are and are working to secure your release. In the first instance, the feeling of isolation and powerlessness—and fear—can be overpowering. In the latter case, the knowledge that people outside are aware of your plight is very nearly liberating in itself—all the more so if the people outside are Americans, and the people who are holding you inside are working for an American "friend" like Mobutu or Samuel Doe.

So Mary Jane and I were eager to contact the U.S. consulate. In Lubumbashi, however, because of the terror sweeping the region, the U.S. consulate had been evacuated. A lone Zairian, Tente wa Tente, was looking after the premises and was authorized to represent U.S. interests in the province. As a routine precaution, we had paid a courtesy call on the Tente soon after our arrival in Lubumbashi. Despite repeated requests, however, we were not allowed to contact him now. We were on our own.

"Who do you work for?" Bob shouted.

"Who did you meet in Kolwezi?"

"How did you meet Maître Kanyama?"

Bob's questions were menacing, but he clearly lacked decision-making authority. He appeared to be paralyzed, stalling for time, awaiting the arrival of a superior. Finally, after four hours of stalemate, the man with authority arrived—in the rotund, swaggering form of the vice governor.

What a relief, I thought. Finally a senior figure was at hand with authority to make decisions. Now we could do business. I assumed that the arrival of a high official would help us get to the bottom of this matter. I assumed that the vice governor of the province, no less, would be smarter, more competent, more cosmopolitan than the blundering characters we'd been dealing with. I assumed, in short, that we were acting in a rational environment.

I was wrong. I had failed to apprehend the perversely sinister, upside-down culture of Mobutu's Zaire. Mobutuism was a system calculated to bring out the worst in people, and it selected for the worst among them. The reality was as vividly surreal as the vice governor's flamboyant purple tunic: in Mobutu's Zaire, the dregs rose to the top.

The vice governor rifled through the contents of my wallet. He found an old laminated press card from the New York City Police Department, which I carry around with a stash of other cards from myriad countries and conferences, the U.N. and such, in the hope that they might satisfy a skeptical official of my journalistic bona fides. The vice governor spoke almost no English. But one word on this NYPD press card looked familiar: "Police." And that was all he needed.

"*Voilà, Voilà!*" he cried in triumph. He jabbed his finger at the incriminating card. "*Police! Police. Vous êtes police!*" Mary Jane calmly explained that, no, I was a journalist accredited to cover the police. The vice governor was adamant. "*Vous êtes police. Vous êtes police. Voilà, Voilà. Vous êtes espion!*"

The vice governor, it now became clear, was a fanatic, maybe even a lunatic. And we were entirely at his mercy. A rational appeal to the man's intelligence would get us nowhere. He was on a power trip, I could see. He was not so foolish as to actually believe that I was "police." But the existence of the word on my ID card gave him his pretext, the leverage he needed to exert his power. Worse, it began to dawn on me that he'd been drinking. He was going to have some fun on this Saturday night. The vice governor reveled in his power over these defenseless Americans. He strutted and preened and slammed his fists on the desk.

My sweat poured. The nausea heaved.

"You will give us those names," he finally declared, striding out of the room. "Or you can forget about the consulate."

"Fire in his wake"

Mobutu Sese Seko was nakedly, flamboyantly evil. Zaire's venerable kleptocrat was one of the longest-surviving five-star despots of the Cold War era: Mobutu Sese Seko Kuku wa za Banga, as he came to be called—"the all-powerful warrior who, because of his endurance and inflexible will to win, will go from conquest to conquest leaving fire in his wake." He was the Guide, the Messiah, the Helmsman, the Leopard, the Sun-President, the Cock who Jumps on Anything That Moves, and—it was Ronald Reagan who said it—"A voice of good sense and good will."

Mobutu was born out of wedlock on October 14, 1930, in the northern town of Lisala in Equateur Province, in what was then the Belgian Congo. His father was a traditional chief of the tiny Ngbaka ethnic group. His mother was a hotel maid. He was adopted in infancy by the man who married his mother, a cook for a Belgian judge. The judge's wife taught Mobutu to read and write in French. Beginning in 1948 he attended a succession of missionary schools in Coquilhatville (now Mbandaka). He was expelled from the last one, reportedly for stealing books from the library. As punishment he was conscripted into the Belgian colonial army, *la Force Publique*.

Mobutu served seven years in the army. In 1956, three years after his discharge, he was caught writing for an underground nationalist newspaper opposed to Belgian rule and was given the choice of prison or exile. He chose exile in Brussels, where he pursued his career in journalism—and developed a friendship with a CIA operative named Larry Devlin. The friendship proved to be opportune. When Devlin was sent to Congo as station chief in 1960, Mobutu followed.

Before independence the Congo had been a backwater. But now it assumed tremendous importance in the new African order, coveted by both the Soviets and the Americans because of its vast size, extending across the heart of the continent and bordering on nine countries, and for its rich deposits of strategic minerals, chiefly cobalt (which is important for aerospace alloys) and uranium. First the Eisenhower administration and then the Kennedy administration feared that Congo was potentially a "Cuba in the making," with huge potential for Soviet expansion across southern Africa in particular. The chief object of their concern was the fiery, charismatic nationalist Patrice Lumumba, who was elected prime minister of newly independent Congo in June 1960.

Devlin famously cabled Washington that the Congo was "experiencing classic communist effort takeover government. Whether or not Lumumba actually commie or just playing commie game to assist solidifying power, anti-West forces increasing power in Congo and there may be little time left in which take action avoid another Cuba."

Whether Patrice Lumumba really was another Fidel Castro in the making is a matter of continuing historical debate. Most likely, he was a naive, parochial idealist, out of his depth amid roiling global currents. In any event, after Allen Dulles, head of the CIA under Eisenhower, presented Lumumba to the president as "a Castro or worse," Eisenhower duly ordered the assassination of the new prime minister. Devlin, by his own account, was given a vial of deadly germs and a kit of hypodermic needles and rubber gloves.

Enter Mobutu. On July 6 and 7, 1960, Mobutu, by then a colonel and chief of staff of the army, staged what he called a "peaceful revolution"—essentially an army coup d'etat. Mobutu was now the effective head of state. Lumumba was placed under arrest. He soon escaped, but Mobutu, working closely by now with Devlin, apprehended him on December 1, 1960. Lumumba was eventually flown in custody to Lubumbashi. Lubumbashi was then the power base of Lumumba's archenemy, Moise Tshombe, and Lumumba disappeared without a trace. The most reliable accounts have it that Lumumba was beaten half to death and bayoneted on the flight to Lubumbashi, and was finished off with a bullet to the head by a Belgian mercenary. Though Devlin has admitted he had carte blanche to take out Lumumba, the CIA was able to claim that in the end it had nothing to do with the murder; it had been taken care of "internally."

"Kleptocracy"

Mobutu soon established one of Africa's archetypal one-party states, in which he tolerated no dissent and encouraged a strong personality cult. The Big Man's picture was plastered on public walls, billboards and even private homes. Stamps, coins, and paper currency all bore his portrait. State television pictured him at the start of each news broadcast descending godlike from the clouds. His rakishly cocked leopard-skin cap and mahogany walking stick were the signature symbols of his power. In rural areas it was rumored that his walking stick had magical powers and was so heavy that only he could lift it.

Under the banner of an ideology he called "authenticity," and later simply "Mobutuism," the Big Man sought to legitimize his rule by reawakening pride in values supposedly unique to Africans, all the while enhancing his own power as the undisputed chief. For two decades Zairians were forbidden to use Christian names, to bleach their skin or to straighten their hair, or even to play most kinds of foreign music on the radio. Congo was renamed Zaire, an old Portuguese corruption of the local name for the country's greatest river. Mobutu decreed his own fashion statement, a two-piece outfit of pants and a tunic, known as an abacost. The distinctive suits were patterned after the Mao suits of China—except that they were worn with an ascot at the neck.

Finally, though, what set Mobutu apart was money. His was the archetypal "kleptocracy"—government by theft. Mobutu's ill-gotten wealth was usually estimated at around $5 billion—roughly equal to the country's national debt. Stories about his bank accounts in Switzerland and his villas, ranches, palaces, and yachts throughout Europe were legion, as were wide-eyed descriptions of his gaudy white marble estate at Gbadolite, his birthplace in northern Zaire; "Versailles in the jungle," it was called. With mansions scattered around the world, he enjoyed extended vacations and lavish shopping trips to places like Disney World or Paris with large coteries of relatives and courtiers, traveling in specially chartered Boeing 747 and Concorde jets. In the 1980s he imported 5,000 sheep from Venezuela for one of his ranches; he did so by dispatching a government-owned DC-8 to make thirty-two roundtrips between Caracas and Zaire.

In Mobutu's Zaire, stealing was not just a distortion of public service but its very purpose. Mobutu reportedly obtained his first few million dollars in the early 1960s from the CIA and a U.S.-dominated U.N. peacekeeping force. He steadily augmented his wealth thereafter by blurring the distinction between public and private funds, dipping often into the national treasury.

Not least among his many lucrative sources of "leakage," as the World Bank and the International Monetary Fund call illegal diversions of money, was Gécamines. By 1980 it was estimated that officials were skimming off at least $240 million a year from the nationalized resource. In 1988 a World Bank investigation estimated that up to $400 million—a fourth of Zaire's export revenues, most of it earned from Gécamines—inexplicably vanished from the country's foreign-exchange accounts.

What was often overlooked in accounts of Mobutu's wealth was the critical role that money played as a political tool. Even as Mobutu accumulated great riches, he spent huge sums to reward his allies and buy off his opponents. The word on the street in Kinshasa when we were there in 1993, impossible to confirm but relayed to me by a diplomatic source who found it entirely credible, was that Mobutu paid an opposition leader, Nguza Karl-i-Bond, $10 million to break with the opposition and become prime minister.

"It's like the Mafia," Kanyama told us. "All Zairian politicians are poor. For survival they have to engage in politics. To earn a living, they have to be on the side of the man in power."

Herman Cohen, Chester Crocker's successor, first met Mobutu almost thirty years earlier. In an interview at the State Department shortly before he left office, Cohen was surprisingly candid with me about Washington's longtime client. He characterized Mobutu's government as "basically a clan, a family of cousins acting like the Mafia in Sicily, making these illegal deals, siphoning the money off cobalt and copper revenues." Cohen stressed that Mobutu did not simply pocket the proceeds, but used them to buttress his power. "Mobutu requires a huge cash flow," he said. "He has to keep the family afloat. In effect he has about three thousand to four thousand dependents, including women and children. It's essentially his own tribe. The attitude is 'We've got to all hang together. If we don't, we're dead.'"

Among the most important of these dependents are, of course, soldiers. A certain amount of cash had to be on hand for them. When money was tight, as it often was with the legitimate economy in ruins, Mobutu's tendency was simply to print more. Hyperinflation generally followed. This was the result in January 1993, when Mobutu tried to meet his military payroll by introducing new five-million-Zaire notes into circulation, worth about two dollars each at the time. The country's fledgling opposition movement, fearing yet another round of hyperinflation, urged shopkeepers to refuse to accept the new notes. Remarkably, the strategy worked. The soldiers found they were unable to spend their money. So they went on a *pillage*, looting Kinshasa. Shopkeepers were shot for refusing to take the new notes. Soldiers in turn were lynched by mobs of angry citizens. Kinshasa's already decimated economy was left in ruins.

Mobutu's elite troops intervened, grabbing their share and then summarily executing hundreds of rank-and-file looters. Nevertheless, the newly printed notes were effectively barred from use—everywhere, that is, except in Mobutu's home province, Equateur, and in Shaba, where Governor Kyungu successfully coerced businesses into accepting them. Prices took off. The black-market value of Zaires, 2.5 million to the dollar in Kinshasa in April 1993, went from 12 million to 24 million to the dollar in Lubumbashi during the two weeks we were there. Mary Jane and I changed money two or three times a day to keep up, carrying around thick bricks of bills bound with rubber bands, the bricks quickly depleted with each purchase of a meal or a bottle of beer.

Mobutu's Zaire was a study in central banking as an adjunct of gangsterism. Few countries have ever witnessed so extreme a case of the monetary system as a pillar of political power—and the riches that come with that power. Zaire's central bank was little more than Mobutu's hip pocket, a ready source of cash with which to reward friends and co-opt enemies.

After the Cold War ended Zaire was effectively cut off from the world financial system. The International Monetary Fund and the United States suspended loans to the country in 1990, after it had run up arrears of $70 million. By then Zaire had already fallen off seven IMF wagons. But its lucrative links with the world's underground economy continued to thrive. Zaire remained a haven for mercenaries, counterfeiters, money launderers and diamond smugglers. Even the central bank had to resort to the black market to buy and sell hard currency.

The central bank had first figured prominently in accounts of misappropriation more than two decades earlier. Albert Ndele, a former governor of the bank, reported that in 1970, the last year of his tenure as governor, he gave the IMF a secret report demonstrating that Mobutu had diverted the entire executive branch budget. Ndele said Mobutu used the money to buy a minor Swiss bank for himself and a $6 million Mercedes-Benz assembly plant for his first wife, Marie-Antoinette Mobutu.

When the IMF deployed a team of technical experts to "reform" the central bank in 1978–79, their leader, Erwin Blumenthal, formerly of the West German central bank, quit in despair after less than a year. He concluded that "control of financial transactions of the presidency is virtually impossible," because "the president's bureau makes no distinction between state expenditures and personal expenditure."

An American investigative journalist, Steve Askin, found that the despot's absolute control of the central bank enabled him to make a mockery of parliamentary budget appropriations and reshape state spending to suit his whims. For example, in 1986 the Office of the Presidency spent $94 million, more than six times its parliament-approved budget. Gross overspending by the presidency was funded in part by gross underspending in education, public health and other human services. Schools and teachers received only $8 million of the $73 million budgeted to them for 1986. Health programs received only $8 million of $24 million.

Mobutu himself provided perhaps the most damning indictment of this system. In a 1977 speech to the legislative council, he declared: "In a word, everything is for sale, anything can be bought in our country. And in this flow, he who holds the slightest cover of authority uses it illegally to acquire money, goods, prestige or avoid obligations. The right to be recognized by a public servant, to have one's children enrolled in school, to obtain medical care, a diploma, etc. . . . are all subject to this tax which, though invisible, is known and expected by all."

The president was ostensibly condemning these practices, yet he clearly condoned them among all except those who showed excessive greed. A year earlier he had warned public servants that "if you want to steal, steal a little in a nice way. But if you steal too much to become rich overnight, you'll be caught."

Participants in Mobutu's predatory racket were not limited to Zairians. As with Firestone and other companies in Liberia, a great many foreign corporations, salesmen and investors were frequently willing to offer secret inducements to Mobutu to obtain plush contracts or access to natural resources or protected markets. The American financier and diamond merchant Maurice Tempelsman, the last companion of Jackie Onassis, was but the most polished in a large cosmopolitan cast. Foreign investors in Mobutu's racket received robust returns on the 10 percent "commissions" they paid to Mobutu and his agents. Bribery, they might say, is a necessary business practice. But their willing collusion reinforced the malady that Westerners so loftily condemned in public.

Mobutu's extravagance was hardly without precedent in Central Africa. It was of a piece with the standard set by King Leopold II of Belgium, who in 1876 claimed the Congo as his private fiefdom, to be exploited for private gain. Leopold managed to extract an enormous fortune in rubber and ivory while leaving behind a legacy of brutality that was virtually unmatched in the colonial era—severed heads to quell resistance, severed hands as a penalty for failure to meet production quotas. The historian and journalist Adam Hochschild, in his excellent 1998 narrative, *King Leopold's Ghost*, estimated that as many as 5 million to 10 million Congolese natives perished from overwork, malnutrition and outright slaughter during Leopold's tenure. It was Leopold's wanton exploitation of Congo that became the subject of Joseph Conrad's 1902 novel, *Heart of Darkness*. In 1904, outraged world opinion forced Leopold to abdicate, and the colony was annexed by the Belgian government.

The Belgian colonial regime was less brutal but not much more enlightened, and it failed utterly to lay a groundwork of legitimate institutions or educate the populace. An infamous statistic neatly summed up the Belgian legacy in Congo: in a population of about 15 million at independence in 1960, there were only sixteen university graduates.

Nearly a century after Leopold departed, Zairians barely eked out a subsistence existence, laboring under the manifold destructive consequences of Mobutu's predatory rule. A nation with seemingly unlimited resources and potential had become one of the world's poorest countries. By the late 1980s, per capita income was less than one tenth of what it had been at independence. In the 1990s, the degree of poverty dropped below measurable levels. The country's infrastructure was finished. Only one paved road in ten that existed at independence survived into the 1990s. The great Congo River became virtually the only viable form of surface transportation, but there were few boats to ply it, and hardly any gasoline to fuel them. Schools and hospitals were closed. Half of the country's children died by the age of five.

During three decades of dramatic decline in living standards, the United States gave Mobutu about $2 billion in foreign assistance. In turn, Mobutu provided Washington with a secure base—in Shaba—for its operations in neighboring Angola, where Jonas Savimbi's UNITA rebels were locked in a prolonged civil war with a Soviet-backed government. The CIA, meanwhile, helped Mobutu with technical assistance for the presidential bodyguard and security apparatus and made available intelligence reports on the machinations of Mobutu's opponents.

Mobutu's role as an ally of the West in its efforts to contain Soviet influence in Africa earned him direct contact with every American president from Eisenhower to George Bush—an achievement unmatched by any other African leader. He made his first visit to the White House in 1963. President Reagan welcomed him twice to Washington. President Bush entertained him at his summer retreat in Maine. Mobutu outlasted a generation of infamously wealthy, pro-Western dictators who ruled over much of the Third World during the Cold War, from the Duvaliers in Haiti to Ferdinand Marcos in the Philippines. Only Fidel Castro of Cuba, from the opposing camp of Third World despots, managed to outlast him.

In the last years of his rule, bereft of his Cold War backing, Mobutu faced mounting anarchy and economic chaos. Yet for seven years he confounded widespread predictions of his imminent demise. I wanted to know how he did it.

"He has his ways and means"

In the convoluted history of Central Africa, the southern Zairian province of Shaba has long been a magnet for swindlers and mercenaries, a center of bloodstained intrigue. Belgian colonizers first exploited Shaba's rich deposits of copper in the late nineteenth century in what came to be called the Belgian Congo—the richest European colony in Africa, and Conrad's "heart of darkness." When the colony achieved independence in 1960, the short-lived secession of the province, then known as Katanga, helped make the Congo a byword for postcolonial chaos and barbarism—and also made it black Africa's first Cold War battleground. It was in Shaba that Patrice Lumumba was famously martyred with the connivance of the CIA and the thirty-year-old Congolese colonel who was then called Joseph Désiré Mobutu.

Two rebel invasions of Katanga from neighboring Angola, in 1977 and 1978, brought Belgian, French, and Moroccan troops to Mobutu's rescue, many of them ferried by U.S. planes. These episodes cemented Mobutu's position as an utterly dependent asset to the West. But he made himself useful. In the 1980s Shaba emerged as a key strategic outpost for the Reagan Doctrine. The CIA used an airstrip in the remote Shaban town of Kamina to channel covert weapons to Jonas Savimbi's UNITA forces in Angola.

So it was no surprise that Shaba emerged as a flashpoint in one of the great unfolding dramas of the post–Cold War era: Mobutu's struggle to remain in power. Buffeted by history's changing winds, bereft of his Western backing, embattled by riotous troops and pro-democracy forces, and squeezed for cash to keep afloat his kleptocratic racket, Mobutu was being tested as never before when Mary Jane and I arrived in Shaba in 1993, seeking clues to his uncanny survival.

"Ethnic cleansing" was the term Zairians used to explain the cramming of tens of thousands of hungry and destitute citizens into two fly-strewn railway stations in the mining towns of Likasi and Kolwezi. They were refugees in their own country, evidence that the time-honored practice of "divide and rule" had been effectively executed. Thumbs were rubbed against forefingers to explain the officially sanctioned looting of the vital state-owned mining installation in Kolwezi, where soldiers, politicians, and all manner of foreign hustlers were operating a none-too-subtle traffic in stolen copper and cobalt and whatever else might earn a few hundred trillion hyperdeflated cash Zaires.

Three years after Mobutu first promised to share power amid a wave of popular euphoria over the news of tumbling regimes in Eastern Europe—"Ceausescu! Mobutu! Ceausescu! Mobutu!" they had chanted in the streets of Kinshasa—he seemed bent on dismembering the country before the country dismembered him. And the strategy was working. Talk of the Big Man's faltering grip, rife in Kinshasa and abroad, had long since ceased in Shaba. In its place was a discourse on the methods of tyranny.

"It's important to know that Mobutu is a great strategist," we were told. "He has his ways and means."

"They will cut our throats"

The train station in downtown Likasi, a two-hour drive northwest of Lubumbashi, is a crumbling edifice built by the Belgians early in the twentieth century. It was part of the sprawling network of rails and roads that linked the Central African copper belt to ports in South Africa and the former Portuguese colonies of Mozambique and Angola. In more prosperous days a substantial portion of the world's copper and cobalt was produced in this part of the world.

When Mary Jane and I arrived in Likasi in April 1993, the station was surrounded by a dense warren of shanties, a maze of burlap and plastic slung over rickety frames fashioned from scrap wood and rusty bedsprings. Across the tracks and beyond a foot-wide open sewer, row upon row of green plastic tents, constructed by Belgian workers from the relief agency Médecins Sans Frontières, extended to the distant horizon. Each tent was crammed with as many as fourteen men, women, and children. The air was filled with the stench of rot and excrement, and with the cacophonous din of scrap metal being pounded into makeshift pots and pans.

Five hours west an equally grim scene was unfolding in Kolwezi. The sidewalks there were piled high with desks, bureaus, sofas, cabinets, and other household goods, all for sale to whoever would buy them. Before relief groups moved in to provide vaccinations and running water, sixty people a day were dying from measles, dysentery, malaria, and respiratory infections.

In both towns the refugees were ethnic Kasaians, born and raised in Shaba but descended from ancestors who were recruited to the mines from the neighboring province of Kasai to the north. Over the previous year, in the worst wave of ethnic violence in the region since the Katangan secession of 1960, more than 100,000 Kasaians had been chased from their jobs and homes by rampaging mobs of indigenous Shabans—or "Katangese," as they call themselves.

The Kasaians had congregated at the train stations of Kolwezi and Likasi in the probably futile hope that one of the infrequent trains would have enough space in its sweltering boxcars to take them and their families away to Kasai at a price they could afford. "We cannot stay, because they will cut our throats," we were told.

The plight of the Kasai in Shaba was not on the scale of unfathomable horrors unfolding elsewhere on the continent during the past decade. The death toll was measured in hundreds, not hundreds of thousands. It received scant attention in the Western press. The *New York Times* published just one article on these events, deep inside the paper, which characterized the crisis as "one of the worst outbreaks of tribal violence in recent memory" but offered few clues to its cause. The *Times* account did note a "political" dimension to the violence but gave no hint that President Mobutu might have had a hand in it. There was a strong suggestion that the proverbial "age-old hatreds" were to blame; the behavior of the Katangese, the *Times* said, was "predictable."

In fact, this little-noted episode in Shaba was a case study in anarchy as a product of tyranny, at once a tactic of an embattled tyrant fighting to preserve his power and a legacy of more than a century of tyrannical rule.

To be sure, there had been a history of enmity between the Katangese and their generally better educated, more successful Kasaian neighbors. The Kasaians have sometimes considered themselves the "Jews of Africa." They predominate among the country's intellectuals, professionals, and entrepreneurs. They had been the beneficiaries of "indirect rule," the bedrock system of the colonial order all across the continent, whereby whites subjugated a vast majority of blacks by enlisting a single minority group from among them—in this case the Kasaians, in Rwanda the Tutsis—and elevating them to a position of privilege, investing them with education and training, sometimes arming them, and using them as proxy agents of domination on the cheap.

The Belgians cultivated the Kasaians as skilled laborers and administrators of the colonial order. Their families were housed by the mining companies; their children were educated in company-built schools, equipped to percolate up through even the most oppressive regimes both before and since independence. Resentment grew accordingly.

"The Kasai are seen as instruments of oppression—on this all Katangese agree," Muyembe wa Banze, a Katangan executive at Géca-mines, the state-owned mining giant, told us. "They seemed to be more attached to the white man—that's what we have seen. They have come from far away and have all the advantages. You'll see that the important positions in society are filled by Kasaians. Mobutu also has used the Kasai to oppress the Katangese."

So there was a reservoir of resentment and mistrust, of envy, stereotyping, even outright bigotry against of the Kasai. Yet in Zaire, as elsewhere, resentment alone cannot explain outright terror. It takes leadership, operating in a context of great political upheaval and insecurity—and impunity—to translate hostility and suspicion into violent conflict. The challenge for the beleaguered despot with his back against the wall is to harness that resentment—to stoke it, chan-nel it, even arm it, in order to destabilize opponents and discredit al-ternatives to the status quo. Mobutu was a master at this. What was striking about the campaign against the Kasai in 1993 was how Mobutu, fighting for his political survival, was able to exploit well-founded bitterness toward his own rapacious regime by deflecting it onto others.

"The Kasai must go"

On April 24, 1990, Mobutu had declared an end to single-party rule and the beginning of a transition to democracy. The Berlin Wall had recently fallen, and the Cold War was over. Mobutu's Western back-ers—the United States, France, and Belgium—had let him know that the years of reliable support were finished. This, together with mounting strikes and protests in Kinshasa and elsewhere, compelled Mobutu to open a "sovereign national conference" to prepare for democratic rule. Opposition leaders returned from exile. Opposition parties proliferated. A raucous public debate enlivened newspapers long subdued by fear.

But problems quickly materialized—especially in Shaba. Barely two weeks after Mobutu's declaration, unidentified commandos went on a nighttime rampage on the campus of the University of Lubumbashi, killing several dozen students (the number is still unconfirmed). There followed a spate of armed attacks on the homes of prominent opposi-tion figures. Opposition rallies were broken up. Arrests and killings multiplied. Transition governments came and went. More than 200 mutually antagonistic political parties entered the fray, many backed with enough cash from Mobutu himself to compound hyperinflation.

Then came the *pillage*. In September of 1991 an astonishing week-long spree of looting and destruction by underpaid troops of the national army laid waste to major cities across the country. Hundreds of civilians were killed. Much of the modern productive sector of the economy was destroyed. The sidewalks next to major military bases became thriving markets for looted goods. Press accounts described the riots as the work of "mutinous" troops. But whether the *pillage* was aimed at toppling Mobutu remains a mystery; no soldier was ever prosecuted or disciplined.

Meanwhile, the major opposition parties had managed to form a coalition called the Union Sacrée de l'Opposition. Its candidate to lead the transition to democracy was a well-known activist named Étienne Tshisekedi. Tshisekedi was from Kasai.

After the *pillage* Mobutu met with representatives of the Union Sacrée and, under pressure from the West, agreed to allow the formation of an opposition government led by Tshisekedi, who was sworn in as prime minister on October 16, 1991. He lasted six days. The problem, like almost all problems in Zaire, boiled down to money. Tshisekedi, with the backing of Western governments, sought control over the Central Bank. This Mobutu could not abide. Control of the printing and distribution of money, as we have seen, was a vital tool of Mobutu's; it was not only the means by which he enriched himself but also his means for supporting his friends and co-opting his enemies. When Tshisekedi arrived at his office one day, he found the doors were locked. A replacement moved in three days later.

Nevertheless, the Union Sacrée continued to have broad popular support. Something needed to be done to break up the opposition alliance. So Mobutu turned to two men from Shaba: Jean Nguza Karl-i-Bond and Gabriel Kyungu wa Kumwanza—the man who authorized our arrest.

Whenever Zairians describe Mobutu's legendary "musical chairs" system of government—the perennial shuffling of his friends and enemies in and out of favor, in and out of money—their first case in point is Nguza Karl-i-Bond. Nguza was Mobutu's foreign minister in the early 1970s. He then became the political director of Zaire's sole political party, the Mouvement Populaire de la Révolution (MPR). In

1977 Nguza was accused of treason and sentenced to death. He is said to have been tortured. But a year later he was freed, and a year after that he became prime minister. Two years after that he fled to exile in Belgium, where he wrote a book exposing Mobutu's corruption. He later testified before a congressional subcommittee in Washington about Mobutu's ill-gotten riches. Then, incredibly, he returned to Mobutu's fold, and in 1986 was sent back to Washington as Zaire's ambassador. Two years later he was foreign minister again.

By 1991 Nguza was out of the loop once more and heading the Union des Fédéralistes et des Républicains Indépendents (UFERI), one of the three main opposition parties in the Union Sacrée.

Gabriel Kyungu wa Kumwanza, who ordered Mary Jane's and my arrest, was one of Nguza's principal allies. He appeared more credible than Nguza as an oppositionist. Along with Tshisekedi, Kyungu had produced a scathing public critique of Mobutu's regime in 1980. The two were imprisoned and tortured. Kyungu was one of the first public figures to decry the massacre of students at the university, and he drew crowds with populist speeches in which he derided Mobutu as an *hibou*, an owl, traditionally associated with black magic.

But that was before November 1991, when UFERI broke ranks with the Union Sacrée. Mobutu appointed Nguza prime minister and Kyungu the governor of Shaba. The violence against the Kasai in Shaba began soon thereafter.

Immediately after Governor Kyungu assumed office, he launched a campaign known as *Debout Katanga!*—"Rise up, Katanga!" Its motto was "Katanga for the Katangese." In a series of public rallies and radio speeches the governor railed against the "enemy within," the Kasai. Bemoaning the misery of the Katangan population, Kyungu repeatedly blamed the Kasaians. He called them *bilulu*, "insects" in Swahili.

"The Kasai are foreigners," he declared. "The Katangese no longer accept the Kasai here. Their presence is an insult. They are arrogant and don't hide it. It is not possible for the tribes to live side by side." In crude harangues that would have been familiar to Asians driven from Uganda by Idi Amin, Kyungu derided the Kasai as money-grubbing exploiters who were lucky to be allowed to flee with their lives. "The Kasai must go, and then the Katangese can have the nice jobs and nice houses," he said.

Then, employing a tactic long used by Mobutu, Kyungu established the JUFERI, a youth brigade in his party, as a vigilante force. This was textbook tribalism: the arming of an ethnically based criminal gang. Mostly unemployed, illiterate thugs from rural villages, the JUFERI provided a violent accompaniment to Kyungu's menacing radio broadcasts. Attacks on Kasaian homes began in late 1991. By April of 1992 the JUFERI, sometimes backed by larger mobs of Katangese, were systematically expelling Kasaians from their homes. Witnesses told Mary Jane and me that the JUFERI were sometimes supplied with gasoline to set houses afire and with beer and marijuana to stoke their aggression. Some Kasaians fought back. The cycle was set in motion.

Meanwhile, on February 16, 1992, hundreds of thousands of people marched through the streets of the capital, Kinshasa, a thousand miles away, in support of a national conference on democracy that Nguza had canceled. Mobutu's troops opened fire on the marchers; according to Human Rights Watch, more than thirty were killed. Mobutu deftly blamed Nguza and soon afterward allowed the national conference to resume. In August the conference nominated Tshisekedi to be prime minister again. Kasaians in Shaba celebrated. Some marched through the streets of Lubumbashi with leashed dogs that wore ties and signs saying "Nguza." Some threw stones at the governor's residence. The JUFERI, armed with knives and machetes, responded predictably. Most Kasaians fled to the train station or to the homes of relatives in town. Those we spoke with had no doubt about who was ultimately responsible for their predicament.

"It's Mobutu," one of their leaders asserted (few Kasaians were willing to be identified by name). "As president of the republic, he can't lower himself into the streets to wage war against the Kasai. He needs someone who is malleable. He uses others, like Kyungu—a pawn of Mobutu."

And who could doubt it? If Kyungu had been doing anything other than the Big Man's bidding, he would have been arrested, along with everyone else responsible for this huge-scale campaign of violent lawlessness in a land where Mobutu himself was the only law.

Kasaians were quick to remind us that not all Katangese approved of what was happening: "It's a false problem," we were told. "It's a manipulation by the politicians." Nevertheless, Nguza and Kyungu had plainly tapped a real vein of resentment. "Monsieur Kyungu expresses the profound aspirations, the soul of the people," Tshibang Kadjat, a Katangan executive at the mining company Gécamines, told us. "From colonization to Mobutu, all the advantages go to the Kasai."

In fact, however, the majority of Kasaians in Shaba suffered as much as most Katangese under a regime that had plundered the province's resources for the benefit of a few. But Katangan leaders made a pact with the devil, calculating that, as one put it, "We have to ally ourselves with the declining dictatorship in order to resist the permanent dictatorship of the Kasai."

"Destabilization"

"You know," a Kasaian prosecutor told us in Kolwezi, "Mobutu is the kind of politician who can profit from any situation to maintain his power. Before, he attacked the Katangese using the Kasai, who were among his closest collaborators. Now he realizes that there were radical political oppositionists among the Kasai. He uses old enmities to destabilize his new enemies. Now he uses Katangese to destabilize the Kasai."

A judge interrupted to clarify: "It was not exactly his goal to dominate the Katangese. Mobutu put Kasaians at the head of many enterprises. But this was so that he could enjoy the riches of the province with the help of the Kasai. Now he says it wasn't he who caused the unhappiness of the Katangese—it was the Kasai. If you look at the situation more closely, both Kasaians and Katangese are in indescribable misery. Those who benefited are Mobutu and his acolytes. It's just that most of his acolytes were Kasaians, especially here in Katanga. This is a region that he has pillaged a lot."

This discussion over dinner in Kolwezi had been organized by our friend Kanyama. Like so much else in Mobutu's Zaire, the dinner had a surreal quality. We had arrived in town just a few hours earlier, exhausted, thirsty, caked with dust, after that grueling eight-hour ride by dirt road from Likasi on the back of a truck packed so tightly with passengers that our legs had fallen asleep for hours on end. Hips wedged against hips, knees gingerly tucked into groins, painfully thin children sitting on our laps, chickens dangling from the canopy overhead, we had bounced and lurched along dirt roads deep into the bush on the only form of public transport available in this part of Zaire. We had crossed the great Congo River itself at one point on a steam-powered ferry.

Now, safe in Kolwezi, we were enjoying beef tenderloin with bernaise sauce and a tasty red wine in Kanyama's private dinner club. The club had been built by the Belgians years ago, and was a reminder that even in these straitened times in impoverished Zaire, someone must be making money, somehow. The dining room was a cozy, oak-paneled affair, with paintings of horses on the walls. The waiters wore immaculate white linen jackets. Our half dozen erudite lawyer companions, in the distinctive style of Zairian elites, wore comically stylish suits that would have fit well in a scene from Batman: one wore a fire-engine red blazer, another, purple velour. Kanyama himself wore a pitch-black double-breasted suit with stark white pinstripes.

But the discussion was deadly serious. It was about the stratagems of one of the world's great tyrants, deftly maneuvering to survive in power by employing time-honored Machiavellian tactics. "Mobutu uses the method of divide and rule to maintain his dictatorship," Kanyama told us "In Shaba today, we have seen the situation between the Katangese and the Kasai. Who benefits from this situation? The answer is simple: Mobutu. He is destabilizing the country."

Kanyama was using a word—"destabilization"—that I had long associated with South Africa, from the years in which Pretoria sought to stem the tide of majority rule by "destabilizing" its black-ruled neighbors. Until now I had never heard the term used in reference to Mobutu.

"Mobutu tries to keep the population in fear," Kanyama explained. "The population is traumatized. Mobutu wants to keep them in this state for a long time. That's how he maintains his position. This is Mobutu's strategy: to make people afraid of democracy, to make people say, before democracy we were okay with Mobutu. People will prefer dictatorship to disorder."

Our dinner club discussion was illuminating and doubly surreal for taking place among lawyers—the rule of law being notably absent in Zaire. In fact, the complete absence of criminal law was what made Mobutu's cynical tactics possible. Soldiers and police, who might have been expected to intervene if Mobutu ordered them to do so, appeared in accounts of the violence only intermittently, most often as criminals engaged in thefts and assaults that provoked reprisals, which merely reinforced the cycle of violence. Lawlessness in general, and lawless soldiers in particular, had been a chronic problem in Zaire ever since independence, when the entire army dissolved in mutiny within a week. Armed shakedowns were commonplace. On that very night in Kolwezi, while being driven home from the club by a Belgian entrepreneur, Mary Jane, Kanyama and I were held up at gunpoint five times by soldiers who emerged like apparitions in our headlights, pointed their rifles menacingly at the windshield, and then gruffly accepted yet another proffer of 5 million or 10 million Zaires—just under a dollar at that week's rate.

"*Pas de problème*," said our Belgian friend with a laugh. "*Pas de problème.*"

"*Who's using who?*"

The Gécamines mining installation is on the edge of downtown Kolwezi. Kanyama drove us there on the dusty thoroughfare that runs through the heart of the city, passing by the train station, which, like its counterpart in Likasi, was overrun with displaced Kasai living in tents and burlap lean-tos. The road itself was choked with refugees silently making their way on foot to the crowded station, their life's possessions on their heads and backs—bundles of clothes, pots and pans, chairs, mattresses, bed springs. The road bank was lined with bureaus, sofas and dining-room sets for sale—furniture too bulky to travel with.

The Gécamines compound is a vast, rocky landscape of open pits and coppery waste dumps. In better days this facility produced up to 80 percent of Zaire's copper and cobalt. Belgians built the mines early in the century, and Belgian spies, financiers, and mercenaries known as *les affreux*—"the dreadful ones"—backed Moïse Tshombe's ill-fated secession movement in 1960, hoping to maintain de facto Belgian control over the lucrative mining industry. Mobutu nationalized the mines in 1967. At its high point, in the mid-1980s, Gécamines produced 480,000 tons of copper a year with 35,000 employees, earned three quarters of Zaire's foreign exchange, and educated 100,000 children in company-run schools.

On the day of our ill-fated visit, the compound was eerily subdued. A half dozen tense JUFERI youths in jeans and sport shirts guarded the entrance against Kasaians. In the two weeks before we arrived, some 7,000 Kasaian workers—half the workforce and most of the skilled employees—had been chased from their jobs at these mines. In all, 40,000 to 50,000 Kasaians in Kolwezi had been rendered homeless. The mines still functioned, we were told, but expatriate company officials doubted that this would last. The production of copper had already declined to 150,000 tons or less in the previous year, because of rampant corruption and mismanagement. A mine collapsed a few years earlier, apparently as a result of negligence. Most of the skilled expatriates fled after the 1991 *pillage*. The company was bankrupt.

A week before our visit ten trucks had lined up along the wall surrounding the plant. Three hundred thieves pushed a hundred tons of copper up to the wall and loaded it into the trucks, and off they drove off to the Zambian border and down to South Africa. This was part of an ongoing traffic in stolen copper, cobalt, electrical wires and pylons, tires, water pumps, and gasoline. Gécamines was being looted down to the ground. Soldiers, the police, workers, company guards, and expatriate Greeks, Lebanese, and South Africans—all were collaborating to ransack Zaire's biggest economic asset.

At the center of the racket, according to company officials, diplomats, and townspeople, was none other than Governor Kyungu. He was said to be getting a $10,000 kickback for each export license granted to truck goods across the border.

It was an old story in Zaire. "Who's using who?" a clergyman asked. "Is Mobutu using Kyungu, or is Kyungu using Mobutu? We ask ourselves this question. If you compare Kyungu when he was in opposition, he was a poor man. Now he is very rich."

Yet there remained the question of why Mobutu tolerated the gutting of Gécamines, a pillar of the economy and an indispensable source of foreign exchange. The answer was diamonds. By all accounts, Mobutu had managed to work out an alternative racket involving the export of diamonds from Kasai. Zaire is one of the world's largest producers of diamonds. The year before our visit, recorded diamond exports came to $230 million. Unrecorded exports? "Anybody's guess," a diplomat told me, "but certainly more, by a substantial margin." An array of mostly Lebanese diamond buyers, working with silent partners in the Central Bank and in the military, were reaping hefty profits in a complex foreign-exchange scam involving a parallel market in checks worth as much as forty times the official exchange rate. They brought in their foreign currency, exchanged it for Zaires with their silent partners, and then headed for the diamond mines. The proceeds leaving via the backdoor of the Central Bank were keeping afloat Mobutu's extended "family" of relatives, elite troops, ethnic kinsmen, and followers. So Gécamines was expendable.

The losers in all this, needless to say, were the long-suffering Zairian people. In the year before our visit inflation spiked by more than 6,000 percent. Unemployment was at 80 percent. Gross domestic product by some estimates had been contracting by as much as 30 percent a year since the *pillage*. Hospitals and schools were repeatedly shut down. Teachers in Likasi had been on strike for more than a month when we were there; their average monthly salary of 30 million Zaires was worth four bottles of beer. Many Zairians were eating just one meal a day, some only one every other day. The public-service sector had largely stopped functioning. Tax collection had ceased— except for the "direct taxation" of army shakedowns. The country's banking system had all but collapsed. The nation of nearly 40 million, four times the geographic area of France, was heading deeper into anarchy by the day.

Yet it was precisely these conditions that made Mobutu's tactics effective. Zairians clearly saw the method in his seeming madness, a deliberate strategy of "destabilization," as Kanyama put it, as a means of discrediting the movement toward democracy and undermining the capacity of the people to mobilize against him.

Foreigners living in Zaire often marveled at the "passivity" of the Zairian people; one I spoke to compared it to "battered-wife syndrome." But Zairians pointed out that Mobutu and his allies still had all the guns and all the money. Hundreds of thousands of people marched in Kinshasa, they reminded me, and more than thirty of them were shot dead. In any event, a clergyman said, "When the population is hungry and tired, it doesn't have the energy to go into the streets."

"Mobutu is the best Machiavellian in Africa over the past thirty years," George Nzongola-Ntalaja, a Zairian scholar now living in Washington, D.C., told me as I set off for Zaire. "He knows when to be the fox and when to be the lion. He has made certain people very rich. They stand to lose everything if he goes. Many around him who have committed crimes fear that they will be pursued judicially. So long as they share the loot with him, they will do anything to keep him in power."

"White man's juju"

I never met Mobutu. My view of the man was from a different perspective than that of my encounters with the other key figures in this book: I was his prisoner. Mary Jane and I spent four days in the custody of SNIP, in Lubumbashi and then in Kinshasa, including five exhausting hours of interrogation about our sources at the Garde Civile. It was a glimpse of tyranny as it looks from underneath, an experience of arbitrary power from a position, albeit fleeting, of powerlessness. It was, for Mary Jane and me, a look at the Big Man from under his boot.

Over the years I've been traveling around Africa, American friends of mine have often asked whether it's dangerous. The answer is: usually not. For one thing, crisis-oriented news coverage notwithstanding, the impression of seemingly constant calamities across the African continent is misleading. Most African countries are at peace, and even in countries afflicted by war, most parts of those countries are spared outright conflict, and the people who live in those regions carry on with their normal lives. In the war zones themselves, it is the Africans who are targeted, not foreigners; the violence is not as random or irrational as it sometimes seems from afar. And whites like me can usually count on "white man's juju"—the unjust but real protection from violence that Africans themselves don't enjoy.[1]

I first learned this lesson in Uganda, in 1983, during Milton Obote's era. At the time Uganda was in thrall to Obote's marauding Ugandan National Army. Pothole-ridden highways were punctuated by police and military checkpoints every ten or fifteen kilometers. Edgy troops in mismatched fatigues and tennis shoes or flip-flops poked their rifles

---

[1]There are exceptions to this rule, chiefly among combat photographers and video cameramen, for whom proximity to the action is more essential than it is for print reporters. In 1993 four photojournalists were killed in Mogadishu, Somalia. Numerous photographers were killed or wounded in the early 1990s in the township wars in South Africa. In 1999 and 2000 three video cameramen, two from Associated Press Television News and one from Reuters, were killed in rebel ambushes in Sierra Leone. See Peter Maass, "Deadly Competition," *Brill's Content*, September 2000.

through your car window. Jam-packed buses and public taxis were forced to disgorge their passengers. The men were shaken down, the women and girls sometimes taken into the banana groves. It was frightful business, and I soon discovered that when I ventured into the vast taxi park in Kampala, the capital, Ugandan travelers would rush toward me shouting "*Mzungu, mzungu!*" eager to share a taxi with a white man. They assumed that the ride would go more smoothly, the checkpoints passed through uneventfully, and they were right. I learned to carry packs of cigarettes for bribes, and made certain never to travel past noon, when the soldiers began to turn glassy-eyed with beer and banana wine. And I was never harmed.

The advantages of being a white man—and an American—were doubly apparent in Liberia on the one previous occasion when I was taken into custody. In 1986, on a steamy Saturday evening in Monrovia, I was arrested in my hotel room along with Jackson Doe, who by all accounts had been the winning candidate in the stolen election the previous year. I had been interviewing Doe and an associate of his, Sammy Dahn, in the hotel bar downstairs when we became aware that we were being watched by plainclothes police. We repaired to my room upstairs to continue the interview. The knock on the door came minutes later. A veritable battalion of police took us into custody. I can still vividly recall the shiver of fear I felt as all those stone-faced men crowded around me, all shiny belts and badges and guns, demanding to know who I was and what I was up to.

But Jackson Doe seemed not the least bit alarmed. The veteran Liberian politician, who was probably twenty years my senior and who by all rights should have been head of state by then, looked at me with absolute calm and announced, "I'm in your hands."

He knew what he was talking about, and so did I. Upon my arrival in Monrovia I had given my business card to the hotel desk clerk, a man named David, and I'd been cultivating him as an ally for a week. David was a Gio man, a friend of Isaac Bantu's, and he was sympathetic to the work I was doing. On the back of my card I had written, "Call the U.S. embassy if anything happens," and sure enough, he did.

Jackson Doe, Sammy Dahn and I were driven off to Monrovia's crumbling police headquarters and interrogated, but the questions were cautious and unthreatening. Like Bob in Lubumbashi, our interrogators seemed paralyzed, unsure how to handle the situation, awaiting instructions from a higher authority. Within a couple of hours, the embassy's political officer, Jannean Mann, had contacted the director of police, Wilfred Clarke, and Doe, Dahn and I were soon released without further ado.[2]

My adventure with Jackson Doe typified the symbiotic relationship between an outsider like me and a native interlocutor. Doe had clearly calculated that he enjoyed a measure of protection so long as he was in the company of an American, both because I could call upon the U.S. embassy in a pinch and because of the attention I might bring to bear if something happened to either one of us. At the same time, I was relying on his judgment of where to meet and when.

A rule of thumb I always adhered to when calculating my own security was, and remains, "Rely on the judgment of natives." The U.S. embassy is required by law to assist American citizens who wind up in trouble. Diplomats, representatives of nongovernmental organizations (NGOs) and other foreigners are worth sounding out concerning the risks, but they have their own interests and agendas. It may or may not be in the U.S. embassy's interest for a journalist to go where he wants to go. And in any case the embassy will usually advise you to stay away from trouble—which makes sense from its point of view but not necessarily from that of a reporter.

A Liberian journalist or a Zairian human rights lawyer, by contrast, knows his territory, speaks the language, and understands the risks. A foreign correspondent rarely travels into dangerous regions, be they war zones or crime-ridden slums, without a local guide of some kind—a fellow reporter, activist, church official, or military escort. I have seen Hollywood movies depicting intrepid war correspondents venturing aimlessly into a battle zone in search of action and footage. In my own experience this is rare—and foolish. In Africa, at least, you rely on a local guide.

"Fixers" they are sometimes called, but the best of them are helpful not just in setting up interviews and finding gasoline on the black market, but in interpreting information, including risk. They are rarely dispassionate. They will often have their own interest in getting

---

[2]Jackson Doe, alas, was also a Gio man, and he was murdered five years later by Charles Taylor's National Patriotic Front of Liberia fighters, apparently for the same reason Sammy Dokie was murdered: he posed a threat to Taylor's legitimacy as self-styled leader of the Gios. Wilfred Clarke, for his part, managed to flee Liberia in 1990 and found his way to New York, where he went to work investigating subway graft for the Metropolitan Transportation Authority.

a story, or in conveying their side of events to a foreign reporter. In a polarized environment—and war is always a polarized environment—it is often impossible to find a dispassionate native interlocutor. Nevertheless the bond that forms between a foreign reporter and his or her local guide often grows strong and deep, all the more so if the latter's judgment of the security situation proves flawed. That is what happened to us with our guide in Kolwezi, Kanyama.

"C'est difficile"

As best we could tell, we had been betrayed by the director of the Gécamines mining compound, a Katangese engineer named Mbaka Kawaya, whom we had interviewed in his office at the mining compound. Kawaya had seemed a straight shooter at first, square-jawed and bespectacled, seated behind his metal desk covered with files and ledgers in his company office. He told us in some detail about corruption in the mines, leaving no doubt about who ultimately was responsible. He told us about a collapse in one of the mines in 1990 in which several hundred miners were killed. "The official line was that it was a 'natural collapse,'" he recalled, "but they were exploiting the mine without security systems. The manager was a close associate of the president."

Featherbedding and cronyism, faked production figures and useless investments—"The whole system was disturbed," he explained. "There were bad investments because people have to make money on the side, following The Guide." The Guide, of course, was Mobutu.

But as our discussion ventured into the recent events in Kolwezi—the routing of thousands of Kasaians from their jobs in the mines, the rampaging mobs of the JUFERI—Kawaya's responses grew hazy and confusing. "Between these young people and the Kasaians, there were disagreements here and there," he conceded, but as he described events it became less and less clear who did what, or why, or who was responsible. It became more and more clear that this man was a Katangan, disinclined to finger his own people, or to accept any responsibility himself for what was happening. "It's not a problem of Gécamines," he insisted. "We don't control the army. We don't control the political party. Security is not our problem. Security is the state, it's the politicians."

I asked Kawaya about a letter we obtained from leaders of the Kasaian community in Kolwezi that was addressed to the directors of Gécamines and signed by more than two dozen Gécamines managers and employees. The letter, written two weeks earlier, protested the growing insecurity in the mines and outlined a number of specific attacks on Kasaian employees. It said the lives and livelihoods of all Kasaians were threatened after Governor Kyungu asserted in a radio address that "Kasaians were not in their own land . . . and they should go back home." The letter protested the "official" presence of JUFERI in mining installations and threats by JUFERI against workers, who were told they should move "to the train station." It documented attacks against Kasaian students in a nearby school and the closing of markets to Kasaians. The signers of the letter announced that they planned to return to Kasai, but also threatened to organize a strike against Gécamines if their security was not guaranteed until their departure. No such guarantee was forthcoming, however, and the signers of the letter were fired from their jobs. As many as 7,000 Kasaian employees then fled or were chased from their jobs, and the exodus was still under way.

"From my point of view," Kawaya told us, "the workers who went to the railroad station are not responsible. The managers who signed the letter are responsible. We suspended them because they engaged in political language. We are a country that is still learning democracy. We don't know how to do it. We haven't learned yet to respect the opinions of others. When the people are free, you have no control. We can't imagine that someone else can think differently."

I asked Kawaya whether he felt any remorse over what was happening. "From a human point of view," he replied, "seeing how we have worked together, there is no reason why this has happened. But we were led by politicians and we play their game. For me, it's a political problem." If it were up to him, I asked, would he allow the Kasaians to come home and return to work? "It's not possible to live under these conditions," he replied.

Kawaya, the manager of the mine, seemed a typical functionary, the kind of character one often finds among those who rise to positions of power in a dictatorship by pretending to see no evil, and accepting no responsibility. Looking back over my notes of our interview, long after it became clear that he must have been the one who betrayed us, I couldn't help but conclude that he knew exactly what was going on, and probably deplored it. I had asked him, finally, who really was responsible for what was going on. *"Tous les politiciens,"* he replied. "Global manipulation, Mobutu, Kyungu, JUFERI." But he added, "I can't change anything. It's a political problem."

We shook hands, and out the door Kanyama, Mary Jane and I went for a brief tour of the mining compound. The manager must have returned to his desk, picked up the phone, and put in a call to the mayor. For as we drove out of the compound in Kanyama's car, we were stopped at the gate by edgy, jeans-clad members of the JUFERI. They were accompanied by two smartly dressed men in sunglasses, who turned out to be SNIP agents. They said they were under orders of the *commissaire urbain*, the UFERI mayor of Kolwezi, P. Anchaire Moji a Kapasu, who was Governor Kyungu's representative in the city. One of the SNIP agents climbed in back of our car, and off we went to meet the mayor.

P. Anschaire Moji a Kapasu turned out to be a squat, beady-eyed and officious gentleman with an air of suspicion. He welcomed us into his living room and immediately asked us why we had not met with him before proceeding to the Gécamines compound. Kanyama explained that we had in fact attempted to see him first thing that morning, but that, not finding him in his office, we had planned to try again after visiting the mines. This was true.

The mayor then told me that Governor Kyungu had been offended that he had not been informed of our presence and considered me to be "reporting without authorization." I explained that we had intended to arrange an interview with the governor upon our arrival in Lubumbashi ten days earlier, but that the governor had been out of town. The mayor informed us that an appointment had been made with the governor that very afternoon in Lubumbashi; in fact, he said, a Gécamines plane would be readied to fly us to Lubumbashi.

As we waited in the mayor's living room to be driven to the airstrip, I took the occasion to ask him a few questions. Exactly what had he done, I wanted to know, to stop the violence in his jurisdiction? He told me that the authorities had done "everything possible" to stop the violence. I asked if anyone had been arrested and prosecuted. He looked at me with a blank expression, as if the idea had never occurred to him. "It's difficult in the mass of people to know who struck whom," he said. "You would have to arrest the whole population. *C'est difficile*."

So much for the rule of law.

"We can't do that"

The interrogation room in the Garde Civile felt dingier, dirtier, and more oppressively humid than ever as the door slammed behind the departing vice governor. "You will give us those names," he had said, "and you can forget about the consulate."

Mary Jane and I sat stunned and appalled. Our hopes for a speedy resolution were dashed. *Is it possible?* I wondered. *Is this what it's like when things are turning out badly?* The gang of SNIP agents circled around us. Bob took his seat behind the battered wooden desk. *How far were they prepared to go? What would they do to get those names?* My stomach churned and heaved. My shirt was drenched. Beads of sweat trickled down my shins. I was angry, alarmed, humiliated.

I looked at Mary Jane. She was as poised as ever—and utterly defenseless.

"We may have to give them something," I ventured, speaking to her in English.

"We can't do that," she replied matter-of-factly.

The daughter of Cuban immigrants to the United States, Mary Jane was not naive about the nature of tyranny. Fluent in French and Spanish, she had by then spent seven years as a researcher for Human Rights Watch, documenting abuses in Cuba, Haiti and the Dominican Republic. She was regularly quoted in the press, and she had been declared persona non grata and barred from Fidel Castro's Cuba. She once succeeded in slipping back into Havana by obtaining a new passport—on which her maiden name, Camejo, by which she was known professionally, was replaced with her married name, Berkeley—and passing herself off as the mild-mannered translator for an American book publishers' association. It took the ever-vigilant, informer-running, eavesdropping, wall-bugging, telephone-tapping agents of Castro's ubiquitous Ministerio del Interior, known as Minint, just four days to figure out who she was and order her out of the country. She spent her last night in Havana tearing pages from her notebooks and flushing them down the toilet.

She was a trouper, I knew. And it was she who supplied the spine for the two of us in the Garde Civile. "We can't give these people any names," she repeated firmly.

Before the questions resumed, I asked Bob if I could use the toilet. To my surprise, he instructed one of the SNIP men to lead me down the hall to a dank, stinking, windowless latrine. The toilet bowl was seatless and half filled with excrement. The air buzzed with flies. I vomited almost immediately, then sat down. I sat for a while in the stench-filled darkness, washing my mouth out with my bottled water, composing myself. It was a thoroughly unpleasant interlude, but also a huge relief and a turning point. The panic dissipated. My strength returned. I pulled myself together and rejoined Mary Jane, Bob and the gang.

The worst, it turned out, was over. Almost as soon as we entered what appeared to be maximum peril, the crisis melted away—at least for Mary Jane and me.

They had gotten what they needed out of Kanyama.

In the days and weeks afterward, I thought a lot about what they could have done to us. Violent physical abuse was commonplace in Mobutu's jails. Beatings with fists, boots, bludgeons and rifle butts, kicking and stomping, electric shock, insertion of sand in the ears, hanging upside down from roofbeams, immersion in septic tanks, whippings with a *cordelette*, a paratrooper's rope with a four-inch buckle—all were utterly routine. But physical torture, I now understood, was but one of the tools Bob and the gang had at their disposal. Others less violent and crude might have worked just as well.

Simple things: They could have taken away my bottle of water. They could have denied my request to use the toilet. They could have confiscated my ever-ready roll of toilet paper. They could have kept us awake all night, and night after night. Fatigue, thirst, hunger and nausea, humiliation, fear above all—my sick and anxious moments with the vice governor had left me with a profound appreciation of the power at his disposal within the four bare walls of that room in the Garde Civile.

And of course they could have separated Mary Jane from me. Had they done so, I would have told them everything they wanted to know.

Kanyama, a human rights lawyer, knew all of this very well. One can hardly blame him for giving Bob and the gang just enough to let us off the hook, if not him. And that apparently is what he did. For as Bob shuttled back and forth between Kanyama and us, he began asking us to confirm our contact with individuals whose names he could only have gotten from Kanyama. We declined to do so, but we knew the game was up. The pressure was off.

We settled in for a long, slow endgame, but the fear had largely subsided. A second officer painstakingly transcribed our innocuous statements in longhand. It took him forever, and he got it completely wrong. He tried again.

At 11 P.M., Kanyama rejoined us. He said he was fine and looked it, but he was deadly serious. We asked whether he had been mistreated, and he said he hadn't. Nor needed he have been. In these circumstances, fear alone is enough. That was what we had learned.

Our status still unresolved, we were driven to the Lubumbashi Sheraton Hotel and held overnight, still in custody of the Garde Civile. The ride to the hotel had a moment of low comedy, of a kind I had come to expect in Zaire. A taxi was commandeered and we all piled in, but then the driver couldn't get the taxi started. Out we got, and we piled onto the back of a battered Toyota pickup truck with our gang of guards. It turned out the truck didn't have operating headlights. There were of course no functioning streetlights in dilapidated, energy-low Lubumbashi. So we rumbled down the road at a snail's pace, in pitch darkness.

"Reporting without authorization"

The following morning, incredibly, we discovered that the telephone in our room was working, and we were able to reach Tente wa Tente, the lone Zairian staffing the evacuated U.S. consulate, whom we had widely checked in with on our arrival in Lubumbashi. Affable, smart, energetic, and utterly professional, Tente had struck us on first meeting as just the kind of man we would want to have on our side in a pinch, and indeed he turned out to be just that.

When we reached Tente by phone from our hotel room at 8 A.M. on the morning after our arrest, he recognized us and immediately swung into action. He sent a cable to his superiors in the embassy in Kinshasa alerting them of our arrest. Then he joined us at the hotel, drove us back to the Garde Civile, and spent most of the next twenty-four hours by our sides—a huge boost to our morale.

Within an hour of Tente's first cable to Kinshasa, we later learned, the embassy had established contact with the Big Man himself, Mobutu. By noon, word had been passed down the line to the Garde Civile in Lubumbashi that the matter had been settled: Mary Jane and I were to be flown to Kinshasa, then expelled from the country. Mobutu apparently had made the simple calculation that he had more to lose than to gain by antagonizing the Americans. It was a calculation he had made many times before, for much higher stakes. I was a bit chagrined to be the beneficiary on this occasion, but I did not complain.

We would spend another day in the Garde Civile, but in a considerably more relaxed atmosphere than the previous evening. Bob interrogated us again, but his questions seemed perfunctory. Our bags were searched and a folder of documents and four rolls of Mary Jane's film were confiscated. These were never returned. Unaccountably, six spiral notebooks containing all of my notes from Likasi and Kolwezi were left undisturbed. It occurred to me later that these men might not know enough about journalism to appreciate the importance of written notes. Bob finally disappeared, and we spent most of the rest of the day sitting around the Garde Civile doing what Zairians spend much of their lives doing: waiting.

There was, however, the remaining open question of what was going to happen to Kanyama. His fate did not appear to have been resolved by Mobutu's little calculation from afar. For much of the day he was visibly anxious, and deadly serious. From time to time he went off to negotiate with Bob and the others, but the negotiations didn't appear to be going anywhere. This being Zaire, Mary Jane had the sensible idea to slip Kanyama a hundred dollars in cash, and see how far it got him. Kanyama took the money and disappeared for a while. When he finally reemerged an hour or so later, the expression on his face was one of utter relief bordering on giddiness. We all had a good laugh. Kanyama had been given to understand that he would be released the following day.

The next morning, the three of us were driven to the Lubumbashi airport. Kanyama was told he would be released shortly, after completing certain formalities in the Garde Civile. Mary Jane and I were asked to sign a statement acknowledging that we were being "invited to leave the country" for "reporting without authorization." Bob gave us a hearty farewell. The gang of guards eagerly pressed forward to shake our hands and wish us well. I think we must have been the most intriguing prisoners to pass through the Garde Civile in years.

We were accompanied on the regular commercial flight to the capital by a plainclothes SNIP agent who sat across from us and ordered two bottles of beer with his breakfast. I took my bag back to the lavatory and proceeded to tear all the pages from my spiral notebooks and conceal them in a bag of dirty laundry—just in case a new team of interrogators in Kinshasa had the sense to confiscate a reporter's notebooks.

At Kinshasa's notorious N'djili Airport we were met by another SNIP agent—and by an American consular official who stayed with us the rest of the way. After another round of rude but nonthreatening interrogation at the SNIP headquarters, we were released—essentially into the custody of the U.S. embassy. We found a room at a Protestant guest house, but our passports were still confiscated, so we were effectively under house arrest. The passports were returned two days later, and we were deposited on the next plane to Johannesburg.

Kanyama, meanwhile, was held one more night at the Garde Civile—no Sheraton for him anymore—and then was permitted to return to Kolwezi. There he was threatened by local Katangese JUFERI and SNIP agents. He managed to send us a communiqué via the embassy in which he said he feared for his life because of the "total insecurity" in Kolwezi. His home had been ransacked by the JUFERI and his car had been confiscated. He had been branded "susceptible" because of his contacts with Americans. Ultimately he was forced to abandon his law practice in Kolwezi and relocate his family to the relative safety of Kinshasa, where he tried to relaunch his legal career from "ground zero." When that failed amid the chaos of war in 1997, he moved back to his roots in Kasai, deep in the interior of what had been renamed the Democratic Republic of the Congo (DRC), where all our efforts to contact him throughout the escalating conflict in 1997 and 1998 were fruitless.

"Après moi, le déluge"

Ever since the collapse of the Berlin Wall in 1989, Zairians and foreigners alike had been predicting Mobutu's imminent demise. That he endured for seven more years—thirty-two years in all—was a measure if his skillful playing of the ethnic card. Mobutu showed himself a peerless master of that delicate and risky maneuver: mobilizing well-founded hatred toward his own rapacious regime and deflecting it onto others.

His method was much akin to Charles Taylor's in Nimba County: tease out someone else's latent prejudice and inflame it with scapegoating rhetoric, mobilize gangs of thugs and criminals and the unemployed, arm them, stoke them with drugs and drink, and loose them upon defenseless civilians with the promise of vengeance and booty. Also like Taylor, Mobutu excelled in the deft orchestration of conduits to the criminal acquisition of wealth.

The ethnic cleansing of Shaba, scarcely noted outside Zaire, was a textbook demonstration of ethnic conflict as both an instrument and a legacy of tyranny, and of the links between ethnicity and organized crime. Three years later Mobutu would try the same tactic again in eastern Zaire, issuing, through yet another provincial governor, an edict to expel—that is, ethnically cleanse—Zairian Tutsis from the region bordering Rwanda and Uganda. Mobutu had for years been a mentor of Rwanda's Hutu leader, Juvenal Habyarimana. In the wake of Rwanda's genocide, Mobutu, with renewed international backing, was providing rufuge to more than a million Rwandan Hutus, including thousands of soldiers and militiamen who had participated in the genocide. In fact, Mobutu was enabling these *génocidaires* to regroup and rearm, in preparation for renewed war in Rwanda. This time, however, Mobutu's recklessness massively backfired. It provoked the armed rebellion led by Laurent Kabila and backed by Uganda, Rwanda, Angola and others, which swept across Zaire and finally toppled Mobutu in May 1997. Exiled in Morocco, he died of cancer just a few months later.

In August 1998, Uganda and Rwanda backed yet another rebel invasion of the Democratic Republic of the Congo, against their erstwhile protégé, Kabila, and the country has been at war ever since, its rich deposits of diamonds and copper plundered by no fewer than six outside states and assorted militias and proxies. As this book was being completed, in the summer of 2000, the United Nations reported that a staggering 1.7 million Congolese had died, mostly from starvation and related disease, in two years of war.

"*Après moi, le déluge,*" Mobutu used to say. Many of his apologists believed him. They imagined that tyranny was an indespensable means of controlling an otherwise anarchic environment. In the violent chaos that consumed Congo after Mobutu's demise, it could be argued that he was right, but for the opposite reason: the tyrant had stoked the forces of anarchy to such a degree that he was no longer able to control them.

Mobutu's belated ouster and Congo's subsequent disintegration highlighted the great risks of anarchy as a tactic of tyranny. There is always the possibility that deliberately provoked chaos will backfire and consume the tyranny it was intended to preserve, as the Hutus in Rwanda—Mobutu's longtime allies—would also learn in 1994. But Mobutu would not have survived in power as long as he did if such tactics had not previously been successful in Shaba. What Mary Jane and I had witnessed prior to our arrest was a compelling argument for anarchy as an instrument of tyranny: sometimes it works.

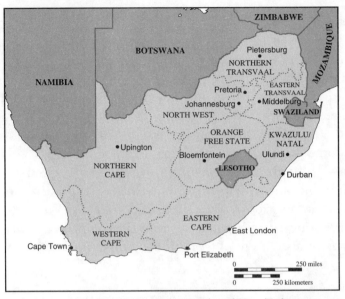

Republic of South Africa, with Natal and KwaZulu, pre-1994

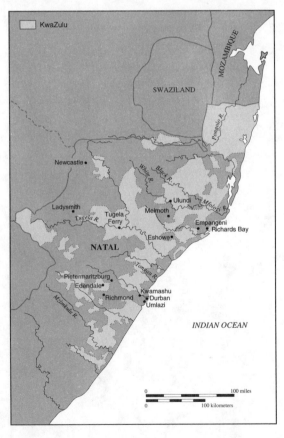

4

THE COLLABORATOR

THE GRANITE COLUMNS of Durban Supreme Court loom imposingly over a well-scrubbed square within view of the Indian Ocean port on the edge of downtown Durban, Natal's principal city. The courtroom on the second floor has the intimate, mahogany-walled feel of the Old Bailey criminal courthouse in London. The lawyers declaim in English and Afrikaans, wearing black robes with frilly white cravats. The Honorable Justice Jan Hugo, rotund and bearded, resplendent in cardinal red, presides from a raised bench with a springbok seal behind him, as he adjudicates from painstakingly construed precedents in the criminal code and common law.

In South Africa's century-long era of white domination, under the British and later under apartheid, it was just this kind of elaborately formal, ritual-bound atmosphere that gave an aura of legitimacy to an otherwise crude and violent system, dressing up in robes and rarefied rhetoric a relentless record of convictions overwhelmingly based on confessions. These were induced, to quote from one of the many human rights investigations of the time, through punching, kicking, slapping, whipping with *sjamboks*, beating with rifle butts, electric shock, enforced standing and exercise, severe food and sleep deprivation, suffocation, enforced nakedness, shackling, stabbing with cigarette butts and the so-called "helicopter"—handcuffing a person at the wrists and ankles and suspending him like a deer from a pole slung between two chairs, sometimes for hours, and pounding with sticks and clubs.

White judges in their flowing red regalia handed down erudite opinions and lengthy sentences, notably unmoved by the parade of dazed defendants with broken teeth and cheekbones, perforated eardrums, cut lips, swollen eyes, slashed backsides and fractured limbs.

The remembered images of perverted justice made all the more remarkable the scene unfolding before us now as Justice Hugo, a veteran of apartheid's bench, gaveled his court to order on opening day of *The State v. Peter Msane & Others.* Thirteen retired white generals, including Magnus Malan, who had been defense minister at the height of emergency rule in the mid-1980s, and seven Zulus, partisans of Mangosuthu Gatsha Buthelezi's Inkatha Freedom Party (IFP), stood accused of complicity in a massacre of thirteen people, ten years earlier, in a remote rural village called KwaMakhutha, in what had been the "homeland" known as KwaZulu.

It was March 1996, two years after South Africa's historic transition to majority rule. The "Magnus Malan trial," as it came to be called, represented a singular attempt by Nelson Mandela's new government to bring to justice those at the very top of apartheid's security forces who, it was alleged, deliberately fanned violence among blacks by arming and training one faction—Inkatha—as a proxy force, in the time-honored tradition of divide and rule.

The proceedings on this opening day were dominated by a motion by the prosecutor, Natal's attorney general, Tim McNally, to add a "conspiracy" charge to the indictment. The 1986 massacre in Kwa-Makhutha was not just an isolated case of mass murder, McNally argued. Rather, it was the logical outcome of a broader conspiracy, a covert alliance of powerful men, black and white, seeking to weaken and discredit Mandela's African National Congress (ANC) and thereby stem the tide of democratic rule. In essence, Malan and his codefendants were accused of building the engine of anarchy that propelled a dirty little war that killed 20,000 black South Africans in ten years—a lethal anarchy among blacks intended to preserve white tyranny.

The alleged conspiracy involved the establishment of a paramilitary capability for Inkatha, comprising two hundred Zulu men covertly trained and armed by the South African Defense Forces (SADF) at a base on the Caprivi Strip in northeastern Namibia. These were the "Caprivi trainees," the death squads that would carry on a proxy struggle against the ANC in the name of Zulu nationalism. This covert collusion between apartheid's security forces and Inkatha, which had come to be known as the "Third Force," epitomized one of the darkest evils of a system of racial tyranny that relied above all, as we have seen elsewhere on the continent, on letting the natives do the dirty work—the cooking and scrubbing and mining, and the fighting and the dying in war.

The twenty defendants marched into a packed courtroom: thirteen silver-haired white men and their seven Zulu codefendants, black and white South Africans standing side by side in the dock. It was an astonishing sight, all the more so since the conspirators had gone to considerable lengths to disguise the link between blacks and whites. The indictment quoted documents seized from South African Military Intelligence headquarters in Pretoria shortly after Mandela was sworn in as president that emphasized: " 'The paramilitary force should not be capable of being linked to the SA Defense Force or the South African State,' " and " 'The impression should rather be created that it had its origin and development within the then KwaZulu.' "

Magnus Malan was all hale and good cheer, dapper in pinstripes and a blue and a red tie. He smiled broadly and waved to supporters in the gallery. Standing silently beside him was the retired general Pieter Hendrik "Tienie" Groenewald. Suave in a dark blue suit, peppery-haired and mustached, "Accused no. 14," as he was called in the indictment, was a central figure in the conspiracy. As chief of South African Military Intelligence in the mid-1980s, the indictment alleged, Groenewald had held a secret meeting on November 15, 1985, with the leader of KwaZulu, Chief Gatsha Buthelezi. Iago-like, the general had informed the chief of plans by Mandela's ANC to "eliminate him and neutralize Inkatha." Buthelezi requested protection. The Caprivi trainees would be Groenewald's answer. Most would be assigned to the KwaZulu Police (KZP), a ragtag homeland militia—not unlike Charles Taylor's NPFL and Mobutu's JUFERI—that turned out to be well suited for the kind of "protection" that is based on taking the fight to the enemy.

The Zulus in the dock, in contrast with their once-powerful codefendants, were mostly poorly educated thugs. They were the accused triggermen, career criminals who allegedly carried out the Kwa-Makhutha massacre—slaughtering a family of thirteen men, women and children suspected of having ANC sympathies—on behalf of the generals in Pretoria and their senior black allies. Only one of the black defendants seemed to be personally acquainted with the white generals. He shook Groenewald's hand and slapped Malan on the back. He was M. Z. Khumalo, for many years Chief Buthelezi's closest confidant and the alleged point man between Pretoria and his boss. Heavy-set, with meaty hands and a paunch, Khumalo had the bearing of a barroom bouncer. His supporters in the gallery in front of me hung an Inkatha banner from the rail.

Conspicuously absent from the proceedings was Chief Buthelezi. He had not been charged, though his name appeared in virtually every paragraph of the indictment. He was clearly at the center of the alleged conspiracy—an unindicted co-conspirator and, by inference, a collaborator. The sensitivity of this black politician's alleged collusion with the apartheid security apparatus was of concern to all involved from the outset. The indictment itself quoted records of a meeting in Durban between Magnus Malan, Buthelezi, M. Z. Khumalo and several others—a meeting at which, it said, "Malan cautioned Buthelezi as to the sensitivity of their relationship. Inkatha should not be linked to the South African government and he [Buthelezi] should not identify himself with the SA government during overseas visits."

"Tribal passions"

Tienie Groenewald and Gatsha Buthelezi would appear at first glance to have little in common. Ostensibly they represented opposite sides of the racial divide in apartheid-ruled South Africa. Yet they forged an alliance, long since drenched in blood, that embodied many of the complex interwoven strands of race, tribe and power. Their relationship was necessarily covert, psychologically complex, and allegedly criminal. Together they produced, in the waning years of white domination in southern Africa, one of Africa's best documented examples of anarchy as an instrument of tyranny.

Tienie Groenewald is not as notorious as some of the other Big Men in this volume, and has scarcely been heard of outside of South Africa. Yet his actions were every bit as cynically murderous as those of Charles Taylor or Mobutu Sese Seko. Groenewald operated in the shadows. He was an important but mostly unseen actor in the netherworld of intrigue and sabotage, death squads and psychological warfare that existed behind the scenes of racial tyranny in the apartheid years, exponentially more lethal than the rawhide whips and rubber bullets whose use made for such compelling drama in the television newscasts of the 1980s.

As a key member of the old apartheid regime's notorious State Se-curity Council (SSC), Groenewald was one of the masterminds be-hind South Africa's ruinous destabilization campaign against its black-ruled neighbors, a campaign that included Pretoria's covert backing of the rebel movements RENAMO in Mozambique and UNITA in Angola.

It was a phenomenon that is still little understood by most Ameri-cans: there *was* a race war in southern Africa. Even as Western on-lookers fretted that "time was running out" and warned that South Africa was ready to "explode," much of the region in which it was the dominant power burned and burned. Possibly a million people died of famine and massacres in Mozambique alone; an estimated half a mil-lion and counting have died in Angola. Few outside the region paid notice, mostly because virtually all the casualties were black.

When the killing extended into South Africa itself in the late 1980s, the world did take notice. For it appeared to be yet another manifesta-tion of the "heart of darkness": inexplicable "black-on-black" violence emerging out of a presumably fractious "tribal" past as the grip of white domination loosened. *The New Republic* editorialized that "the passions driving black men to kill other black men are the tribal pas-sions to which they were born. In that sense, South Africa, though more advanced than its neighbors, replicates their experience." The *New York Times* described the fighting of that era as "a resurgence of earlier battles between rival ethnic groups." The *Washington Post* re-ported the flaring up of "age-old hatreds." The *Los Angeles Times* char-acterized the violence as "tribal killings." *The New Yorker* lamented what it called "historical tribal animosities."

Actually, no such historical animosities existed. South Africans were indeed replicating the experience of their neighbors. But that experi-ence had little to do with "tribal passions to which they were born" and everything to do with racial tyranny. Tienie Groenewald and his confederates were replicating the tactics of tyrants across the conti-nent through the decades: divide and rule; arm the criminals; let the natives do the dirty work.

Apartheid in many ways typified Africa's most self-destructive ten-dency. It was tribalism codified. "Tribalism," as we have seen, is not an exotic habit of hatred but rather a method: a cynical means of acquir-ing or holding on to power by exploiting or magnifying ethnic differences. South Africa's southeastern province of Natal was a good place to learn about tribalism because the fighting in Natal pitted Zulu against Zulu. So the most obvious and superficial explanation for conflict—ethnicity—fell away in Natal. One could focus instead on all the myriad other elements in the picture which in the end explain tribalism's potency in much of the rest of Africa as well: the tactics and legacies of tyranny, the absence of legitimate law, the machinations of opportunists and their proxies, the fusion of politics with crime, poverty, and ignorance.

Natal's dirty war was steeped in the violent history and self-fulfilling prophesies of apartheid. Like the former Soviet Union, South Africa in transition provided a sobering illustration of the links between tyranny and lethal anarchy. White South Africans tended to think of black-on-black violence as an alien phenomenon that had nothing to do with them; "You can't take the bush out of the African," they used to say. But the war in Natal had quite a lot to do with whites, and with the methods they used to dominate blacks for more than a century.

"Loyal natives"

From the bustling port of Durban on the Indian Ocean coast, Port Shepstone is an hour's drive south along a highway that still evokes the stark contrasts of the old apartheid era. You drive from the First World in and out of the Third World—through the lush green sugar estates of irrigated, segregated white South Africa, and in and out of the bleak and impoverished rural hills of what was then KwaZulu, the Zulu "homeland" and power base of Chief Buthelezi and his Zulu-based Inkatha.

Port Shepstone is a modern seaside town with paved streets, trimmed lawns and an air-conditioned shopping mall. It is named after the nineteenth-century British secretary for native affairs, Theophilus Shepstone, who developed South Africa's version of "indirect rule." It was an ingenious delegation of repression whereby traditional chiefs were coerced or co-opted into governing their native subjects on behalf of the white authorities. Shepstone's indirect rule was the forerunner of the "homeland," or bantustan, system, Hendrik Verwoerd's epic vision of divide and rule known as "separate development." Beginning in the early 1960s, more than 3.5 million black

South Africans were forcibly removed from their homes to "self-governing," nominally independent "homelands"—one of history's great campaigns of "ethnic cleansing" before the term was coined.

Chief Buthelezi and his Inkatha confederates derived their power from the bantustan system. KwaZulu, with some 8 million Zulus, was the largest of ten bantustans. It stretched across an archipelago of mostly barren land along the eastern edge of the country. Although Buthelezi famously refused the independent statehood envisioned for all the homelands by apartheid's architects—accepting a bogus independence would have discredited him as an avowed opponent of apartheid—KwaZulu, like the others, endured as a reservoir of cheap migrant labor and as an ethnically based center of power for those who would wield it.

Buthelezi was once lionized by white South Africans and Western conservatives as a "moderate" alternative to Nelson Mandela's African National Congress. He opposed sanctions and favored free enterprise. He rose to power with the acquiescence of the ANC, and throughout the 1970s and 1980s he appealed for Mandela's release from prison. He said he opposed apartheid.

Yet Buthelezi was fundamentally a creature of the bantustan system. He was appointed chief minister of KwaZulu in 1972 and later, importantly, minister of police as well. He used his position as the head of KwaZulu to build up a formidable power base.

While the ANC was banned (1960–90), and its partisans jailed and tortured, Inkatha was free to carry on its activities. Relying on funds—and guns—provided by Pretoria, and on the virtually unlimited police powers and taxing authority provided by the system of indirect rule, Inkatha evolved into an impressive political machine with exclusive channels of patronage. In KwaZulu, Inkatha controlled the allocation of land, health care, pensions, education, travel documents, and police officers. Inkatha was less a "party" or a "movement" than a syndicate of rural Zulu chiefs and urban bosses backed by the coercive power of the KwaZulu Police (KZP).

Buthelezi lorded over the KwaZulu "homeland" like a petty despot. He wore the badge of ethnicity, militant Zulu nationalism, as his source of legitimacy. Over the years, much was made—mostly by whites—of Buthelezi's tangled roots in the Zulu royal family and of his inheritance of a Zulu tradition of militarism. But the exotic leopard-skin trappings in which Buthelezi wrapped himself in the name of African "tradition" masked the violent source of his power: the armed forces of white tyranny.

In the spring of 1993, when Mary Jane and I first visited KwaZulu, Buthelezi was struggling to hold on to power. As befits a durable survivor in the land of apartheid, Buthelezi was playing the ethnic card. He mobilized the mostly illiterate Zulu population much as the Serb nationalist leader Slobodan Milosovic was mobilizing Serbs in the former Yugoslavia during those same years: by propagating a highly romanticized version of his people's history and tradition, and by stoking their fears. A sinister theme running through the rhetoric of Buthelezi and his Inkatha chiefs and warlords—and of the police—in the waning days of apartheid was that the ANC, South Africa's leading black nationalist organization, was nothing more than an agent of the Xhosa, bent on "genocide"—Buthelezi's word—against the Zulus. Without Zulu "unity" under his leadership, Buthelezi warned, Zulus would be subjected to "ethnic cleansing" at the hands of what he characterized as the Xhosa-dominated ANC. (The Xhosas—Nelson Mandela was Xhosa—had their own "homelands," Transkei and Ciskei, farther down the Indian Ocean coast.) Buthelezi decried the ANC's "campaign to annihilate the Zulu nation." He declared, "They want to leave us homeless so that we too will be forced to wander in the desert, as the people of Israel did after their emancipation from Egypt."

The deadly fallout from this cynical game was replayed in countless rural villages and townships across KwaZulu that year. Mary Jane and I got our own introduction to its complex dynamic at a funeral outside the town of Eshowe, about an hour's drive north of Durban.

"In a moment"

On the day they buried Jacky Ntebela, South Africa's slanting winter sun gave an incandescent glow to the rolling green cane fields of northern Natal. It was a Saturday afternoon in June. Jacky's "Comrades," as ANC partisans called themselves, held aloft the black, green, and yellow banner of the ANC as they followed his hearse out of the mean smattering of matchbox houses and rutty dirt roads known as Gezinsila township, on the outskirts of Eshowe. The Comrades shuffled in the familiar rhythmic *toyi-toyi* and lifted their voices in the stirring funeral dirge of the armed struggle against apartheid:

Monrovia, Liberia, April 1996. "Many of these boys are orphans of the war," the Liberian rebel leader Charles Taylor told the author. "Some of them saw their mothers wrapped in blankets, tied up, poured with kerosene and burned alive. We keep them armed as a means of keeping them out of trouble. It's a means of control." (Christophe Simon/AFP)

Charles Taylor *(above)*, whose rebellion against Samuel K. Doe would leave as many as 150,000 Liberians dead. It was Taylor's signature insight that someone else's will to mass slaughter, that of the aggrieved Gio people toward Doe's minority Krahn, could be harnessed to his own will to power. "Kill the Krahn!" was his battle cry. (Bhasker Solanki/FSP/Liaison)

Ronald Reagan and Liberian President Samuel K. Doe at the White House in 1982. President Reagan introduced Doe as "Chairman Moe." (Barry Thumma/ AP) Chester A. Crocker *(right)*, assistant secretary of state for African affairs, said to the author, "I would never in a million years tell you I was seeking what was in the best interests of Liberia. I was protecting the interests of Washington." (Barbara Adams/Liaison)

Likasi train station *(above)*, Shaba Province, southern Zaire, April 1993. Before relief groups moved in, sixty people a day were dying from measles, malaria and respiratory infections—evidence that the time-honored practice of "divide and rule" had been effectively executed. "It's important to know that Mobutu is a great strategist," one man told the author. "He has his ways and means." (Scott Peterson/Liaison)

President Mobutu Sese Seko of Zaire had direct contact with every American president from Eisenhower to Reagan. Over three decades the United States gave Mobutu $2 billion. President Reagan called Mobutu "a voice of good sense and good will." (Dirck Halstead/Liaison)

Chief Mangosuthu Gatsha Buthelezi (*left*, Tait Selwyn/Liaison), leader of South Africa's Zulu-based Inkatha movement. His war with Nelson Mandela's African National Congress (*below*, Georges Merillon/Liaison), killed 20,000 Zulus. "I'm not the sort of person who gets in bed with anyone," he assured the author. General Pieter Hendrik "Tienie" Groenewald (*right*, Peter Magubane/Liaison) was chief of South African military intelligence in the mid-1980s. "Naturally, certain assistance was given to Inkatha," he said. "After all, we were both fighting the ANC."

Hassan al-Turabi (*left*, Scott Peterson/Liaison), leader of Sudan's National Islamic Front. "Islamic Leninism" was the term Sudanese used to describe Turabi's ruthlessly cunning rise to power. Riek Machar (*right*, Mary Jane Camejo), the rebel whose failed coup against the mainstream guerrilla leader John Garang (*below, top row center, with confederates*, Anthony Suau/Liaison) triggered an internecine bloodbath that killed tens of thousands. "It was a big fight," Riek told the author. "We are certainly not angels," Garang conceded.

François-Xavier Sibomana (*above*), a Rwandan Hutu farmer and father of eight, and an admitted member of an Interahamwe militia, one of the Hutu death squads that massacred upward of 500,000 ethnic Tutsis in 1994. "Everybody had to join," he told the author. "It was the thing to do." (Mary Jane Camejo)

In March 1998 President Bill Clinton stopped in Kigali, the Rwandan capital, and acknowledged that the United States "did not do enough" to halt Rwanda's genocide. He appeared with General Paul Kagame (*at right*), the Tutsi military strong man, and President Pasteur Bizimungu, a Hutu. (C. Johnson/Liaison)

President Yoweri Museveni of Uganda (*right*) was embraced by the Clinton Administration as the prototype for a "new Generation" of African leaders, the harbinger of an "African renaissance," before he plunged Uganda into war in neighboring Congo. "There is responsibility of regional leaders to attack dictatorship," he told the author. (Lebrun/Photo News/Liaison)

The United Nations International Criminal Tribunal for Rwanda began trying top conspirators in the genocide in 1996, in Arusha, Tanzania. Jean-Paul Akayesu (*above*, Jean-Marc Bouju/AP), a former small-town Hutu mayor and archetype for the indispensible middle management of the genocide, was convicted of genocide and crimes against humanity in September 1998. "Honestly speaking, frankly speaking, there was never any question of Tutsis being killed, never, never," he claimed. Judges Lennart Aspegren of Sweden, Laity Kama of Senegal and Navanethem Pillay of South Africa (*below, left to right*, Sven Bloch) presided. Pierre-Richard Prosper of Los Angeles led the prosecution. (*below right*, Sven Bloch)

More than 100,000 Rwandan children were orphaned in the genocide and
its immediate aftermath, including these Hutus (*above*, Antonin Kratochvil),
who were herded into a makeshift orphanage run by Unicef after watching
their parents die of cholera in Goma, Zaire, in July 1994. Back in Rwanda,
surviving Tutsis and moderate Hutus (like this one, *below*, James Nachtwey/
Magnum Photos) deemed too sympathetic to the Tutsis bore the scars from
machete wounds inflicted by the Interahamwe militia.

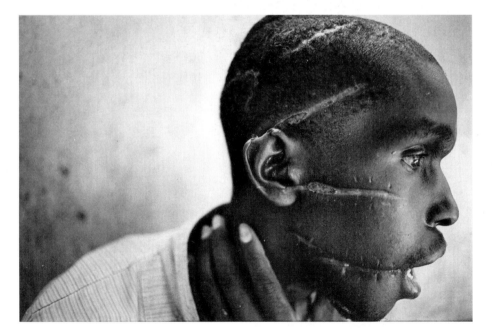

"*Hamba kahle Umkhonto, Umkhonto we Sizwe,*" they sang—"Go well the spear, the spear of the nation."

The tiny rural cemetery was tucked into the bush off the side of the road, a humble collection of unkempt, weed-covered mounds and crude wooden crosses. Jacky's open grave was at the end of a row of four fresh mounds of copper-colored soil. These were the brand-new graves of men whose deaths in the previous fortnight had something to do with Jacky's violent demise. They were partisans of Inkatha. The murder of one of these men, a Mr. Ngema, whose unmarked grave lay adjacent to the hole around which the dancing, chanting Comrades now paid their last respects, had set in motion a chain of attacks and counterattacks in which Jacky's death was but the latest and probably not the last.

"You can't tell if it was retaliation," one of the Comrades advised me as the casket was lowered into the ground. "The area is a bit tense."

The events around Eshowe, a picturesque, placid-seeming rural white farming community with the smudge of Gezinsila on its periphery, typified the mosaic of discrete miniwars that made up the wider pattern of conflict in Natal. Eleven people had been killed around Eshowe in the two weeks before Jacky Ntebela's funeral. Behind these murders was a complex saga involving alleged warlords, hit squads, and police complicity—most of it impossible to confirm for lack of any lawful accountability in South Africa's shifting ground between tyranny and anarchy.

The local Inkatha warlord was a man named Gideon Zulu, a prince in the traditional Zulu royal family. Gideon Zulu was a member of the KwaZulu legislative assembly and also a member of Inkatha's central committee. He had been a feared participant in Natal's running battles at least since August of 1985, when he led a vigilante *amabutho* (pronounced "amabootoo"), a regiment of Zulu warriors, in a club-wielding, spear-carrying rampage against funeral-goers from the ANC-aligned United Democratic Front (UDF) in the huge Durban township of Umlazi.

Among Gideon Zulu's former bodyguards, neighbors told us, was a man named Xolani Ngema. He was the son of the murdered man whose fresh grave we found adjacent to Jacky Ntebela's grave. Xolani Ngema was a special constable—"*kitskonstabel*" in Afrikaans—in the KwaZulu Police. The KZP was an adjunct of the South African Police (SAP), funded by Pretoria. It was supposedly responsible for neutral law enforcement in KwaZulu; in reality it was Chief Buthelezi's personal militia. Thus does crime become combustibly blurred with politics, when the rule of law becomes identified with a partisan political interest. The KwaZulu Police, and the *kitskonstabels* in particular, were implicated in innumerable crimes of commission and omission; "*kits*" means "in a moment" in Afrikaans, a reference to the minimal training the *kitskonstabels* received.

After the attack on the elder Ngema, in which three others were also killed, Ngema's son Xolani rounded up a gang of KZP veterans and embarked on a reign of terror. They attacked the Mazmuku family first, killing three, including a seventy-nine-year-old grandmother who had only recently joined the ANC. Then they attacked Sipho Mthiyana—a former *induna*, the Zulu equivalent of a ward boss—and his son, Lucky.

The attack on Sipho Mthiyana had happened in the night ten days earlier, when, he told me, Xolani Ngema and two others had set upon him and his son with bush knives and shot him three times with a .38 caliber revolver. He was sitting now on the front porch of his plain cement-block house, with chickens darting around the dirt yard. Portly and bespectacled, Sipho Mthiyana, fifty-one, spoke with evident discomfort, his head still wrapped in gauze and three bullet wounds healing on his buttocks. Lucky, twenty-three, wearing an ANC T-shirt, sat in silence. He had hideous scars across his face and on a grossly swollen elbow.

"Xolani believes the ANC killed his father," Mthiyana said. "After the violence started last year, the IFP leaders alleged that I was with the ANC. At the time Xolani said to me, 'You didn't do anything to stop the ANC from growing.' He said, 'Next time I will kill you.' "

Sipho Mthiyana's power to stop the ANC, had he chosen to do so, derived from his position as an *induna*. According to traditional Zulu custom, *indunas* have, among other responsibilities, the power to mobilize their respective warrior regiments, the *amabutho*, should the safety of their constituencies be threatened. Many *indunas*, like their chiefs, received salaries from the KwaZulu government and were thus, by necessity, aligned with Inkatha. After the ANC was unbanned in 1990 and its representatives began organizing in rural Natal for the first time, Sipho Mthiyana was instructed by his superiors in Inkatha to mobilize the *amabutho* against the ANC. "The chairperson of the

IFP told me to keep the ANC out," Sipho Mthiyana recalled. "They asked for my permission to use the *amabutho* to fight to keep the ANC out. I denied that authority. I was trying to avoid the violence between the ANC and Inkatha. As a result, they started saying, 'No, you are not with us; you are sympathetic to the ANC.'"

Sipho Mthiyana was soon ousted as an *induna*. "They have started to threaten people," he said. "They have hired gangsters. They go out at night to assault and shoot and burn homes, to show people this is what will happen if you join the ANC." Had he reported the attack on him to the police? "It would be useless to pursue the matter with the police," Sipho Mthiyana said. "The SAP cops used to say, 'The ANC must go back to Transkei.'"

This was the ethnic card. Zulus who supported the ANC, by many accounts a majority among South Africa's 8.5 million Zulus, were branded *amaXhosa* (literally, "Xhosas"), betrayers of their Zulu brethren.

"I am living in fear," Sipho Mthiyana told us. "I am not sleeping in my house. My family sleeps in the Methodist church. No one sleeps here anymore."

"Justice organizations"

As many as 20,000 black South Africans were murdered in internecine political violence among blacks in the decade between 1985 and the 1994 election. In Natal alone nearly 2,000 were killed in 1993, a figure well above a decade-long average of about a hundred a month—three or four a day. At least as many people were wounded, by everything from bush knives and spears to hand grenades and automatic gunfire. More than 100,000 were driven from their homes.

The ANC's war with Inkatha began in Natal during the township uprising of the mid-1980s, when the ANC's campaign to render the townships "ungovernable" evolved into an often violent effort to destroy the structures of the state and its clients, including the police, suspected informers, township councilors seen as puppets of Pretoria and rural bantustan officials. To this day ANC partisans regard their war against Inkatha as the last chapter in the long struggle to destroy apartheid and all its agents, black and white.

"The killings relate to the struggle for liberation in this country," said Harry Gwala, the militant patriarch of the ANC in Natal before his death in 1995. "The background to the violence is the intensification of the struggle against apartheid. It is a war of liberation."

Whether Inkatha's partisans were in fact stooges or collaborators, when they were attacked, necklaced, or driven from their homes by arsonists, their survival interests coincided with those of the state and its security forces. They fought back, sometimes in league with the police, sometimes by mobilizing mobs of vigilantes who gave as good as they got—and often much more.

Of course, even if the conflict pitted the forces of change against forces with a stake in the status quo, not all those fighting for change were notably enlightened, and not all those who found themselves defending the status quo were sinister. Most of the latter were cannon fodder, duped or press-ganged into fighting for interests they were bound to defend for their own survival. All manner of gangsters and opportunists jumped into the fray on both sides, and the methods they employed brought out the worst in each other.

Quite apart from the covert role of elements of the security forces in influencing the conflict, another engine propelling the cycle of violence—akin to those in Liberia and Congo/Zaire—was the absence of legitimate law enforcement, a problem inherent in the absence of legitimate government. Natal's war was a textbook case of anarchy as a product of tyranny. The ANC saw the police as the enemy, and vice versa. Anarchy compelled people to seek allegiance with political parties for refuge, vengeance or both.

"You're talking about a high-crime situation," said a police detective who believed that incompetent and indifferent police were the primary cause of the violence. "People are looking for justice. They turn to political parties, or to an armed wing, or to returned political exiles who can achieve justice for them. Political parties have become justice organizations for millions of people because there is a big vacuum that the police are either unable or unwilling to fill."

The failure of the police derived from a number of factors. Apart from the partisanship of many police officers, to whom the ANC was always a murderous and—until 1990—illegal organization, there was outright racism among many white and Indian officers, who imagine that blacks killing blacks is the natural order of things. There was also severe understaffing and pervasive incompetence in investigative work. Under South Africa's draconian security laws and extended states of emergency, the police never had a legal incentive to develop evidence beyond what could be beaten out of a suspect with no lawyer, no right to remain silent and no limit on how long he could be detained without charges.

And there was the problem of finding witnesses. "People are understandably afraid to testify," said Justice John Didcott, a respected judge in Natal who went on to serve as one of the original justices on South Africa's post-apartheid Constitutional Court. "Many fear that people who are in trouble will come back and not only kill you but kill your family as well. It has a snowball effect. People are likely to be acquitted because witnesses are afraid to give evidence against them, and people are reluctant to give evidence because they believe people are likely to be acquitted. It's important for the police to provide protection for witnesses, but police protection might put you in even greater danger, because people would suspect you are an informer."

There is no question that the conduct of many comrades, dating back to the era of "necklacing" and "people's courts" in the township uprising of the mid-1980s, drove people into Inkatha's arms. Senzo Mafayela, Inkatha's chief organizer in the Durban area, told me, "I did not agree with how the ANC were running things. People were being intimidated, stoning transport, burning houses, making threats that interfered with my life—you had to participate. If you didn't, you were the enemy. You were a stooge. You were a sellout."

Justice Richard Goldstone, the South African jurist who went on serve as the original chief prosecutor for the International Criminal Tribunal for the former Yugoslavia, chaired a judicial commission investigating the causes of the violence in Natal. In a conversation I had with him in July 1993, he spoke of the political rivalry between Inkatha and the ANC as "the trigger, not the cause" of violence. "It's the last of a series of causes that go back a century," Goldstone told me. "You have a century of racial discrimination, of dehumanizing the victims to justify discrimination. You have forty-five years of apartheid, including the repression of black political representation. You have the use of the South African police and security forces for repressive purposes. You have tremendous unemployment, poor education, and discriminatory education. If you add all of these things up, it would be strange if this were not a violent society."

Indeed, South Africa's anarchy was as much a legacy of white rule as it was a tactic. Political killings accounted for only a fraction of the violence in South Africa. By some estimates, purely criminal murders out-numbered politically motivated murders by five to one. South Africa's murder rate doubled between 1990 and 1994; it was reckoned to be ten times that of the United States. Unemployment surpassed 50 percent among black South Africans, and reached 90 percent or more among the so-called "lost generation" of black youths in some areas. The fail-ing economy drove hundreds of thousands from the rural homelands into crowded shantytowns outside the townships in a largely futile search for jobs. These slums had all the social pathologies of urban slums and shantytowns the world over: acute housing shortages, lack of schools and transport, the breakdown of families and other traditional sources of authority. Organized crime flourished, with "shacklords" running protection and gambling rackets and trafficking in drugs and, above all, guns. High-powered firearms poured into the country; an AK-47 could be bought in the townships for about fifty dollars.

Justice Goldstone provided an example of the blending of crime and politics in a 1993 report of his commission's findings regarding a criminal gang known as the Black Cats, which terrorized Wesselton Township, outside Ermelo, just north of Natal. The commission was unable to substantiate the claims of two Black Cats—later confirmed by subsequent investigations—that the gang had been trained as a hit squad by South African Military Intelligence. But it found that the Black Cats were eventually recruited as members by Inkatha, appar-ently to establish an Inkatha presence in that area. The commission reported, "For some time Wesselton . . . had been the scene of violent confrontation between a number of criminal gangs. . . . The position was exacerbated by the gangs attracting the attention of political orga-nizations, which used them in order to enlarge their political support and power. All of these factors combined and led to violence and ruth-less murder."

"I support apartheid"

Zulus in the ANC were quick to remind me that Zulu chiefs were among the founders of the ANC. The president of the ANC before it was banned, in 1960, was Albert Luthuli, a Zulu chief who won the Nobel Peace Prize. The ANC's problem with chiefs was not with their role in traditional structures but with the marriage of those structures with the structures of apartheid.

Under Theophilus Shepstone's system of indirect rule, chiefs were placed on the government payroll and subordinated to the colonial governor. Shepstone recognized some traditional chiefs and appointed others. The chiefs exercised absolute authority over their subjects, though they were accountable not to their own people but to the colonial government. Shepstone's genius was in persuading Africans that they were governing themselves. Through a succession of acts and amendments over the next century, indirect rule grafted state structures onto the traditional system, in the process creating a bureaucratized chieftainship with unaccountable power. When the homelands were created, chiefs became powerful employees of homeland governments. Since in KwaZulu most chiefs were members of Inkatha, they became instruments of Inkatha's power.

To be sure, KwaZulu's chiefs were and remain a mixed lot. Many served their subjects as best they could under the circumstances imposed upon them by apartheid. Whether they were puppets, collaborators, agents, dupes, opportunists, or well-meaning victims of apartheid—it could be a difficult call amid the tangle of bribery and coercion. The complexity of their position was brought home to me in a conversation in Umgababa, a semirural KwaZulu township south of Durban, where two senior advisers of an embattled Inkatha chief, Philbert Luthuli, waxed nostalgic for the days of Hendrik Verwoerd and Jan Smuts, two paragons of white domination.

John Luthuli, seventy-one years old, the chief's uncle, perhaps noticing my dropped jaw, explained, "They were using the law, and a person grew up knowing himself quite well. He knew that he didn't have to do something bad because he is going to go to jail." But Verwoerd was the architect of apartheid, was he not? "I support apartheid," Luthuli replied. "It makes you have an identity. You knew that you are an African, and an Indian is an Indian, and a white man is a white man. People have lost their identity now."

Albert Mchunu, seventy-three, the chief's white-bearded counselor, added, "The whites were making us clever by treating us like that. We have planted sugar because of such things." Luthuli continued, "We won't survive without that presence of the whites. We are like animals."

I must have looked startled.

"I'm not saying this to bribe you because you are white," Luthuli assured me. "I'm saying this because of what I've seen of black people killing each other."

Mchunu brought up the by now familiar ethnic issue: "Since Transkei and Ciskei have their own governments, they must remain like this. It is [the Xhosas] who are causing the conflicts here. They must remain in their areas and don't interfere with what is happening here." That sounded like an argument for apartheid, I noted. "Yes, we are fighting to maintain apartheid," Mchunu replied. "We don't want the whites to go away from here. We fought the Boers. We fought the British. And then we were living in peace. It is the ANC which is causing this war."

Luthuli's attitude was perhaps an extreme example of abasement, but it wasn't uncommon, I was told, among older, mostly illiterate peasants in rural Natal. A word like "collaboration" probably applied less than "adaptation" or "accommodation" to a harsh life of subservience.

"The police vanished so we could kill each other"

Minutes away from the chief's kraal, across the road and in the ANC's turf, one of the Comrades, Thomas Mdluli, denounced the chief and his allies. "Those people are believing in the bantustan, in the apartheid system," he declared. Mdluli, twenty-seven, a life-raft repairman, was the ANC's branch organizer in Umgababa and the local chairman of the South African Communist Party. Sitting in his cramped bedroom, bearded, bespectacled, wearing a red Communist Party T-shirt and a black leather jacket, Mdluli looked every bit the militant as he described a long succession of what he said were indiscriminate police-backed attacks on his area.

But his tone softened when he spoke of his parents, still living on Chief Luthuli's side of the road. "On the other side of the road are the parents only, the poor people like my mommy and pappy. They are controlled by the IFP, because the old people know how to tolerate the apartheid system. They think, 'While I'm here, to keep peace I will stay here and accept what is happening.' Like my father—he said, 'On that side we listen to one man.' My dad is not educated. He has standard three [fifth grade]. My mom was standard two [fourth grade], because at that time they were not permitted to go to school. I'm talking about what I have experienced in my own family.

"My mommy, she's a domestic worker. She works under a white man, a member of the National Party. She used to say, 'Listen, boy.'

My mommy's boss used to drive me to school for seven years. She used to say, 'Because they were good to me, I support their party.'"

Inevitably, many chiefs and their *indunas* over the years operated like bosses and capos with their own little mafias. In the KwaZulu precincts around Port Shepstone more than 135 people were killed in four months of bloodletting in 1993 that began with a popular revolt against an *induna* accused of extorting "taxes" from his impoverished constituents while failing to account for where the money was going. The *induna's* chief was later charged with eleven counts of murder.

In the late 1980s a group of dissident chiefs formed with the aim of abolishing the bantustan system. The Congress of Traditional Leaders of South Africa (CONTRALESA) inevitably gravitated toward the ANC and the UDF; Buthelezi denounced CONTRALESA as a "spear [in] the heart of Zulu unity." CONTRALESA's first president, Chief Mhlabunzima Joseph Maphumulo, was assassinated in 1991. The crime was never solved, but evidence pointed to agents of the South African Police. Earlier, in 1988, a close ally of Maphumulo, Chief Msinga Mlaba, had been assassinated. That crime, too, was never solved, though Mlaba's younger brother and successor as chief, Zibuse Mlaba, told me he had "information" that the murder was the work of an Inkatha hit squad.

Chief Zibuse Mlaba, thirty-eight, gave me a firsthand account of the covert pressures brought to bear on rural chiefs by security-force agents working in collusion with Inkatha. After he became chief, he said, he was approached by a captain in the South African Police who promised to give him weapons if he would join Inkatha's chiefs and fight the United Democratic Front. "They didn't know I was with the UDF," Mlaba told me. "They were trying to project me against my own people to get rid of the UDF Comrades. They offered me any help I needed." He was given a pistol and a shotgun. The chief reached in his pocket and pulled out three gun licenses issued by SAP, and drew back his windbreaker to reveal a pistol, which he said he had accepted to protect his wife and children. "They said I would no longer have control over my own people if I allowed the UDF to be active in my area. They said, 'You are going to be ruled by foreigners.' They said the only solution was to join the other chiefs in Inkatha and fight the UDF." Few chiefs resisted these entreaties, Mlaba said. "When you refuse, they threaten you. Some joined in because they feared for their lives."

When Chief Mlaba refused to send his *amabutho* to an Inkatha "prayer rally" in 1989, buses filled with warriors and vans filled with SAP men descended on his area. "They were shouting at us that we have allowed the Xhosas to invade the Zulus' land," Mlaba recalled. When his own youthful followers counterattacked, "The police vanished so we could kill each other."

"As fire drives out fire, so pity, pity"

Natal's warlords could be compared to fourteenth-century Italian *signori*, twentieth-century Chinese and Lebanese warlords, Colombian drug lords, and Mafia racketeers. Like all of these, the warlords of Natal controlled fiefdoms through a mixture of terror and patronage. In their own fiefs they could tax and recruit, run protection rackets, hire hit men, and finance private militias by extorting tribute from their subjects, whether peasants or squatters. The warlords exploited the corruption inherent in unaccountable power. The old Shepstonian system was designed to make the administration of Africans pay for itself by permitting chiefs to rule over their own tribesmen and collect taxes from them. *Indunas* were the collection agents, and many emerged as warlords. Likewise, urban councilors, local Inkatha chairmen, and members of the KwaZulu Legislative Assembly monopolized the structures of power and patronage in their areas.

In the vast squatter settlements that mushroomed outside Durban after the lifting of Influx Control in 1986, urban shacklords moved into the vacuum of lawless power. They organized vigilantes to curb crime—or perpetrate it—and paid them by creating an informal tax base from "rents," or household levies. By the mid-1980s, greater Durban was one of the fastest-urbanizing areas of the world; the squatting problem was second only to that of Mexico City. Refugees from rural poverty flooded into Durban at a rate of 100,000 a year. By 1985 the number of people living in squalid, anarchic shantytowns on the outskirts of Durban had reached a million.

The proliferation of warlords in Natal also had roots in the political unrest that swept the townships and rural areas in the 1980s, and in the use of vigilantes by various groups, primarily Inkatha, in reaction to the unrest. Warlords who first emerged as gangsters or who served a vigilante function against crime, or both, were inevitably drawn into the political struggle. Certainly the ANC produced or rode on the backs of township toughs with tax bases of their own: "If you want us to defend you, you must pay us so that we can buy bullets," the Comrades used to say.

The struggle against apartheid was long exploited by criminals who, in the name of the struggle, looted, extorted, and murdered for personal gain. These were the *comtsotsis*—unemployed, illiterate gangsters who flourished when tens of thousands of UDF activists were detained during the mid-eighties uprising. Amorphously organized self-defense units, unemployed veterans of Umkhonto we Sizwe—the ANC's armed guerrilla wing, popularly known as MK—and common criminals alike, all heavily armed, fought in the name of the struggle. Lines of authority were blurred; legal accountability for abuses was nil.

ANC partisans took some comfort in pointing out that the ANC's violence was generated primarily at its fringes, whereas Inkatha's violence flowed from the center outward. But the ANC's leadership in Natal, if not directly linked to specific acts of violence, hardly worked to prevent violence. Quite the contrary. "We will not meet them with Bibles in our hands," Harry Gwala, the ANC's militant Natal Midlands leader, told me when we discussed Inkatha in 1993. "If they come with fire, we will quash them fire with fire. Even Shakespeare said that 'as fire drives out fire, so pity, pity.' "

Gwala, accused of sabotage, spent twenty years on Robben Island with Nelson Mandela. Now seventy-four and increasingly hampered by a neurological disease that left his arms dangling uselessly by his sides, Gwala since 1990 had carved out a role for himself as the father figure for the young Comrades who carried on the decade-long struggle against Inkatha in Natal.

"We have nothing to hide," Gwala assured me. "We would be happy if allegations are made in public." Was it not true, I asked, that the ANC had given as good as it got in Natal? "At no time have we had an expedition to go out and kill people," Gwala replied. "But when we have been attacked, we have defended ourselves. We have been open about that."

Indeed, Gwala at least had the advantage of relative candor. He never denied inciting the comrades to do battle against Inkatha's warlords, if not the rank and file. "What we have said is that people who have been used by Inkatha, the *amabutho*, they are victims of apartheid. They are not our enemies. We said, 'Peace among the people, war against the warlords.' "

"In fact, sir, I am a strong man"

The most notorious of Natal's warlords were aligned with Inkatha, and many had murky links with the security forces. Chief among them was David Ntombela, an *induna* who was involved in nearly all the bitter struggles that wracked the Natal Midlands. Ntombela was the archetype of the rural Inkatha warlord, an *induna* who emerged as a dominant figure in the Pietermaritzburg region in the late 1980s. He became notorious for leading *amabutho* into battle against UDF strongholds, most memorably in the "Seven Days War" in the Edendale Valley, in March of 1990, in which more than a hundred died. Ntombela's reputation as a strongman was secured on Christmas Day of 1984 when, in front of many witnesses, he shot and killed his own brother after an argument. He was implicated in at least eight murders, including those of a woman and her eleven-year-old daughter in 1987, but he was never convicted. Witnesses were loath to come forward.

Ntombela's well-documented connections with the security forces included participation in the planning of a 1986 massacre of eleven people in the KwaZulu town of Trust Feed, which led to the first judicial confirmation of collusion between high-ranking Inkatha officials and the South African Police. He was a member of the KwaZulu Legislative Assembly and of Inkatha's central committee. In 1993 he became Inkatha's regional chairman for the Natal Midlands.

I met Ntombela in June 1993 on his sixty-seventh birthday, in a bare-walled office at Inkatha's headquarters in Pietermaritzburg. He turned out to be a coarse, high-strung man with peppery gray hair and wary, milky eyes. He was missing a couple of front teeth. He spoke with passion in a high-pitched smoker's voice, pounding on his desk to make his points. Two plainclothes bodyguards, who said they were KwaZulu policemen, guarded the door. A pile of government-issue firearms lay on the floor in the corner. Ntombela wore a windbreaker indoors to conceal what he conceded with a smile was his ever-present pistol. He went through most of a pack of Rothmans over the course of an hour-long interview.

"They say Ntombela is warlord number one just to damage my dignity and my leadership," Ntombela asserted indignantly. "In fact, sir, I am a strong man. No one will push me. My strategy is, I don't shoot first but I don't run away."

I asked Ntombela what the conflict was all about.

"The peace-loving people were against what the UDF was doing," he explained. "They demanded to join Inkatha, because Inkatha was against what was going on with the UDF. If you ask anyone, 'Who started burning people alive?' they will tell you it was the ANC and the UDF. They forced people not to go to work, attacked people's houses, and burned their cars. They want to get freedom out of violence, while Inkatha is totally against violence. But every time the ANC would attack, Inkatha would defend themselves."

Ntombela heatedly disputed the charge that Inkatha was a proxy of Pretoria—"No one who's got a brain can support apartheid," he scoffed. "We all reject apartheid." Yet minutes later he embarked on a long soliloquy that sounded as if it could have been written by apartheid's visionaries: "Two years back, pamphlets were distributed in Transvaal by the ANC that said 'Kill the Zulus.' A lot of Zulus were killed in Transvaal because Zulus believe they have got their own government. Xhosas have their own government, which is Transkei. They've got their own government, which is Ciskei. Now people have been learning that history. The ANC, they've got one Zulu, which is Jacob Zuma. The rest are Xhosas."[1]

The apocalyptic rhetoric of the warlords had long since been absorbed by the rural men who were doing most of the fighting and dying in Inkatha's name. After my meeting with Ntombela I spent an evening in a "hostel" on the edge of KwaMashu Township. South Africa's notorious single-sex hostels were monuments to a migrant worker system that tore men of all ages from their families and housed

---

[1]Jacob Zuma was the lone Zulu on the ANC's national executive committee. Zuma used to be the chief of intelligence for the organization in exile. After the 1999 elections he was named deputy president by Thabo Mbeki. When I spoke with Zuma in Johannesburg, shortly after my meeting with Ntombela, Zuma dismissed the supposedly ANC pamphlets as obvious police forgeries used in the time-honored tradition of divide and rule.

them like animals near the mines or factories where they worked, in conditions of unspeakable squalor. The men who lived in KwaMashu's hostel were members of an *amabutho* that had engaged in bloody clashes with the comrades, who controlled most of the rest of Kwa-Mashu. They took me on a sobering tour of their dehumanizing living quarters.

"Bad, bad, bad," one of them whispered, his voice a mix of shame and resignation, as he showed me the cramped, dark, cell-like room in which he had lived with three other men like chickens in a coop since 1964. Dirty laundry hung from chords overhead. The cement walls were covered with grime. Spears leaned against one wall. The communal shower was filthy. The toilet was filled with days-old waste. I was speechless.

"We oppose apartheid," a man with a white beard told me. "Zulus, Xhosas, all suffered the same under apartheid." Everyone nodded in agreement.

But then the subject turned to the comrades. What was the fighting all about? I asked. A man with a scar on his jaw from a bullet wound replied, "The ANC campaign seems to be directed at the Zulu man. That makes us fear that if the ANC takes power, the Zulus would have no land and no place to stay." A man in a red leather jacket spoke up: "There is a serious problem. We have the Umkhonto we Sizwe [MK] and the SADF [South African Defense Force]. They will be joined after the elections. That will create serious problems." All the men were murmuring their assent. The man went on, "MK has been trained to kill the ANC's political enemies. So we fear that if MK is joined with the army, then the Inkatha leadership will be eliminated." Everyone vigorously agreed.

Did they fear for their own lives under an ANC-led government? Everyone nodded. *Yebo! Yebo!* all agreed. "Yes! Yes!"

Natal's war pitted Zulu against Zulu, yet each side demonized the other by projecting the malevolent image of another tribe onto its Zulu brothers. Zulus aligned with Inkatha were agents of the white man; Zulus aligned with the ANC were agents of the Xhosa. It was a kind of race war by inverted proxy—a measure of apartheid's sinister resilience. There was truth in Harry Gwala's view that Inkatha was doing the dirty work of apartheid. But most of those who were fighting and dying in Inkatha's name, like the men in KwaMashu hostel, were merely cannon fodder, exploited as much by their own Zulu leaders as by the white man. Much like Samuel Doe's Krahn in Liberia, though, the logic of ethnically based politics can be self-perpetuating. The violent conduct to which Chief Buthelezi drove his Zulu followers in a decade of conflict with the ANC made them ever more dependent on Buthelezi's survival in power. As the elections approached in 1994, Zulus like those men in KwaMashu hostel appeared to have good reason to fear the ANC. At issue was not whether South Africa would explode but whether it would continue to burn.

"Total strategy"

By the time Magnus Malan, Tienie Groenewald and their codefendants filed into the Justice Hugo's crowded courtroom two years later, it was no longer a matter of serious dispute that elements in South Africa's old security forces played an important role in stoking political violence. In 1992, President F. W. de Klerk had tacitly conceded that high military and intelligence officials had sought to establish a covert "Third Force" to thwart the ANC, and he dismissed or suspended twenty-three officers.

The only documentary evidence of the existence of an explicit, calculated "Third Force" was uncovered by the Investigative Task Unit (ITU), a body appointed by Mandela shortly after the 1994 elections to investigate hit-squad activity in what was now called KwaZulu-Natal. It was headed by a human rights lawyer in Durban, Howard Varney. In June 1995 Varney and his colleagues conducted a search of Military Intelligence headquarters in Pretoria. They discovered State Security Council documents in which the creation of a *Derde Mag*, a Third Force, was proposed and then researched by a "Third Force working group." In minutes of a State Security Council meeting dated May 12, 1986, at the very height of the township violence and while Groenewald was still chief of Military Intelligence, the gathering approved a proposal for the creation of a "Third Force," parallel to the army and the police, which would have the capacity to "effectively wipe out terrorists" and which would utilize security forces "in order that the underminers are countered with their own methods."

But the specific proposal for setting up such a force never got off the ground. One reason, Varney and his colleagues concluded, was that existing projects among the myriad security forces were already accomplishing the same objective. A web of clandestine state structures was already deeply involved in disabling and eliminating enemies of the apartheid state. These structures included the army's Special Forces, the South African Police's Special Constables, front companies run by South African Military Intelligence, and all manner of assistance rendered to surrogate armed factions through the euphemistically named Directorate of Special Tasks and Joint Management Centers. Taken together, this multiplicity of covert structures formed a "hidden hand" that relied extensively on violence among blacks as a means of preserving white domination.

So the Third Force in South Africa was not a discreet, identifiable covert entity. Rather, it was inherent in the system, permeating all parts of the security apparatus. The Third Force, such as it was, embodied the multiple coercive dimensions of white domination at its furthest extremes as well as in its deepest subterranean depths, direct and indirect, at once cracking heads and manipulating what was inside them.

The documents uncovered by Howard Varney's unit formed the basis for the prosecution of Malan and his confederates. The authenticity of these documents was never seriously disputed. The authors confirmed their contents. Only their interpretation was subject to debate. Ultimately, the outcome of the trial would hinge on a seemingly sterile and probably specious distinction between "offensive" and "protective" measures—that is, the motives of those who set mass slaughter in motion. What no one could dispute was the long-standing pattern of collusion between Inkatha, ostensibly a black nationalist movement, and the most violent institutions of white tyranny.

The pattern dated back as far as the early 1970s, an era in which Inkatha was still nominally allied with the ANC as confederate black nationalist organizations struggling to bring down apartheid. The former Inkatha central committee member Walter Felgate, himself a long-standing police agent, who defected to the ANC in 1997, told South Africa's Truth and Reconciliation Commission in a closed hearing that Buthelezi maintained a close relationship with the notorious Bureau of State Security (BOSS) dating back more than twenty years. He said that for two decades Buthelezi received monthly briefings from top intelligence agents of former Prime Minister B. J. Vorster. Felgate said Buthelezi held meetings with BOSS operatives on a regular monthly basis as far back as 1973.

Beginning in the 1970s South Africans were deeply involved in the futile campaigns to stave off the advancing tide of black rule in the re-

gion. They formed intimate alliances with the old Portuguese counterinsurgency police known as PIDE (Policia Internacional e de De-
fesa do Estado), and with the old white security forces in Rhodesia
during the Rhodesian civil war. When those efforts failed, many veterans of PIDE and the Rhodesian secret police moved to South Africa,
where they joined South African operatives in the ruinous destabilization campaigns of the 1980s.

The plot thickened during the tumultuous regime of P. W. Botha,
who took power in 1978. Botha had been minister of defense before
he became prime minister and then state president. During Botha's
eleven years at the helm, real power in South Africa resided in a body
called the State Security Council, through which Botha ruled with his
generals. All significant decisions of state were subordinated to what
they called a "total strategy" aimed at staving off a "revolutionary onslaught" of armed insurgencies across the frontline states of southern
Africa.

Throughout the 1980s the South African Defense Force and South
African Military Intelligence waged four wars abroad and one at
home. South Africa backed Jonas Savimbi's UNITA rebels in Angola
and the notorious RENAMO insurgency in Mozambique. Ultimately
more than a million black Africans died in Angola and Mozambique in
the 1980s, and the number was still climbing in Angola as the 1990s
drew to a close. To be sure, the wars in Angola and Mozambique had
local causes and homegrown villains, but there can be little doubt that
the struggle to preserve white tyranny in South Africa magnified those
causes and empowered the villains.

The notion of "total onslaught" against South Africa was a product
of Cold War thinking, which had embedded itself in the minds of
apartheid's securocrats in the 1950s and 1960s. The onslaught was en-
visaged to be Communist-inspired and directed at all spheres of the
security of the state. The ideologues portrayed it as an attack on the
Christian principles and democratic values supposedly upheld in the
Republic of South Africa. The Soviet Union, they believed, was bent
on establishing its influence on the subcontinent, using black nationalist organizations such as the ANC as surrogates.

There was always a question as to the extent to which Pretoria's securocrats really believed their own propaganda. For although black
nationalist insurgencies in the region, including the ANC, did receive
backing from both Moscow and Beijing, they were clearly home-

grown movements whose chief aim, as history has since shown, was not the spread of communism but the dismantling of white tyranny. Whether Pretoria's generals grasped this fact or even cared, they found ample support for their view—and guidance—from anti-Communist allies in the West, not least the United States.

Magnus Malan had been trained at the U.S. Army Command and General Staff College, an institution renowned for formulating the "indirect" methods of counterinsurgency warfare.

In a document introduced in the Malan trial, President Botha referred to the 1966 classic, *The Art of Counter Revolutionary Warfare*, by J. J. McCuen, a lieutenant colonel in the U.S. Army. His book had been paraphrased and widely distributed within the military and intelligence structures in South Africa. A key element of McCuen's strategy was the establishment of "counter guerrilla" or "middle groups" to mobilize politically and to act violently against revolutionary forces. Botha's summary of McCuen's ideas highlighted "[t]he development of a counter-revolutionary guerrilla force which is employed according to guerrilla tactics to annihilate revolutionary guerrillas and take control over the population." Another document advocated the creation of guerrilla forces as an "adjunct to a government's strategic force."

This was the basis for Pretoria's support for RENAMO and UNITA; it became the basis for its support for Inkatha as well. Pretoria viewed Inkatha as it viewed RENAMO and UNITA: as a bulwark against internal revolution. Its aim was to build up Inkatha as an anti-revolutionary force.[2]

A key revelation of the Malan trial was the link between Inkatha and the larger campaign to destabilize southern Africa during the 1980s. Brigadier J. P. Opperman, the prosecution's first witness, detailed the close-knit relationship between military officers who ran clandestine supply lines to RENAMO rebels in Mozambique and the covert plan to use Inkatha as a surrogate offensive force against the ANC inside

---

[2]This is clear from an SSC memorandum, dated February 27, 1986, titled "Die Rewolsionare Bedreiging teen die RSA" ("The Revolutionary Movement in the Republic of South Africa") and circulated to all members attending the March 1, 1986, SSC meeting. The document said in Paragraph F: "Structures such as Inkatha must be built up to be an obstacle to radicalism." Another SSC document, dated April 24, 1986, described "anti-revolutionary groups such as Inkatha" as part of the "RSA's capacity in countering the revolutionary war."

South Africa itself. Opperman corroborated the widely held belief that support for RENAMO and support for Inkatha were two sides of the same coin.

Much of the information contained in secret military documents placed before the court detailed how Operation Marion, as the effort to train the "Caprivi trainees" was called, was seen by its architects as a strategy to use the RENAMO option, which had brought Mozambique to its knees, inside South Africa itself. The Directorate of Special Tasks was the special forces unit that ran RENAMO operations for many years in Mozambique, and this was the same unit that set up Operation Marion. Three of Tienie Groenewald's co-accused—Brigadier Cornelius van Neikirk, Brigadier John More and Cornelius van Tonder—had been directly involved in coordinating support for RENAMO.

The Directorate of Special Tasks also was in charge of training UNITA soldiers in the same Caprivi Strip base in northern Namibia where the two hundred Inkatha fighters were trained. Opperman, the witness, was the commander of seven UNITA bases in the Caprivi Strip before he applied for a transfer to the base that had been set up in the same area for Inkatha's paramilitary squads.

"Certain assistance was given"

In November 1985 Tienie Groenewald, then director of South African Military Intelligence, prepared a memo that clearly reflected the offensive intent of Buthelezi's request for assistance. "Buthelezi expressed the view," Groenewald wrote, "that the ANC should realize that if it uses violence against KwaZulu and its people, the Zulus, KwaZulu is prepared to use violence against the ANC." Groenewald expressed concern that in training the Caprivi group in lethal techniques and weaponry, it was running the risk of creating a "potential monster"—*"potentsiele monster"*—which might someday be used against Pretoria, should Buthelezi abandon his preference for "peaceful change."

In another memo that Groenewald wrote to Andries Putter, chief of staff of the SADF, dated February 14, 1986, Groenewald described meeting alone with Buthelezi to discuss the "broad extent of the assistance in setting up a para-military capability" in order to reach a "principled agreement." Groenewald reported that Buthelezi had accepted a plan for two hundred individuals chosen by him, covertly, with the full cooperation of the SADF, to be trained at the Caprivi Strip.

Nearly two years before these documents were introduced as evidence in his trial, I spoke with Groenewald at the headquarters of the Freedom Alliance, a new right-wing political party, in Pretoria. This was in December 1994. Mandela had been in office for eight months. The Freedom Alliance was led by retired military men bent on protecting Afrikaner interests—"We are very much like the Jews," Groenewald explained to me. "Survival is a very important issue."

Always in the shadows, Tienie Groenewald wielded as much backroom influence as any other single person in South Africa's far-right sphere. A former fighter pilot and military attaché, Groenewald was born in 1937 on a farm outside Koster in the western Transvaal. He joined the air force in 1955 and obtained an honors degree in military science. He excelled in the field of "communications operations"—"comops" it was called, a euphemism for psychological warfare. After rising to the rank of major general, he was appointed security adviser to the State Security Council by P. W. Botha in 1982, and then chief director of Military Intelligence in 1985, at the very height of Pretoria's destabilization campaigns abroad and emergency rule at home. Groenewald briefed the SSC, the junta of elite generals who essentially ran South Africa through the 1980s, at 8 A.M. each morning from 1984 to 1986. By his own account, he was the SSC's top expert on the ANC.

"A lot of people were extremely dedicated people," Groenewald told me. "They weren't all murderers. Ninety percent of these people were honest police or soldiers doing their jobs." But then he added, "If you had witnessed a necklacing, you're not going to have too many scruples about killing the person responsible for doing that."

The Freedom Alliance operated out of a shiny glass building in an office park on the outskirts of Pretoria. The headquarters had the prim, bland feel of an insurance agency office. Groenewald, then fifty-seven, was pink-cheeked and avuncular in post-apartheid retirement, genial, smart, articulate, and generous with his time. He wore a grayish-blue suit and tie, and soft gray Hush Puppies. Our conversation took place more than a year before he was indicted for his alleged role in Operation Marion. At the time he appeared to have nothing to fear, and he made no attempt to deny his covert alliance with Chief Buthelezi.

"Naturally," he told me, "in the struggle against the ANC, certain assistance was given to Inkatha. It was never official policy and it was never the policy of the Defense Force that this should be assistance in creating a military infrastructure. What we did do, at the time when the ANC was assassinating Inkatha leaders, was to assist Inkatha in setting up a self-defense capacity."

The general added, "Whether there was 'close alliance' between Inkatha and the SAP or the SADF, it certainly did happen at one stage that these forces were biased in favor of Inkatha. After all, we were both fighting the ANC."

Groenewald was frankly conceding what would be the central component of the Malan prosecution: "The military men created the military infrastructure," he said. "But look at the police. Look at National Intelligence. I'm not saying we had a completely clean bill. I was involved up to 1986 in various forms of support for Buthelezi. We were involved in training, propaganda, hearts and minds kind of ops. Remember: Buthelezi was the prime minister of a state."

KwaZulu was not an independent state, of course, but that was beside the point. Groenewald's candor reflected the underlying premise of this covert alliance: it was inherent in the system. I was reminded of an earlier conversation I had with another of Buchner's and Groenewald's infamous colleagues, a former South African Police operative named Philip Powell, who went on to become a senior Inkatha figure and admitted gunrunner in the early 1990s. "What you call a military alliance between Inkatha and the security forces—it was not an alliance," Powell told me. "It was an institutional relationship. There is a simple explanation: the KwaZulu Police was not an independent agency. The KZP was actually an extension of the SAP. So there's nothing sinister."

Nothing sinister at all. From the point of view of the generals, the chief was a cog in the system.

"Things happen"

When I asked Groenewald to talk about apartheid, he pleaded ignorance. "The biggest problem with apartheid was the fact that most whites were ignorant of the socioeconomic conditions of black people. Because of apartheid, you could have a black community living within five kilometers of a white community, living in absolute poverty, and whites wouldn't know about it." But, he added, "Apartheid was never aimed at destroying a culture. Apartheid was really only aimed at giving black people what Afrikaners had. What we should have done was create a homeland for Afrikaners just like the others. The intention was never to take away."

I reminded the general that 3.5 million blacks had been forcibly removed from their homes, leaving whites—15 percent of the population—with more than 80 percent of the land.

"Forced removals—that was wrong," the general conceded. "But you're looking at negative aspects of apartheid."

And the positives? He wouldn't take the bait. Like Jenkins Scott in Monrovia and Chester Crocker in Washington, Groenewald wanted to stress the "context" in which things turned problematical "It was the nature of unconventional warfare that led to the ignoring of human rights," he said. "This has happened throughout the world. And after all, assassinating someone isn't the same as dropping an atomic bomb on Hiroshima."

Actually, he added, the ANC was to blame. "The ANC created a culture of revolution within the African people, to make the country ungovernable."

Torture? Mass arrests? Death squads?

"When you have unconventional warfare based on terrorism, that happens," the general averred. "Under certain circumstances, things happen which shouldn't happen. Under normal circumstances, it would not happen." This was almost an exact echo of Jenkins Scott. "Under the circumstances," Scott had told me, "it looks like human nature."

Groenewald was eager to highlight what he called "foreign involvement" in South Africa, and the sense of his own covert campaigns as part of the global struggle against communism. "Don't underestimate the involvement of foreign intelligence in Third Force operations: MI6, the CIA."

The CIA?

"I know of CIA operations," he replied coyly. "Supplies, financial involvement through a network of fronts. South Africa was a pawn in the struggle between the big powers."

Groenewald's claim is plausible but difficult to substantiate, but there can be little doubt that Groenewald and his confederates relied heavily on the CIA as a source of legitimacy. Again and again in my conversations with white South African securocrats, I was struck by the lengths each one went to minimize the importance of apartheid as a motivating factor. "Our assistance to RENAMO and to Savimbi was based on our struggle against communism," Groenewald told me. "Our original involvement with UNITA was in support of the United States and Kissinger, to neutralize Soviet involvement in Southern Africa."

I asked Groenewald if he had any regrets. By then 20,000 people had been murdered in KwaZulu-Natal.

"I have no personal regrets," he replied. "Fortunately, I participated in the Defense Force at a time when the Defense Force *as such* did not engage in any form of violations of human rights. So, my conscience is clean." The emphasis was his, and it went to the heart of the conspiracy he initiated and the system it was designed to preserve: in Operation Marion, the natives did the dirty work; whites "as such" stayed clean.

As to the problem of his own accountability, Groenewald demurred: "Let people on both sides who made political decisions—let them be punished. If that is the case, very few political leaders will come out with clean hands."

"Let them kill one another"

Details about the Third Force first appeared in the public confession of Dirk Coetzee, a former policeman who was commander of the SAP's notorious Vlakplaas base. In a newspaper interview in 1990, Coetzee admitted to a series of hit-squad murders aimed at creating a climate in which violence flourished. Coetzee has since become something of a celebrity in South Africa. He is a voluble, high-strung character who seems to have found his life's calling as a nonstop and frenetic confessor of his own past sins—and those of his erstwhile confederates. On the morning in 1994 when I met him in Pretoria, he had scheduled two interviews for the same hour, the other with a British television crew. It was one of the peculiarities of the new South Africa that Coetzee was now on the payroll of the ANC, advising the new government on intelligence matters.

In our interview in Pretoria, Coetzee explained the Vlakplaas mentality this way: "The underlying premise was 'Let the blacks kill themselves, the bastards. Let them kill one another. Divide and rule, destabilize, discredit the ANC. Make sure there is no peace between the ANC and Inkatha." Coetzee described Inkatha's leaders as "power-hungry bastards, complete opportunists."

Coetzee also spoke more broadly about the ethos within the security forces in their regionwide campaign to stem the tide of majority rule. "We were told this was the last white Christian outpost on the southern tip of Africa, threatened by the Communist terrorist onslaught," he said. "I didn't run up and down this country killing people just for the fun of it. It was either them or us."[3]

It was in the rural KwaZulu township of Trust Feed that longstanding suspicions of covert collusion between Inkatha and South African Police officials received judicial confirmation for the first time. There, on the night of December 2, 1988, a gang of men descended on the mud-walled home of a suspected ANC activist and murdered eleven men, women, and children. Three years later a white South African Police captain, Brian Mitchell, and four black *kitskonstabels* in the KwaZulu Police were convicted of the murders. Notwithstanding an extensive cover-up by senior police officials, the court found that the massacre occurred in the context of "the counterrevolutionary strategy" that Captain Mitchell perceived himself to be conducting against "the enemies of the state." Among those present at the meeting where the massacre was planned, witnesses testified, was the Inkatha warlord David Ntombela.

In a cascade of disclosures in 1991 that came to be known as Inkathagate, it was established that in 1990, very soon after lifting the ban on the ANC, the South African Police began secretly funneling at least $600,000 to Inkatha so that Buthelezi could hold large rallies to counter the ANC's shows of strength. There were further disclosures of police payments to other conservative groups, including the Inkatha trade union UWUSA.

Justice Goldstone's report on the Third Force, published barely a month before the 1994 election, concluded that Coetzee's old unit,

---

[3]Coetzee had admitted involvement in twenty-seven hit-squad incidents, including ten murders. "I'm prepared to face the music," he told me. "Up until this day I haven't asked for immunity. I say, 'Charge me.' But if I go to jail, then de Klerk must go with me." In the event, Coetzee did ask for immunity, and the South African Truth and Reconciliation Commission granted it in 1997.

Vlakplaas, which fell under the command of Colonel Eugene de Kock, was involved from 1989 in violence aimed at the "destabilization" of South Africa.

"I find that I'm an easy man to talk to"

One of the twenty-three officers dismissed by President de Klerk in 1992 personified the collusion between Inkatha and the covert warriors of earlier campaigns. Major General Jac Buchner served as commissioner of the KwaZulu Police from 1989 to 1992. He was previously chief of the Special Branch of the South African Police in Pietermaritzburg. By then he was already a veteran operator in South Africa's covert wars against the ANC and its allies in neighboring states.

His claim to covert fame derived from his service as commander of a unit of the Special Branch in Pretoria responsible for "turning" captured guerrillas of the ANC and the Namibian nationalist group SWAPO (South West African People's Organization) and then training them to serve as informers and carry out death-squad attacks. Buchner's eventual posting as Special Branch chief in Pietermaritzburg and his three-year stint as Buthelezi's police commissioner coincided exactly with the escalation of the conflict in Natal.

Like so many of the key figures engaged in conflicts across the continent, Buchner was anything but a thug. "I would use the term 'evil' with Buchner," said John Aitcheson, a professor at the University of Natal in Pietermaritzburg who closely tracked Natal's conflict from the beginning. "He's not just rough and tough. Buchner is as bad as they get precisely because he is clever. He was the security police's intellectual. Early in his career he was the state's chief witness on the ANC. He is said to have the most amazing library."

I had a chance to meet Jac Buchner in March 1996—the very week the Malan trial was getting under way. I had spent several years trying in vain to track him down, finally succeeding with the help of a source involved in the Malan prosecution. The day before our meeting Buchner's name had come up in the Malan trial. A witness had testified that Buchner took part in a meeting at which the need to kill an informer was discussed. I had missed that day's trial proceedings, and the reference to Buchner was not in the morning papers, so I was not aware of it when I met with him. He made no mention of it in the course of our three hours together. Buchner had not been indicted and he told me he did not fear indictment. He had not applied for immunity with South Africa's Truth and Reconciliation Commission.

"I never asked for immunity," he explained. "I don't think I have done anything wrong."

Buchner and I met for coffee and, in his case, a tall glass of fresh orange juice, at the neo-Gothic Imperial Hotel in Pietermaritzburg. We sat in an airy, glass-ceilinged breakfast room with ferns and a gurgling water fountain. Buchner turned out to be a disarmingly hale fellow, fifty-seven years old and deeply tanned, with a warm, ready smile, penetrating blue eyes and a shock of long, wavy silver hair. He was dressed for an afternoon of golf: white polo shirt, blue plaid shorts, blue kneesocks and Topsiders. He told me he was planning a walking trip around England that summer. His dream, he said, was to walk around the Isle of Man in the Irish Sea.

Buchner was a charmer, a schmoozer, smooth as vintage whiskey. He gave me a sense of being taken into his confidence. A natural raconteur, he spun out his brutally eventful life's story in a mellow honey-rich baritone voice. In the manipulative genre of police interrogations, I imagined, Buchner must have been the good cop, handing out cigarettes and soothing reassurance.

Buchner grew up in the Eastern Cape and in what was then called South-West Africa, now Namibia. He joined the South African Police in 1955, when he was sixteen. He began as a patrolman in Pretoria and then a fingerprint expert, and then moved to Durban as a detective. In 1964, four years after the ANC was banned and launched its armed struggle, Buchner was selected for the Special Branch, where he became a star. He established himself as a top expert on the activities of the ANC and its military wing, Umkhonto we Sizwe (MK).

"My role was investigating the activities of MK," he recalled nostalgically, "intelligence, running sources, investigating cases as a detective, and also, interrogation of all the guys who we detained and getting to know the organization."

In 1968 Buchner was posted to Victoria Falls, in what was then Rhodesia, and he would spend much of the next decade there as South Africa's point man in the Rhodesian bush war. He was highly decorated in Rhodesia. He supervised covert South African support for the Selous Scouts, the infamous Rhodesian counterinsurgency force, and he developed close ties with a number of Rhodesian operatives who went on to play key roles in South Africa's destabilization wars throughout the region, notably in Namibia, Mozambique, and later in Natal.

But Buchner's real claim to infamy was his exceptional skill in "debriefing" captured ANC cadres. He was said to have an uncanny ability to "turn" captured ANC guerrillas into police agents, or *askaris*. He was the mastermind of the police *askari* units that worked with Vlakplaas to infiltrate and assassinate ANC-aligned activists throughout the 1980s.

"I find I'm an easy man to talk to," Buchner explained with a smile.

In November 1987, Buchner was posted to Pietermaritzburg as head of the Special Branch for the Natal Midlands. "There was nothing sinister," he assured me. But the posting put him at the center of the escalating war in Natal. It was widely assumed even at the time that Buchner, his reputation by then well established, used that office to provide clandestine support for Inkatha. His role became more explicit when he took over the KwaZulu Police in 1989.

How did it work? I asked him. Here he was, by all accounts one of apartheid's craftiest spies, now serving as chief of Gatsha Buthelezi's personal militia. Exactly what was his relationship with the Zulu chief who claimed to be engaged in a nonviolent struggle against white tyranny?

"From the day I was appointed until the day I left, he never gave me an instruction," Buchner replied. "He left the running of the police force entirely to me."

Imagine that, I thought. Buthelezi left the running of his personal militia entirely to Jac Buchner. One can hardly blame the ANC for regarding Inkatha as a tool of apartheid, with or without secret documents later confiscated from Military Intelligence. There was nothing subtle about it.

From his days in Rhodesia, Buchner had maintained a close friendship with Eugene de Kock, who later went on to achieve infamy—and a conviction for 157 murders—as commander of the notorious Vlakplaas death-squad unit. Buchner introduced de Kock to the woman de Kock eventually married in Rhodesia, and Buchner also married a Rhodesian woman. When de Kock applied for amnesty before the Truth and Reconciliation Commission, he detailed the clandestine gunrunning operation from Vlakplaas to Inkatha in the early 1990s, but he pointedly omitted Buchner from his list of top conspirators. But other former Vlakplaas agents told the Truth Commission that Buchner was deeply involved in supplying truckloads of assault rifles, rocket launchers, land mines, and ammunition to Inkatha paramilitary units while he was in Pietermaritzburg and then commissioner of the KwaZulu Police.

"It was an open life"

Buchner repeatedly tried to impress upon me that he was an outsider, not part of the "clan," as he put it, meaning the inner circle of Afrikanerdom. His motives were strictly professional. "I didn't do any of this because of ideology," He said. "I always worked for the government of the day."

But the government of the day was a racial tyranny fighting a brutal war of survival, I noted.

"A job was a job," Buchner explained. "Through the years, especially when I became a detective, once I joined the Special Branch, what motivated me was mostly contact with people, people of opposing beliefs, having the opportunity of sitting with someone far from home and picking their brain, finding out what makes them tick. I found it interesting."

Buchner was waxing nostalgic now. "It was an open life," he mused. "It was exciting, exhilarating at times, and interesting. Eventually, when I was doing the 'turnings,' as they call it, trying to turn people, it nearly became too easy."

Then how did he do it? I asked. What was the secret to "turning" hardened black nationalist guerrillas into traitors, informers for apartheid's secret police?

"I used to spend hours with these chaps. I thought it was a waste to send them to prison. Many were disillusioned. After talking with them I was able to convince them that they should turn. Especially in the late 1980s, many who came back saw that there were changes. Many were kept in horrendous conditions in the camps."

Buchner took a sip from his orange juice.

"I remember one chap came into our office. He had been arrested with explosives. He said, 'I'm not going to speak to you.' I said, 'I don't want you to speak to me. I already know more about you than you do. You have two choices. Either you go to jail or you work with me.'"

He looked me in the eye with those deep blue eyes. "You're a Caucasian," he said. "You grew up in Western circumstances. Everything you do is written down. With the black man nothing is written down. Everything is committed to memory. I'm speaking very generally. My point is, you would be taken to a camp of five hundred people. Everybody's got a false name. Three months later, you won't be able to remember anyone. But this chap will be able to remember everything. So you give this man his whole history. You tell him, 'You grew up here, you left home in thus and such a year, you went to this place, then you went to that one, you trained with this one and that one.' Before you know it, he's ready to work with you. They're all starved for conversation. They have sat in a cell for three days or eleven days. I would offer them cigarettes, beer."

The general paused for a moment, reaching down to pull on his kneesocks.

"So it does work," he finally said. "Or, let's put it this way, I had success."

Indeed, by all accounts, he did. What he was leaving out, of course, was the rougher treatment in which he may or may not have been directly involved, but which pervaded the police culture in which Buchner was a star, and which undoubtedly was used to extract this man's "whole history" from other prisoners. Without at least the threat of this brutality, no amount of beer, cigarettes and conversation would have persuaded a committed black nationalist to betray his cause on behalf of white rule. The Truth and Reconciliation Commission would confirm in gruesome detail, on the basis of the confessions of the torturers themselves, the full extent of brutality in apartheid's interrogation rooms: everything from beatings and sleep deprivation to slamming penises and breasts in drawers. Between 1960 and 1990—Buchner's era exactly—about 80,000 people were held in South Africa's prisons without trial, of whom 10,000 were women and 15,000 were children.

What about it? I asked. The South African Police had a reputation for playing pretty rough in those days, beatings and such, I noted. Did he have anything to do with that?

On the contrary, Buchner assured me, "My dealings were always above reproach. You had to take the cases to court. If you used such methods, the case would be thrown out of court."

This was nonsense, of course. Apartheid's courts for years relied on confessions in the overwhelming majority of cases, and most confessions were extracted by means of torture or the threat of it. Emergency laws reinforced the practice by providing for weeks-long incommunicado detention, during which suspects had no access to counsel, nor anyone else on the outside.

What about apartheid? I asked. Was Buchner ever bothered by the fact that he was fighting to uphold racial tyranny? "I did not see it as upholding apartheid," he demurred. "In 1982–83, when we went to the U.S., but even in Rhodesia, it's stupid to say now, but I shared a room with blacks. In my whole working career, I spent more time with blacks than with whites. I didn't see it as upholding apartheid. You were upholding law and order."

Could he understand at all with what the ANC was fighting for?

"Oh yes," Buchner replied. "If I was a black man, I would have been the first one to join the organization. But my position was, they shouldn't do it through guerrilla warfare. My feeling was, you should settle this matter through dialogue. I never believed in apartheid and I never supported it. That also counted against me. I was always judged as too friendly with them."

Dialogue, friendship—whatever. In what had by now become a familiar pattern, Buchner stressed that his covert career was of a piece with the global struggle against communism. In March 1983, he recalled, he was asked by the CIA to bring six witnesses before U.S. Senator Jeremiah Denton's Senate Subcommittee on Terrorism. He spoke warmly of his confederates in the CIA, with whom, he said, he sought to root out Cuban-Soviet influence in liberation movements across Africa.

"Look," he said, "our training was mostly from you guys, and the Brits. By that I mean American techniques, not men. Everybody knew you. It's a brotherhood—we in the police of the various intelligence offices overseas, including ones in Washington."

In three hours Buchner uttered not a word of remorse. A career immersed in wars that killed hundreds of thousands of civilians, in which tens of thousands were maimed in custody, untold blameless lives destroyed in the name of racial domination—"an open life," he called it, wistful at the memories, "interesting," "exciting," "exhilarating." Yet I had very nearly fallen for it. He was so smooth and intimate and seductive that I almost felt like I'd bonded with the man. I had laughed at his humor. I had told him about my family. We had talked effortlessly for three hours, and parted warmly. I was nearly smitten. I can only imagine how I might have felt if the bad cop was waiting in the wings.

As we parted, Buchner and I exchanged business cards. I tucked his into my pocket and forgot about it. Later I pulled it out. Buchner's card was plain white with black script. It gave his name and a post office box—but no address and no phone number.

"No reason to doubt"

In May 1996, Tienie Groenewald was acquitted of all charges against him. His lawyers produced a document proving that he had asked to be transferred off the Inkatha death-squads project before the Kwa-Makhutha massacre was carried out. Then, in October 1996, Malan and the rest of the accused were acquitted as well. Justice Jan Hugo concluded that the 1986 KwaMakhutha massacre at issue in the trial had indeed been carried out by an Inkatha death squad created and trained by the South African army to fight the ANC. But, he said, the prosecution had failed to link the defendants to the massacre. Justice Hugo concluded that the testimony of two key state witnesses, both of them top security officers who were confessed accomplices in the 1986 massacre, could not be relied upon. He also said that a key document presented to the court and signed by nearly all of the top defendants, which explicitly proposed the training of Inkatha partisans in "offensive" military techniques, did not by itself constitute a conspiracy to murder.

The Malan verdict was not the last word on justice for apartheid's criminals. Prominent—albeit midlevel—security officials were convicted and others may still face trial. But the acquittal represented the last chance for criminal prosecutions against those at the very top, including Buthelezi himself, who played a central role in fomenting the violence in KwaZulu-Natal.

The acquittals were a major blow to the credibility of South Africa's criminal justice system, long associated in the minds of black South Africans with the arbitrary enforcement of apartheid's security laws. It was not lost on black South Africans that both the chief judge and the prosecutor were white holdovers from the old regime. South Africa's courts had not been purged, and prosecutors enjoyed protection from dismissal under laws that were passed by the white-led National Party in the waning days of the old order.

The evidence against Malan and his codefendants had been assembled by an independent team of investigators appointed by Mandela— Howard Varney's ITU. But then it was handed over to a prosecutor appointed by the old white regime, the KwaZulu-Natal attorney general Tim McNally. Both Justice Hugo and McNally had a history of skepticism about the existence of state-sponsored death squads. In the view of many critics of the verdict, both the judge and the prosecutor, like white South Africans generally, seemed intuitively unable to grasp the malign intentions of the old apartheid security forces. They seemed unable to fathom the grubby world of covert operatives waging unconventional war during the years of what the securocrats called "total onslaught" against white rule. It was a world of murderers, psychopaths, and gangsters—a far cry from the more recognizable picture painted by the defense counsel of starched uniforms and military discipline. Justice Hugo, for example, said he found "no reason to doubt" the credibility of one defense witness who admittedly played a leading role in covert operations in support of RENAMO in Mozambique.

Justice Hugo acknowledged that Inkatha death squads were trained at the same South African army base where Mozambican and Angolan rebel forces were trained. But he rejected on technical legal grounds what has long been obvious to most black South Africans: that the army deliberately stoked violence among blacks in South Africa by backing a surrogate force, Inkatha, just as it had done in Mozambique and Angola.

The Magnus Malan trial resonated in South Africa much as the O. J. Simpson trial resonated in the United States, with blacks and all but a small minority of whites forming completely different judgments of guilt or innocence on the basis of the same set of facts. The difference was that in South Africa, the stakes involved not two but 20,000 unsolved murders.

Meanwhile, KwaZulu-Natal's dirty war festered on. At least 148 people were murdered in politically related attacks in the three months prior to the Malan verdict.

The Truth and Reconciliation Commission, for its part, found "overwhelming evidence" that Inkatha was "the primary non-state perpetrator" of human rights abuses prior to 1994 and was responsible for more than a third of all violations committed during the thirty-four-year period the commission was mandated to investigate. Inkatha's own submission to the commission, it found, was "singularly unforthcoming, evasive and defensive." It found Buthelezi personally accountable for "gross violations of human rights."

The Truth and Reconciliation Commission essentially confirmed all the elements in the Malan indictment. "In 1986," it said, "the SADF conspired with Inkatha to provide Inkatha with a covert, offensive paramilitary unit [hit squad] to be deployed illegally against persons and organizations perceived to be opposed to or enemies of both the South African government and Inkatha."

Magnus Malan, Tienie Groenewald, Jac Buchner, and Philip Powell were all identified as "Chief Buthelezi's co-conspirators."

Remarkably, the Truth and Reconciliation Commission reported that the entire cost of the Caprivi trainee program was only 5.1 million rand, equivalent to about $2 million. In an environment where the institutions of accountability for crime were extremely weak, it seems that a sum not much greater than it would take to build a small factory was all that was needed to train two hundred thugs and supply them with automatic weapons, and thereby set off a spiral of violence that killed thousands of civilians and nearly derailed South Africa's progress toward democratic rule.

"I've always espoused nonviolence myself"

I spoke with Buthelezi in March 1996 in his office in Cape Town, where he was serving as minister of home affairs in Mandela's government of national unity. That very morning, testimony had begun in the Malan trial. Buthelezi was essentially an unindicted co-conspirator in the trial: his name appeared twenty-seven times in the indictment, beginning with the very first sentence. The indictment began: "In an address to the KwaZulu Legislative Assembly on 28 May 1984, the Chief Minister of KwaZulu, Prince Mangosuthu G. Buthelezi ('Buthelezi') stated: 'In fact, I believe that we must prepare ourselves not only to defend property and life, but to go beyond that and prepare ourselves to hit back with devastating force at those who destroy our property and kill us.'"

Buthelezi's domain in the Home Affairs Ministry was a vast, plush, wood-paneled corner office with two immense sofas upholstered in blue, gold and crimson stripes, a large glass coffee table and two luxurious flower arrangements on the windowsills. It overlooked the stately Cape Dutch–style Houses of Parliament in the shadow of Table Mountain. The walls were lined with enlarged, framed photographs of Buthelezi with Ronald Reagan in the Oval Office, Buthelezi with Margaret Thatcher, Buthelezi with Helmut Kohl, Buthelezi with the Pope. There were signed pictures of Jimmy Carter and John Major. His polished mahogany desk and a matching side table were piled high with papers. On the windowsill in the corner farthest from Buthelezi's desk, barely visible from where I sat, there stood a small black and white picture of Buthelezi with Nelson Mandela.

Buthelezi has a reputation for volatility, but as we shook hands and exchanged pleasantries, he seemed courtly, almost diffident. There were no leopard skins for this American visitor: instead it was a gray business suit, blue-and-white-striped shirt, and a subdued print necktie, with paisley socks and black loafers with tassels.

I began by lobbing him a softball about his long-term vision for South Africa. The chief settled into an oft-repeated mantra about federalism, and he went on in this vein without interruption for half an hour. There was a strangeness to his delivery. He seemed to be talking by rote, as if he were reciting lines from memory for an invisible teacher. And for long stretches—ten minutes here, another fifteen there—he spoke with his eyes closed.

"What I support is classic federalism, like in the U.S. or Germany," he droned, as bored with his own delivery as I was. "I cannot articulate it any further than that."

He never looked at me. He made no attempt to engage, no effort at personal rapport or persuasion. There was no sense of animation whatsoever, no feeling, no passion. He was totally lost in the details of an endless, familiar saga of long-ago convoluted debates.

"He's weird," I scribbled in my notebook.

Worried that I might run out of time, I cut to the chase. What about the violence in KwaZulu-Natal? Buthelezi brushed the question aside. "It has been going on for ten years," he said with a perfunctory sigh. "There is no easy answer. You should know. If you have been covering it then you know. Members of both parties are in conflict."

Buthelezi eyed me warily. He had often clashed with South African reporters. He seemed to suspect my question was loaded, not meriting a detailed answer.

"I've always espoused nonviolence myself," he declared. "I've always been a proponent of peaceful change." He walked me through the history of his early alliance with the ANC and subsequent falling out. There was a hint of bitterness, but mostly he spoke in a wooden monologue, as if he was weary of retelling the same old story and had little confidence that I would get it right.

I had neither the time nor any real interest in rehashing this endlessly disputed history. Regardless of who was right or wrong, a personal feud over tactics couldn't explain the mass killings in Natal. I wanted to know what Buthelezi had to say about collaboration. There was no secret about it anymore: Inkatha, ostensibly a Zulu nationalist anti-apartheid movement, had entered into a covert military alliance with apartheid's security forces, organized by some of the most notorious covert operatives of the apartheid era. Did Buthelezi have no qualms about this alliance?

"There was no choice about it," he replied, in effect conceding the essential point. But his tone of voice had changed. He was quickly worked up when I used the word "collaboration." He was looking me in the eye for once—a cold, penetrating stare.

"The government created these structures. My leadership did not depend on that. In all this time, I rejected independence because I rejected apartheid."

Then what happened? I asked. How could one be opposed to apartheid while simultaneously entering into a military alliance with its security forces?

"There were plots to murder me," Buthelezi replied. "What happened is that in 1984, the UDF was founded [as a surrogate for the banned ANC]. Very strangely, in their very first statement, they said they would welcome all black organizations except Inkatha. Before that I had welcomed the emergence of the UDF."

He made no mention a notorious episode in 1983, on the campus of the University of Zululand, of which Buthelezi was chancellor, in which Inkatha *impis* killed six student demonstrators in the first outright confrontation between Inkatha and the newly formed UDF.

"From that point on," Buthelezi continued, "members of my party were assassinated. There were plots to come and kill me. Because I rejected independence, I didn't have an army. An army was always given as a reward for accepting independence."

"They were hit squads too"

All possibly true. What was striking, though, was that Buthelezi was no longer denying what he had denied for many years: that he had in fact aligned himself with apartheid's security forces. The newspapers in South Africa that week were filled with damning details of the Malan indictment and its extensive documentary evidence. There no longer seemed to be any point in Buthelezi's disputing the substance of his pact with the devil, and he did not do so. Instead he rationalized it.

When I pointed this out, Buthelezi grew agitated and hostile, but he kept on talking.

"It was only after they [the UDF] started killing my colleagues that I started to consult with the government. They were necklacing people. They would kill anyone they would label a collaborator. That label included anyone who would not agree to their strategy of violence. People were coming to me and I had nothing to protect them with. My police could not protect them."

There was an element of truth in Buthelezi's avowal—and an element of tragedy. Whatever his opinions about apartheid may have been when he entered politics in the 1960s, clearly Buthelezi found himself trapped in a murderous logic not entirely of his own making. Militants in the ANC may well have had it out for him; Harry Gwala's admonition to the comrades to go after Inkatha's warlords was surely grounds enough to target the chief himself. One could hardly blame Buthelezi for fearing that his survival was at stake. In response, he did what survivors always do: he found protection wherever he could get it.

But in doing so—and in doing so secretly—he allowed himself to be an instrument of white tyranny. It was a measure of his cynicism—not his personal tragedy—that in securing both his personal survival *and* his political survival, he was prepared to drag into a violent abyss the very Zulus in whose name he claimed to be fighting. He put not just himself but his constituents in the service of apartheid. He put his appetite for power above the lives of his people.

"There was nothing hanky-panky," Buthelezi insisted, his voice rising now. "There was nothing treacherous about that." But he knew enough when he made his deal with Magnus Malan and Tienie Groenewald to keep it secret, at all times masking his struggle for survival as a struggle for the survival of the Zulus. The very morning of our meeting in Cape Town, the newspapers featured accounts of an amendment to the Malan indictment which featured evidence of a meeting in March 1998 in Durban between Magnus Malan, Brigadier Opperman, M. Z. Khumalo and Buthelezi, at which Malan cautioned Buthelezi about the "sensitivity of their relationship." Malan warned Buthelezi that he should not allow himself to be identified with the government, and "should not identify himself with the South African Government during visits overseas."

Had Buthelezi ever stopped to question the motives of men like Malan and Groenewald?

"But why should I?" he replied. "The ANC had MK, which was organizing hit squads which killed a lot of people, white and black. I didn't have any means of protecting myself and my people. I'm telling you straight away, the ANC was trying to kill me. Inkatha's actions were of a self-defense nature."

What could he tell me about gunrunning? I asked.

"I know nothing about that. If it happened, I knew nothing about it."

What about the Caprivi trainees, the heart of the Malan indictment?

"I know nothing about how they were deployed. When people were actually being killed by hit squads, there is no time to think about those niceties, about the ethics of things like that. When you declare war—the atomic bomb also killed people."

That was interesting. Tienie Groenewald had also mentioned the atomic bomb to me.

"I think they [the Malan prosecution] are just trying to rewrite history," Buthelezi concluded. "They are saying that the violence started with those two hundred people, which of course is laughable."

What about the prosecution's contention that the Caprivi two hundred were trained as offensive forces—hit squads—rather than a purely defensive force?

"I'm a South African citizen. Being put in charge of protecting the population is a moral duty. The details of how they [the Caprivi 200] were trained—I was never given a manual."

Then he added, "What about the hit squads of the ANC? They were hit squads too."

With this last sentence—"They were hit squads *too*"—Buthelezi conceded a central element of the Malan indictment, which the judge ultimately ruled that the prosecution had failed to prove.

"Ordinary common sense"

Sitting now with Buthelezi, comfortable in his stuffed, striped sofa in the spacious corner office of the minister of home affairs, I was reminded of a conversation I'd had with a former Inkatha ally who had fallen out with Buthelezi, who told me he believed Buthelezi had been, in effect, "turned" by Jac Buchner and Tienie Groenewald. "They colonized his mind," the erstwhile ally told me, explaining that, in a classic ploy, apartheid's spies had preyed on Buthelezi's insecurity—and his blind ambition—and magnified his fear. "They made him think that his salvation lay with the security police."

Had Buthelezi in fact been turned? Maybe so, but it occurred to me now that Buthelezi had hardly been consumed by the devil he danced with. On the contrary, he had survived and even prospered, outlasting his former allies and enjoying the trappings of power in the new order. And he appeared to have won a de facto immunity from prosecution that even the old white generals did not enjoy. Machiavellian to the core, he had excelled as a black politician in the land of apartheid by doing the white man's dirtiest work, and had gotten away with it—albeit with the blood of thousands of his own people on his hands.

So, finally, I asked, what about indirect rule? Wasn't that what the fighting was all about?

"If you have certain theories, I'm not prepared to cooperate," he snarled. The question had touched a nerve. For the first time in our hour-long conversation, Buthelezi turned openly hostile. "My ancestors suffered from the time the British attacked the Zulu nation. My grandfather was exiled. Now if you generalize about indirect rule, it's a lot of nonsense! It's nonsense!"

What about "Operation Marion?" I asked. The actual code name for the alleged Malan conspiracy, derived from "Marionette" and implying that Buthelezi was a puppet, had only emerged in the public domain within the previous week. Was Buthelezi a puppet? A stooge? A collaborator?

"I'm not going to respond to the propaganda of my enemies!" he seethed. "I'm not going to get into these insults! Everybody knew I was anti-apartheid," he said. "Everyone knew!"

What about Jac Buchner? I asked. One of apartheid's most notorious torturers in charge of his own KwaZulu Police? How could Buthelezi have Jac Buchner running his police and still claim to be "anti-apartheid"?

"What of it? He was appointed by Pretoria."

Had it never occurred to him that he had gotten himself in bed with the devil?

Buthelezi looked at me with an expression of pure malice. "I'm not a person who gets in bed with anyone," he huffed, turning his head away.

It was clear my time was up. All pretense of courtesy had evaporated. I wanted to know just one more thing. What about Buthelezi's repeated threats of further bloodshed if Third Force prosecutions were not suspended?

"It's not a threat!" Buthelezi cried, eyes ablaze, fairly shaking with rage that made me wonder whether he was about to assault me. "I've never threatened! To say I'm inciting is just nonsense! It's just ordinary common sense!"

With that, Buthelezi rose from his sofa and ushered me to the door. I thanked him for his time. There was no eye contact. I offered my hand but he declined it, swiftly turning away and returning to his desk. That would be all.

"Incipient anarchy"

In fact, Buthelezi was right. It *was* just common sense. Violence had always been the currency of power in South Africa. The vaunted negotiations between the National Party and the ANC, which paved the way for the 1994 elections, were very much driven by the fear on all sides of escalating violence—and by the demonstrated capacity of all sides to engage in it. The Truth and Reconciliation Commission was established in large part to accommodate the controversial guarantee of amnesty for political crimes, which was written into the transitional constitution under threat of violence.

The ANC's decision to include Inkatha in the Government of National Unity was likewise driven by fear of violence. The decision not to indict Buthelezi along with Malan and the other codefendants was widely assumed to have been made out of fear of violence. The Truth and Reconciliation Commission in turn never compelled Buthelezi to testify: in its final report it characterized its failure to do so as "probably an incorrect decision." In its defense it noted that the issue had been intensely debated within the commission, "which ultimately succumbed to the fears of those who argued that Buthelezi's appearance would give him a platform from which to oppose the Commission *and would stoke the flames of violence in KwaZulu-Natal, as indeed he himself promised*" [emphasis added]. Buthelezi's implicit threat of violence saved him.

South Africa thus far had avoided the fate of its neighbors in part because of the wisdom of its leaders, most notably Mandela and the former president F. W. de Klerk, and because of the vigor of its independent civil society: human rights groups, church organizations, a vigilant press. And Buthelezi turned out to be more buyable than many expected, allowing himself to be co-opted with a cabinet position in an ANC-dominated government. Political violence in KwaZulu-Natal festered well beyond the 1994 elections; as many as three thousand were murdered in the ensuing five years—a staggering figure by any standard save that of South Africa's neighbors elsewhere in Africa, and a measure of how difficult it can be to arrest such a cycle.

By 2000 the killings had largely subsided. There remained, however, deep structural problems that will threaten stability for years to come: gross disparities of wealth and poverty, acute housing shortages, unemployment as high as 50 percent among blacks. The arithmetic is daunting.

On top of what may be the world's most horrific AIDS epidemic, perhaps the most pressing problem for South Africa after five years of majority rule was the proliferation of organized crime. Indeed, the *Sunday Times* in Johannesburg warned in 1998 of an "incipient anarchy" nudging the country toward "the brink of a gangster nation." That may have been too strong, or it may not have been. But the widely held view among white South Africans and many foreigners that South Africa had solved the problem of apartheid only to be saddled with an entirely new problem of crime was far off the mark. In South Africa as elsewhere across the continent, this "incipient anarchy" was very much a product of a long history of tyranny.

The growth of organized crime had clear roots in the political violence of the late apartheid era, and in the vacuum of criminal law that
helped to spawn it. Criminal gangs that sprang up on all sides as
armed wings of political factions during the struggle over apartheid
segued after 1994 into private practice, active in everything from car
theft and gunrunning to extortion and narcotics trafficking. The
country was awash in firearms, many of them smuggled in by the various political factions in the late 1980s and early 1990s. Many of the
guns had been manufactured by the police themselves.

The increase in crime, and the failure thus far of the police to effectively combat it, was in some areas leading to a revival of so-called
"people's courts"—summary mob justice filling in for an absence of
due process—and revenge attacks. In what had come to be called
"community policing," vigilantes of all colors were bypassing police
and courts and meting out their own rough justice. In one notorious
incident in July 1999, neighbors of a gang leader arrested on charges
of raping and murdering a fourteen-year-old girl raised $670 and
bailed him out of jail—then they stabbed him, doused him with gasoline and set him on fire.

The police, stripped of their extraordinary powers and subjected to
relentless public scrutiny, have been exposed as hopelessly incompetent. Where once they could rely on confessions, dubiously extracted
but usually upheld by apartheid's courts, they now faced the awkward
demands of constructing cases on evidence. Often they failed. The
courts, flooded with half-baked cases, were releasing criminal suspects
on low bail and returning them to the communities.

South Africa's murder rate in 1997 was 52 people per 100,000, compared with 6.8 per 100,000 in the United States. Armed militias or
gangs dominated poor black communities and extracted tribute from
fearful residents. Some reached understandings with local police officers. Some have developed vertical alliances with national political
parties and individual politicians who encouraged violence in various
ways over many years, or with businessmen who could import the
goods which they most required—guns—and who could wholesale
other goods for export.

Prominent among the latter are marijuana (of which South Africa is
now the world's leading producer, according to police statistics) and
stolen cars. Some criminal middlemen have good connections in poli-

tics and the security services, especially those who are veterans of the covert actions of the past. Many of the security and intelligence forces of the region had been penetrated by criminal groups in a complex network of relationships.

During the end phase of apartheid, the police were so intent on the struggle with the ANC that they failed to halt an influx of sophisticated professional criminals from abroad who, after 1994, based themselves in South Africa. Enterprising gangsters from across the continent gravitated southward, transforming South Africa in just a few years from a country in which heroin and cocaine were almost unknown to a leading transit point and a significant market for these products.

The countries of southern Africa are linked in a highly integrated economic system constructed by the British and the great mining houses of the late nineteenth and early twentieth centuries. As the outlying parts of the southern African economic system have grown poorer, their formal economies have shrunk, to be replaced by informal, illicit trade. South Africa remains at the hub of the region's formal economy, but it is also at the center of this burgeoning smuggling economy and even plays a role in the smuggling networks of the Great Lakes region of Central Africa. According to Stephen Ellis, a British researcher, it was South African Military Intelligence officers, colleagues of Tienie Groenewald, who succeeded in establishing Johannesburg as the hub of the ivory and rhino horn trades in the late 1970s, with the personal approval of Magnus Malan.

The formation of new power blocks by professional criminals, secret service officers and senior officials working together has not claimed control of the state itself to the same degree as in Russia, for example. Nor have South African politicians combined public office with personal enrichment to anything approaching the degree of their counterparts in other important African countries, such as Nigeria and Congo. Countries like Mexico or, worse, Colombia may be more analogous to South Africa in showing how a highly developed system of criminal syndicates with connections to political factions and the security forces can corrode conventional economic activity and subvert democracy.

South Africa's constitutional transition represents the triumph of reason and compromise over violence and revenge, but over the long haul the country's problems are formidable. It is not for me to make a prediction. In the 1980s and early 1990s, I was among the many who forecast a bleaker future for South Africa than what has thus far come to pass. The conventional view back then was best articulated by J. M. Coetzee in his 1983 novel, *Life and Times of Michael K*, in which he envisioned a South Africa "torn by civil war . . . an anarchic world of roving armies." Thankfully, that has not come to pass—not in South Africa, anyway. For a glimpse of the road not taken, of a future that looks very much like Coetzee's nightmare vision, one must travel northward, to the anarchic world of roving armies that is Sudan.

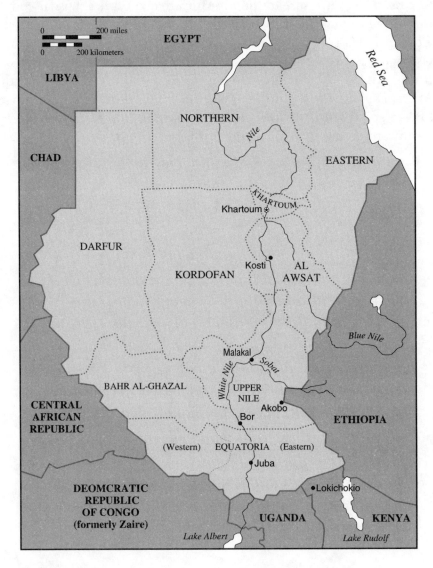

Sudan

5

THREE PH.D.S AND
A NEW KIND OF AFRICAN LEADER

THE BORDER BETWEEN Kenya and southern Sudan is a harsh, dry, fly-ridden semidesert inhabited by nomadic cattle herders. The village of Lokichokio sprouts up incongruously, a surreal boomtown where huge growling cargo planes lift off from a world-class landing strip, fuel trucks clog the dirt roads, and sunburned Europeans and Americans, wearing shorts and hiking boots and carrying walkie-talkies, populate a steadily expanding metropolis of safari-like huts and trailers. Lokichokio is the staging ground of Operation Lifeline Sudan, the United Nations' long-running $2 million–a–week relief program that year after year brings precious little relief to the famished victims of Sudan's civil war, the longest war in the world.

On a slow afternoon in Lokichokio, a half dozen jaded relief workers were sipping Cokes in "the clinic," a thatch-roof, gravel-floor canteen with dartboards and a Ping-Pong table. The talk was angry, demoralized, and frankly cynical. It was about the Big Men in southern Sudan, or, as one of them put it, the "little dictators": the myriad chiefs and warlords and rebel faction leaders with whom the U.N. and independent relief agencies were engaged in an insidious dance.

"They use our food to fuel their war," someone said. "It's a racket with the chiefs. It's like a business cartel."

Feeding civilians was being held hostage to feeding soldiers first, all agreed. The worst offenders were the two main guerrilla faction leaders, Riek Machar and John Garang.

"They don't care how many people die," an American lamented. "The lesson they have learned is that if you keep fighting, the West will keep feeding you."

A Frenchman confided, "I make deals with Garang. To get ninety percent to my people, I let him have ten percent. If you don't feed the soldier, you push the soldier to rob the civilian. If you stopped any assistance, it would be the children who would die. It's a vicious circle. You cannot solve it."

An exasperated Brit had an idea: "Has anybody said to Garang or Riek, 'Here's a million dollars. Please go away'?"

Sudan has been at war for thirty-five of the last forty-five years, thirteen of the last seventeen decades. The current round of fighting is entering its sixteenth year with no end in sight. The best guess is that upwards of 2 million have died since 1983; 85 percent of southern Sudan's population has been displaced. Southern Sudanese, with a mix of sorrow and shame, reckon they've been bludgeoned nearly back to the Stone Age.

Sudan's war is usually explained as a clash between the Arab and Islamic north and the long-subjugated Christian and animist black African south. There is truth in this view. But another way of looking at Sudan is as a textbook case of Big Men using little men, a handful of elites endlessly maneuvering for power and booty while millions perish.

For generations of Sudanese, war has become a self-perpetuating industry. Many suffer, but more than a few are benefiting. Politicians, soldiers, weapons merchants, warlords, gangsters and famine profiteers—all tirelessly jockey for advantage, heedless of the suffering they cause. What's left of the Sudanese state is a composite of predatory interests; whoever is on top is the faction most skilled at preying on others. It is as if Sudan were not a country anymore but a process: it exists through the fact that people are fighting and exploiting each other.

Sudan, Africa's largest country, is a laboratory for disorders common to many of its most intractable sectarian and ethnic conflicts. Sudan's Big Men personify a particularly ruinous symbiosis of ethnicity and organized crime—with an added dimension, religion. I had come here in May 1994 to meet some of these men: John Garang and Riek Machar in their southern guerrilla redoubts, and in Khartoum, the "spiritual leader," Hassan al-Turabi, perhaps the Biggest Man in Sudan—the cast of characters at the top, on all sides, whose interests and machinations and evasions of responsibility might illuminate the pathology of an endless war.

I had already met with another Big Man in this war, and Khartoum's avowed archenemy: Yoweri Museveni, the president of neighboring Uganda. Widely hailed, not least in Washington, as the prototype for a New Kind of African Leader, Museveni had brought of a measure of peace to Uganda, a country that had been riven by what seemed like its own endless war under Idi Amin and Milton Obote. What did it take, I had hoped he could tell me, to arrest this kind of malignancy?

"Submission to God exclusively"

Slouching languidly in its desert isolation at the confluence of the Blue and White Niles, sand-strewn, dilapidated, oven-hot Khartoum seemed a universe apart from the war in southern Sudan. The cry of the *muezzin* wafted across the capital, calling the Muslim faithful to prayer. Women in veils, men in long, white djellabas, their heads wrapped in twisted turbans, made their way through sluggish traffic amid taxis honking, donkeys bleating. Apart from the moonscape of fetid refugee camps on its distant periphery, where a million displaced southerners languished in humiliating beggary, Khartoum did not have the feel of a capital at war. The edge in its otherwise somnolent air derived from the pervasive presence of informers for Hassan al-Turabi's secret police.

Turabi greeted me in a plain stucco villa on a quiet side street near the center of Khartoum, the headquarters of his power base, the National Islamic Front (NIF). His office was cool, with Venetian blinds shut tight against the midday sun and air-conditioner humming. There were few outward signs of power. The walls were bare, the desk, uncluttered. The interview had been speedily arranged through the government's otherwise obstructionist press office, and Turabi appeared to have all the time in the world for a foreign journalist, the better to cultivate his messianic image.

"Islam is a current," he told me in fluent English. "Islam means submission to God exclusively, submission to a higher power."

Turabi is a diminutive man with soft hands and a white wisp of a beard, bespectacled, urbane, resplendent in a flowing white robe and turban. A lawyer by training, with a doctorate from the Sorbonne, he spoke in a deep, sonorous voice, his undulating sentences punctuated by a nervous giggle and an ingratiating smile that gave an impression of trying to seduce.

Sitting behind his polished desk, Turabi would have talked without interruption for two solid hours if I had let him. He said things like "Of course you know very well who controls American foreign policy. Zionists of course. Among lawyers, bankers, journalists, their number is very big. I know who is a Jew among them. Many people know it of course."

Turabi was the brains behind the military regime of General Omar al-Bashir, which seized power in a coup in 1989 and has ruled Sudan ever since through sheer terror. Turabi achieved international notoriety—and the abiding enmity of Washington—because of his alleged support for terrorists and because of his avowed ambition to lead an Islamist crusade from Algiers to Damascus. But the threat he posed to the rest of the world through terrorism paled in comparison to the terror he inflicted on his own population, from purges and torture to state-induced famine. His power was rooted in the skeletal remains of Sudan. It was at a rare moment when peace appeared to be at hand, in May 1989, that Turabi's Islamists moved to seize power and reignite the war. They had scuttled all efforts to end it ever since.

"There is a vacuum now," Turabi told me. "That vacuum is being filled by an Islamist spirit. I just happened naturally to have been on the track where history is moving."

"Islamic-Leninism" was the term some Sudanese were using to describe Turabi's years-long, ruthlessly cunning rise to power. Under the cloak of piety, Turabi and his military allies fashioned a modern, highly sophisticated fascist movement and turned Sudan, or at least the territory under its control, into a vicious police state. They imprisoned hundreds in "ghost houses," shot, whipped and beat dissidents, banned the independent press and trade unions, dismantled the judiciary, and purged the military, the civil service and the universities.

"Don't reduce currents to conspiracy," Turabi snarled when I asked whether he was using Islam as a political tool. "Islam represents a wave of people," he declared. "When people sense injustice, an individual starts to represent them. They say, 'He speaks for us.'"

I pointed out that this "wave of people" came to power in a military coup. The NIF won less than 20 percent of the vote in Sudan's last election, in 1985. Turabi rose to the bait with coiled intensity: "This is stupidity by people who don't understand the nature of history," he hissed. "It's so stupid. Most journalists are very superficial observers of facts."

"He is the enemy of Islam!"

Hassan al-Turabi did not start Sudan's war. Five successive governments in Khartoum have prosecuted the fighting with wanton indifference to the suffering of southern civilians. But Turabi, like his rebel counterparts, John Garang and Riek Machar, was an especially cunning creature of a war-driven political culture, in which southern Sudanese casualties are so many logs in the boiler. All three, like their contemporaries across the continent—Charles Taylor and Mobutu Sese Seko, Tienie Groenewald and Gatsha Buthelezi—have been survivors, outlasting innumerable rivals through sheer ruthlessness and guile.

Turabi's National Islamic Front was ideally suited to the demands and opportunities of permanent war. It was quite literally a front, and an ingenious hybrid, a cross between theocracy and a Mafia syndicate. True believers provide the cannon fodder in the form of a heavily indoctrinated Islamist militia modeled after Iran's Revolutionary Guards. These young men and boys are dropping like flies in southern Sudan. Meanwhile, an elite cabal of generals, Islamic bankers, arms merchants, currency swindlers, land appropriators, cattle raiders, oil prospectors, and outright slave traders—through the patronage of their godfather, Turabi—muscled their way into the profits of war.

Sudan's Big Men have excelled in their peculiar environment by mastering two intertwined requirements of power. The first is the art of manipulating potent symbols, masking one's personal agenda in a larger, legitimating cause. It must be a cause which justifies extreme measures, and for which people are willing to sacrifice their lives.

The second requirement is to accommodate this larger cause to the economic forces that predominate in conditions of total anarchy. In the war-ravaged wilderness of southern Sudan, where most of the country's natural resources are located—including gold, arable land, and, not least, oil—the formal economy has long since collapsed. The criminal acquisition of wealth is the only game in town. The challenge for the successful power broker is to ride the predatory elements: to harness them, tax them if possible, arm them if necessary, and amass enough power to liquidate them before they can liquidate you.

"If you don't have one of the mafias on your side, you won't get anywhere," I was told.

For Turabi, the mask was Islam. There was speculation in Khartoum about whether Turabi holds genuine religious beliefs. Some said he does. But many Sudanese across a broad spectrum, in the watchful privacy of their homes, vehemently mocked his pretensions to piety.

"He is not an Islamist, he is the enemy of Islam!" I was told.

Harold Isaacs, in his 1977 book, *Idols of the Tribe*, described religion as a "tool of power, blesser of the banners of conquerors and consolers of the conquered, upholsterer for the seats of the mighty, cushion maker for the weak, a system for keeping masters undisturbed in their mastery and subjects (quoting Machiavelli) 'well-conducted and united,' or (quoting Marx) 'the opium of the people.' " Alternatively, Isaacs noted, religion can be a "source of challenge to authority, as in the Chinese idea of the transferable Mandate of Heaven, and in the many millenarian revolutionary movements that joined religion and politics in holy and sanguinary assaults on power in many different societies over many centuries." Turabi's Islam embodied both of these age-old uses.

Religion has long been the political lever of last resort in Sudan. Chronic economic crises and interminable war have long since eroded the legitimacy of the Sudanese state. The majority of northern Sudanese are deeply religious Moslems, and Islam is the one potent symbol on which northern Arab political forces have been able to rely for popular support.

The nineteenth-century Sudanese nationalist Muhammad Ahmad, known as "the Mahdi"—"the messiah"—first invoked Islam as a unifying force in the popular uprising against Turko-Egyptian rule, which yielded Sudan's first theocratic state. The British, in turn, during their subsequent half century of colonial rule, cultivated Islamic sects as the basis for rival political parties. The longtime military dictator Jaafar Nimeiry, when his regime began to crumble in 1983, played the Islamic card, declaring *sharia*, the law based on the Koran. He thereby relegated Sudan's 4 million non-Moslem southerners to second-class status. That was the start of the current round of war.

War legitimizes an Islamist regime with a cause that faithful Moslems cannot oppose. Turabi's relentless and highly sophisticated propaganda portrayed the war as a Western and Zionist plot against

Islam. A typical *fatwa*, or religious decree, exhorted the faithful to *jihad*, or holy war, on the grounds that southern rebels "directed their major efforts toward the killing of Moslems, the sabotage of mosques, the burning of the Koran and its desecration with filth. Zionists, Crusaders and the Arrogants incited them to do this and provided them with arms and supplies."

Such a war justifies total control—and any atrocities necessary to prevail. And it makes the regime less amenable to compromise. A regime bent on Islamizing Sudan cannot allow one-third of the country to go its own way.

Then of course there's money to be made. Islam is a tool for securing the petrodollar. As far back as the 1970s, Turabi and his allies, deftly applying Saudi-backed financial favors and ideological indoctrination, began systematically insinuating themselves into key institutions, notably the military and the banking system. Through Islamic banks, they came to exercise a virtual monopoly on access to capital.

As we have seen elsewhere across the continent, the business of Sudan's war is central to its longevity. In the byzantine world of Sudanese politics north and south, conduits to wealth are the Big Man's stock in trade. One of the most lucrative and time-honored privileges is that of waging war: the right to raid and plunder, or otherwise prey on marginal constituencies. Merchants, militia leaders, politicians and army officers connive together. They arm militia groups, organize the sale of looted livestock, put captive labor to work on commercial farms, create artificial shortages by blocking relief supplies. There is virtually no cash economy in southern Sudan: no banks, zero employment. But there are commodities for theft or barter: soap for chicken; cassava flour for peanuts; secondhand clothes, beer, tea, sugar, cigarettes; cattle for women and girls.

All sides manipulate famine relief. Because Sudan has been blacklisted by Western lenders, foreign relief agencies and the U.N. are sometimes the country's largest sources of hard currency. When I was in Khartoum, Turabi's government was requiring relief agencies to deposit their cash in one of two Islamic banks and exchange it for Sudanese pounds at half the commercial rate. The government used most of the resulting windfall to purchase fuel and arms for the war. "It's blackmail," one livid relief official told me. "It amounts to collusion between us and the government. We are totally revolted, but there are no alternatives."

Estimates of the war's cost that year ranged from $1 million to $4 million daily. The government's published budget was $5 million daily. The donors were paying $4 million a week.

Turabi, however, was bored with my questions about the war. As we talked, the Sudanese air force was bombing refugee camps in southern Sudan, scattering 200,000 into the bush. Turabi preferred not to dwell on it. "Now, I'm really not too involved in the south," he sighed, waving aside my questions with his soft hand. A war in his own country, one of the great humanitarian catastrophes of the late twentieth century—but Turabi was a very busy man.

"Maalesh"

I had first traveled through Sudan in February 1983—five arduous weeks that tested my endurance and opened my eyes to extremes of human history and experience of which I had been all but completely oblivious. Sudan, covering more than a million square miles, is nearly twice the size of Western Europe, larger than all of the United States east of the Mississippi. The country was at peace that year, but it wouldn't be for long. Only months after my visit, the country would slide back into a war it has been fighting ever since.

I traveled by train through Egypt from Cairo to Luxor and Aswan; by steamer-towed barge, deck class (sleeping bags *al fresco*), up the length of Lake Nasser from the Aswan Dam to Wadi Halfa on the northern Sudanese border; then by train again, third class, thirty-one hours across 560 miles of the Nubian Desert to Khartoum. The train was a turn-of-the century relic of the British colonial era: wood-clapboard sides, wood-slatted seats and glassless, open-frame windows in the third-class section. It was packed so tightly with passengers that most could scarcely find a seat and many rode on the roof, where I encountered two uniformed police officers rolling a joint of "bongo"—marijuana—and smoking it as they watched the desert go by.

I spent the last six hours down below, wedged into place with perhaps a hundred dusty, filthy, sweaty, exhausted fellow third-class passengers pressed against and on top of one another, in the aisles, on each other's laps, in the vestibules and in the Turkish latrines, even lying on the baggage racks overhead. All were so immovably compressed that I, half standing, found room enough on the floor for only one of my feet; the other was wedged against the hip of an elderly Nubian who sat in the aisle for thirty-one hours with his grandson in his lap. In the pair of seats across from me—two facing, wood-slatted benches designed, it appeared, for two persons each, I counted eleven people: three actually seated on each bench, two more lying on the floor underneath the seats, and three babies. One of these had so much dust in his nostrils and throat that he simply could not stop coughing and gasping; another cried competitively for an hour and a half. It must have been 110 degrees. The passenger cars had no electricity, and we traveled the last six hours in pitch darkness. The only light came from a tea vender who periodically waded through the throng with a flashlight dangling from his mouth, pouring tea into a half dozen filthy glasses and serving them to parched-throated passengers for a few shillings each. The train lumbered through the desert, kicking up copious amounts of sand and dust that settled on the third-class cars in the rear. By the time I reached Khartoum, I, too, appeared to be composed primarily of sand and dust.

Half standing for the last several hours of a thirty-one-hour journey through the desert, filthy and exhausted, I dreamed with increasing fervor of what a sumptuous cosmopolitan oasis Khartoum must be. A hot shower, clean sheets, a decent meal, a frosty beer perhaps—alas, the capital offered anything but. Emerging from the main gate of the train station at midnight: nothing. Total blackness. No cars, no people, not a single light either in a building or in the streets, dirt avenues and sidewalks, a veritable ghost town on the edge of the desert. The explanation, not immediately forthcoming, turned out to be that, because of severe gas shortages created by a crushing balance-of-payments deficit, the government had simply cut off the electric power generators after dark, throwing the entire capital into darkness. Combined with the requisite, heat-induced five-hour siesta each afternoon, the nightly blackout surely made Khartoum the most lethargic, unproductive, almost completely inanimate capital city in the world.

Then of course there was the poverty. It was noticeable not so much in the kind of hideous squalor that I'd seen in Cairo and Alexandria. In Sudan you saw it in the details: the ubiquitous open sores on small children's shins and knees, oozing and festering with flies, unwashed, uncovered, and likely to remain that way for weeks or months or even years. You noticed it in the multitude of polio victims hobbling around using their thickly callused hands as crutches, or conversely, in the virtual absence of people with gray hair, there being so few people in Sudan who live long enough to have gray hair. The average life expectancy at birth in Sudan after a decade-long ceasefire was forty-six years. The best estimate was that half the population was under fifteen. And among so many of these, indeed among nearly all of those under ten, there were the huge distended bellies, evidence of kwashiorkor, the severe protein deficiency that causes the children's bellies to swell with excess water.

Even then, before the fighting resumed and huge-scale famine recurred, malnutrition was nearly universal in Sudan. The infant mortality rate of 141 per 1,000 births was ten times that of the United States; half of all children died before the age of five. In the southern provincial capital of Juba, some eight hundred miles south of Khartoum, I was told that an effort to start a blood bank had been foiled on two accounts: the predictable one was that they couldn't refrigerate the blood for lack of petrol to keep an electrical generator going; the surprise was that the healthy people in Juba, those volunteering to give blood, turned out to have 30 percent fewer red blood cells than the average European, too few for a healthy donation. There was one physician for every 35,000 Sudanese.

Logistics in the Sudan were so impossibly convoluted that after a few days you found you hadn't given a moment's thought to anything else. There were no set rules, no procedures, nothing more sophisticated than a piece of carbon paper. Setting the wheels in motion required infinite patience, tolerance and a tremendous amount of personal diplomacy: a little banter, some cigarettes, possibly a cup of tea or a little baksheesh—a gratuity. Yet, in the course of spending three arduous days in Khartoum just trying to register with the police, obtain the necessary travel permits in duplicate copy with two photographs, gather information about possible trains, buses or boats to Juba, change money on the black market (it evolved, after strenuous inquiries, that the best deal was to be had on the semilegal black market, a peculiar institution whereby the government, realizing it could never eliminate the black market, sought instead to cash in on it)—after three days of this, aggravating as it was, I found I had spent many pleasant and enlightening hours drinking sweet tea and conversing with all manner of police, truck drivers, black-marketeers, transport officials, immigration bureaucrats and the like, as well as various assorted hucksters and Good Samaritans. And I found that the Sudanese, for all their problems, and for all the evil that was soon to consume their country, were possibly the most hospitable, generous and humorous people I had ever met.

I had intended to take a paddle steamer up the White Nile, from Kosti to Juba, reputed to be a glorious and relaxing five-day journey through Dinka country and the Sudd, the world's largest swamp. But the boat was canceled that week—no fuel. By then I was already well accustomed to the experience of being foiled again and again in the course of trying to accomplish basic things in a country where almost nothing works. "*Mafishe*" is the Arabic expression with which I was by now thoroughly familiar. It means "finished," all over, come back another day. Arriving at the station at noon to catch a scheduled 1 P.M. train to Kosti: *mafishe*, no train today, brakes not working. Arriving at the immigration office to register with the police: *mafishe*, closed, breakfast break from 9 to 10:30 A.M.; returning shortly after noon: *mafishe*, closed for the day, come back tomorrow. Planning a trip from Nyala to Wau: *mafishe*, road impassable because of guerrilla disturbances (the beginning, I would later learn, of the latest round of war).

"*Insh'Allah*" was another essential term, as in "Everything in Sudan is *Insh'Allah*." It means, roughly, "God (Allah) willing," or, for the non-devout, "Maybe." So the boat has been canceled this week for lack of fuel—what about next week? "*Insh'Allah*." Maybe, God willing. So you say there is no running water today. When might we be able to take a shower? "*Bokoran*." Tomorrow. "*Insh'Allah bokoran*." Is it safe to travel through Uganda these days? "*Insh'Allah*."

The translation is not exact because it expresses a state of mind, well adapted, it seemed, to a part of the world where almost nothing worked and no one had control over anything. Nor did anyone expect otherwise. At home in America, people imagine that there are rational explanations for things like shortages and delays, and that with time and work and resources the problems can be identified and overcome. In Sudan, it appeared, there was no such feeling of efficacy. "*Maalesh*" was the rule—meaning, roughly, "What can you do?" Your family and half your village has been wiped out by cholera, or Green Monkey disease? "*Maalesh*." The hotels are all full, the train has been canceled, the water is contaminated: "*Maalesh*." Time and again, my expressions of impatience or exasperation were met with the same uncomprehending reply. "*Shwaya, shwaya*," I was advised. Slowly, slowly.

I learned to adjust my expectations. In particular, I learned to adjust my sense of time, to think not in terms of minutes, as I was accustomed to do at home, nor even in terms of hours, as one might in Egypt or Kenya, but rather in terms of days. The train is scheduled to leave on Monday, but if there's a delay it might not leave until Wednesday or Thursday, *Insh'Allah*. It is supposed to take three days to reach your destination, but it has been known to take as long as a three weeks. You would like to take a shower today but there might not be running water until tomorrow or the day after, *Insh'Allah*.

So, "*mafishe*," there was no boat to Juba that week, no fuel. *Maalesh.* Instead, I took a truck, along with about two dozen northern Sudanese men, most of them traders, all of us swaying and pitching and jolting on top of huge stacks of canvas teabags that served both as cushions and as handles to clutch on to. The driver estimated the trip would last three days—"*Insh'Allah*." We traveled mostly at night, since it was far too hot to do much of anything during the day.

The journey took us down flat dirt tracks through camel-colored desert and gray-green savanna, past stark, thatch-roof, fly-strewn villages inhabited by incredibly tall, thin, pitch-black people with parallel ritual scars on their foreheads—the signature of the Nuer. There were some indelible images. One, viewed from the top of the truck as we lumbered down a track through the bush just east of the Nile, was of a Nuer woman, perhaps six feet tall and antenna-thin, charcoal-black, naked from the waist up, barefoot, a long brass tobacco pipe protruding from her mouth. She was calmly balancing an immense sack of what appeared to be maize on top of her head, bearing a small child on her back with a cotton sling, and carrying a five-gallon Jerry can of water in one hand and a slightly smaller jug in the other. Slim as she was, she must have been strong as a bull. She was walking across the parched, flat savanna at dawn, with no village nor sign of life nor even a single conical thatch-roof hut visible in either direction from where I watched her, on top of the truck, to the horizon many miles away.

The trip was plagued with mishaps: countless breakdowns and prolonged, inexplicable delays at the many police checkpoints. A knifing incident at one checkpoint resulted in the jailing of one of our drivers and a three-hour delay while a sufficient bribe was negotiated. At midnight on our second night we ran into a ditch and had to unload the entire truck in order to haul it free. In Malakal, a new passenger boarded the truck with a load of dead fish, befouling the air and attracting a swarm of flies (he received cool stares from the rest of us). Needless to say there was no running water outside the towns and cities, and there was none between Kosti and Juba. We carried Nile River water in a large rawhide pouch strung to the side of the truck. Every half hour or so I filled my canteen with this milky liquid, adding so many water purification pills that it tasted like swimming-pool water.

Remarkably, all of the delays not withstanding, we rolled into Juba at nightfall on the third day as promised. Evidently the driver's original projection assumed there would be innumerable calamities, and he was right.

"Abid"

Two more images from that exhausting trip made a lasting impression. The first, glimpsed from the same position on top of the truck as the Nuer woman, impressed me more for the reaction of my fellow passengers than for what I saw. Early on the morning of our second day on the truck, we finally left the relentlessly bare desert behind us and entered the scrubby, still hot, but blessedly green savanna of Upper Nile Province. This was the divide between northern Sudan and southern Sudan. We were leaving the Arab world behind and entering black Africa, in my case for the first time.

We were traveling through the bush on a track of red clay, two dozen Sudanese Arabs and two Americans, myself and my friend Pete Leyden of Minneapolis, our sunburned heads ineptly wrapped in twisted turbans as protection from the heat (it actually works, we found) and noses comically covered with Nivea cream. I was still drowsy as we got under way, and benumbed by the monotony of the red dirt track slicing through pale-green scrub brush. I looked up and was astonished to see a Nuer man walking up the track. He was buck naked and barefoot, tall and thin and pitch black, with typically narrow slits for eyes and huge bucked teeth, and ritual parallel scars across the forehead. Sure enough, he was even carrying a spear.

It should be clear by now that the stereotypical image of Africans as naked spear-carrying primitives has few real-life counterparts across the continent. Even in Sudan's timeless war, the combatants are mostly camouflage-clad fighters wielding Kalashnikovs over their shoulders, led by erudite men with doctorates. Yet in the vast remoteness of southern Sudan, stunted by decades of war and scarcely touched by development, nomadic cattle herders carry on much as they have through the ages, bonded in work and ritual to the long-horned cattle they both worship and thrive on.

Astonished and delighted as I was at this remarkable sight, with its implicit confirmation of my own arrival on the farthest edge of the back-of-beyond, I was taken up short in my wide-eyed enthusiasm by the white-robed passenger beside me. As the Nuer man glided graceful as a gazelle by the side of the truck, barely acknowledging us, the man beside me nudged my arm and grinned mischievously. He made a dangling gesture with his forefinger—a reference to the Nuer man's naked penis. He glanced back at the other passengers and they all roared with laughter. He repeated the gesture and again the others roared.

It was an expression of none too subtle racism—*those primitive brutes*—which seemed retrograde even by the standards of all the racism I had already seen both at home and abroad. I would encounter something close to it among whites further south, while hitchhiking in Zimbabwe and South Africa. But in Sudan, there was an unabashed quality to it, an absolute contempt, which even the most bigoted ex-Rhodesian rugby player or Afrikaner cop could be counted on to conceal from an American visitor.

I had spent my college years in Boston when that city was in the throes of violent resistance to court-ordered busing. In my first newspaper job I had covered the police in Montgomery, Alabama, where the robbery-homicide detectives would try to goad my nice northern liberal sensibility with occasional talk about drunken "spear-carriers"—yes, spear-carriers—caught up in domestic disputes in public housing projects on the black side of town. So I was not naive about bigotry even in my own country. Yet, as enduring and destructive as our own problems with bigotry have been, they also have been the subject of political struggle and legal challenge. No such struggle or challenge has occurred in northern Sudan.

At least since the Ottoman Turks instituted slavery in the nineteenth century, racism has played a corrosive role in southern Sudan. The Mahdi's Islamists proved themselves even more brutish than the Ottomans. After the Mahdi's *jihad* routed the Ottomans and their British advisers from Khartoum in 1885, the Mahdi's followers expanded the slave trade in the south and compelled conversion to Islam. When the British returned fifteen years later and routed the

Islamists, they were welcomed at first by southerners who knew of their laws against slavery. But the Brits compounded the racism. Their "southern policy" in the 1920s was to seal off southern Sudan as a "closed district." It was textbook divide and rule, intended to isolate north from south, Arab from Christian. Northern Sudanese traders were denied access to southern markets. Marriage was forbidden between northerners and southerners. Across southern Sudan English was taught in the schools. Islam was suppressed. Djellabas and turbans were forbidden. A pass system was created, not unlike the one used to enforce apartheid in South Africa.

And, yes, a system of indirect rule was elaborated. As in South Africa, traditional chiefs were co-opted or coerced into dominating their subjects on behalf of the British. In Sudan, indirect rule both discredited and calcified indigenous political structures. By the time of independence in 1955, a half century of British rule had left Sudan with two mutually estranged regions divided by language and religion—and racism. Britain's southern policy had reinforced Arab stereotypes of blacks as primitive brutes by stunting development across the south, yielding a backward, isolated region, overwhelmingly illiterate, deeply poor, and shunted out of power.

Ever since independence, in war and in peace, northern Arabs have dominated all spheres of Sudanese life. Northern Arab Sudanese across a broad spectrum still think of black southerners as subhuman; many still refer to them as "*abid*"—literally, slaves. Even among the most sophisticated and liberal-minded in Khartoum, the awesome suffering of black southerners, their fellow countrymen, scarcely registers. Racism, I came to believe, is an indispensable piece of the engine propelling Sudan's war without end. Racism is undoubtedly magnified and exploited by cynical leaders like Turabi, but there it is.

"One of those countries"

The second image was of President Reagan. On the night before we set out for Juba, I was eating dinner, fried fish and rice, in a outdoor, dirt-floor café in Kosti, a remote riverside trading post about an hour south of Khartoum. Kosti has little to recommend itself other than the fact that it lies at the intersection of Sudan's main north–south transportation route (the White Nile) and its only east-west route, a bumpy, barely navigable road to Port Sudan, on the Red Sea (across the million-square-mile expanse of Sudan there are but seventy-five miles of paved road—and the pavement ends south of Kosti). There is virtually nothing in Kosti: no pavement, no sidewalks, no street lights, no store fronts—nothing save a few rows of white stucco one-story buildings, a police station, a railroad track, a truck yard, a freight dock—and a single black-and-white television.

The television, I discovered, was set up and successfully flickering (by means of a gas-powered generator that competed with the audio) in the only restaurant in town, the very café at which I was now seated. When I arrived, some two dozen Sudanese men in turbans and djellabas (no women, for this was still the Moslem-dominated half of Sudan, and you never saw woman out of their homes after dark) were seated in metal chairs arranged in a semicircle around this impressive miracle of modern technology, intently watching what appeared to be an Arabic soap opera. Halfway through my meal, the news came on and the volume was turned up. An intense-looking anchor, wearing the standard turban and robe, delivered the news in Arabic. Suddenly, as if out of some parallel universe, there appeared the familiar bobbing head of President Reagan. And he was talking about Sudan!

Or at least he was trying to. Over the course of about fifteen minutes, the familiar faces of Leslie Stahl, Chris Wallace, Sam Donaldson and Lou Cannon of the *Washington Post* appeared as well, putting questions to the President, making me feel right at home here in parched, remotest Kosti. The questions all seemed to revolve around Libya and Muammar Qaddafi, and something about AWACs and troops being massed on the border of Libya's neighbor—Sudan. I'd missed the Arabic explanation for all of this, but I could tell from the questions that something problematical to American interests was afoot, and that Sudan appeared to be on our side.

Finally the President put it in perspective: "We do know," he began, "that Colonel Qaddafi has been and will continue to be a destabilizing force in the region, so nothing would surprise us, and we do know that Sudan is . . ." And here the President faltered for a moment, and you could see him groping in his mind for that map of Africa that some aide—very likely his assistant secretary of state for Africa, Chester Crocker—had shown him. "Sudan is"— the President faltered again, and you could imagine him struggling to visualize that huge, featureless space just south of Egypt and east of Libya—". . . Sudan is one of those countries in that region of Africa."

The American president may have known next to nothing about this obscure, impoverished African country, and cared even less. But his flickering image on that generator-powered television screen in Kosti—and his meaning—gave evidence that Sudan was anything but an isolated outpost at the end of the earth, untouched by and irrelevant to the modern world. On the contrary, and central to it troubles, Sudan, like Liberia and Zaire, was very much connected to the rest of the world, a key strategic player in the great competition between the superpowers and their proxies.

The president of Sudan in 1983—Washington's man in Khartoum—was Jaafar Nimeiry. It was Nimeiry who would reignite Sudan's civil war only a few months after I left. Nimeiry had seized power in a coup in 1969 and had evolved into a ruthless military dictator. When he made his coup he was allied with the Sudanese Communist Party, but in 1976 he switched sides in the Cold War, becoming Washington's ally and a reliable check on Qaddafi, as well as on potential Soviet designs on the Nile and on the vital Horn of Africa. In 1979 Sudan was the sole member of the Arab League to support the Camp David agreement between Israel and Egypt.

Nimeiry had not always been a tyrant. Through most of his first decade in power, he had no outside backing to rely on, and he skillfully diffused domestic conflicts and accommodated many of his adversaries. In 1972, in a landmark achievement, Nimeiry was able to negotiate a ceasefire in the war, the fabled Addis Ababa accords, under which the south achieved a measure of self-government. In 1977 he reached an agreement with his principal political rival, Sadiq al-Mahdi, that made it possible for opposition forces to participate openly in national politics. Sudan's prospects appeared bright, and it was during this era that Washington began to reach out to Nimeiry as a potential ally.

But by the time of my visit in 1983 President Nimeiry had devolved into an archetypal strongman. His dour, bespectacled image—light-skinned, formal in full-scale military regalia or casual in turban and robe—was a ubiquitous presence in framed portraits in every store and office, printed on every Sudanese pound. He held all the strings of power; he was the head of the state, head of government, leader of the only legal party (the misnamed Sudanese Socialist Party), commander-in-chief of the armed forces. Regularly "reelected" president with majorities in excess of 99 percent, Nimeiry made all the decisions.

The president maintained his personal following by adhering to an age-old formula—reward the faithful handsomely, and punish the disloyal ferociously. A meticulous man, the president's recipe was finely honed: to each new cabinet minister the gift of a Mercedes-Benz; to each new general a Peugeot; and to each new minister at the regional level a Renault. His erstwhile colleagues on the original Revolutionary Council of 1969 were not dispatched empty-handed when they were removed from office. While taking all the power for himself, he appeased them with a house, a car and a pension each. Later, when three of these comrades dabbled in a coup attempt, they were hanged.

In time, repression became Nimeiry's only recourse as he alienated one group of allies after another from the Communist left to the Islamic right, and survived repeated coup attempts. His prisons bulged with political prisoners. To travel within Sudan, both foreigners and Sudanese had to obtain special documents and citizens even had to obtain a special pass to enter the international departure terminal at the Khartoum airport. Police at frequent roadblocks checked identity cards. Plainclothes security men were everywhere. In 1983, well-placed Sudanese estimated that 30,000 informers were operating in Khartoum alone. Each neighborhood had its own plainclothes policeman and each university class was assumed to harbor an informer. Many Sudanese intellectuals recounted tales of harassment by the secret police. One graduate student in sociology, for instance, had her notes confiscated while researching Khartoum's informal economic sector. A car washer she interviewed was, in fact, a plainclothes policeman who arrested her for "asking questions without a permit."

Nimeiry was a mercurial figure, and increasingly erratic, given to making policy on the basis of dreams and messages he claimed to have received from Allah. His regime degenerated into a melange of opportunists, military officers on the make, a diminishing few leftists—and the Muslim Brothers, Hassan al-Turabi's growing political base. Turabi had gone into exile after the 1969 coup, but he returned after Nimeiry's switch of allegiance, and he would serve as Nimeiry's attorney general.

Notwithstanding Nimeiry's repressive and increasingly erratic conduct, the Reagan administration stood by him as an important strategic ally. A steady flow of U.S. aid greased the wheels of his patronage machine, and it would enable him and his successors to wage war on the south. Washington, in return, got what it paid for: Sudan's loyalty and a regional base of operations.

Sudan's slide into renewed war that year had many complex causes and ample candidates for blame in addition to Nimeiry. But it was probably not a coincidence that the war reignited after the United States began providing large amounts of assistance to Nimeiry's government—nearly $1.5 billion in total. The aid contributed to Nimeiry's recklessness and subsequent downfall by rewarding him for focusing on external adversaries like Libya's Qaddafi, and by encouraging him to believe that he could count on Washington to bail him out of his mounting internal problems. As with Liberia and Zaire, American officials were more concerned with Sudan's potential as a diplomatic ally and strategic asset than they were with how well Khartoum managed its economy or settled its domestic political problems.

It was the Carter administration that first decided to sell arms to Nimeiry's regime and make it the principal African beneficiary of American foreign assistance. Carter was concerned about growing Soviet influence in neighboring Ethiopia. He also wanted to ensure that Khartoum would support U.S.-Egyptian initiatives in the Middle East. Nimeiry's value as a client became that much greater when he agreed to grant the United States military access to his country in order to facilitate the development of a Persian Gulf rapid deployment force. After the Reagan administration took over in 1981, Sudan, like Samuel Doe's Liberia, also became an important base of operations for William Casey's covert CIA campaign against Libya's Qaddafi.

In April 1983, Assistant Secretary of State Chester Crocker summed up Washington's opinion of Nimeiry, declaring that the United States had become "Sudan's closest friend." Two months later, in June 1983, Nimeiry unilaterally abrogated the Addis Ababa accords, and the following September he imposed *sharia*, Islamic law, on the whole country, in effect relegating non-Moslem southerners to second-class citizenship and thereby reigniting the war he had helped to end a decade earlier. These moves were widely unpopular even in the north, and Nimeiry's hold on power grew ever more tenuous, and ever more dependent on the *jihad*, holy war, against the infidels for his legitimacy.

Two years later, on April 1, 1985, Nimeiry met President Reagan in Washington. The White House announced that it was releasing $67 million in aid to Khartoum because Sudan's President Nimeiry's government was taking "the steps required to bring its economy under control." But the aid came too late to save Nimeiry. Five days after his meeting with Reagan, Nimeiry, still in the United States, was ousted from power in a bloodless coup.

"An autonomous affair"

Unlike most African coups, the coup in Sudan in 1985 was prompted by a genuine popular uprising, and the generals who ousted Nimeiry—he wound up in exile in Egypt—paved the way for a more or less legitimate election the following year. The winner was Nimeiry's longtime nemesis, Sadiq al-Mahdi, an articulate career politician who had briefly served as prime minister in the 1960s in an earlier failed experiment in parliamentary democracy. Sadiq's election was widely applauded at home and abroad amid hopes that he might bring an end to Nimeiry's war. It was not to be. Five chaotic years later, Sadiq was ousted in the military coup spearheaded by Turabi's National Islamic Front. The war smoldered on, since then claiming perhaps a million lives and counting. Sadiq's failure served to underline the enduring pathologies that perpetuate Sudan's endless war through one government to the next, from military dictatorship through parliamentary democracy to Islamist tyranny.

I had a chance to meet Sadiq al-Mahdi at the time of my visit with Turabi in 1994. A great-grandson of the legendary Mahdi, Sadiq remained a important figure in Khartoum, though he had been in and out of detention since his ouster in 1989. He had spent four months in prison not long before we met, accused of plotting a coup. For the moment he was free, albeit effectively under house arrest, and he received me in a cone-shaped straw gazebo at his spacious compound on the bank of the Nile, in Omdurman, the vast residential township that in colonial times was Khartoum's equivalent of Soweto.

Sadiq had often impressed Western visitors with his sharp intellect and engaging, cultivated manner. His doctorate comes from Oxford. He spoke with livid passion about the police state repression of Turabi, who was Sadiq's brother-in-law and once served in *his* government as justice minister—a measure of the incestuous character of Sudanese politics among the small circle at the top.

"What's happening has nothing to do with Islamic principles," Sadiq told me. "It is more akin to the practices of totalitarian states as developed by Hitler and Stalin. It's a coalition of totalitarian forces."

But when my questions turned to the war, Sadiq was every bit as mendacious as Turabi. "To look at it positively," he ventured, "how could Sudan with its diversity hold together for so long? Just as you may speak of the empty half of the glass, there has been real achievement of the Sudanese people over the years."

This was hard to swallow. A quarter of a million southern Sudanese starved to death in 1988–89, Sadiq's last full year in power. I was in Sudan that harrowing year. There was a sense that Sadiq was not just dithering but actively thwarting all possibilities for peace that might enable his political opponents to claim credit for ending the war. His government was also notably obstructionist when it came to famine relief. An exasperated American relief official, echoing a widespread sentiment, told me at the time, "There is no will on the part of Sadiq's government to do anything about this problem. It's more than casual indifference. There is something approaching outright hostility towards people who are concerned about the problem. Why? Because the people who are hungry and dying are southerners. They are not considered to be Sudanese."

I had spent a week in Juba between Christmas and New Year's 1989. It was one of the darkest periods of the war, and one of the few when famine was so acute that Sudan briefly captured the world's attention, resulting in the creation by the U.N. of Operation Lifeline Sudan. Southern Sudan that year seemed to be eating itself alive. Southern groups had fallen to fighting among themselves, settling scores with automatic weapons, SAM-7 missiles, land mines, and other armaments supplied by Libya and the United States—both jockeying for influence with the government—and Ethiopia, backer of the rebel Sudanese People's Liberation Army (SPLA), led by John Garang.

At that point Sadiq was our ally, and John Garang, then based in Soviet-backed Ethiopia, was our enemy. The enemy of our enemy was our friend. The SPLA's strategy at the time was to destroy the government's capacity to govern in the huge and already impoverished southern half of the country. It had succeeded in gaining control of most of the south, confining government troops and officials to a few remaining outposts like Juba. But hunger and indiscipline among the SPLA's 30,000 mostly illiterate rank and file had led to widespread looting and pillaging, effectively destroying not only the government's ability to govern the region but the people's ability to live in it.

Both the rebels and the government were using food as a weapon, destroying crops and then blocking humanitarian efforts to deliver famine relief. Juba itself was completely isolated for two months after the rebels ambushed a food convoy. The people survived on a diet of boiled water lilies and roasted rats.

Sadiq's government, meanwhile, was waging a proxy war. It was a textbook example of anarchy as an instrument of tyranny, and a reprise of the divide-and-rule strategies of Sudan's slave-trading era. Much as Magnus Malan and Tienie Groenewald armed and trained Gatsha Buthelezi's KwaZulu Police as a vigilante proxy force against the ANC, Sadiq's military created ethnically based militias across southern Sudan, providing high-powered weapons and ammunition to traditional ethnic rivals of Sudan's largest southern group, the Dinka, who predominate in the SPLA. These modern weapons, nominally provided for self-defense against the SPLA, quickly ratcheted up the stakes of traditional conflicts over land and cattle—conflicts that until only a few years earlier were waged with sticks and spears and settled through negotiation by tribal elders. Now they were being waged with automatic assault rifles and hand grenades in an escalating spiral of attack and revenge.

Among the earliest southern groups to be armed by the government were the Mondari, pastoral nomadic cattle herders like their Dinka neighbors, with similar physical features—they are tall and thin, pitch black, with distinctive ritual scars on their foreheads. As in Natal, ethnicity in lawless, war-ravaged, famine-plagued southern Sudan was above all a means of protection. Even amid famine, what little food was available went first not to the women and children but to the young Mondari men, the warriors, on whom the rest depended for protection. And indeed, when I visited the main Mondari refugee camp outside Juba, the young men look fit for a fight. On Christmas Day the young Mondari men, having set aside their automatic weapons, dressed in leopard skins and gaudy sashes and paraded through the streets of Juba. They waved flags, blew whistles, chanted traditional African call-and-response holiday greetings, and staged wrestling matches in a downtown square.

Depending on who was reciting the history of what followed after the government armed the Mondari in 1983, the Mondari militia either raided neighboring Dinka for their cattle or resisted SPLA raids, and the fighting continued for two years. The Mondari finally retreated with their cattle to the outskirts of Juba, where they set up camp. In 1988 the SPLA attacked the camp and drove the Mondari farther into town, to a ragged assemblage of green plastic tents and thatched-roof huts barely a mile from its center. So the Mondari, in spite of—and perhaps because of—their government-sponsored militia, had been twice displaced by the war.

Juba's inhabitants were no strangers to war. It was there in Sudan's southernmost province of Equatoria that most of the fighting occurred in Sudan's earlier seventeen-year round of war, which began with independence from Britain and Egypt in 1955. That war went almost completely unnoticed in the West, though it cost half a million lives. Then as now, hunger was the worst killer.

On a quiet night between Christmas and the New Year in 1989, I shared a meal of roasted goat meat and maize porridge in a lightless thatched-roof café with middle-aged veterans of the old *Anyanya* guerrilla movement, as the earlier rebels were called. The *Anyanya* sought to liberate the south of Sudan and create a separate African nation. Instead, the 1972 Addis Ababa accords with Jaafar Nimeiry established limited southern autonomy. Eating with their fingers and washing their food down with smuggled whiskey, these Equatorian *Anyanya* veterans told me that the SPLA was not much more than a Dinka militia. They said that Equatorians like themselves initiated that earlier campaign. The Dinka, they argued, formed the SPLA to fight the government only after the government threatened to diminish Dinka power by subdividing the south into three separate provinces, a move that seemed to benefit Equatorians.

The Dinka, needless to say, told it differently.

The irony was that most southerners, then as now, readily identified with the cause of the SPLA. All shared the deeply held grievances of the African south against the dominant Arab north—much as Zulus left and right shared a common grievance against white tyranny and Kasaians and Katangans shared a common grievance against Mobutu. But from the vantage point of besieged Juba on New Year's 1989, just as in Lubumbashi or Durban, the larger issues of tyranny and oppression seemed remote. There was a lot of talk about how there were "no good guys," in the war, that "both sides are to blame."

"We believe they [the SPLA] have not considered the welfare of the population," one embittered *Anyanya* veteran told me. "The issue of injustice, the issue of discrimination, the issue of *sharia* laws—these causes are shared by many. But the SPLA has looted, killed, raped. They put antipersonnel mines under trees where people sit for shade. They place them in the paths leading to boreholes. They place them in fields for cultivation. Every time they have attacked, they have attacked innocent civilians, not the army. So they will never convince the people, whom they kill and rape and whose villages they burn, that they are fighting the northerners."

For nearly six years since 1983, the government's cynical strategy of divide and rule had, in effect, been a substitute for bargaining in good faith with the SPLA. Even if Garang, the SPLA's leader, had managed to come to terms with the government, it is doubtful that he or any other leader could have controlled more than a limited number of the armed combatants. The forces of anarchy had taken on a momentum of their own.

On Christmas Day, Juba seemed momentarily to forget about the war. In a camp for displaced people on the outskirts of town, men, women and children gathered on rows of log benches under plastic canopies and celebrated the holiday with remarkable cheer. But even as Mass was being held, the singing was disrupted by the blast of an exploding land mine. SPLA rebels had entered the camp on Christmas Eve and kidnapped a dozen young women and boys. They had buried mines along their route to secure their getaway, and four people stepped on them the next day. All were killed. For a bemused Equatorian relief worker, the news seemed to capture the war in a microcosm. "The government wants the people in the south to die," he said. "And the SPLA has done the government's job for them."

In Khartoum in 1994, I asked Sadiq, now six years out of power, why he had failed to end the war. "The conduct of the war was really an autonomous affair by the generals, not by civilians," he said, passing the buck. But what about arming militias? That was the responsibility of his government. "This is war. Those tribal groups came to the government and asked for arms to protect themselves. This war was a very nasty business and should be stopped. We tried to keep it a clean war but we invested very heavily in the war process."

Sadiq sounded very much like South Africa's Tienie Groenewald talking about the origins of Inkatha's death squads in the name of "protection" from the ANC. In countries where all citizens enjoy equal protection under the law, it is the state's responsibility to protect them from violence. In racist states, on the other hand, where blacks are regarded as second-class citizens, the responsibility to protect blacks from other blacks is fobbed off on black vigilantes who claim to be acting in "self-defense." The resulting cycle of anarchy serves to reinforce racism by disabling and discrediting its opponents and confirming stereotypes. In this sense Sudan has indeed realized the nightmare J. M. Coetzee envisioned for South Africa, one with roots in a comparable kind of racism. Sadiq al-Mahdi and Hassan al-Turabi were creatures of the same racist political culture and the same "war process." Opposition and government alike in Sudan viewed southern lives as beside the point.

Like the Kasai refugees in Lubumbashi's train station who fingered Mobutu, southern Sudanese had little doubt about who ultimately was responsible for their predicament. "I say that the prime minister [Sadiq] is just a man who is willing to exterminate southerners," Archbishop Paolino Lukudu of the Roman Catholic diocese in Juba told me. We were sitting in his spare living room on Christmas Day sipping Tang by candlelight. I had accompanied him for much of the day as he delivered Christmas sermons in refugee camp after refugee camp on Juba's periphery, sheepishly apologizing that all he could offer his famished listeners was "spiritual food, not actual food, unfortunately." Now he was walking me through his own bitter analysis of what this war was all about—"a political war," he stressed, "a war of domination."

But, I asked, "extermination?

"I am not exaggerating," the archbishop replied. "I'm saying that the situation in the south is genocide, indeed. There is a saying by the Arabs: '*Aktul al-abid bil abid*'—kill the slave through the slave. That's what he's doing. With the militias he is succeeding. He has not killed any of us. It is we who are killing ourselves."

On my last morning in Juba, when I visited Juba Hospital, a crumbling green wood-frame establishment with stained walls and torn screen windows. I met a patient named Santino Remo, seventeen years old. Two weeks earlier Santino had stepped on a land mine planted by the SPLA. When they brought him into the hospital, it was late at night and there were no lights to illuminate the wards—the generator was shut down for lack of fuel. The blood bank was closed for lack of a functioning refrigerator. There were no medicines or painkillers, no antibiotics, no syringes, no dressings, no sterilized equipment of any kind because the coal was finished, not even running water because the pump had broken down.

Now, Santino was sleeping on a grimy mattress on the floor of the emergency ward. A nurse washed Santino's wounds with cloudy water drawn from the Nile. A doctor told me Santino was "going downhill," too weak from hunger to survive a needed amputation. The nurse sprayed bug repellent near Santino's shrapnel wounds to ward away the flies. That would be the abiding image I carried with me when I returned to southern Sudan six years later.

"I really don't have any regrets"

From the window of a ten-seater prop plane circling high over southern Sudan, the village of Akobo, on the Ethiopian border, appeared to be an orderly constellation of circular huts with straw fences and dirt paths meandering across a vast flat savanna. As the plane began its descent, you could see signs of the malignancy that had brought us there. Rows of blackened, roofless huts came into view, and the fields were abandoned. Internecine fighting among local clans in Akobo had scattered more than 24,000 people from their homes in the weeks just prior to our visit.

A blizzard of flies wafted over us as we disembarked on a sodden grass landing strip. Faces pressed all around: taut with hunger, wide-eyed and expectant, electric with the promise of manna from heaven. Operation Lifeline Sudan had sent this plane to deliver medicines for the local clinic run by the French relief agency Médecins Sans Frontières.

It was June 1994, not long after my visit with Hassan al-Turabi. The Big Man in Akobo was Riek Machar. Riek, as he is commonly called, was the leader of the South Sudan Independence Movement, a breakaway faction of the SPLA, John Garang's main rebel movement, which once controlled nearly all of southern Sudan and now controlled almost none of it. In August 1991, Riek had made a fateful bid to seize control of the SPLA from Garang. It didn't work. Instead, Riek's failed coup metastasized into a catastrophic internecine war between the Nuer and the Dinka, the two largest ethnic groups in southern Sudan. Tens of thousands were slaughtered; several hundred thousand starved to death in the resulting famine. The rebels were split in two, then in three, then four fighting factions. The southern cause was reduced to where it had been around 1960.

"I really don't have any regrets," Riek assured me.

We were sitting now in his dirt-floor and mud-walled compound, swatting the flies, guarded by a dozen listless teenage rebels in shorts and flip-flops, Kalashnikovs slung over their shoulders. Riek is an attractive man in his forties, smoothly affable, a little cocky. He, too, has a British Ph.D., from the University of Bradford. He was wearing pressed battle fatigues with a red beret and bright red monogrammed shoulder boards that set him strikingly apart from the rabble around us. A barefoot boy shined the Big Man's combat boots as we talked.

"Garang was responsible for the ills of the movement," Riek continued. "It's his leadership that was responsible, not mine."

A particularly wanton massacre by Riek's troops was "unfortunate," he admitted, but it wasn't his fault. "I don't feel responsible for the deaths. We all went to fight for our liberation. So we pay a high price."

Riek had once promised to investigate the massacre. The result?

"If any atrocities were committed, it was not necessarily sanctioned by the leadership."

Anybody held accountable?

"In a big fight, you don't know who did this. It was a big fight."

If Hassan al-Turabi's mask was religion, the symbolic cover for Riek and Garang was race. Theirs was the cause of black southerners against historic injustice. No southerner could fail to identify with the southern cause—especially after years of enduring Khartoum's well nigh exterminative war tactics. Garang and Riek undoubtedly believed in it too. Yet for them the legitimacy of the southern struggle against northern Arab domination was not just a goal worth fighting for but an inoculation against any personal accountability for crimes committed in its name. "We all want to fight for our liberation, so we pay a high price" was Riek's alibi. Garang, when I asked him about the suffering of the southern Sudanese, would reply, "The Islamic Arab agenda is the cause of the war and the source of the suffering. It is a choice between slavery and freedom. What is life worth to be at peace when you are a slave in your own country?"

Garang and Riek both talked a good game. Yet they, like Turabi, relied on utter ruthlessness to survive in it. Like Turabi, they were masters of the Machiavellian arts: of purges and shifting alliances, playing rivals off against each other—and riding the criminal class.

Like Turabi's NIF, the SPLA was a well-adapted hybrid, at once a genuine liberation movement and a confederation of criminal gangs. The disastrous 1991 split, with its bifurcation along ethnic lines, was akin to what happens when Mafia dons fall out. It paralleled the experience of Liberia after Samuel Doe and Thomas Quiwonkpa fell out in the mid-1980s. When the Big Man's survival was at stake, ethnicity became useful, indeed mandatory—a badge of legitimacy and protection, as we have seen, and of justice. A violent struggle for power between two individuals ramified outward to consume their respective groups. In their lawless, gun-saturated environment, murder was piled on murder, massacre on massacre.

"I was with Garang for eight years," Riek told me. "I have witnessed the lack of democracy, his dictatorial measures. I had seen the abuses of human rights."

It took him eight years to see the light, but Riek was right about Garang. The SPLA began its war with broad popular support across the south. But its character was shaped by its principal backer, the former Ethiopian dictator Mengistu Haile Mariam, and by Mengistu's backer, the Soviet Union. Garang would belatedly discount his pact with the devil as a "marriage of convenience," given Khartoum's Cold War alliance with the West. But with the SPLA able to sustain itself in Ethiopia, it never developed the grassroots support of a classic guerrilla struggle. SPLA leaders never pursued hearts and minds. They took the race card for granted.

Across the south, the SPLA in its heyday behaved like an occupying army. Civilians were the main military targets. All factions sought to destroy communities presumed to be supporting their opponents. In far-flung, scorched-earth sweeps, minimally trained, totally illiterate, heavily armed fighters torched villages, stole the livestock and food, planted land mines, conscripted the young men and boys, and raped the women and girls.

Human Rights Watch reported in 1994 that "all parties have waged war in total disregard of the welfare of the civilian population and in violation of almost every rule of war applicable in an internal armed conflict." Garang's explicit strategy was to render southern Sudan ungovernable, and in that he succeeded. The south became not only ungovernable, but virtually uninhabitable.

Garang, by way of self-exculpation, would tell me that "for every hundred men I recruit I may have two thieves." By then he had recruited roughly 180,000 men in twelve years. That would mean 3,600 thieves. Heavily armed by Garang, and deployed in conditions of absolute lawlessness, many became powerful thieves indeed.

It was the collapse of Mengistu's regime in Ethiopia in 1990 that precipitated the split in the SPLA. The new Ethiopian regime kicked the SPLA out and a power struggle within the movement ensued. It became the Nuer chief, Riek, against the Dinka chief, Garang. Khartoum, true to form, pumped in guns and bribes—divide and rule, the enemy of my enemy is my friend, let the natives do the dirty work.

In my conversation with Turabi in Khartoum, I had asked him about the split in the SPLA. He told me, "There is a measure of ethnic feeling, not only in the south but all across Africa. It explains most of it. Everybody knows it's a Dinka-Nuer affair. It's tribal. Just like Rwanda. I'm sorry to say, that's a very important aspect."

Turabi's notion about "ethnic feeling" reflected a widely held prejudice. Like whites in South Africa seeking to explain black-on-black violence, many northern Sudanese Arabs believe Africans possess some inherent disposition for conflict based on ancient, inscrutable hatreds. Yet Turabi and his military allies, like their white South African counterparts in the waning days of apartheid, were doing everything in their power to exploit and magnify ethnic divisions. By arming ethnically based militias and bribing chiefs and warlords, northern governments through the years stoked the engine of anarchy in which appeals to ethnicity become lethal.

"War is regrettable"

Three hundred miles southwest of Akobo, John Garang held court in a makeshift, thatch-roof-and-canvas guerrilla command post in the rugged bush near the Kenyan border. The SPLA commander was reachable after weeks of persistent schmoozing with his allies in Nairobi, drinking round after round of warm beer with his press aides in Lokichokio, and several hours of bouncing and lurching in a four-wheel-drive vehicle along dirt tracks through the remote mountain reaches of southern Sudan. Garang's turf, after four years of fighting with Riek's breakaway faction and renewed government offensives, had been reduced to a tenuous sliver on the southernmost frontier.

"Of course we are not trying to achieve a military victory," Garang told me. "We cannot win this war."

Garang was a big bull of a man, charming, smart, even funny, dressed in pressed camouflage fatigues. His doctorate comes from Iowa State University. He received military training at Fort Benning, in Georgia. Like so many of Africa's warlords, he did not appear to be a thug, and he certainly didn't talk like one. He said things like "The engine that drives the war is injustice. The regimes since independence have failed to evolve a sociopolitical commonality which transcends localism. Governments have moved toward parasitism, Arabism, Islamism."

I asked Garang about the rampant criminality of troops under his command. He dodged and wove, blamed Khartoum, and changed the subject. "We are certainly not angels," he finally conceded. "You will hear these charges. You will also hear about the popularity of the SPLA. There are positive things, and there are negative things. There are individuals who rape and steal. But what I want to underline is that it is not the movement."

On the one hand, on the other hand. I asked Garang if he had any regrets.

"I don't believe so," he replied thoughtfully. "War is regrettable. It results in destruction and suffering. But human beings have gone to war from time to time. People have fought for ideals that are worth fighting for."

Not long after our meeting, Garang's forces attacked the Nuer village of Ganyliel, killing 210 villagers, including 127 children. In a new offensive, his forces recaptured parts of the south from which they had been expelled three years earlier, advancing to within twenty miles of Juba. Garang was being rearmed with help from Sudan's neighbors. Uganda, Kenya, Ethiopia, Eritrea, and Egypt all feared Khartoum's support for armed Islamist groups; Egypt would blame Turabi for an attempt the following year to assassinate Hosni Mubarak.

Few doubted that the United States had a hand in Garang's revival. Garang passed through Washington just before Christmas 1995. The Clinton administration denied giving arms to Garang, but admitted it did not discourage others, notably Israel, from doing so. Americans and Israelis shared an interest in containing a hostile Islamist regime. Indeed, Secretary of State Madeleine Albright met with Garang in Uganda in 1997 and warmly endorsed his movement.

The plot would thicken in 1998, when the United States attacked a pharmaceutical factory in Khartoum with cruise missiles. President Clinton accused Turabi's regime (on what would turn out to be shaky evidence) of backing Osama bin Laden, the Saudi-born financier suspected of plotting the terrorist bombings of American embassies in Kenya and Tanzania, which killed more than two hundred people, mostly Kenyans. Bin Laden had lived in Khartoum in the early 1990s. He owned an Islamic bank, a construction company, and investment firms in Turabi's Sudan, where he and his associates secured a near monopoly on gum Arabic, Sudan's leading export.

Bin Laden shared roots with Turabi among the so-called "Arab Afghans"—the tens of thousands of volunteers from across the Arab world who fought alongside the CIA-backed Afghani *mujahideen* in their 1980s war against the Soviet occupation of Afghanistan. Flush with Islamist zeal and the sweet taste of victory over one superpower, they had turned against the other and fanned out across the Middle East, the Balkans, parts of Central Asia and Pakistan, and Africa, staging deadly attacks on targets affiliated with their former sponsor, the infidel United States. Sudanese with links to Turabi's secret police were among those convicted of conspiring to bomb the World Trade Center in New York in 1993.

The underlying premise of Washington's support for the *mujahideen* in their war against the Soviets was the same as the premise of our support for Samuel Doe, Mobutu, Nimeiry, and the rest: the enemy of our enemy is our friend. Milton Beardon, a former CIA official who ran the agency's covert operations in Afghanistan from 1986 to 1989, put it this way in an interview with the *Washington Post*: "Sometimes you work with unsavory people to deal with acute evils." A decade later, the Cold War was over, the tables had turned, and "rogue" terrorist states were now the enemy, but the underlying premise of American policy was the same: the enemy of our enemy is our friend.

That Hassan al-Turabi, our erstwhile friend, now turned out to be an acute evil is a lesson in the law of unintended consequences. Bombing him on shaky evidence was another: it unwittingly reinforced his stature in the Moslem world as an Arab leader standing up to the enemies of Islam, and it undermined Washington's stature as a peacemaker in Sudan, however unpromising that might have been. John Garang may not have been as bad as Turabi, but helping to arm him as the enemy of our enemy merely poured more fuel on Sudan's endless fire. His cause may have been just, but in the logic of his environment, he was in too deep with the bad guys to disentangle himself. Sudan's Big Men adjusted their calculations; the little men kept on dying.

"A new kind of African leader"

So what is to be done? How do you arrest this endless cycle of war? If armed insurrection merely brings out the worst in its leaders, what are the alternatives?

The Clinton administration seemed to have found a compelling answer in Yoweri Museveni, the Ugandan leader who was Garang's main military ally and Turabi's most potent enemy in the region. Museveni, through Garang and with Washington's blessing, has been waging a proxy war of his own with Khartoum for over a decade. And he has likewise produced ample evidence of the law of unintended consequences.

Museveni is a bear of a man with a shiny bald pate and an avuncular style that has disarmed many a visitor. Politician, intellectual, ex-guerrilla leader and, since 1986, the president of Uganda, Museveni was embraced by Bill Clinton's administration as a new kind of African leader, the darling of Western donors, a man who minces no words about the "backwardness" of Africa. He says things like "I have never blamed the whites for colonizing Africa, I have never blamed these whites for taking slaves. If you are stupid you should be taken a slave." Sitting in the shade of a huge flame tree on his cattle farm in southwest Uganda, sipping from a glass of piping hot fresh cow's milk, the president spoke ironically, Socratically, turning questions back on his questioner, slyly chuckling at his own answers.

But his mission could not have been more serious. He was trying to achieve what many feared no one could: to bring Uganda back from the abyss of its own huge-scale mass slaughter. Amid the litany of horrors that have befallen so many countries in postindependence Africa, Uganda occupies a singular place. In the 1970s and early 1980s, Idi Amin and the less notorious but no less wanton Milton Obote plunged Uganda into a nightmare every bit as dark and sinister as the ones that unfolded across its northern border in Sudan or across its southern border in Rwanda in 1994. Possibly a million Ugandans died in two decades of sheer terror.

The road from the capital, Kampala, to Museveni's farm cuts through lush tropical mountains straddling the equator along the edge of Lake Victoria, not far from the headwaters of the White Nile and the Mountains of the Moon. Dense green forests and red earth, banana palms, coffee plantations, crested cranes and spotted guineafowl, bougainvillea in perpetual bloom—this was the hauntingly beautiful landscape that moved Winston Churchill to call Uganda the "pearl" of East Africa. When I first traveled this road in 1983, it was riddled with potholes. Teenage soldiers in baggy battle fatigues and rubber flip-flops with bloodshot eyes and slurred speech, manned dozens of checkpoints, poking great big, heavily used Kalashnikovs into taxis and buses, shaking down travelers, often raping women and girls. Kampala had crackled with gunfire at night. The trading centers of Masaka and Mbarara were sullen, bombed-out ruins.

A decade later, in 1994, the road was newly paved and there were no roadblocks. The streets were safe at night, markets bustled, and nightclubs pulsated to the twangy rhythms of the latest hits from neighboring Zaire. Nearly all of Uganda's immediate neighbors were in turmoil. To the south, Rwanda and Burundi were convulsed by civil war and genocide. Zaire, on Uganda's western border, was in the throes of "ethnic cleansing" as Mobutu maneuvered to survive in power. To the north, tens of thousands of Sudanese were in flight from Khartoum's latest offensive against southern rebels as Sudan's endless war entered its second decade. Even Kenyans, on Uganda's eastern border, who for years had viewed Uganda's agony with a mixture of horror and disdain, were beset by yet another round of state-induced ethnic "clashes" that had shaken that nation's reputation for stability. Uganda, of all places, looked like a model of tranquillity.

A decade earlier I had felt a rush of relief when I exited Uganda into what was then pacific Rwanda; in 1994 I experienced precisely the same sensation moving in the opposite direction.

"Uganda is out of the woods," Museveni told me. But the twinkle in his eye masked toughness, arrogance, even ruthlessness. He had not stayed on top in Uganda by being soft. Almost alone among African leaders, Museveni had managed to secure broad international support while defying Western pressure for multiparty democracy. He argued that multipartyism aggravates ethnic divisions. It was a familiar argument, made by many a cynical African tyrant bent on rationalizing unaccountable power. But such was Uganda's uniquely fractious past that in Museveni's case the argument could not be dismissed out of hand. Uganda was the kind of place where a top-ranking Western diplomat, while lamenting the arrests of three leading "multipartyists" on sedition charges, could nonetheless suggest that "Museveni may have calculated that it is time to demonstrate power, and he may be right—safety first."

At the time of my visit Ugandans were electing members of a constituent assembly that would ratify a new constitution. It was a "dress rehearsal" for parliamentary elections later that year. The central issue for voters was whether to elect candidates who favored "multipartyism" or those who favored continuing for five more years with Museveni's all-inclusive—some said *too* inclusive—"movement" system. Unfortunately, most of the "multipartyists" looked less like Jeffersonian democrats than like partisans of the old Obote regime, determined to reclaim power by stoking ethnic divisions. The campaign opened a window on a still stubbornly polarized country at a crossroads—battling AIDS, still very poor, and still largely dependent on the personal authority of one man, Museveni. Most Ugandans were living in peace. The question was how long it might last.

The Buganda crisis

At independence from Britain in 1962 Uganda was already a fractious polity, vulnerable even by the standards of postcolonial Africa to the destructive forces of sectarianism and ethnicity. Its borders had been drawn up by the European colonial powers at the oft-lamented Berlin conference of 1884, with little regard to interests of the indigenous peoples. Some forty distinct ethnic groups were roped together, and, as elsewhere, a system of "indirect rule" accentuated ethnic differences by vesting unaccountable power in tribal chiefs and by divvying up schooling and jobs according to the time-honored method of divide and rule. The Bantu-speaking Baganda in the south, whose kingdom was most advanced and whose lands in the fertile mountainous region around their capital, Kampala, were best suited for export crops, were favored for posts in the colonial service—and thus for the schooling needed to fill them. The Nilotic-speaking groups of the north—the Acholi and Langi, and also those known as Kakwa, Idi Amin's group—were stereotyped as "warlike"; they filled the ranks of the colonial army, along with Nubians from southern Sudan brought in as mercenaries.

Cutting across these fissures was the overlay of religion. Catholics and Protestants, proxies for the French and British, respectively, clashed in the nineteenth century; the British political triumph yielded a legacy of discrimination against Catholics that persists to this day. A small Moslem minority, meanwhile, including Idi Amin's Kakwas, endured third-class status. The one glue that might have fastened some of these cleavages, an entrepreneurial middle class, was made up mostly of outsiders, Ugandans of Indian descent who were later to be expelled by Amin.

Comparable conditions existed in nearly all the countries of post-colonial Africa, yet not all degenerated to the depths that Uganda did. Again, it is not true that Africa's many ethnic groups are inevitably prone to conflict and bloodshed; most, even among Uganda's forty-odd tribes, live side by side in relative harmony. In Uganda as elsewhere, though, the potential for conflict was compounded by a third important legacy of colonial rule: the absence of legitimate institutions of law and accountability. Competition for power took place in a Hobbesian vacuum; only the most ruthless and cunning need apply. This left Uganda especially vulnerable to the idiosyncratic personalities of its leaders.

Milton Obote now lives in Zambia in what is by all accounts a mostly drunken exile; Ugandans say he was often publicly drunk while in power. Obote never achieved the worldwide infamy of Idi Amin, yet his two terms as head of state (1962–71; 1980–85) were just as destructive. Unlike Amin, Obote was a weak and paranoid leader who handled the army with kid gloves. He created the opening for the rule of the gun. Idi Amin was Obote's hatchet man.

The descent into chaos began in earnest in 1966 with the so-called "Buganda crisis," when Obote, the country's first prime minister, suspended the constitution and ordered army units led by his army commander, Amin, to attack the palace in Buganda of the popular hereditary king of the Baganda, Uganda's largest and most prosperous tribe. The Baganda were the proud and privileged, and thus resented and feared, beneficiaries of indirect rule. Over the next five years Obote oversaw the cumulative militarization of power, which became blatant when Amin seized power in a coup in 1971. The militarization of politics fragmented the army and security forces, largely along ethnic lines according to the same Mafia logic as in Liberia. Anarchy alternated with tyranny. As each faction assumed power, it set about liquidating its predecessors, their families, and their presumed civilian supporters, as well as the supporters of new insurgencies, which inevitably arose in response.

For the next fifteen years the theater of carnage shifted from one region of Uganda to another as each regime in turn sought to consolidate its power. Amin's forces massacred tens of thousands of Acholi and Langi from the north, who predominated in the armed forces of Obote's regime. In 1972 Amin expelled Uganda's 70,000 Asians, the country's entrepreneurs, plunging the country into economic chaos from which it is only now beginning to recover. Amin's soldiers, mostly Kakwas, Nubians, and mercenaries from Sudan and Zaire, as well as agents of Amin's notorious State Research Bureau, the secret police, rounded up scores and then hundreds and then thousands of suspected enemies, finally unleashing a campaign of wholesale violence in which an estimated half a million people were killed. Of course the more people Amin killed the more enemies he made. There were twelve attempted coups in all, and plots aplenty involving dissidents near and far. One of them allegedly involved Amin's own wife, Kay Amin, who was murdered and dismembered.

After Amin's ouster in 1979 and Obote's return to power a year later, Obote's newly constituted army, made up as before mainly of Acholi and Langi, took their revenge in Amin's home region, massacring thousands. Soon Obote's poorly trained, ill-fed, irregularly paid army, swollen by the urban unemployed, was fighting three separate insurgencies, including Museveni's National Resistance Army (NRA).

"Backwardness"

A decade after Museveni ousted Obote, most Ugandans were living in peace. The economy was picking up. Roads were being built. Children were going to school. Hospitals had medicines. Refugees had returned. An independent press was flourishing, and other independent civic and political associations were emerging. People walked the streets at night without fear of soldiers or criminals. Ugandans were living with hope.

It was a remarkable achievement which no one would have predicted, and it showed that Africa need not be as hopeless as it sometimes seems.

"Let's agree on the essential points," Museveni told me. "Regular elections, universal franchise, free press, separation of powers."

I asked the president what it took to arrest so entrenched a cycle of ethnic violence. "What Europeans and Americans call ethnicity in this context is actually backwardness, social and economic backwardness," Museveni replied "Africa is preindustrial. It does not have a middle class. Its dominant opinions are held by peasants. Their attitudes are often parochial. They do not have a vested interest in cosmopolitanism, or in nationalism."

The president was, obliquely, making the case for his economic program as a key to stability; it is a virtual textbook adaptation of the International Monetary Fund's Structural Adjustment Program: free markets, a convertible currency, an independent central bank, selling off state-owned companies, tight budgets and downsizing the civil service and the army. Inflation, at the time of our visit, was down to single digits (from an annual high of 300 percent the year before Museveni took over). The black market for hard currency was gone (when I first visited Uganda a decade earlier, the spread was ten times the official rate). Annual growth exceeded 5 percent.

Museveni invited back Uganda's Asians, whom Amin expelled in 1972, and he returned their property. His aim is to attract investors and build a middle class. "If there is a middle class, it will cut across ethnic groups," Museveni told me.

"Backwardness" was also Museveni's explanation for the dangers of multipartyism. His argument was simple: multiparty democracy works where social divisions are horizontal, based on class. In Africa the divisions are vertical, based on tribe, and political parties inevitably reflect that vertical division. In Uganda this is not just an academic point. The existing parties are in fact closely identified with ethnic and sectarian interests, and with the regimes that represented those interests to the detriment of others. Milton Obote's Uganda People's Congress (UPC), identified with northern Protestants, mostly Acholis and Langis, remains a force in Ugandan politics.

Earlier in our visit, three top UPC leaders were arrested and charged with sedition. The charges stemmed from a manifesto published by the UPC alleging that Museveni's government was dominated by people of Rwandan origin. Many top officials in Museveni's old guerrilla army were in fact Rwandan refugees. In 1982, in an episode scarcely noticed by the rest of the world, President Obote expelled more than 80,000 Banyarwandans from southwest Uganda. Many returned to the country as NRA guerrillas, and when Museveni took power they took power with him.

Now Obote's old UPC allies, campaigning as "multipartyists," were playing the ethnic card, raising doubts about Museveni's ethnic loyalties as a means of discrediting his government. Museveni ordered them arrested.

"They are criminals," Museveni told me with evident bitterness. "These multipartyists are not committed to multiparty politics. It is a means of dividing the people. We look at them as traitors. They want power because they cannot live without power." He emphasized that the matter was now in the hands of what he said was an independent judiciary. "We insist on discipline," he continued. "If you say something which assaults the dignity or acceptability of a group of the Ugandan population, the state should arbitrate. I am a manager. They are opportunists manipulating ethnic divisions."

Clearly Museveni had an authoritarian streak, but his comments highlighted the complexity of Uganda's predicament. What he said about the multipartyists undoubtedly was true. Those who were claiming a right to free speech and advocating "multiparty" democracy had a history of extreme authoritarianism; they were cynical partisans of a recent regime that did not merely arrest but summarily murdered thousands; they were seeking to exploit ethnic divisions that they only recently had used to destroy the country.

"The Lord's Resistance Army"

After Museveni's NRA forces took power in 1986, remnants of Obote's UNLA, in a continuation of the familiar cycle, went back into the bush in the north and waged yet another guerrilla campaign. Museveni's NRA forces spent five years battling a succession of insurgencies in the north, by turns crushing and co-opting their fighters and supporters.

Now, well into the 1990s, Museveni's army was battling in the north against yet another remnant of the old insurgent forces, a tiny guerrilla faction known as the Lord's Resistance Army. The LRA, led by a messianic psychopath named Joseph Kony, was being armed, financed and fed by Hassan al-Turabi and Sudan's armed forces. "They are the ones who launched the rebellion," Museveni told me. "The Sudan army has

always had malevolent intentions." In fact, it was textbook proxy warfare on both sides, with Turabi on the one hand and Museveni—and
Washington—on the other,—each arming "the enemy of my enemy."
The Lord's Resistance Army—its mask of religion, Turabi's signature,
notwithstanding—would achieve notoriety in subsequent years by kidnapping children and transforming them into murderers. It was hardly
a sympathetic cause, yet Museveni's sometimes heavy-handed counterinsurgency campaign was reviving old enmities.

"This fear is coming up again," I was told when I visited the north.
People told me Museveni was no better than Amin. "Museveni is
more educated," I was told. "Museveni is a learned killer."

I was speaking with a dozen Acholi UPC "multipartyists" gathered
in a dirt yard in the northern provincial capital of Gulu. The men sat
on stools in a circle around a pot of steaming traditional beer known
as *marwa*. They sipped the muddy brew through long straws fashioned from hollowed-out reeds called *icike*. The men insisted they not
be identified by name. "There is talk of freedom, but freedom has a
limit," one of them said.

The talk that evening was of the army's latest campaign against the
Lord's Resistance Army. By all accounts these so-called "Kony rebels"
were not much more than bandits, a last remnant of the earlier northern insurgencies, with no discernible ideology and little popular support. They had alienated the local population by kidnapping and
killing civilians, raping women and girls, and cutting off the ears,
noses and lips of captives.

Reports of army abuses against the local population soon emerged.
The previous year Amnesty International had reported: "Massacres of
unarmed civilians and prisoners by soldiers of the government's National Resistance Army (NRA) have taken place every year. The victims have included children and whole families. Some have been
burned to death in their homes; others have been suffocated to death
after being crammed into pits or other confined places of detention.
Yet others have been beaten or shot to death by soldiers who apparently believe they are above the law. Thousands of people have been
unlawfully detained without charge in military barracks where many
have been tortured or ill-treated."

When I asked Museveni about Amnesty International's allegations,
he told me, "I don't dispute them. What I don't agree with [Amnesty]

on is the charge that we condone abuses, that we know about but ignore abuses, that we cover up abuses. In fact we have executed soldiers who committed abuses." Indeed Amnesty International, which opposes the death penalty, protested in 1992 that over forty soldiers had been executed since 1987. "Amnesty says executions are too harsh," Museveni continued. "We still apply the law of Moses. We still say an eye for an eye. If you kill someone, you must die."

The NRA's abuses in the north were not on a scale comparable to the wanton abuses committed by Amin's and Obote's troops, but comparisons of scale and severity are hardly meaningful to the victims. A man sipping *marwa* on my left drew a parallel between Museveni and Amin, and he added, "We are even deeper into the vicious circle that we thought we were out of."

Hassan al-Turabi was playing this vicious circle like a violin.

"Buying peace"

Uganda's continued polarization was worrisome not just because of the legacy of past ethnic conflict but because of the continued absence or weakness of the mediating institutions of civil society. Amin and Obote destroyed what little the British left behind of the rule of law in Uganda. Police, courts, the army—all were either politicized along ethnic lines or eviscerated. It was the rule of the gun, the law of the jungle—the pattern we have seen across the continent. For years state crimes went unpunished. And in the absence of individual accountability for these crimes, groups were blamed—and groups were relied upon to obtain justice.

Museveni, to his credit, made it a priority to reestablish the rule of law. He virtually scrapped the discredited police force he inherited in 1986 and hired and trained a new force of 20,000. He set about rebuilding a cowed and withered judiciary with the help of Western aid—he told me there were only "three or four" high court justices left in the entire country when he came to power. He worked to diversify and professionalize the army. By all accounts (except in the north), the progress on these fronts had been remarkable. The wholesale criminality by the state and its agents was gone for now. But there was still a long way to go, and abuses still occurred.

Meanwhile, there was the problem of legal accountability for the many crimes committed under past regimes. One of Museveni's first acts when he came to power in 1986 was to establish a Human Rights Commission to document the country's history of abuses and, it was hoped, identify and prosecute the culprits. The aim was to clearly identify his regime as a "break from the past." Eight years later the commission's findings had yet to be published, and very few individuals had been successfully prosecuted.

There were logistical problems. Money and resources were limited. Evidence was poor. The continuing fragility and incompetence of the law undermined efforts to successfully prosecute even those individuals whom the Human Rights Commission recommended prosecuting. A few prominent individuals were arrested and tried, only to be acquitted for lack of sufficient evidence. These failures discredited the process and discouraged witnesses.

But the main problem was political. Inevitably, past regimes were closely identified with different regions and tribes; going after accused human rights abusers was perceived in those regions as persecuting their tribes. In some instances communities refused to cooperate with investigators, shielding criminals in their midst on grounds of ethnic solidarity. And there was concern that so many people had blood on their hands that settling accounts would be impossible. "Where will it end?" we were told.

The recurring insurgencies in the north also created problems. Many northern insurgents, former Obote fighters, were motivated by fear that they would be brought to account by a government dominated by southerners. In 1987 a general amnesty was declared in hopes of luring northern rebels out of the bush. This was Museveni's strategy of "buying peace." He offered rebels a chance to come out of the bush and be integrated into the national army. Many took it. "We thought that trying to punish everybody—it would be an endless process," Museveni told us.

Under Museveni's policy of "co-optation rather than confrontation," hundreds of soldiers and their leaders from the myriad fighting forces, police and intelligence units, private militias, and bandit gangs, as well as numerous civilian officials from previous regimes, were lured out of the bush or exile and were integrated into Museveni's umbrella-like National Resistance Movement (NRM) and its soon-bloated army.

The goal, as in Mandela's South Africa, was peace and reconciliation. The problem, also as in South Africa, was that very few people have been held accountable for past crimes; a great many Ugandans have gotten away with murder.

"My cows are crying for me"

Is Uganda out of the woods? Ugandans need only look across their northern border at Sudan to know how fleeting peace can be. Sudan had seventeen years of war, then ten years of peace, and then, since 1983, years more of ruinous war with no end in sight.

Uganda and its army still revolve around the personal leadership of Museveni, who has shown, for better or worse, that he can be as authoritarian as he is visionary. Museveni said in 1994 that he would step down after five more years. "My cows are crying for me," he told me with a chuckle. "My mission is now almost accomplished, which is to orient my people toward modernization. We shall complete this process of democratization."

Five years later, Museveni remained in power and had no apparent plans to leave. He had, to his credit, submitted to a relatively free and fair election in 1997, and he won a five-year term. Even so, not many Ugandans I spoke with were so confident that his mission was almost accomplished. "The stability of Uganda hinges on one man," said Billy Okadimiri, an Acholi journalist in Gulu whose support for the "movement" has put him at odds with many of his neighbors. "National sanity and international respect revolves around one man. In a situation of a vacuum of leadership, there will be a direct slide to anarchy. People are still not sure that if Museveni is not there, would the army behave as it is behaving now? These are their fears."

Justice Arthur Oder of the Uganda Supreme Court and chairman of the Human Rights Commission put it this way: "Uganda as a state has been identified with individuals. But the pillars of civil society are institutions, not individuals." I asked Justice Oder what was to stop Uganda from sliding back? "Nothing," he said. "In Africa, power is controlled by whoever has the gun. It is still the case."

Museveni scarcely blinked when I ran these doubts by him. "When we defeated the dictatorship," he said, "our first task was to put these pillars in place: to restore the police, to restore the rule of law, to restore the civil service, to restore the army, and to restore the judiciary." One can only hope he succeeds in this task above all others.

Uganda will have real peace, I suspect, only when its stability depends not on the character of its leaders but on the quality of the institutions those leaders are a part of. History will judge Museveni not according to the measure of peace he has achieved while in power but on whether the peace survives after he steps down—if and when he finally does so. Time will tell whether the "pillars" he is setting in place remain standing after he leaves.

"A new generation of African leaders"

Doubts about Uganda's fragility notwithstanding, Museveni emerged as the poster boy for the Clinton administration's trumpeted enthusiasm for a "new generation" of African leaders, a veritable pan-African alliance of enlightened men bent on rooting out the corrupt and brutal era of strongman politics that had blighted the continent for a generation. Credulous diplomats and smitten journalists hailed the "euphoria" sweeping the continent as these erudite new leaders seized its destiny in their supposedly nimble hands.

The climax of this short-lived euphoria was President Clinton's historic trip to Africa in April 1998—the first by an American president since Carter touched down briefly in Liberia in 1977. At a meeting in the president's mansion, the State House, in Entebbe with six of these newfound allies, Clinton embraced this "new generation" as harbingers of an "African renaissance." Secretary of State Madeleine Albright had previously signaled a wholly new American policy toward Africa, after frankly acknowledging the damage Washington had contributed to in Africa by embracing dictators like Doe and Mobutu. Now, she said at the conclusion of a seven-nation tour of Africa in 1997, "Africa is very fortunate to have a group of strong leaders working in favor of regional cooperation."

In addition to Museveni, the dashing warrior princes included Paul Kagame of Rwanda, whose Tutsi-led rebel forces put an end to the genocide in 1994; Issaias Afwerki, the quietly charismatic guerrilla leader turned president of Eritrea; and Ethiopia's Prime Minister Meles Zenawi, another former guerrilla fighter who was trained as a physician and whose "soulful, calm speeches and Western suits," said the *Washington Post*, "describe the antithesis of the Soviet-backed dictator whom he overthrew, Mengistu Haile Mariam."

Within months of Clinton's visit, nearly all of these leaders were at war with one another. Kabila of Congo, who with Washington's blessing had liberated that vast nation from America's longtime client, Mobutu, turned out to be a predatory thug. Then the dean of the "new generation," Museveni, and his protégé, Kagame of Rwanda, who had backed Kabila's war against Mobutu, grew disillusioned with their progeny and launched yet another armed insurrection within Congo, yielding the current intractable conflict that has drawn in a half dozen surrounding countries and claimed, as of mid-2000, 1.7 million civilian casualties from fighting and famine.

In the Horn of Africa, meanwhile, Ethiopia and Eritrea set upon each other in a remote border conflict that claimed tens of thousands of lives in trench combat reminiscent of World War I but that featured twenty-first-century weapons and nineteenth-century medical facilities.

The new leaders had clearly made a hash of it, and the talk in Washington shifted from a "pan-African alliance" to "transcontinental war."

What went wrong? For all their impressive talk, our African allies had little in common save their success at beating discredited predecessors at their own game. They all achieved power through the use of force, and that is how they were inclined to hold on to it. Ultimately they, like those whom they ousted, were accountable to no one save their own armed constituencies.

Washington was understandably eager to do business with a new generation of articulate leaders who at least embraced market-oriented economic reforms if not democratic systems of accountability. To be sure, Museveni had brought a measure of stability to his own war-battered country. General Kagame drew sympathy as a leader of Rwanda's decimated Tutsis after the genocide of 1994. But the Clinton administration was slow to come to terms with the fact that all these men had time and again shown a reckless disregard for the lives of defenseless civilians that is the hallmark of men grown accustomed to unaccountable power. The names and faces had changed, but the rules of the game remained the same.

And of course, all of the players, including Washington, were operating according to the time-honored principle that "the enemy of my enemy is my friend." Even the best-intentioned among them were trapped in mafia logic, compelled to shed ever more blood merely to survive. The faces had changed, but the rules of the game remained the same.

The Clinton administration belatedly distanced itself from Kabila in Congo, but it remained closely identified with Museveni and General Kagame to the end, even as they launched or provoked one bloodbath after another and finally, in 1999, fell to fighting against each other in eastern Congo. The administration rarely rebuked them for their recklessness, maintaining strong diplomatic, military and economic ties that left the impression that they enjoyed unwavering American support. They in turn behaved as if they believed they had carte blanche to pursue their adventures.

The Clinton administration's enthusiasm for "strong" new leaders left many Africans and longtime Africa watchers at home with a disquieting sense of déjà vu. There was a whiff of an all-too-familiar sliding scale of standards that for years formed the basis for the very coziness toward despots that the administration sought to disavow.

For instance, when Secretary of State Albright made her comments about "strong leaders," she was standing beside Laurent Kabila in Kinshasa. She said she hoped that with a "commitment to open markets, honest government and the rule of law," Congo would emerge as an "engine of regional growth." With Kabila beaming at her side, she added, "President Kabila has made a strong start toward these goals."

Even as Albright spoke, Congolese opposition leaders were languishing in jail without being charged with any crime, having been arrested and beaten by agents of the renamed but scarcely retooled secret police force that, as the SNIP, frequently jailed and beat them under Mobutu's rule. Businesses were being shaken down for huge bribes in exchange for government contracts.

"There is a long way to go to reach those goals," Albright conceded to reporters who challenged her optimistic assessment, "but I am encouraged by a number of positive steps."

In the face of arbitrary arrests, beatings and widely reported massacres in northeastern Congo by troops under Kabila's command, the reference to "positive steps" toward honest government and the rule of law carried a disquieting echo of Chester Crocker's enthusiasm for "steps in the right direction" and "noteworthy positive aspects" in connection with Samuel Doe's brazenly stolen election in 1985.

There were other echoes of Chester Crocker. "You need to look at the evolution of democracy in terms of a movie, not still photographs," said National Security Adviser Anthony Lake during the first Clinton administration, "Or, in other words, in dynamic and not static terms." This was almost an exact replica of one of Crocker's statements in his letter to the Lawyers Committee for Human Rights, in 1987, in which he wrote of "movement in a positive direction" in Samuel Doe's Liberia, suggesting that "if you take a moving picture, it shows a trend which we think is a positive one."[1]

The Clinton administration was slow to recognize that a well-intentioned effort to forge special relationships with less malevolent but no more accountable leaders had failed to arrest the continent's destructive tendencies. Africa's problem is not just a problem of leadership, it is a problem of institutions—or, rather, the absence of institutions of law and accountability that make enlightened leadership more likely. In the absence of individual accountability for serious crimes, groups get blamed. The cycle of ethnic slaughter goes unchecked.

The truly radical thing for the United States to do is to invest its resources and its credibility not in individual leaders but in the fledgling attempts across the continent to build institutions of law and accountability; in the end, these represent the only real hope for lasting positive change in Africa.

"We cannot have this blackmail"

I had an opportunity to meet again with Museveni in New York in January 2000. By then I was writing editorials for the *New York Times*, and I had written a signed piece a week earlier in which I questioned the wisdom of the Clinton administration's close identification with the so-called "new generation" of African leaders, including Museveni and Kagame. Museveni made no mention of the piece, but his tone was notably cooler than it had been when we met on his farm six years earlier.

Museveni was in town for a summit meeting of African heads of state who were involved in Congo's festering civil war, which in two years would kill an estimated 1.7 million people, mostly from starvation and disease. The New York meeting had been organized by Richard Holbrooke, Washington's ubiquitous and energetic ambassador to the United Nations, who was using his month as president of

---

[1]Lake left the Clinton administration in 1997 and joined Chester Crocker on the faculty at Georgetown University.

the U.N. Security Council to focus the world's attention on the problems of Africa. He called it the "Month of Africa."

I met Museveni in his suite at the Waldorf Astoria. His own ambassador had suggested the interview and made the arrangements, but the president showed no sign of recognizing me.

I asked Museveni about the law of unintended consequences. He had waged an armed rebellion against Idi Amin, and then another against Milton Obote. Now he was backing Garang's armed rebellion against Islamist tyranny in Sudan. He had backed Laurent Kabila's armed rebellion against Mobutu's tyranny in Zaire. Now he was backing an armed rebellion against Kabila's tyranny. In 1990 Museveni had backed the Rwandan Patriotic Front's (RPF) armed invasion of Rwanda from Uganda, led by men who were among Museveni's closest military confederates.

Had it not occurred to Museveni and his friends, I asked, that armed rebellions provoke massive violent reprisals against defenseless civilians? What was he thinking in 1990? I wanted to know. Surely he was mindful that a Tutsi-led armed rebellion in Rwanda was likely to result in the mass murder of Tutsi civilians. That had been the pattern in both Rwanda and Burundi, not to mention in his own war in Uganda itself: huge-scale mass slaughter of civilians in response to ethnically based armed rebellions.

"We did not conspire with the RPF in 1990," Museveni demurred. "But after they went, we did not want them to come back. We said stay there."

Did Museveni accept no responsibility for the bloodshed that followed? For that matter, did he accept no responsibility for the bloodshed unleashed in his own war against Obote? Does one who engages in violent rebellion—even justified armed rebellion against tyranny—bear no responsibility for the unintended consequences of his rebellion? When those consequences are foreseeable, as surely they were in Rwanda and Congo, as well as in Sudan, does the rebel bear no responsibility for protecting those who bear the brunt of the tyrant's repression?

Museveni was plainly contemptuous of this line of questioning.

"There is a thief who grabs a briefcase in the street," he said, eyes alight, staring me down. "When I try to restrain him, he starts shooting passers by. And then the journalist from New York [meaning me] says, 'Why did you try to restrain him? You are the one who provoked him.' Don't you think that's a bit . . ." He shook his head incredulously. "The authors of the genocide are to blame. We cannot have this blackmail."

Blackmail?

"Amin said on the radio, 'Museveni will be killed. His family will be killed.'" He was recalling his first armed rebellion in Uganda, against Idi Amin. "That was blackmail—if you resist dictatorship your family will be killed. The threats to my family should not doom resistance to dictatorship. I do my duty. If you want to kill innocent people, that's your own responsibility."

The president concluded with vehemence, "But I will not accept blackmail. Every dictator says, 'If you attack me, I will kill you.' Before 1986, one hundred thousand children were dying of six preventable diseases in Uganda. So people in a bad system are dying every day. That is the basis for deciding to resist a dictatorship. You are mistaken. The people who are killed in reaction to resistance are not as many as by dictatorship itself. There is responsibility of regional actors to attack dictatorship."

Museveni had a point, of course. Even the best-intentioned of Africa's leaders must choose between painful alternatives. Meek submission to tyranny would be unacceptable, yet nonviolent resistance would likely be ineffectual. That is why outside powers are essential, from the point of view of the tyrant as well as that of his subjects. Outside powers possess the resources and the clout that nonviolent regional actors otherwise lack. Without the backing of an outside power, Africans have long since learned, nonviolent resistance to tyranny is futile.

"I hope he will survive"

Barely a month before my meeting with Museveni in New York, Hassan al-Turabi was being maneuvered out of power in Khartoum, betrayed by his allies in the military regime of his former confederate, General Omar al-Bashir. The general took over Turabi's party, renamed the Popular National Congress, and the companies that financed it. In the game of musical chairs that is Sudanese politics, however, Turabi was hardly out of the picture. He was left free to speak, apparently to prevent him from being seen as a martyr. There was speculation in Khartoum that Sadiq al-Mahdi, presently in exile and allied with John Garang, might return to Khartoum and form an alliance with Turabi. In the meantime, reported *The Economist*, "Mr. Turabi's talk is peppered with new words and phrases: democracy, tolerance, rights of women, free and fair elections. The man who set up Islamic militias to fight a *jihad* in the south is now telling young people not to give up their lives for oil."

Meanwhile, Sudan's endless war simmered on. Government forces continued bombing civilians, driving thousands from their homes, and in August 2000 Bashir's air force bombed United Nations aircraft delivering emergency aid to the south. The bombings led the U.N.'s Operation Lifeline Sudan to suspend relief flights to hundreds of thousands of people newly threatened with starvation. Flush with new oil revenues secured in partnership with the Chinese army and a Canadian firm, Talisman Energy Corp., Bashir's regime was busily rearming, press-ganging young men for the army and pouring out militaristic propaganda on its radio and television stations. John Garang's SPLA was attacking the government-controlled oil fields. Garang was newly allied with Riek Machar, who had signed a peace accord of his own with the regime in 1997 and openly joined forces with Khartoum before things turned sour and he returned to the bush.

As I learned of these doings from afar, I found myself thinking not of Riek, or Garang, or Turabi, or even Museveni, but of a twenty-four-year-old U.N. radio operator named Peter Gatreak. He had been my guide in Akobo. Peter was a delightful companion, warm, curious, and, like so many in that part of the world, physically striking: tall and thin as a toothpick, pitch black, with huge teeth and four parallel scars across his forehead—the markings of the Nuer. Like everyone's in Akobo, Peter's life had been one long series of uprootings and losses. He was a refugee in Ethiopia for seven years. His father was killed in the war. His mother died from hunger. Aunts and uncles, brothers and sisters, in-laws, cousins, friends—"so many" also died. "We are suffering indeed from hunger," Peter told me. He'd never been to school. He had no memory of peace. He had no ambitions for his week-old son, beyond "I hope he will survive."

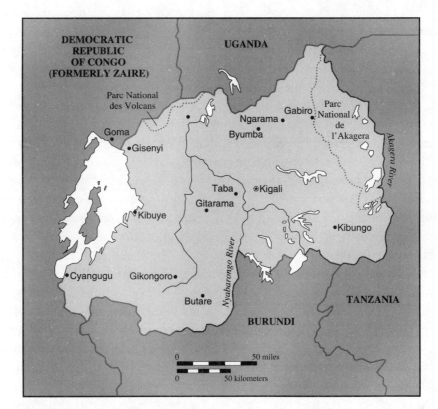

Rwanda

6

THE DEFENDANT

On that Friday morning in March 1998, at the moment just before noon when his defense against the charge of genocide began to fall apart, Jean-Paul Akayesu dabbed his brow with a folded snow-white handkerchief. He took a sip of his bottled water. He straightened his necktie and fingered the lapels of his smart blue suit. On the floor beneath the witness stand, Akayesu's wingtip-clad right foot vibrated rhythmically, the heel bouncing up and down so violently that his entire body shook.

"I did not hold a meeting," he said. "I did not participate in a meeting."

His words by themselves were innocuous. But in the packed spectators' gallery behind him, behind the ceiling-high wall of bullet-proof glass, the simultaneous translation filtered through our head-sets with the impact of an electrical charge. Jaws dropped. Eyes exchanged astonished glances.

The meeting in question occurred on April 18, 1994, in Akayesu's native Rwanda, in a town called Giterama. This was two weeks into Rwanda's three-month genocide. The bludgeoned and severed bodies of the country's Tutsi minority were piling up three times as quickly as Jewish dead accumulated in Nazi Europe; upwards of half a million Tutsis would be killed by the end of June. The meeting in Giterama was chaired by Rwanda's prime minister at the time, Jean Kambanda. By all accounts save Akayesu's, Kambanda's message was simple: it was time for the assembled Hutu government officials to put aside their differences, to "come together and fight the enemy"—that is, to exterminate the Tutsis without further delay.

Akayesu at that time was the *bourgmestre*, or mayor, of Taba Commune, a rural farming community set amid banana palms and eucalyptus trees in the mist-shrouded hills just west of Kigali, the Rwandan capital. He was forty-one years old, a father of five. He had been a popular mayor from a fledgling opposition party, a schoolteacher by training, well educated, articulate, with no known history of criminality or bigotry. By all accounts he actually resisted the genocide in those first two weeks.

But after that fateful meeting in Giterama, according to the many survivors and witnesses who testified against him, Akayesu changed. He appeared to have made, they said, a cynical calculation that the wind was blowing in favor of genocide and the time had come to get with the program. He decided to lead the killings in Taba, and with his decision, hundreds of his constituents obediently picked up their machetes and joined him.

Exchanging his civilian coat for a camouflage military jacket, Akayesu made speeches denouncing Tutsi men, women and children as *ibyitsu*, "accomplices," of a Tutsi-led rebel insurgency. He set up roadblocks where Tutsis were identified by their pale-green identity cards and hauled away to their deaths. He personally hunted down fellow Hutus who were in hiding and beat them into betraying their Tutsi neighbors. Then he tracked down those neighbors and ordered them shot or hacked to death by the hundreds. And as the slaughter intensified, several witnesses recalled with chilling precision, Akayesu incited his men to gang-rape Tutsi women, gloating, "Never ask me what a Tutsi woman tastes like."

"Betrayal" was the word survivors used to account for Akayesu's conduct at the Bureau Communal, Taba's humble government compound of brick-and-stucco buildings around a red dirt courtyard. Hundreds of Tutsis had sought refuge there, assuming Akayesu would protect them. "I went to the Bureau Communal to alert Akayesu so that he would be helpful to us," said one. Instead, "He killed us and killed our people."

Another recalled Akayesu telling them, "Wicked people, wicked people no longer have a right to shelter."

The images of calculated evil were difficult to square with the cornered figure squirming in the witness stand in front of us now at the United Nations International Criminal Tribunal for Rwanda, in Arusha, Tanzania. Akayesu had spent eight hours on the stand the previous day giving his own version of events. He had portrayed himself as an ineffectual, indecisive, powerless man dominated by a murderous superior. "I was completely overwhelmed," he claimed.

But now, on this cathartic final day of testimony in his fifteen-month-long trial, Akayesu was ensnared in a web of deepening contradictions. To begin with, the issue was not *whether* the defendant had actually attended a meeting in Giterama. He had spent most of the previous hour recounting the meeting in detail. His characterization of what transpired was implausible. He described a bewildering, seemingly pointless gathering of high Rwandan officials at a time of widespread mass slaughter in their country, in which, to hear him tell it, the fact that most of the victims were Tutsis never came up, and the identity of the "enemy" was ambiguous. Then, under intense questioning from prosecutor and judges alike to account for his own role in the meeting, Akayesu blurted out, incredibly, that he had actually stood up and denounced the killing of Tutsis. But only the day before he had testified that there was no mention of the killing of Tutsis. "No, no," he had said, "honestly speaking, frankly speaking, there was never any question of Tutsis being killed, never never." As for himself, he testified, "I said nothing."

Now, finally, he was confronted with the fact that he originally had denied ever attending such a meeting.

The prosecutor bearing down on Akayesu was an American, thirty-four-year-old Pierre-Richard Prosper of Los Angeles. Prosper asked Akayesu to read aloud from the transcript of a nine-hour interview he gave to investigators for the tribunal who first interviewed him after his arrest in 1996. They, too, had asked Akayesu about the Giterama meeting. Akayesu now read his reply to the court: " 'I did not hold a meeting. I did not participate in a meeting.' "

Whether he was lying now or lying before was immaterial: he was cooked. After listening for fifteen months to a parade of witnesses testify in detail about his conduct after that meeting, Akayesu had now completely changed his story.

"Well," he stammered, "I put aside the fact that I participated in a meeting. Ask me why. Ask me why I didn't talk about having participated in a meeting."

Prosper put the question this way: "Is it because you knew what the message was at this meeting? The message of 'come together and killing the Tutsis'? And is it because you knew that by admitting you were at that meeting, it would become evidence of your guilt, that you received the message and went out and implemented the plan in Taba? And are you changing your testimony today because we heard witnesses who testified and placed you at the meeting? Is that what's happening here, Mr. Akayesu?"

"You are interpreting me completely differently," Akayesu protested. But now the judges piled on. One by one they ridiculed the accused. The presiding judge, Laity Kama of Senegal, was first: "Did he or did he not attend a meeting?" he asked. "That's the question."

Prosper: "You heard the president, Mr. Akayesu."

Akayesu: "Yes I attended a meeting."

Judge Kama: " So what do you mean by 'I did not participate in a meeting'? Because people say that you changed after that meeting."

Akayesu was silent for a moment. His foot vibrated frantically. Finally he replied.

"Ah, Mr. President, I can't remember."

"Our last redemption"

Four years after Rwanda's genocide established a new standard for state-orchestrated barbarity on a continent plagued by such crimes, the United Nations International Criminal Tribunal for Rwanda had received precious little attention in the west—lamentably so. For unlike its counterpart for the former Yugoslavia taking place in The Hague, the Rwanda tribunal held out the promise of bringing to book some of the most notorious accused war criminals in its mandate. It also had the potential to demystify the "Dark Continent": to document for an international audience—and for history—how "tribalism" in Africa is a product not of ancient, inscrutable hatreds but of calculated tyranny.

The Arusha tribunal, poorer cousin of its counterpart in The Hague, was established in October 1994 after a United Nations Commission of Experts found that the "concerted, planned, systematic and methodical" acts of "mass extermination perpetrated by Hutu elements against the Tutsi group" in Rwanda "constitute genocide." Together the two tribunals represented the first international attempt since the Nuremberg and Tokyo trials to prosecute suspects for war crimes, crimes against humanity, and genocide. Their aim was to document atrocities and hold individuals accountable and thereby to arrest a culture of impunity that has been the bane, as we've seen, not just of Rwanda but also of much of the rest of a continent where time and again entire ethnic groups have been blamed for the crimes of their leaders.

The tribunals were at the cutting edge of a growing movement to establish international institutions of justice and accountability for mass violence—a movement that began with the Nuremberg and Tokyo war crimes trials a half century ago. The trials that convicted Nazi war criminals at Nuremberg were, as the chief prosecutor, the former U.S. Supreme Court justice Robert Jackson, famously argued, "one of the most significant tributes that Power has ever paid to reason." Jackson also asserted the importance to history of an irrefutable body of evidence about Nazi barbarism. "We must establish incredible events by credible evidence," he wrote.

Generations of historians have been grateful for his success, but political support for such trials languished throughout the half a century of the Cold War. The idea of international institutions of accountability for mass violence was viewed as a naive pipe-dream in a period in which anticommunism (or anticapitalism) was the only goal of foreign policy; neither side wanted its own conduct, or that of its clients, exposed to legal scrutiny. In the decade since the collapse of the Berlin Wall, however, the idea had gained widespread support, and the tribunals themselves, though far from perfect, had taken on a life of their own.

The two tribunals were seen as trial runs for the permanent International Criminal Court endorsed by 120 nations at a conference in Rome in July 1998. The Clinton administration was opposed to a permanent tribunal, fearing that U.S. troops around the world could be hauled before it on specious grounds, but it supported the tribunals at The Hague and in Arusha. Secretary of State Madeleine Albright was an early outspoken advocate. When she was ambassador to the United Nations in the first Clinton term, she repeatedly invoked the Nuremberg precedent. Prosecutions before an international tribunal, she said, "will establish the historical record before the guilty can reinvent the truth." The United States was the largest contributor to the Rwanda tribunal, putting up more than $45 million in the tribunal's first four years. David J. Scheffer, the Clinton administration's ambassador at large for war crimes, spoke of what he hoped would be "a powerful Nuremberg-like signal sent to the people of Rwanda."

Of course, international support for the tribunal was not purely a function of high-minded idealism. As world leaders including President Clinton belatedly conceded, the international community failed abysmally in 1994 to prevent the genocide in the first place. The world quite literally stepped aside when the massacres began, leaving Rwandans to their fate.

We now know that the United States actually blocked the U.N. from intervening in Rwanda. The Clinton administration, soured by its experience in Somalia, was reluctant to intervene in another African nation in which American interests were not obvious. It ignored powerful warnings of impending genocide in 1993 and early 1994, including a Central Intelligence Agency report that half a million people could die. Even when it became clear that thousands of Rwandan civilians were in mortal danger, the United States blocked the U.N. from taking action. President Clinton told the U.N. in 1994 that it had to learn "when to say no." At the height of the killings, State Department spokesmen were instructed not to use the word "genocide" for fear that such a term would create pressure to act. Later, in March 1998, when Clinton visited Rwanda briefly during his tour of the continent—three months after Akayesu's testimony—the President acknowledged, "We did not act quickly enough."

France was more directly implicated. France was closely allied with the embattled Rwandan regime of President Juvenal Habyarimana, which carried out the genocide. The government of the former French president François Mitterrand armed and trained Habyarimana's army and allied militias, and there were reports, denied by the government, that France continued to arm the regime throughout the genocide. France finally sent troops into Rwanda in June 1994 in a controversial intervention that helped to put an end to the massacres but enabled the perpetrators to flee the country.

Akayesu's trial bequeathed to history dramatic evidence of the world's acquiescence in the genocide. The week before my visit to Arusha, the former commander of a United Nations peacekeeping force in Rwanda in 1994, Canada's Maj. Gen. Romeo Dallaire, was called to testify. He asserted that his force could have halted the genocide had it committed sufficient troops and given them the authority to aggressively pursue those carrying out the massacres. In five and a half hours of emotional testimony, Major General Dallaire reminded the judges of a by now infamous fax he sent to his superiors at U.N.

headquarters in New York in January 1994 warning, on the basis of information obtained from an informant, that large-scale massacres were imminent. He insisted that if the U.N. had taken the steps he called for at the time, his peacekeepers "would have been able to save the lives of hundreds of thousands of Rwandans."

"Seems as though you regret this, major general," one of Akayesu's lawyers said to Dallaire at one point.

"You cannot even imagine," Dallaire replied.

With this sorry record in mind, the chief prosecutor for both the Hague and Arusha tribunals at the time of Akayesu's trial, Judge Louise Arbour of Canada, compared the role of the tribunals to that of domestic criminal courts. "Criminal law kicks in when all other institutions have failed," she said. "This is our last redemption, our last chance to contribute toward some sort of resolution of these situations. We should not short-change history by failing to show the magnitude of the criminal organization, and the criminal drive."

The Arusha trials have already had a profound impact on the nature of human rights investigations in Africa. In the 1970s and 1980s, human rights investigations aimed at simply establishing that abuses had occurred, so as to provide grounds for pressuring governments to curtail abuses. Now, with the establishment of war crimes tribunals, human rights investigations are implicitly aimed at developing evidence for prosecution. The implications of this change could be seen in the experience in early 1998 of the U.N. team investigating the alleged massacres of Hutu refugees in northern and eastern Congo. The main suspects were troops loyal to the rebel leader Laurent Kabila and the Rwandan army leader, Gen. Paul Kagame, during the seven-month war that brought down Mobutu of (then) Zaire. The U.N. team was finally withdrawn from Congo in April 1998 after months of futile attempts to carry out their investigation. There seemed to be little doubt that the obstacles encountered by the U.N. team in Congo were linked to the proceedings in Arusha—to the fear among those allegedly responsible for the massacres that the investigation might lead to their indictment for war crimes. To no one's surprise, when the U.N. team issued its admittedly incomplete report in June accusing Congolese and Rwandan troops of massacring an unknown number of Hutu civilian refugees, it explicitly called for establishment of a tribunal to prosecute those responsible.

Notwithstanding corruption scandals and management problems in its first two years (most of which had been cleaned up by the time Akayesu took the stand, according to a U.N. audit) and continuing inexcusable delays, the Rwanda tribunal had a chance to produce what the Yugoslav tribunal probably never will: a measure of justice for top conspirators, and a coherent narrative of how the conspiracy was organized. Many of the most senior figures in the genocide were already in custody, including the former defense minister, Theoneste Bagosora—Rwanda's Himmler—and the notorious radio propagandist Ferdinand Nahimana.

Barely two months after Akayesu's dramatic testimony, the former prime minister Kambanda pleaded guilty to six counts of genocide—the first guilty plea in an international court and a landmark in the history of war crimes prosecutions. His cooperation with prosecutors yielded ever-stronger evidence against his co-conspirators.

Akayesu's trial was notable for another reason: it set a precedent for the prosecution of sexual violence as a component crime of genocide. Tens of thousands of Tutsi women were raped during the massacres. This was itself a method of tyranny. Military and political leaders like Akayesu specifically encouraged sexual violence as a means of terrorizing and degrading the Tutsi community and furthering the ultimate goal of the genocide: the destruction of the Tutsis as a group. The Hutu propagandists specifically targeted Tutsi women, portraying them as calculating seductress-spies bent on undermining the Hutus. The propaganda was based on a widespread stereotype of Tutsi women as desirable—the Kinyarwanda word is *ibizungerezi*, beautiful and sexy. The notorious *Kangura* ("Wake-up") newspaper edited by another defendant in Arusha, Hassan Ngeze, warned Hutu men to be on guard against Tutsi women. The newspaper warned that a Tutsi-led rebel insurgency will not hesitate to transform their sisters and wives into "pistols." Rape survivors interviewed by investigators for Human Rights Watch recalled comments such as those chillingly recounted by one Tutsi woman, identified as Witness JJ, who testified she heard Hutu men say: "We want to see how sweet Tutsi women are"; or "You Tutsi women think you are too good for us."

Akayesu was not accused of directly participating in rape, but he allegedly incited his men to rape and was a witness to numerous rapes. An early witness testified that she had seen rapes by men under Akayesu's command. Judge Navanethem Pillay of South Africa, the tribunal's only female judge, wanted details. Another witnesses described gang-rapes at the Bureau Communal. After Human Rights Watch and women's groups pressed the tribunal to take rape seriously, the court adjourned for more investigation, and Akayesu's indictment was finally amended to include rape.

"From time immemorial, rape has been regarded as spoils of war," Judge Pillay told me. "Now it will be considered a war crime. More and more evidence is emerging in Yugoslavia and here that rape was part of the general plan: targeting a group. We want to send out a strong signal that rape is no longer a trophy of war."

I was attending Akayesu's trial on my first trip back to Central Africa since 1994, when I witnessed Rwanda's genocide and its immediate aftermath. Those few weeks in June and July 1994 had left me haunted and bewildered. Churches filled waist-high with decomposing corpses, orphans pulled from the piles of their murdered relatives, mass cholera, all those hideous machete wounds—there was a weird, surreal, science fiction quality to Rwanda's catastrophe that defied easy emotions.

I had no real desire to go back. It was not so much the scale of the crime as the breadth of complicity that soured me. But the search for justice was something I couldn't ignore. It had become clear early on that the massacres were state-orchestrated. In the years since the genocide, commentators had rarely failed to note that what happened in Rwanda was not "just another tribal slaughter." But after a decade of reporting on Africa's conflicts, I knew that there was in fact no such thing as "just another tribal slaughter." They are all provoked from on high. What set Rwanda apart, and what drew me back, was not the fact of a conspiracy but the belated recognition of that fact by the world at large, and the decision—in the form of the Arusha tribunal—to try to do something about it.

Akayesu's trial promised to be especially interesting for the light it would shed on the ultimate mystery of Rwanda: How was it possible? Rwanda's genocide killed more people more quickly than any other mass slaughter in recorded history. The unprecedented velocity of killing would not have been possible without the participation of hundreds of thousands of ordinary civilians. Neighbor turned against neighbor. This trial might help to answer the question I had put to François Xavier Sibomana, the Hutu farmer and father of eight who admitted to me in that vacant lot in Kabuga, in June 1994, that he had killed his own brother-in-law: How could so many ordinary people participate in so monstrous a crime?

"They must respect the rules"

Akayesu was neither a twisted psychopath nor a manipulated simpleton. He was not a top figure like Bagosora, nor a lowly, illiterate, machete-wielding peasant like François Sibomana. He was, instead, the link between the two: an archetype of the indispensable middle management of the genocide. He personified a rigidly hierarchical society and a culture of obedience, without which killing on such a scale would not have been possible.

"It wouldn't have happened without him," said Ephraim Karangwa, Akayesu's successor as *bourgmestre* of Taba. "Two thousand wouldn't have died. At the beginning, people here did not want to kill each other. But when Akayesu started holding meetings and pushing people to kill, the killing started. The *bourgmestre* is a person whom people respect."

Karangwa and I were sitting in Akayesu's old office at the Bureau Communal, a week after Akayesu's two days on the stand in Arusha. The *bourgmestre*'s office was a spare, bare-walled room with a metal desk, patent leather couch and a coffee table, but no electricity or telephone. The window behind me looked out on the red-dirt courtyard where four years earlier Akayesu made his speeches beseeching the *Interahamwe* militia—the name means "those who attack together"—to hunt down and kill the "enemy." Across the road, in a leafy grove where barefoot boys tended cattle, two mass graves rimmed with wildflowers held the remains of the two thousand Tutsis murdered in Taba in 1994.

Karangwa is a slightly built man with a scraggly beard and wary, darting eyes. Like most officials who wield real power in Rwanda today, including judges, jailers and prosecutors, Karangwa is Tutsi, a survivor of the genocide who lost many relatives. He had served under Akayesu as a police inspector. In April 1994 he watched from a hiding place as Akayesu ordered the murder of his two brothers. He says Akayesu sought to kill him too but couldn't find him.

In the middle of our discussion, the *bourgmestre* abruptly rose from his seat and dashed out of the room. Upon returning, he explained matter-of-factly that he had spotted a stranger in the courtyard and dispatched his aides to investigate. It was a startling illustration of the tight control the *bourgmestre* exercises over his tiny rural community—and of the tense security situation in Rwanda four years after the genocide, as an ongoing Hutu-led insurgency and government reprisals deepened mistrust.

"When you are a leader," Karangwa continued, "if you are in a position of authority, every time you tell the people something, they consider it the truth because you are an authority. They know you are there to lead them, and if you tell them to do anything, they know it is the truth."

Even killing? I asked.

"Yes. If you are the *bourgmestre* and you tell people that the Tutsis want to kill us so we must kill them, do you think that the people won't do that?"

No one really knows what proportion of Rwanda's Hutus participated in the genocide. My driver and my translator that day, who were both of mixed parentage and had fled the country during the massacres, debated the matter over a lunch of roasted beef *brochette* in a roadside café. Deo, the translator, estimated no more than 5 percent participated; Yayah, the driver, said 40 percent killed. The discussion went back and forth without result, except to conclude, as Yayah put it, "This is a country where every Tutsi lost a relative in the genocide, and every Hutu has a relative in prison. It's an impossible situation."

Karangwa, the *bourgmestre*, attached a rational motive—self-defense—to an ingrained inclination to obey an "authority." But Rwanda's culture of obedience goes deeper than that. I would encounter a vivid illustration of this phenomenon later that week when I visited one of the provincial prisons in search of François Sibomana. Rwanda's prisons were then holding some 130,000 accused *génocidaires*. In the eastern province of Kibungo, the main prison is a squat brick edifice built to house 1,000 detainees. On the day of my visit there were 3,196 inmates, virtually all of them genocide suspects, including 112 women and 132 minors. There were also 25 infants, growing up in confinement with their imprisoned mothers.

Conditions were typical of prisons across the country, which is to say: unspeakable. An overpowering stench of weeks-old sweat and filth and urine hit me as I waded into the densely packed dormitories.

As my eyes adjusted to the dark, I became aware of hundreds of eyes peering out of the blackness, some within inches of my face. There were no lights or toilet facilities. Prisoners used chamber pots to relieve themselves. The sleeping quarters were pitch dark but for slim window slits. Ventilation was nil. There were no beds or mattresses. The prisoners slept shoulder to shoulder on flattened cardboard boxes arrayed on shelves akin to a chicken-coop. Their clothes and other belongings hung like stalactites from the ceiling. The prison yard was packed to overflowing, covered with a coat of soot from smoke billowing out of the cooking tent at one end of the courtyard, where inmates stirred massive vats of beans and rice. Streams of fresh sewage dribbled around me. Lice, malaria, ringworm, typhoid, and dysentery were rampant.

In 1995 as many as nine prisoners per day were dying in Rwanda's prisons. Conditions were said to have improved by the time I arrived, but disease, dehydration and suffocation remained common. It was hard not to imagine that, guilty or not, these people were enduring a fate worse than death. This really was hell on earth.

My guide through Kibungo prison was the elected leader of the prisoners, a thirty-eight-year-old former businessman named Joas Kaburame, himself accused of genocide. He told me he was framed by a former lover who was jealous of his marriage to another woman. It could be true—who knows? No trial was imminent, he said. The Rwandan government was estimating that at the current rate it would take four hundred years to try all those accused of complicity in the genocide.

I asked Kaburame what seemed to me an obvious question: Was there ever any violence in this awful place?

"There are no fights," he replied matter-of-factly, without a trace of irony. "It's forbidden to fight. They must respect the rules."

This was the culture of obedience, chillingly illuminated, at the very heart of Rwanda's darkness: three thousand accused mass murderers packed in horrendous conditions like snakes in a bottle—and no violence. They are forbidden to fight, and so they don't. It goes a long way toward explaining the velocity of a mass slaughter that was orchestrated on high but implemented by tens of thousands of ordinary civilians at the grass roots. It also underscores the critical importance of local middlemen like Jean-Paul Akayesu. Rwanda is a nation of followers, people who "must obey the rules," and do.

The "Hamitic hypothesis"

Of course, many other factors also contributed to the genocide: a menacing insurgency, external arms deliveries to all sides, economic insecurities and acute population pressures. There was chicanery and lack of nerve by leading Western states, and the dereliction of duty by the United Nations peacekeeping force on the ground in Rwanda at the start of the massacres. Not least, there was real bigotry.

As we saw in Liberia and Zaire, in Sudan and Uganda, it was a bigotry born of history. In Rwanda the bigotry was amplified by an elaborate system of myths built up around that history and broadly accepted by Hutus and Tutsis alike. It has often been remarked that Hutus and Tutsis—the latter make up roughly 15 percent of the population—meet none of the conditions normally associated with distinct tribes. For centuries they have spoken the same language, lived on the same hillsides and intermarried to such an extent that the physical characteristics stereotypically attributed to them—tall, thin and lighter-skinned for the Tutsis; short, stocky and darker-skinned for the Hutus—are often blurred. Specialists on the region often protest that the distinctions between the two groups are artificial. But sixty years of colonial rule and thirty-five years of Hutu domination yielded real divisions: deep-seated stereotypes, and reservoirs of envy, fear and mistrust that were ripe for exploitation. The fact that leaders manipulated ethnic divisions for their own cynical ends does not change the fact that the divisions were there to be manipulated, in the hearts and minds of those below. Yes, Rwanda was a land of followers, but they were followers prepared to hate and fear.

Rwanda was a textbook example of the destructive legacies of "indirect rule." Before colonial rule, Rwanda was a highly organized feudal kingdom. Tutsi chiefs were overlords, but ethnic distinctions were fluid, and social mobility was commonplace. First the Germans and then the Belgians introduced a system of indirect rule whereby the Tutsi chiefs controlled the Hutu majority and extracted its labor on behalf of the colonial power. Indirect rule, as we've seen across the continent in the colonial era, was a means my which minority groups and traditional chiefs were vested with power and privilege, educated and trained, and subcontracted to do the dirty work on behalf of the white man. Resentments grew accordingly, nowhere more so than in Rwanda and neighboring Burundi.

In Rwanda the malignant consequences of indirect rule were magnified by an explicit racial ideology known as the "Hamitic hypothesis." European racial theorists concocted out of thin air the "scientific" notion that "white Africans" from the northeast had brought civilization to the rest of the primitive continent. The Tutsis of Rwanda were held up as just such a superior race, intellectually gifted, morally uplifted, born to rule. The Hutus, on the other hand, were considered dumb beasts of burden, ill suited to be anything more than soil-tilling subjects. Education privileges for the Tutsis reinforced these stereotypes. A system of population registration, including ethnically based identity cards, cemented them.

Tutsis, not surprisingly, embraced these myths as justification for their privileged position. Generations of European and Rwandan Tutsi intellectuals elaborated on a pseudo-anthropology of Tutsi superiority and Hutu incompetence. Elitism evolved into racism, and a myth of historic Tutsi domination—and cunning—came to be broadly accepted by Hutus and Tutsis alike. Sixty years of humiliating subjugation yielded among Hutus what the French scholar Gérard Prunier has called "an aggressively resentful inferiority complex," which their leaders were keen to exploit.

In the "social revolution" of 1959–62, in which the Belgians were driven out, upwards of 10,000 Tutsis were murdered, and as many as 300,000 were driven into exile in neighboring countries. Thousands more were murdered and exiled in subsequent waves of repression. For the next three decades Hutu politicians, no more democratic than their Tutsi predecessors, justified their rule by reinforcing Hutu fears of Tutsi perfidy.

The slide toward genocide began in October 1990, after the Rwandan Patriotic Front (RPF), a rebel insurgency led by Tutsi exiles, invaded from Uganda. Their aim was to pressure the government of President Juvenal Habyarimana to allow Rwanda's exiled Tutsis to return. Three years of fighting ended in a stalemate, and President Habyarimana was forced to enter into a power-sharing agreement with the Tutsi rebels. By then extremists within Habyarimana's embattled regime had begun formulating a plan to subvert the agreement and destroy the rebels by exterminating their base of support.

A key component of the plan was a virulent propaganda campaign, crafted by prominent Hutu intellectuals like Ferdinand Nahimana, now in custody in Arusha, which tapped into and inflamed the old

Hutu fears and resentments and stereotypes—and the campaign worked. On April 6, 1994, President Habyarimana's plane was shot down—most likely by his own hard-line allies. The president's assassination was immediately blamed on the Tutsis and pointed to as proof of Tutsi deviousness; it provided the pretext for the massacres to begin.

Within days, neighbor turned against neighbor, friend against friend. It was a measure of the psychosis that gripped Rwanda then that some of Taba's Tutsis returned again and again to the Bureau Communal even as the killing accelerated, in the hope, they said, of a swifter end to their agony. "I sought refuge there because I knew that people who were going there would be killed by bullets," testified the thirty-five-year-old mother of four who was identified in the vernacular of the tribunal's precarious witness protection program as Witness JJ. "I didn't want to be killed by machetes and clubs."

It was Witness JJ's graphic testimony that finally conveyed the unfathomable horror of those events in Taba. She had been raped six times by stoned and drunken Hutus wielding clubs, machetes and pickaxes in the compound's cultural center, while Akayesu looked on.

"It was very difficult for me indeed to put my legs together, to put my thighs together," she recalled. "I felt so weak, I was so weak. I had lost my mind. I was wishing I had died at that time."

Witness JJ watched helplessly as her sister was raped and then hacked to death with machetes. Her husband had already been shot. In all, seven of ten in her immediate family were killed. But perhaps the worst betrayal was that of a Hutu couple with whom she had left her twenty-month-old son. She thought she could trust them to protect him; instead they killed him.

"I hate myself," she whispered on the witness stand.

When Akayesu's lawyer asked Witness JJ why she repeatedly returned to an area where she had already been beaten and raped, she replied, "Well, we would come there actually to seek out our own deaths. We had commanded and demanded that we be killed, but our death kept being postponed to tomorrow and the next day."

"Progress along a continuum"

In July 1994 the Rwandan Patriotic Front finally routed the Hutu regime and ended the genocide, and a million Hutus fled the country, including many of the *génocidaires* and their leaders. In a familiar pattern, the latter rearmed, using United Nations refugee camps as a base, and they had been fighting ever since to return to power and finish what they started. This had led to the present intractable situation. A minority-led regime was compelled by circumstances beyond its control to govern indefinitely as a military dictatorship, in which even the best-intentioned leaders were trapped by inescapable logic, compelled to shed ever greater quantities of blood merely to survive.

Many advocates for justice in Rwanda, including supporters of the International Criminal Tribunal, believe that justice will lead to "healing" and "reconciliation" between Hutus and Tutsis. That is an unrealistic goal. There are too many other factors in play, and many of them, as in an ongoing civil war, are hardening mistrust. The history is accumulating, and so is the bigotry.

But bigotry alone does not explain mass slaughter. Racial stereotypes, envy, resentment, scapegoating, fear—all helped to make genocide possible, but not inevitable. They help to explain why people followed, but that is not enough to explain what happened. They were there to be manipulated and exploited by cynical and desperate leaders. But what sort of environment spawns such leaders in the first place, and rewards such tactics?

Rwanda was a textbook case of ethnic conflict as a product of tyranny, and of the links between tyranny and anarchy, and those between ethnicity and organized crime. As we noted earlier, there is a widespread misconception of the post–Cold War era that ethnic conflict is a by-product of "failed states." Rwanda represented the opposite: a state that was all too successful in mobilizing along rigidly hierarchical lines from the top down, from the head of state and his ruling clique of co-conspirators down to the last village mayor, making possible the slaughter of hundreds of thousands in barely three months, mostly with clubs and machetes.

Rwanda was a model of order. The country was divided into twelve *préfectures* led by *préfets*; 154 *communes* led by *bourgmestres* like Akayesu; 1,600 *secteurs* led by *conseillers*; and tens of thousands of *cellules*, or groups of households—a top-down network of control rooted in the precolonial kingdom, codified by colonizers, and preserved after independence. Once Hutus had vanquished the Tutsi elite in the early 1960s, they used the preexisting social structure to exercise complete control over the populace. This rigid hierarchy was not to be confused with the rule of law. The rule of the gun was paramount; enforcement was arbitrary.

The psychologist Ervin Staub, in his valuable book *The Roots of Evil: The Origins of Genocide and Other Group Violence*, examined mass slaughters in this century, from the Turkish genocide of the Armenians to the Nazi Holocaust to Pol Pot's genocide in Cambodia. Staub found not just "certain characteristics of a culture and the structure of a society"—such as obedience and hierarchy—that enhance the potential for group violence, but also "a progression of actions," in response to which "the perpetrators change, as individuals and as a group, as they progress along a continuum of destruction that ends in genocide." Rwandans experienced just such a "progress along a continuum of destruction."

In the years leading up to the genocide, massacres of Tutsis had been perpetrated across Rwanda with increasing frequency—and with impunity. Four hundred were slaughtered in Kibilira in 1990, five hundred in Bigogwe in 1991, three hundred in Bugesera in 1992. No one was ever held accountable. The rest of the world paid no heed.

"People had been taught for a long time about killing," Ephraim Karangwa, Akayesu's successor in Taba, reminded me. "People were already sensitized to kill. Akayesu said that the Tutsis had planned to kill Hutus. If you told a Hutu that the Tutsis want to kill people, the Hutu must react."

In Rwanda—very much as in Liberia, Zaire, Sudan, Uganda, and KwaZulu-Natal—the law of the jungle, a culture of impunity, obtained. Rwanda's Hutu elite, those whose excelled in this lawless culture, established a clear example of the state as a racketeering enterprise. Juvenal Habyarimana had governed Rwanda for twenty-three years after the model of his mentor, Mobutu of Zaire. Amply funded and armed by the French, Habyarimana ran lucrative rackets in everything from development aid to marijuana smuggling. He and his in-laws operated the country's sole black-market foreign exchange bureau in tandem with the Central Bank. Habyarimana also was implicated in the poaching of mountain gorillas, selling the skulls and feet of baby primates. Habyarimana's brother-in-law was the principal suspect in the murder of the American anthropologist Dian Fossey.

This was the criminal culture in which the genocide was hatched. Like gangsters and despots through the ages, Habyarimana apparently was consumed by the monster he created.

On the afternoon before Akayesu took the witness stand, I had lunch in Arusha with Pierre-Richard Prosper, the prosecutor. The son of Haitian immigrants, he is an affable, intense, athletic-looking man with piercing brown eyes and a boyish smile. His main prior experience was prosecuting members of Colombian drug cartels and street gangs in Los Angeles. I asked Prosper about the political culture in which Akayesu operated. He replied by comparing it to the criminal culture in Colombia that evolved out of the civil conflict known as *la violencia*, which claimed some 200,000 to 300,000 lives between 1948 and 1953.

"In Colombia, businessmen are opportunists taking advantage of a criminal environment for personal gain," Prosper said. "It was the same for politicians in Rwanda. Akayesu was an opportunist, completely amoral." He compared the *Interahamwe* militias to the ethnically based street gangs he had prosecuted in Los Angeles. "In gangs, it's more criminal-minded. They live in a criminal world. Ties of blood and ethnicity are huge. It's a family. People will go to any extreme to protect their turf and reputation."

Akayesu, Prosper said, was "like a businessman with two faces, an opportunist who joined a criminal enterprise. He's doing business in an environment where part of doing business is killing people. It was a cold, calculated political decision. He thought he was joining the winning side. It was all about power." Rwanda, Prosper added, was a case of "smart people taking advantage of a criminal environment." There were true believers, he conceded—the fanatical racial theorists of Hutu Power. And there were a great many common criminals who used the genocide as a pretense to loot and steal. But in the final analysis, Prosper said, "You need all three: the ideologues *and* the opportunists *and* the thugs. Otherwise it just won't happen."

I asked Prosper about Akayesu's claim that he had no choice, that he was "completely overwhelmed" by his superiors. "He's showed zero remorse," Prosper replied. "He could have done nothing. He could have gone into hiding. If he had some moral value, he could have fled." Indeed, some 2 million Rwandans, Hutu and Tutsi alike, fled the country in the first two weeks of the genocide—possibly the largest movement of refugees anywhere in the world in history. Two hundred and fifty thousand people entered Tanzania in just forty-eight hours.

There was another dimension of Rwanda's slaughter that goes to the heart of the Arusha tribunal's mission. Justice Richard Goldstone of South Africa, who served as chief prosecutor of the tribunals until 1996, once said that its central mission was to arrest the historic cycle of vengeance-inspired ethnic slaughter. "For the great majority of their histories, the Croats and Serbs and Muslims, and the Tutsis and Hutus, have lived in relative peace with one another," Goldstone said. "Such interethnic violence usually gets stoked by specific individuals intent on immediate political or material advantage, who then call forth the legacies of earlier and previously unaddressed grievances. But the guilt for the violence that results does not adhere to the entire group.

"Specific individuals bear the major share of the responsibility, and it is they, not the group as a whole, who need to be held to account, through a fair and meticulously detailed presentation and evaluation of evidence, precisely so that the next time around no one will be able to claim that all the Serbs did this, or all Croats or all Hutus—so that people are able to see how it is specific individuals who are continually endeavoring to manipulate them in that fashion. I really believe that this is the only way the cycle can be broken."

Justice Goldstone was talking about the devastating cycle of slaughter among Hutus and Tutsis not just in Rwanda but also in neighboring Burundi. Rwanda's border with Burundi is not much farther from downtown Kigali by car than Coney Island is from midtown Manhattan by subway—about an hour. Beginning in 1959, at least 10,000 Rwandan Tutsis were killed by Hutu insurgents, and several hundred thousand were driven into exile. At the time, the late English philosopher Bertrand Russell called those killings in Rwanda "the most horrible and systematic human massacre we have had occasion to witness since the extermination of the Jews by the Nazis." No one was ever held accountable for these massacres, and they could have hardly have been reassuring for the Tutsi oligarchy still holding on to power in neighboring Burundi.

In 1965, some 5,000 to 10,000 Burundian Hutus were killed by a Tutsi-dominated army. That turned out to be a premonitory sign of the awesome carnage of 1972, when upwards of 100,000 Burundian Hutus—some say 200,000—were killed. Then in 1988 Burundi's army killed 20,000 Hutus, and in 1991, another 3,000. As many as 50,000

Burundians—Hutus and Tutsis—were butchered after a Tutsi-led coup in 1993, and perhaps 100,000 have died in Burundi's continuing bloodshed since then. Finally, between 500,000 and 800,000 Rwandan Tutsis and dissident Hutus were killed in the 1994 genocide.

Tutsis killing Hutus, Hutus killing Tutsis—the common denominator in all this slaughter, until now, was the total absence of legal accountability for a single perpetrator at any stage over four decades. In the absence of individual accountability for even one general, tyrant, militia leader or gangster, and with no commonly agreed-upon set of historical facts based on a "fair and meticulously detailed presentation and evaluation of evidence," as Goldstone put it, Tutsis and Hutus alike have blamed each other as a group. And so each has been prepared to believe the worst about each other's intentions in times of chaos, making both groups especially vulnerable to the machinations of the propagandists, and especially amenable to the protection that those sharing the same ethnicity claimed to afford.

Fear, not hatred, was the dominant theme of the Hutu propagandists in Rwanda, who relentlessly terrorized their listeners on two state-allied radio stations both before and throughout the genocide. These propagandist broadcast fabricated tales of harrowing massacres attributed to Tutsi guerrillas and civilians. They warned Hutus that Tutsi-led rebels were bent on reimposing feudalism, wiping out all the Hutus and taking all their land. Many Hutus, looking across that nearby border at what happened in Burundi, believed what they were told, and they did what they thought they must to survive.

Who is fit to judge?

This history raises the question of who is fit to judge. General Paul Kagame, leader of the RPF rebel army that invaded Rwanda in 1990 and now the Big Man in Kigali, is keen to draw parallels between the Tutsis' experience of genocide and that of the Jews. He and his fellow Tutsi generals point to Israel's conduct in the Middle East as a model for their own behavior. Indeed there are legitimate parallels, and they help explain why policy-makers in Washington are reluctant to pass judgment on those who claim to be acting on behalf of Rwanda's Tutsis, survivors of genocide.

But the parallels are not exact. The Jews of Europe were never armed. There was no Jewish conspiracy to dominate Europe, nor had there ever been one. There had been no Jewish tyranny in Germany, as there were Tutsi feudal tyrannies in Rwanda and Burundi, and there had been no Jewish-perpetrated genocides in, say, Austria, as there were Tutsi-perpetrated genocides against Hutus no fewer than three times in a generation in Burundi, just an hour's drive down the road.

These differences by no means absolve Hutus who participated in the genocide, but they underscore the transcendent recklessness of the Tutsi refugees like General Kagame who, in 1990, thought the solution to their exile was an ethnically based armed insurgency against an entrenched and brutal, Hutu-dominated regime in Kigali. No rational man could have looked at the history of repeated mass slaughters in Rwanda and Burundi since 1959 and doubted for a moment that at least one likely outcome of such an invasion was massive violent reprisal against defenseless Tutsi civilians.

General Kagame was not himself a victim. To suggest that he was is to adopt the same logic that informed the genocide, namely that a Tutsi is a Tutsi is a Tutsi, whether armed or unarmed. Kagame and his RPF confederates were armed. The victims of the genocide were unarmed. Kagame may argue, like Museveni in Uganda, that armed rebellion was his only alternative under the circumstances; he surely did not intend for his rebellion to provoke a genocide. He points out that Westerners, including Americans, have often resorted to violence to achieve our ends. Fair enough. But Kagame bears a measure of responsibility for the unintended consequences of his choice of violent means.

The French writer Gérard Prunier, author of an outstanding history of the genocide, *The Rwanda Crisis*, tells the story of the RPF occupation of a town in western Rwanda during the early stages of the war. An old Tutsi man remarked to one of the young guerrilla fighters who had come to "liberate" him: "You want power? You will get it. But here we will all die. Is it worth it to you?" Prunier went on to say, "It is improbable that in late 1990 when Paul Kagame was working day and night to turn the RPF from an alienated band of exiles into an efficient fighting machine, he ever stopped to ask himself what was really going to happen. And in a way it is quite normal. Action carries with it its own logic, and in such situations men who stop to think for too long are likely to end up dead. But given the peculiar nature of the Hutu/Tutsi historical conundrum, historical myths, Belgian colonizers and all, any military action in this context had the inescapable quality of a bull let loose in the proverbial china shop."

Prunier concluded, "There is no reason to doubt the genuineness of the political ideals motivating the front's leaders when they launched their action. But . . . their rock-hard conviction of being right both morally and politically seem to have caused them to underestimate the depth of the irrational myths, fears and hatreds they were about to confront—including probably those lurking on their own side."

For a decade since that first invasion in 1990, Rwanda has been at war, first with itself, then not once but twice with what is now Congo, in each case with staggering costs in civilian casualties. In the pantheon of African rebels who could likewise claim a just cause, General Kagame and his confederates were not as cynically opportunistic as Charles Taylor in Liberia, not as heedlessly brutal as John Garang in Sudan. But Kagame's recklessness was comparable to theirs. Like his mentor and erstwhile ally, Museveni of Uganda, Kagame has shown that even well-intentioned leaders must abide by the murderous logic of the environment in which they are operating: the faces may change, but the rules of the game remain the same. This may be the most important objective of the Arusha tribunal: to begin to change the rules, not just for Rwanda but for much of the rest of Africa as well; to replace the rule of the gun with the rule of law.

"I began to feel some kind of fear"

"I was very much surprised," said that man with the quizzical eyes. "Looking at my neighbors, I thought they were friends. I was very much surprised that they were among the people who came to try to kill us."

Isadore Munyakazi was forty-two years old and balding. He wore a dirty blue shirt and faded brown, threadbare trousers and rubber flip-flops. It was June 1994. We were sitting on benches in the filthy remains of an abandoned corner store, in Kabuga, the rubble-strewn, rebel-held town on the outskirts of Kigali where I had met François-Xavier Sibomana. Rwanda's genocide was still unfolding in the south. The climactic siege of Kigali was under way. Hundreds of dazed survivors of the massacres, some of them wrapped in gauze that barely concealed their ghastly machete wounds, loitered amid the wreckage of their lives in the looted and gutted ruins nearby. Isadore and a friend of his, Bonaventure Niyibizi, both Tutsis, were trying to explain to me how tens of thousands of their fellow countrymen could have been lured, incited or coerced into participating in mass murder.

Isadore, a career civil servant, had survived with his wife and children but lost twenty immediate relatives. Bonaventure, forty, had been the top Rwandan working for the United States Agency for International Development in Kigali before the Americans, along with most other foreigners living in Rwanda, were evacuated in April 1994, leaving their Rwandan colleagues to their fate. Like Isadore, Bonaventure had managed to survive with his wife and three children, but his mother, who was seventy, was killed in what he later learned was sadistic three-day execution: the killers severed her Achilles tendons the first day, hacked off her legs the second day, and returned on the third day to dump her body into a river. His sister was killed with her five children. His wife's sister and *her* three children, his wife's four uncles and all of their children—as many as fifty relatives in all—had been murdered.

"Really," Bonaventure sighed, "I cannot understand it myself."

Rwanda in the spring of 1994 was a place where extreme stories like this—unspeakable, unbelievable, inexplicable—were numbingly commonplace. For me the tone had been set at eight o'clock on my very first morning in May 1994, at a makeshift hospital ward set up in a churchyard in Byumba, high in the heartbreakingly beautiful hills of northern Rwanda—the Switzerland of Africa, they used to call it. Amid the stench of fresh machete wounds and the hollow stares of children with stumps for limbs, I met a thirty-year-old woman named Odette, who carried a baby on her back named Dominique, aged two. The baby wasn't hers. The Presidential Guard had killed Dominique's parents, neighbors of Odette, on the same day they broke into Odette's home at five o'clock in the morning, grabbed her husband and bayoneted him to death, then rounded up her three brothers and four children—ages thirteen, eleven, eight and four—and shot them to death in the living room. Odette had fainted behind the sofa and was left for dead. She wept quietly as she told me her story. "I too find it unbelievable that somebody can have the cruelty of killing even a baby," she said. I asked what should happen to the killers. "They should be punished with the weight that their crime deserves. They should be taken to court and given the death sentence."

On the day before my meeting with Isadore and Bonaventure, I had visited that plain brick church by a dirt road south of Kigali, in a village called Nyamata, that was filled waist-high with several hundred decomposing corpses. The pattern across Rwanda was that many thousands of Tutsis sought refuge in churches or were herded there by Hutu government officials promising protection. One of Akayesu's fellow detainees in Arusha, Clement Kayishema, the alleged "butcher of Kibuye," a pediatrician-turned-*préfet*, stood accused of ordering more than two thousand Tutsis into a Catholic church on April 17, 1994, with a promise that he would protect them there. Instead, witnesses testified, Kayishema fired a gun in the air and ordered members of the army, the communal police, the *Interahamwe* militia and armed civilians to set upon the trapped Tutsis with guns, grenades, pangas, machetes, spears, and cudgels.

The day before, I had met that wide-eyed eleven-year-old girl, Umulisa, with her smudged cheeks and a luminous smile, who had laughed hysterically rather than tell me in her own words about the day two weeks earlier when she fled from her home as the militia arrived, then returned an hour later and discovered her mother and father, brothers and sisters, aunts and uncles in a heap of severed heads and arms and legs on the floor of her living room. This too would become familiar. Hundreds of thousands of Hutu and Tutsi children were orphaned, abandoned or separated from their families in the genocide and subsequent mass exodus and cholera epidemic. Even those lucky enough to avoid being attacked or who survived their machete wounds were tormented by severe psychological trauma. Many had seen their entire families massacred before their eyes. Others had possibly more complicated memories: Hutus who watched their own fathers and uncles and brothers participate in mass murder. Some, including children as young as eleven, were themselves lured into committing acts of butchery.

Dazed and destitute, Rwanda's lost children could be found wandering aimlessly through refugee camps and makeshift orphanages, tense with hunger, wracked by dysentery and malaria, and haunted by images of unspeakable horror.

"I don't miss my parents because they have died," one of them told me.

In a vacant lot less than a block from the store where Isadore, Bonaventure and I were sitting, I had interviewed six admitted members of the Interahamwe militia—François-Xavier Sibomana was one of them—who had been captured days earlier by the Tutsi-led rebels. They were illiterate peasants, husbands and fathers, with thickly callused hands. Most of them, like Sibomana, had spent their entire lives cultivating sorghum and sweet potatoes on the steep mountain slopes of Kibungo Prefecture in eastern Rwanda. Defeated, scared, disheveled, wearing grimy secondhand clothes and sneakers or rubber flip-flops, they spoke in dull monotones under the watchful eyes of their Tutsi captors. They appeared to be men of the herd; each one said he had never killed before. Evidently calculating that it was pointless, and might be fatal, to deny their crimes, they spoke with surprising candor about joining up with the "*Igitero*": a group of attackers, the leaders and the led acting as one.

"Many people contributed to killing one person," one of them told me. "Because they feared the blood of the victim ["a guilty conscience," my translator explained] each person feared to kill alone. We would kill in groups. Even that old man hiding in the sorghum plantation—when we discovered him, Leonard, the militia leader, ordered everybody to hit the old man. Even after he was dead, everybody was supposed to take part in the killing. I used a club."

Another said, "If someone was discovered, we would surround him with sticks and start beating him. Then the rest would come with sticks and machetes and finish him off."

I asked this gentleman if he felt any remorse. "I felt guilty and I felt I was committing a crime," he replied. "I had never killed before so I did not feel comfortable to kill, because I knew these people had committed no crime. But I had to save myself. I had only to do as I was told."

This was the line: they killed because they were forced to. Many were killed for refusing to kill, they said. But further questions yielded a more complicated picture. Fear, not hatred, may have driven them to kill, but it was fear not just of their leaders. It was also fear of those whom they sought to exterminate.

Emmanuel Kamuhanda, eighteen years old, wore a mangy purple corduroy jacket, blue jeans, and plastic high-top sneakers. Sullen and withdrawn, he spoke very quietly, and did not look me in the eye. "I did not want to kill," he told me. "I was just compelled to kill by the leader of the militia." When I asked how many people he had killed, Emmanuel replied, "There were many. Perhaps those who had the lists know better. I can tell you in my village we killed fifteen people.

After my village we went to other villages and killed many. To say there were hundreds would be an understatement. The top leaders of the militia, when they marched us to kill, they had a list of the victims. We were shown who to kill on the list. If you resisted, they would threaten you. They said you must kill or you will be killed."

Yet when I asked Emmanuel *why* he was forced to kill, his reply suggested that he understood the reasons for killing, and that they made sense to him: he believed in what he was doing when he was doing it.

"The government always told us that the RPF was Tutsi and if it wins the war all the Hutus will be killed," he said. "As of now I don't believe this is true. But at the time, because it was the government saying so, using the radio, and because I had not known the RPF before, I believed that the government was telling the truth."

His confederate added, "They were always telling people that if the RPF comes, it will return Rwanda to feudalism, that they would bring oppression."

A third put it this way: "I did not believe the Tutsis were coming to kill us and take our land, but when the government radio continued to broadcast that the RPF is coming to take our land, is coming to kill the Hutus—when this was repeated over and over, I began to feel some kind of fear."

"Accusation in a mirror"

Even as we spoke, I could hear a broadcast of Radio-Télévision Libre Mille Collines (Thousand Hills Free Radio-Television) coming from a transistor radio behind me. RTLM was the main state-aligned radio station, established by hardliners in August 1993, whose virulent propaganda played a central role in the genocide, very much as Joseph Goebbels's broadcast propaganda fueled the Nazi genocide. There was nothing subtle about it.

"Since they are a single ethnic group, we can exterminate them easily," Hutu listeners were told. "Just look at the height and appearance of a person and then mash his pretty little nose. . . . We can't let them attack our country while we cross our little arms and flee in every direction. We must take sticks, clubs, machetes, and stop them from destroying our country."

Rwanda's radio propagandists reinforced the old myths. A mimeographed document entitled "Note Relative à la Propagande d'Expansion et de Recrutement," found by Alison des Forges of Human Rights Watch in Butare Prefecture, shed fascinating light on the calculation behind the radio broadcasts. The author of the document, clearly someone who had studied at university level, tells his colleagues how to sway the public most effectively, conveying lessons drawn from Lenin and Goebbels and from a book called *Psychologie de la publicité et de la propagande,* by Roger Mucchielli, published in Paris in 1970. He advocates using lies, exaggeration, ridicule and innuendo to attack "the enemy." Moral considerations are irrelevant except when they may offer a weapon against the other side. The aim, says the author, is to persuade the public that the "enemy" stands for war, death, slavery, repression, injustice and sadistic cruelty.

A particularly revealing proposal is called "accusation in a mirror," meaning that the propagandists should impute to the enemy what they themselves and their allies are planning to do. "In this way," he explains, "the party which is using terror will accuse the enemy of using terror," and thereby convince even "honest" listeners that they would be justified in taking whatever measures are necessary "for legitimate [self]-defense."

Such "accusations in a mirror" were much in evidence before and during the slaughter. Indeed, much of the propaganda accused the Tutsi-led rebels of seeking to accomplish precisely what the Hutu regime was seeking to accomplish. A week before the massacres began, for example, the state-run station Radio Rwanda attributed to the RPF an ideology of "ethnic purification" that the Habyarimana regime itself was preparing to carry out. The station reported that the Coalition for the Defense of the Republic (CDR), a virulently racist offshoot of Habyarimana's National Republican Movement for Democracy and Development, was "pacifist and realistic because it recognizes the ethnic problem which has been eating away at our country for centuries." The CDR "denounced the ideology of ethnic purification preached by many extremist RPF members," and "urged the RPF to renounce once and for all its ideology of power struggle based on vengeance and revenge."

"Remember the rule of law"

Sitting now in that abandoned store in Kabuga, I put the old familiar question to Isadore and Bonaventure: How is such a horror possible?

"We cannot understand it ourselves," Isadore conceded. When I pressed him, he began by stressing subjective factors peculiar to Rwanda. "Illiteracy is part of it," he said. "Politicians say, 'If you don't do this, it will go back to the fifties. You will be like a slave.' Illiterate people will believe it. They believe what they hear on the radio. They believe what their leaders say. They cannot discover the truth for themselves because of the low level of their education. There is ninety percent illiteracy in some of these areas." An edge of bitterness crept into Isadore's voice. "We are still at a primitive level," he said, "where people think they have to resolve a misunderstanding with a machete."

I asked Bonaventure if he agreed with Isadore that illiteracy explained the disaster. Nazi Germany was one of the most highly educated countries on earth. For that matter, the former Yugoslavia was hardly an illiterate society. Yet both these nations in the heart of Europe had descended into barbarism as extreme as what was now unfolding in Rwanda. Did Bonaventure agree that Hutus were slaughtering Tutsis because Rwanda was "still at a primitive level"?

Bonaventure was silent for a moment. Finally he shook his head. "Remember the rule of law," he said. "It did not exist. People in the country have not learned about the rule of law. There has been no justice in Rwanda. For all the killings and massacres over the years, there has been no justice."

I asked how Rwanda could possibly overcome this disaster.

"There is only one way," Bonaventure replied. "That is to find the people who have been responsible for this and to bring them to trial according to the law."

Isadore agreed, abruptly revising his theory about illiteracy. He drew me up a list of those he would bring to trial. At the top was Colonel Bagosora, the notorious defense chief widely viewed as the mastermind behind the genocide. Isadore scribbled more names. The list grew, until finally he wrote: "all the *préfets*, all the *bourgmestres*, all the *conseillers*."

"Educated people," he explained. "The administrative chain from the president on down. The *préfets* are like governors. The *bourgmestres* are like mayors. They are galvanizing the killers."

I asked Isadore if he would bring his neighbors to trial—the ones he thought were his "good friends." He thought for a moment and shook his head. "To me, they are just instruments," he said. If you will bring these people to justice, you'll take everybody. It will be an endless process. But if the people at the top are punished according to the law, and the population knows that, that is the only way."

Bonaventure vehemently disagreed. "People who have murdered have to be punished," he said. "The level of responsibility is not the same, but you cannot say this person who took a machete and killed this baby—that he is not responsible. He must be responsible for his acts. Ignorance is no defense."

Ubutabera is the Rwandan word for justice. Four years after the genocide, more than 130,000 accused *génocidaires* were in custody in Rwanda itself, housed like vermin in those stench-filled, disease-ridden, densely packed prisons. The new Tutsi-led government was gamely endeavoring to try them, but the results were not pretty. Rwanda's judiciary, like most of the rest of the state, was dismantled, looted and abandoned in 1994. Even with $18 million in foreign support, much of it from the United States, Rwanda's newly created system of poorly educated, hastily trained judges, prosecutors and investigators was hopelessly out of its depth. And in any case, the ongoing civil war was incompatible with basic standards of due process—for example, witness protection was impossible. By the end of that year Rwanda's makeshift domestic courts had tried some 330 people for genocide and condemned 116 to death. In April 1998, firing squads executed 22 of them.

There is a saying in Kigali that life expectancy in Rwanda is twelve hours renewable. Even the government belatedly recognized that the best hope for justice lay outside its borders, under international auspices.

"Sharp force injuries"

The International Conference Center in Arusha, Tanzania, is a musty, rundown cement-walled facility built by the Chinese in the 1970s. Arusha is a faded provincial backwater, about an hour's drive south of Mount Kilimanjaro and the Kenyan border. You get to the conference center in dilapidated taxis that bounce and lurch along a tree-lined, pothole-ridden thoroughfare running the length of the city. Electricity is erratic. The phones are unpredictable. My evening interview with the South African judge, Navanethem Pillay, who in 1999 would succeed Judge Kama as chief judge of the tribunal, was briefly thrown off track when the lights went out; she and I chatted in pitch darkness for a few minutes before an emergency generator rumbled on and the lights returned.

Judge Pillay is a petite, bespectacled, dark-skinned woman whose soft-spoken manner on the bench belies a steely-tough legal mind and an earthy, schmoozing temperament after hours. She has jet-black hair and a luminous smile. A product of apartheid's despised Indian community, Judge Pillay made her name in South Africa representing jailed anti-apartheid activists like Harry Gwala in her native Natal Province in the 1970s and 1980s. She lost far more cases than she won. Many of her clients were brutally tortured in police custody, and she claims credit for being among the first defense lawyers to introduce evidence in court of systematic torture in South Africa's jails, an achievement she recalled two decades later with evident pride.

Sitting in her spare, bare-walled chambers on the night before Akayesu took the stand, Judge Pillay spoke to me at length about her hopes for the tribunal. She left no doubt that she is aiming for history. "Why did this happen?" she said of the genocide. "Our judgement will certainly answer that question. We're addressing history. We won't just say the accused did this or did not. We're a tribunal, not a court."

Judge Pillay was one of those who saw the Rwanda and Yugoslav tribunals as trial runs for a permanent International Criminal Court: "I believe we need an international judicial system," she said. "Too many major criminals, some of whom are heads of state, are protected by other governments. The objective of the International Criminal Court would be to end the culture of impunity on the part of the macro-offenders."

I asked Judge Pillay about the quality of justice coming out of the Arusha trials. "This is an emerging process," she conceded. "There have been many problems, due to the lack of resources and experience. But I'm sure it's going to shape up. The fact that we're here is significant in itself. It's a learning experience. This is why it's slow."

By then everyone agreed that Arusha was a disastrous choice of location for the tribunal. It is hours from Rwanda itself, which was considered too insecure, and witnesses and investigative staff had to be flown back and forth, though the airport does not meet international standards. It is a five-hour bus ride from the regional hub, Nairobi, Kenya, the base for the international press corps, which was thus unable to give it regular coverage. Nairobi, with its easy access and relatively sophisticated infrastructure, would have been the logical choice for the tribunal. It was rejected for political reasons: Kenya's president, Daniel arap Moi, was an ally of the late Rwandan president, Juvenal Habyarimana, and when the tribunal was established in 1994, Kenya was protecting a number of accused war criminals. So the tribunal carried on in isolated, inconvenient Arusha, largely out of sight and out of mind.

The tribunal's lawyers and supporting staff worked in basic offices with stains on the walls and boxes strewn about. The law library, at the time of my visit, was a single spare room with one long table and mostly bare book shelves with a smattering of legal texts (there was, at least, a complete set of the Nuremberg trial transcripts). Everything from computers to stenographic equipment to slide projectors to microphones had to be airlifted in, not to mention staff qualified to operate and maintain them. At the time of my visit there was still no forensic lab.

The establishment of a third trial chamber in May 1998 helped to speed up the tribunal's work, but the inevitable delays and miscues associated with establishing a sophisticated courthouse operation from scratch in this remote Third World outpost had taken their toll. An audit released in February 1997 by the United Nations inspector general found rampant mismanagement and waste. The audit concluded that "not a single administrative area functioned effectively," though none of the tribunal's six judges was implicated. In response, the U.N. secretary general fired the tribunal's registrar and its deputy prosecutor. A more recent audit, released in February 1998, found that "improvements were observed in virtually every area surveyed by the team of investigators and auditors."

The improvements came too late to prevent one disastrous miscarriage of justice that nearly derailed the tribunal. In November 1999 the appeals court in The Hague, which oversees both the Rwanda and Yugoslav tribunals, ordered the release of Jean-Bosco Barayagwiza, a notorious former *préfet* who had been charged with genocide and crimes against humanity. The appeals court said his due process rights had been denied because he was held for nineteen months in Cameroon before being handed over to the tribunal and formally charged—apparently because of the tribunal staff's own negligence. The appeals court eventually reinstated the indictment, but not before an understandably outraged Rwandan government, dominated by now by Tutsi survivors of the genocide, suspended its cooperation with the tribunal for almost six months.

Apart from administrative problems, deeper structural problems were inherent in the context in which the tribunal was operating. Chief among them was witness protection. Rural Rwanda was an intimate society radically polarized by an ongoing civil war. The tribunal's ability to guarantee the safety of its witnesses was limited, especially for defense witnesses. The tribunal had gone to considerable lengths to ensure adequate defense counsel for the accused. It paid more than $1 million to defense lawyers during Akayesu's trial. But defense was not an arm of the tribunal, and states were not inclined to assist defense counsel, especially not for Rwandans accused of genocide. It was all but impossible to investigate the reliability of witnesses who are under protection orders.

For all its problems, the tribunal buzzed with high-stakes drama in the days leading up to Akayesu's appearance on the witness stand. Three other defendants were also on trial that week, and several others from among the twenty suspects in custody appeared in court. In trial chamber 2, Clement Kayishema, the alleged "butcher of Kibuye," sat stone-faced with his co-defendant, Obed Ruzindana, a businessman, as witnesses recalled the massacre of 2,000 Tutsis at the Catholic church in Kibuye. And Bagosora himself made an appearance in trial chamber 2.

Bagosora is widely believed to have been the central figure in the genocide, as well as the main conspirator in the event that triggered it: the shooting down of President Habyarimana's plane on the night of April 6, 1994. Bagosora had been President Habyarimana's right-hand man, a key figure in the infamous "*clan de Madame*," the tight circle of racketeers surrounding the late president's wife, Agathe Habyarimana. Bagosora was arrested in 1996 in Cameroon. Stocky and aloof, he appeared in court looking incongruously professorial in a blue suit and crimson bow tie and wearing wire-rim glasses.

Alternating with Akayesu in trial chamber 1 was Georges Rutaganda, former vice president of the *Interahamwe*, who was accused of genocide and crimes against humanity. Rutaganda's initial defense lawyer, Luc De Temmerman of Belgium, achieved a measure of notoriety early on when he claimed, "There was no genocide. It was a situation of mass killings in a state of war where everyone was killing their enemies."

Testifying for the prosecution that week in the Rutaganda trial was Dr. William Haglund, an American forensic anthropologist from Seattle who had played an important role in the Yugoslav tribunal as well. Haglund had examined the remains of twenty-seven men and women in a mass grave behind Rutaganda's garage in Kigali, where Tutsis apprehended at a nearby roadblock allegedly were disposed of. "See the fracture line around nearly 180 degrees of the skull?" Haglund asked the judges, narrating slides in a darkened courtroom. "The whole left side of the face is missing, with extreme fractures extending to the nose and eye socket." On another slide he noted "massive blunt-force traumas, multiple convoluted complex fractures . . . possibly caused by a large limb or club, something with a broad surface, swung with considerable force." On another skull he found "sharp force injuries, two separate blows by a linear sharp object, possibly by a bladed instrument."

I watched Haglund's testimony from the spectators' gallery, surrounded by a class of Tanzanian schoolgirls dressed in matching blue skirts, white shirts and socks, and black oxford shoes. They observed the proceedings in rapt fascination. The girl to my left commented during a break that Rutaganda, the defendant, "looks like a murderer." Her classmate to my right objected that "you can't judge people by their looks." The first girl replied, "Yes, but he still looks guilty."

"He was my boss"

But the main event on that Friday afternoon in Arusha was Jean-Paul Akayesu's last stand in his own defense. The defendant was already badly shaken by the end of that morning's testimony. His conflicting accounts of that crucial April 18, 1994, meeting in Giterama had left his credibility in shreds. No, he had told investigators in 1996, "I did not participate in a meeting". Yes, he testified in the morning, "I attended a meeting." No, he testified the day before, "honestly speaking, frankly speaking, there was never any question of Tutsis being killed, never, never." Yes, he said in the morning, "very honestly, I took the floor, your honor," to denounce the killing of Tutsis.

At issue on that last afternoon was Akayesu's personal relationship with the leader of the *Interahamwe* in his region, a notorious thug named Silas Kubwimana. In effect, Akayesu was being asked to account for the awkward personal logistics of his pact with the devil.

During his eight hours of direct testimony the previous day, Akayesu had portrayed himself as a well-intentioned if bumbling Good Samaritan who housed and fed refugees, borrowed mattresses, gave people money, issued fake identity cards, and wandered about the commune at the height of the massacres beseeching people to be reasonable and stop killing each other. "I gave lessons," he recalled. "When I found a group that was not aggressive or that was not interested in killing I talked to the group. I put the message across and I told them, should we now be killing one another?" When he encountered killers, he asked them, "Why did you kill them?" or "Why are you creating these habits of killing?" He said he did not listen to the radio. He had no power to make arrests. But, he asserted, "I condemned their actions."

But a parade of prosecution witnesses testified that, after that April 18 meeting in Giterama, Akayesu began appearing at public meetings in Taba wearing his camouflage jacket, standing side by side with Silas Kubwimana and urging his constituents to "fight the enemy." Kubwimana, meanwhile, was urging the same audiences to "kill the Tutsis." Akayesu's public alliance with Kubwimana, witnesses said, legitimized the massacres in the minds of an otherwise reluctant public. (Kubwimana remains at large.)

How, Pierre Prosper, the prosecutor, wanted to know, did Akayesu expect the population to interpret his message any differently?

"I worked with the population, Akayesu replied. "The population knew my stand. . . . As *bourgmestre*, even though a weakened one, I am sure the population understood my message. Whereas this Silas, whose behavior and character was well known, I am sure that a large number of the population, those who were present, were just jeering at him. I am sure of that."

Prosper: "You were opposed to what Silas Kubwimana was saying . . . Is that correct?"

Akayesu: "Completely."

Prosper noted that Akayesu continued to travel throughout the commune and giving speeches side by side with Kubwimana, each one urging the crowds to fight the enemy and kill the Tutsis. "You didn't walk away did you?" he asked.

"I really don't know how you interpret things," Akayesu replied. "I had to diffuse the message and the message I gave was at no time a bad message, and I was before a receptive population. I am sure that I was understood a thousand times better than Silas."

Prosper reminded Akayesu of what the prosecution witnesses had understood from those speeches: "This is what the witnesses say you said at this meeting. They say you, meaning the population, should pursue the Tutsi wherever they are because they are still hiding. There are young people who have taken the habit to marry a Tutsi woman. If we find someone with a woman like that the person will be punished and we can even destroy their houses because this person will have become then an accomplice of the Tutsi. You continue by saying, even a woman who was married to a Tutsi and who is pregnant was to be looked for and her pregnancy removed. . . . I mean, that's how they understood your message."

"That was false," Akayesu responded.

Finally, Prosper asked Akayesu to describe his relationship with Kubwimana. Akayesu replied: "Mr. Kubwimana . . . He was a leader of all killing activities. He was all-powerful. . . . Silas Kubwimana was all-powerful in the commune. . . . He was all powerful in Taba."

Prosper turned the court's attention to the transcript of that nine-hour interview with tribunal investigators in 1996. Then as now, Akayesu was asked: What was the role of Silas Kubwimana in Taba? The prosecutor asked Akayesu to read his reply to the court.

"Silas Kubwimana . . . He told us that he had been assigned the responsibility of keeping the peace in Musambira, Runda and Taba communes." A mandate for peace? the investigators had asked. "Yes," Akayesu had replied, "That means holding meetings with people and things of that sort."

There was a buzz in the spectators' gallery. The absurdity of Akayesu's earlier story was all too obvious.

Prosper was poised for the kill: "You were specifically asked the role of Silas Kubwimana and in this interview you never mentioned that he was the leader of the *Interahamwe* in charge of the massacres, and this big powerful person that you tell us today. Is it because now you have heard the testimony where people say you and Silas were side by side? So this is a new defense?"

Akayesu dabbed his brow. He reached for his bottled water. His foot vibrated frantically. "Not to say that Silas was a leader of the *Interahamwe*?" he finally ventured. "That would not be surprising. Even a small child would tell you that. And to say that he was all-powerful—was I asked to describe Silas as you asked me now? I don't think so. The question was not to describe Silas."

It was too late. As he had been that morning, Akayesu was confronted with the fact that had had completely changed his story. One by one the judges piled on.

Judge Kama was first: "Mr. Akayesu, since yesterday your defense is that you were emptied of your powers by Silas Kubwimana. . . . The question [in 1996] was, 'What was the role of Silas Kubwimana in the commune of Taba?' The question was clear. On the occasion of that question you had the opportunity of saying what you have been saying since yesterday, but when that question was asked you didn't say it and the prosecutor is right to express surprise. I am also expressing surprise."

Akayesu: "I will explain, Mr. President. What is my answer? I said that he was mandated for peace although he did not work indeed for the maintenance of peace but he had a mandate for peace. Is that not a role? I think it is a role. It is also a role. Maybe it would be said that I did not say all that had to be said but this was a role. He was in charge of peace."

Judge Kama: "As compared to what you have said, you described Silas, that he was a real demon and you even said yesterday that he was a hired killer. That is to show how dangerous he was. [But in 1996] you were asked to give his role and you said that he had a mandate for peace? This hired killer, he had a mandate for peace? I am surprised."

The spectators around me were in an uproar. Judge Kama was mocking the defendant in open court. Akayesu was only deepening his humiliation by seeking somehow to reconcile his flagrantly inconsistent statements. He appealed to the judges to "look at the context in which we are. . . . Indeed Silas knew his role. He had a mandate. He had a role. The role was to preach the message of peace."

Judge Kama was incredulous, his voice dripping with sarcasm: "Should I understand that there was—he had changed his role? From being a hired killer he became a dove bringing the news of peace?"

"I did not say everything." Akayesu replied. "We are in a definite context. A specific context. His role was to maintain peace although that is not what he did."

Judge Lennart Aspegren of Sweden was equally incredulous. He asked Akayesu if there was any possibility of a misunderstanding. "The question is clear," he said. "Is your answer also clear?"

"Maybe it is not exhaustive," Akayesu stammered. "But I think it is somehow my answer. I limited myself to saying that he had a mandate for peace."

The audience was aghast. A Reuters reporter sitting behind me leaned over and whispered in my ear, "He's finished."

But Prosper wasn't finished. He turned the witness's attention to yet another excerpt from Akayesu's by now disastrous interview with tribunal investigators in 1996. The question put to Akayesu then was "What was your relationship with Kubwimana?" Prosper asked the defendant to read his reply to the court. "In fact," Akayesu read, "we know each other very well but we are not close. I kept my distance from him."

Prosper: "And in response to that question again you never mentioned that Silas Kubwimana was responsible for the terror in Taba or in intimidating you or in threatening you?"

Akayesu: "What paragraph are you referring to, Mr. Prosecutor?"

Judge Kama interrupted to help him out: "The paragraph twenty-four that you have just read," he said. "The prosecutor says you never spoke of the strange relationship between you and Mr. Kubwimana that we have been talking about since yesterday. You said he threatened to kill you. Was that [the interview in 1996] not the opportunity for you to say a little bit about it when you were asked about your relationship?"

"Well," Akayesu replied, "I didn't know that you wanted me to go into the depth of the matter."

It was left to Judge Pillay to deliver the final blow. "Mr. Akayesu," she began, in her quiet, unassuming manner, "you say you kept your distance from Silas Kubwimana. So when did you associate with Silas?"

Akayesu: "In fact, it was due to those meetings, . . . on those dates that Silas could be found standing next to me or being next to me and it didn't last, and it didn't last long. It didn't take much time. I hope I have responded to your question, Your Honor."

Judge Pillay: "Did he ever visit you in your home?"

Akayesu: "I know he went to my house but when you talk of a visit you are thinking of a friendly relationship. He did go to my house but I wouldn't say he came to visit me, no."

Pillay noted that Akayesu had just moments earlier insisted that he had associated with Silas only at meetings. Now it turned out that Silas had been in Akayesu's house as well.

"Why did Silas come to your house?" she asked. "I ask you this because you mentioned that you associated with him at the meetings and now it turns out that he was in your house. So what was he doing there?"

Akayesu replied, "The origin of the question is in terms of the distance. You see, he is the one who came to my house. I didn't go to his house. I didn't go to look for him and besides it depends on the period we are talking about. It was the beginning of May and that was the time when meetings had to be held. The boss comes to my house and then we go to the office because meetings were being held at that time, peacekeeping meetings."

Judge Pillay paused for a moment. There was a stir in the spectators' gallery. The English translation filtered through our head-sets. The word "boss" seemed to come out of nowhere, so much so that Judge Pillay asked Akayesu whether the translation was correct. He said it was.

Judge Pillay: "When did he become your boss?"

Akayesu: "Well, I used the expression 'boss' to show what he was doing because indeed on that same morning he told me very ironically, 'You continue resisting the *Interahamwe* and very soon you are going to see, you are going to see what would happen.' You see, he was making verbal threats. He was threatening me verbally. He arrests and imprisons people. It is what I mean when I say he was my boss. Maybe it has the same—I don't know if it has the same meaning and connotation in English as in French, but he has become the Big Boss."

Judge Pillay: "And Mr. Akayesu, you didn't say that when the prosecution's investigators asked you what is the relationship between you and Silas. You should have said, 'He is my boss.'"

Akayesu reached for the water bottle. "Your Honor," he said at last, a note of desperation in his voice. "I must say that all these things that I'm said to have said, I did not say them either. It is not possible. In fact, in this interview there is something lacking."

Judge Pillay: "Mr. Akayesu, just one last question from me is, are you asking then that before this chamber comes to a decision we should check on the tape, we should check your voice and test this particular piece of evidence that's recorded in the transcript? Are you challenging this part and you want to check it on the tape?"

Akayesu: "Your Honor, that is far from my intention, of asking this chamber to go and verify through the tapes. What I said is that I haven't—I did not say everything, every single thing . . . I couldn't have said everything."

Pillay: "You are giving more details in your testimony today you say?"

Akayesu: "That is correct your honor."

A glimmer of light

At 10 A.M. on September 2, 1998, the gallery filled to overflowing in trial chamber 1. The mood was tense and expectant. The Rwandans in the crowd—some two dozen survivors, witnesses and government officials were flown in for the occasion, including Taba's *bourgmestre*, Ephraim Karangwa—seemed particularly on edge. A hush fell over the chamber as the judges in their scarlet robes filed in. The defendant rose, impassive in his smart blue suit.

Judge Kama delivered the verdict: guilty as charged on nine counts of genocide, crimes against humanity and war crimes, including rape. It was the first conviction after a trial for genocide by an international court, and the first time that rape was defined as an act of genocide. Akayesu winced briefly as the verdict was announced, but otherwise he betrayed no emotion. A month later he was sentenced to a maximum penalty of life in prison.

In the guilt-ridden wreckage of contemporary Rwanda, Akayesu's conviction was a drop in the bucket. Four years after the genocide, there remained more than half a million unsolved murders. There were still 130,000 Hutu suspects in custody, with little hope of proper trials. In Arusha, higher-ups in the old Hutu Power chain of command, like Bagosora, had yet to be tried. And the country was still at war. The conviction of a single village mayor was scant justice indeed when measured against the scale of Rwanda's crime, and no amount of justice will bring back the dead or heal the awesome wounds of a shattered nation.

But Akayesu's trial and conviction had meaning beyond Rwanda. The world stood by and watched in 1994, in part because of deep-rooted stereotypes of Africa as a subrational zone of ancient hatreds impervious to outside intervention. The Arusha tribunal grew out of a belated recognition from afar of what Africans like Bonaventure and Isadore knew all along: that bigotry in Africa, no less than elsewhere in the world, is fueled by injustice. A half century after the Nuremberg trials, the Arusha tribunal's judgment against Akayesu established justice in its most basic sense—accountability to the law for criminal acts—as an answer to bigotry in its most monstrous form, genocide. That is a small measure of justice for Rwanda: that at the end of a blood-drenched century, in which some of the great civilizations of the world have likewise descended into barbarism, this tiny, tragic speck of a country, tucked away in a part of the world long maligned as the heart of darkness, has yielded a glimmer of light.

ACKNOWLEDGMENTS

My first thanks go to the scores of Africans who shared their time and wisdom with an inquisitive American reporter, often in circumstances of acute distress. I can only hope this book does justice to their experience, and that it adequately reflects the humility I have so often brought home from my encounters with these remarkable people. I won't begin to enumerate them here, and in any case, for reasons that should be clear, a great many of them spoke to me on the condition that they not be named. But I would like to single out a handful of African journalists and activists who played an especially valuable role in shaping this work, as companions, as guides, and as inspirations. They are Isaac Bantu, Gabriel Williams and Tiawan Gongloe in Liberia, Kanyama Mbiyabu in Zaire, S'Kumbuzo Miya, Wally Mbele and Howard Varney in South Africa, Suliman Baldo of Sudan, and Charles Onyango-Obbo and Joe Oloka-Onyango in Uganda.

A number of colleagues and Africa hands over the years made particularly useful contributions to my work. Mark Huband and Edith Odemo were extremely generous and helpful, not least in sharing their office in Nairobi. Richard Carver has been a true confederate and sounding board since our days together in Matabeleland. The folks at Human Rights Watch—Peter Takirambudde, Bronwen Mamby, Binaifer Nowrojee, Janet Fleischman, Jemera Rone and Alison Des Forges—have been invaluable. Will Reno, when he's not cavorting with warlords, has been endlessly intriguing. Peter Rosenblum was especially helpful in Zaire. John Prendergast shared abundant insight on Sudan. Diane Orentlicher first helped me understand the importance of accountability.

This book grew out of a series of assignments for *The Atlantic Monthly*. William Whitworth, the long-time editor of *The Atlantic*, took a chance on a stranger, for reasons known only to him, and that has made more difference than he will ever know. Jack Beatty and Amy Meeker, veteran *Atlantic* hands, were shrewd and skillful with my copy. Editors elsewhere who helped to subsidize the reporting and shape the writing include Kyle Crichton, David Shipley, James Gibney and David Ignatius. Most recently, Howell Raines and Philip Taubman have given me the opportunities of a lifetime, for which I am profoundly grateful. Steve Pickering solved a problem at the last minute that had bedeviled me for five years.

Throughout the long struggle to produce a manuscript, three friends who knew how to do it served as mentors, fixers and pep talkers. Dan Swanson read draft after horrendous draft and made countless superlative suggestions. Tina Rosenberg, in ways too numerous to mention, bestowed one life-altering favor after another. Glenn Frankel, who never lost faith in me despite all the evidence, assigned and edited what would become the final chapter.

The bulk of the manuscript was written in a cluttered cubicle at the World Policy Institute at the New School for Social Research. I am grateful to Myra Kamdar and Stephen Schlesinger for affording me the chance to make my intellectual home there. Four intrepid interns at the institute—Amy Frumin, Michelle Ciarrocca, Rudee Roth and Mirko Dakovic—searched, surfed, sifted and distilled far beyond the call of duty. Belinda Cooper included a pilot chapter in her own fine book on war crimes. Bill Hartung, "the other Bill," was a steady source of encouragement. My students at the New School, where for three years I taught a course on ethnicity and conflict in Africa, stimulated my mind and boosted my morale. Sophie Mineut translated French press coverage of Rwanda with nimble enterprise. Alison Morley found the photographs.

The Alicia Patterson Foundation gave me a fellowship that allowed me to report systematically on ethnic conflict for a solid year and landed me in Rwanda in the spring of 1994. My thanks especially to Margaret Engel there. The Open Society Institute, in turn, gave me an Individual Project Fellowship, which supported much of the writing. I am grateful to George Soros, Aryeh Neier, Gara LaMarche and Gail Goodman.

My agent, Wendy Weil, has been helpful throughout in ways large and small. Alex Stille, Silvana Paternostro, Jennifer Washburn, Gene Ely and my sister, Dr. Annie B. Berkeley, read some early drafts of chapters and offered much-needed feedback. Dan Swanson, Glenn Frankel and Suliman Baldo read the entire manuscript in draft, making many valuable suggestions.

At Basic Books, Tim Bartlett inherited an orphaned project and guided it with intelligence and infinite patience. Vanessa Mobley fought many battles on my behalf, and earned my lasting devotion. The copyeditor, Katherine Scott, made some stupendous catches that saved me from professional ruin, as did the project editor, Richard Miller. Needless to say, they bear no responsibility for what errors of fact or judgement have survived.

The same cannot be said of my wife, Mary Jane, who accompanied me on much of the reporting and, along with our daughter, Carmen, bore with me through the long years of writing. As my editor of first and last resort, interpreter, photographer, transcriber, consciousness raiser, jailmate and convicted co-conspirator, she must bear credit or blame for every last word. I could not have written the book without her.

BIBLIOGRAPHY

General

Adorno, Theodor W., et al. *The Authoritarian Personality*. New York: W. W. Norton, 1982.

Anyang' Nyongo, Peter, ed. *Arms and Daggers in the Heart of Africa: Studies on Internal Conflicts*. Nairobi: Academy Science Publishers, 1993.

Arendt, Hannah. *The Origins of Totalitarianism*. 2d ed. Cleveland: World Publishing, 1958.

———. *Eichmann in Jerusalem: A Report on the Banality of Evil*. New York: Penguin Books, 1977.

Bayart, Jean-François, Steven Ellis, and Béatrice Hibou, eds. *The Criminalization of the State in Africa*. Bloomington: Indiana University Press, 1999.

Brown, Michael E., ed. *Ethnic Conflict and International Security*. Princeton: Princeton University Press, 1993.

Browning, Christopher R. *Ordinary Men: Reserve Police Battalion 101 and the Final Solution in Poland*. New York: HarperPerennial, 1993.

Chalk, Frank, and Kurt Jonassohn. *The History and Sociology of Genocide: Analyses and Case Studies*. New Haven: Yale University Press, 1990.

Clarridge, Duane R. (with Digby Diehl). *A Spy for All Seasons: My Life in the CIA*. New York: Scribner, 1997.

Clough, Michael. *Free at Last: U.S. Policy Toward Africa and the End of the Cold War*. New York: Council on Foreign Relations, 1992.

Cooper, Belinda, ed. *War Crimes: The Legacy of Nuremberg*. New York: TV Books, 1999.

Davidson, Basil. *Let Freedom Come: Africa in Modern History*. Boston: Atlantic Monthly Press, 1978.

———. *The Black Man's Burden: Africa and the Curse of the Nation State*. New York: Times Books, 1992.

Foltz, William J., and Henry S. Bienen, eds. *Arms and the African: Military Influences on Africa's International Relations*. New Haven: Yale University Press, 1986.

Fukui, Katsuyoshi, and John Markakis, eds. *Ethnicity and Conflict in the Horn of Africa*. London: James Currey, 1994.

Gutman, Roy, and David Rieff, eds. *Crimes of War: What the Public Should Know*. New York: W. W. Norton, 1999.

Harden, Blaine. *Africa: Dispatches from a Fragile Continent*. New York. W. W. Norton, 1990.

Harding, Jeremy. *Small Wars, Small Mercies: Journeys in Africa's Disputed Nations*. London: Penguin Books, 1993.

Horowitz, Donald L. *Ethnic Groups in Conflict*. Berkeley: University of California Press, 1985.

Human Rights Watch. *Playing the Communal Card: Communal Violence and Human Rights*. New York: Human Rights Watch, April 1995.

Huntington, Samuel P. *Political Order in Changing Societies*. New Haven: Yale University Press, 1968.

Ignatieff, Michael. *Blood and Belonging: Journeys into the New Nationalism*. New York: Farrar Straus & Giroux, 1993.

———. *The Warrior's Honor: Ethnic War and the Modern Conscience*. New York: Metropolitan Books, 1997.

Isaacs, Harold R. *Idols of the Tribe: Group Identity and Political Change*. Cambridge: Harvard University Press, 1975.

Jackson, Robert H., and Carl G. Rosberg. *Personal Rule in Black Africa: Prince, Autocrat, Prophet, Tyrant*. Berkeley: University of California Press, 1982.

Kapuscinski, Ryszard. *The Emperor*. New York: Vintage International, 1989.

Kwitny, Jonathan. *Endless Enemies: America's Worldwide War Against Its Own Best Interests*. New York: Congdon & Weed, 1984.

Lamb, David. *The Africans*. New York: Random House, 1982.

Mamdani, Mahmood. *Citizen and Subject: Contemporary Africa and the Legacy of Late Colonialism*. Princeton: Princeton University Press, 1996.

Marnham, Patrick. *Fantastic Invasion: Dispatches from Africa*. London: Jonathan Cape, 1980.

Mazrui, Ali. *The African Condition*. London: Heinemann, 1980.

McCuen, John J. *The Art of Counter-revolutionary War: The Strategy of Counter-insurgency*. Harrisburg, Pa.: Stackpole Books, 1966.

Meredith, Martin. *The First Dance of Freedom: Black Africa in the Postwar Era*. London: Hamish Hamilton, 1984.

Neier, Aryeh. *War Crimes: Brutality, Genocide, Terror, and the Struggle for Justice*. New York: Times Books, 1998.

Pakenham, Thomas. *The Scramble for Africa: White Man's Conquest of the Dark Continent from 1876 to 1912*. New York: Avon Books, 1991.

Persico, Joseph. *Nuremberg: Infamy on Trial*. New York: Penguin Books, 1994.

Rodney, Walter. *How Europe Underdeveloped Africa*. Washington, D.C.: Howard University Press, 1982.

Sandbrook, Richard. *The Politics of Africa's Economic Stagnation*. New York: Cambridge University Press, 1985.

Staub, Ervin. *The Roots of Evil: The Origins of Genocide and Other Group Violence*. Cambridge, U.K.: Cambridge University Press, 1989.

Taylor, Telford. *The Anatomy of the Nuremberg Trials*. New York: Knopf, 1992.

Ungar, Sanford J. *Africa: The People and Politics of an Emerging Continent*. New York: Simon & Schuster, 1985.

Vail, Leroy, ed. *The Creation of Tribalism in Southern Africa*. London: James Currey, 1989.

Ward, David. *Chronicles of Darkness*. London and New York: Routledge, 1989.

Weschler, Lawrence. *A Miracle, a Universe: Settling Accounts with Torturers*. New York: Pantheon Books, 1990.

Woodward, Bob. *Veil: The Secret Wars of the CIA 1981–1987*. New York: Simon & Schuster, 1987.

Young, Crawford. *The Politics of Cultural Pluralism*. Madison: University of Wisconsin Press, 1976.

Liberia

Ellis, Stephen. *The Mask of Anarchy: The Destruction of Liberia and the Religious Dimension of an African Civil War*. New York: New York University Press, 1999.

Huband, Mark. *The Liberian Civil War*. London: Frank Cass, 1998.

Human Rights Watch/Africa. *Easy Prey: Child Soldiers in Liberia*. New York: Human Rights Watch, September 1994.

Johnson, Charles S. *Bitter Canaan: The Story of the Negro Republic*. New Brunswick, N.J.: Transaction Publishers, 1987.

Lawyers Committee for Human Rights. *Liberia: A Promise Betrayed*. New York: Lawyers Committee for Human Rights, 1986.

Liebenow, J. Gus. *Liberia: The Quest for Democracy*. Bloomington and Indianapolis: Indiana University Press, 1987.

Reno, William. *Warlord Politics and African States*. Boulder: Lynne Rienner, 1998.

Sawyer, Amos. *The Emergence of Autocracy in Liberia*. San Francisco: Institute for Contemporary Studies Press, 1992.

Congo/Zaire

Hochshield, Adam. *King Leopold's Ghost*. New York: Houghton Mifflin, 1998.

Kalb, Madeleine G. *The Congo Cables: The Cold War in Africa, from Eisenhower to Kennedy*. New York: Macmillan, 1982.

Lawyers Committee for Human Rights. *Zaire: Repression as Policy*. New York: Lawyers Committee for Human Rights, August 1990.

O'Brian, Conor Cruise. *To Katanga and Back*. New York: Simon & Schuster, 1962.

Schatzberg, Michael G. *The Dialectics of Oppression in Zaire*. Bloomington and Indianapolis: Indiana University Press, 1990.

Winternitz, Helen. *East Along the Equator: A Journey up the Congo and into Zaire*. New York: Atlantic Monthly Press, 1987.

Young, Crawford, and Thomas Turner. *The Rise and Decline of the Zairian State*. Madison: University of Wisconsin Press, 1985.

South Africa

Africa Watch. *The Killings in South Africa: The Role of the Security Forces and the Response of the State*. New York and London: Africa Watch, 1991.

Amnesty International. *South Africa, State of Fear: Security Force Complicity in Torture and Political Killings, 1990–1992*. London: Amnesty International, June 1992.

Biko, Steve. *I Write What I Like*. London: Heinemann, 1978.

Boraine, Alex, Janet Levy, and Ronel Scheffer, eds. *Dealing with the Past: Truth and Reconciliation in South Africa*. Cape Town: Institute for Democracy in South Africa, 1994.

Crocker, Chester. *High Noon in Southern Africa*. New York: W. W. Norton, 1992.

Finnegan, William. *Dateline Soweto: Travels with Black South African Reporters*. New York: Harper & Row, 1988.

———. *A Complicated War: The Harrowing of Mozambique*. Berkeley: University of California Press, 1992.

Fredrickson, George M. *White Supremacy: A Comparative Study in American and South African History*. New York and Oxford: Oxford University Press, 1981.

Hanlon, Joseph. *Apartheid's Second Front: South Africa's War Against Its Neighbors*. London: Penguin, 1986.

———. *Beggar Your Neighbors: Apartheid Power in Southern Africa*. London: James Currey, 1986.

Haysom, Nicholas. *Mabangalala: The Rise of Right-Wing Vigilantes in South Africa*. Johannesburg: Centre for Applied Legal Studies, 1986.

Hochschild, Adam. *The Mirror at Midnight: A South African Journey*. New York: Penguin Books, 1990.

Johnson, Phyllis, and David Martin. *Frontline Southern Africa: Destructive Engagement*. New York: Four Walls Eight Windows, 1988.

Kentridge, Matthew. *An Unofficial War: Inside the Conflict in Pietermaritzburg*. Cape Town and Johannesburg: David Philip, 1990.

Lawrence, Patrick. *Death Squads: Apartheid's Secret Weapon*. London: Penguin Books, 1990.

Lawyers Committee for Human Rights. *The War Against Children: South Africa's Youngest Victims*. New York: Lawyers Committee for Human Rights, 1986.

Lelyveld, Joseph. *Move Your Shadow: South Africa, Black and White*. New York: Times Books, 1985.

Mare, Gerhard. *Brothers Born of Warrior Blood: Politics and Ethnicity in South Africa*. Johannesburg: Ravan Press, 1992.

Mare, Gerhard, and Georgina Hamilton. *An Appetite for Power: Buthelezi's Inkatha and the Politics of "Loyal Resistance."* Johannesburg: Ravan Press, 1987.

Meer, Fatima, ed. *The Codesa File.* Johannesburg: Madiba Publishers, 1992.

Meredith, Martin. *Coming to Terms: South Africa's Search for Truth.* New York: PublicAffairs, 1999.

Minnaar, Anthony, ed. *Patterns of Violence: Case Studies of Conflict in Natal.* Pretoria: Human Sciences Research Council, 1992.

Minnaar, Anthony, Ian Liebenberg, and Charl Schutte, eds. *The Hidden Hand: Covert Operations in South Africa.* Pretoria: Human Sciences Research Council, 1994.

Morris, Donald R. *The Washing of the Spears.* London: Sphere Books Ltd., 1965.

Mzala. *Gatsha Buthelezi: Chief with a Double Agenda.* London: Zed Books, 1988.

North, James. *Freedom Rising: Life Under Apartheid Through the Eyes of an American on a Four-Year Clandestine Journey Through Southern Africa.* New York: Macmillan, 1985.

Pauw, Jacques. *In the Heart of the Whore: The Story of Apartheid's Death Squads.* Johannesburg: Southern Book Publishers, 1991.

Reed, Daniel. *Beloved Country: South Africa's Silent Wars.* Johannesburg: Jonathan Ball Publishers, 1994.

Sparks, Allister. *The Mind of South Africa.* London: Heinemann, 1990.

———. *Tomorrow Is Another Country.* Johannesburg: Struik, 1995.

Taylor, Stephen. *Shaka's Children: A History of the Zulu People.* London: HarperCollins, 1995.

Thompson, Leonard. *The Political Mythology of Apartheid.* New Haven: Yale University Press, 1985.

———. *A History of South Africa.* New Haven: Yale University Press, 1990.

Vines, Alex. *Renamo: Terrorism in Mozambique.* London: James Currey, 1991.

Winter, Gordon. *Inside Boss: South Africa's Secret Police.* New York and Harmondsworth, U.K.: Penguin Books, 1981.

Sudan

African Rights. *Facing Genocide: The Nuba of Sudan.* London: African Rights, July 1995.

Africa Watch. *Denying the Honor of Living: Sudan—A Human Rights Disaster.* New York and London: Africa Watch, March 1990.

Amnesty International. *Uganda: The Failure to Safeguard Human Rights.* London: Amnesty International, 1992.

Avirgan, Tony, and Martha Honey. *War in Uganda: The Legacy of Idi Amin.* Dar-es-Salaam: Tanzania Publishing House, Ltd., 1982.

Beshir, Mohamed Omer. *The Southern Sudan: Background to Conflict.* London: Hurst, 1968.

Bukenya, Alex B. *Inside Luwero Triangle*. Kampala: Kitata, 1992.

Deng, Francis M. *The Dinka of Southern Sudan*. New York: Holt, Rinehart and Winston, 1972.

———. *War of Visions: Conflict of Identities in Sudan*. Washington, D.C.: The Brookings Institution, 1995.

Hoagland, Edward. *African Calliope: A Journey to the Sudan*. New York: Random House, 1978.

Holt, P. M., and M. W. Daly. *The History of the Sudan*. London: Weidenfeld & Nicolson, 1979.

Human Rights Watch/Africa. *Civilian Devastation: Abuses by All Parties in the War in Southern Sudan*. New York: Human Rights Watch, June 1994.

———. *Children of Sudan: Slaves, Street Children and Child Soldiers*. New York: Human Rights Watch, September 1995.

———. *Behind the Red Line: Political Repression in Sudan*. New York: Human Rights Watch, May 1996.

Khalid, Mansour. *The Government They Deserve: The Role of the Elite in Sudan's Political Evolution*. London: Kegan Paul International, 1990.

Keen, David. *The Benefits of Famine: A Political Economy of Famine and Relief in Southwestern Sudan, 1983–1989*. Princeton: Princeton University Press, 1994.

Kyemba, Henry. *A State of Blood: The Inside Story of Idi Amin*. London: Paddington Press, 1977.

Martin, David. *General Amin*. London: Faber & Faber, 1985.

Mamdani, Mahmood. *Imperialism and Fascism in Uganda*. Nairobi: Heinemann, 1983.

Miller, Judith. *God Has Ninety-nine Names: Reporting from a Militant Middle East*. New York: Simon & Schuster, 1996.

Museveni, Yoweri K. *What Is Africa's Problem?* Kampala: NRM Publications, 1992.

Voll, John O., ed. *Sudan: State and Society in Crisis*. Bloomington and Indianapolis: Indiana University Press, 1991.

Rwanda

African Rights. *Rwanda: Death, Despair and Defiance*. London: African Rights, September 1994.

Des Forges, Alison. *Leave None to Tell the Story: Genocide in Rwanda*. New York: Human Rights Watch, 1999.

Destexhe, Alain. *Rwanda and Genocide in the Twentieth Century*. London: Pluto Press, 1995.

Gourevitch, Philip. *We Wish to Inform You That Tomorrow We Will Be Killed with Our Families: Stories from Rwanda*. New York: Farrar Straus & Giroux, 1998.

Human Rights Watch/Africa. *Beyond the Rhetoric: Continuing Human Rights Abuses in Rwanda*. New York: Human Rights Watch, June 1993.

―――. *The Aftermath of Genocide in Rwanda: Absence of Prosecution, Continued Killings.* New York: Human Rights Watch, September 1994.

―――. *Rwanda: A New Catastrophe?* New York: Human Rights Watch, December 1994.

―――. *Rwanda/Zaire: Rearming with Impunity—International Support for the Perpetrators of the Rwandan Genocide.* New York: Human Rights Watch, May 1995.

―――. *Shattered Lives: Sexual Violence During the Rwandan Genocide and Its Aftermath.* New York: Human Rights Watch, 1996.

Kamukama, Dixon. *Rwanda Conflict: Its Roots and Regional Implications.* Kampala: Fountain Publishers, 1993.

Keane, Fergal. *Season of Blood: A Rwanda Journey.* New York: Viking, 1995.

Lemarchand, René. *Rwanda and Burundi.* London: Pall Mall, 1970.

―――. *Burundi: Ethnocide as Discourse and Practice.* Cambridge, U.K.: Cambridge University Press, 1994.

Malkki, Liisa H. *Purity and Exile: Violence, Memory, and National Cosmology Among Hutu Refugees in Tanzania.* Chicago and London: University of Chicago Press, 1995.

Newbury, Catherine. *The Cohesion of Oppression: Clientship and Ethnicity in Rwanda, 1860-1960.* New York: Columbia University Press, 1988.

Prunier, Gérard. *The Rwanda Crisis: History of a Genocide.* New York: Columbia University Press, 1995.

INDEX

Abacha, Sani, 54, 60
Accountability for crimes, 14, 16, 44,
    51, 69, 89, 100, 151, 157, 160,
    161, 173, 183, 221, 229, 234, 236,
    238, 240, 248, 249, 263, 264, 284
"Accusations in a mirror," 271
Acholi ethnic group, 228, 230, 231,
    233, 236
Addis Ababa accords (1972), 211, 213,
    217
Afghanistan, 13, 69, 79, 82, 225
AFL. See Liberia, Armed Forces of
    Liberia
Africa, 4(map), 35, 64, 76, 78, 119,
    129–130, 192, 225
    Africans characterized, 6–7, 8–9, 10,
    12, 13, 87, 207, 209
African Americans, 17, 87, 89, 90, 91,
    92, 94
Africa News, 77, 84
African Mining Consortium, Ltd., 53
The Africans (Lamb), 8–9
Afwerki, Issaias, 237
Ahmad, Muhammad. See Mahdi
AIDS, 6, 190, 228
Aitcheson, John, 175
Akayesu, Jean-Paul, 245–248, 250,
    254, 256, 259, 262, 276, 277–284
Albright, Madeleine, 224, 237, 239,
    249
Amin, Idi, 8, 84, 122, 197, 226, 228,
    229, 230, 231, 234, 241, 242
Amin, Kay, 230
Amnesty International, 233–234

Anarchy, 13–14, 128, 144, 155, 199,
    218, 219, 223. See also Tyranny
ANC. See South Africa, African
    National Congress
Angola, 18, 77, 80, 81, 95, 96, 98, 116,
    117, 118, 140, 167, 182
    Movimento Popular de Libertação
    de Angola (MPLA), 80
    National Union for the Total
    Independence of Angola
    (UNITA), 77, 80, 81, 95, 98, 116,
    117, 147, 167, 168, 169, 173
Arab-Israeli war of 1973, 76
Arab League, 211
Arabs, 11, 14, 196, 208, 209, 219, 221,
    223, 225
    Arab Afghans, 225
    See also Islam
Arbour, Louise, 251
Arendt, Hannah, 7
Armaments. See Weapons
Arthur, Chester, 70
*The Art of Counter Revolutionary
    Warfare* (McCuen), 168
Arusha, Tanzania, 273
Arusha tribunal. See United Nations,
    International Criminal Tribunal
    for Rwanda
Askin, Steve, 114
Aspegren, Lennart, 280–281
Assassinations, 110, 159, 171, 172,
    177, 185, 224, 259
Atlanta Journal-Constitution, 8
Atlantic Monthly, 9, 18, 104

295

Baganda ethnic group, 228, 229
Bagosora, Theoneste, 252, 272, 276, 283
Balkans, 13, 49, 225
Bank of Credit and Commerce International (BCCI), 33
Banks, 34, 37, 50, 52, 111, 128, 201, 231. *See also* Zaire, central bank
Bannings, 21
  of academic activities, 33
  of political activity, 32, 33, 65
  of press and trade unions, 199
Bantu, Isaac, 37, 39–41, 130
Banyarwandan ethnic group, 232
Barayagwiza, Jean-Bosco, 275
Bartering, 201
Bashir, Omar al-, 198, 242
BBC radio broadcasts, 39, 48, 68
BCCI. *See* Bank of Credit and Commerce International
Beardon, Milton, 225
Belgian Congo, 9, 109, 115. *See also* Congo; Zaire
Belgium, 9, 11, 115, 119, 120, 127, 257
Berkeley, Mary Jane, 104, 106, 118, 129, 135, 138, 150
Best, Kenneth, 78
Bethlehem Steel Company, 41
Beukes, Herbert, 98
Bigotry, 257, 284. *See also* Racism
Bikindi, Simon, 2
Bin Laden, Osama, 225
Bishop, James, 84–85
Black Cats gang, 156
Black market, 113, 204, 231
Blame, 51
Blood banks, 204, 220
Blumenthal, Erwin, 114
Boley, George, 55
BOSS. *See* South Africa, Bureau of State Security
Botha, P. W., 98, 100, 167, 168
Botswana, 95
Bribery, 115, 206, 223, 239
British colonial rule, 8, 11, 12, 229. *See also* Sudan

Buchner, Jac, 10, 99, 170, 175–181, 183, 189
  "turnings" of, 177, 178, 188
Burkina Faso, 52, 53
Burundi, 17, 227, 241, 257, 263, 264, 265
Bush administration, 80, 82, 85, 116
Buthelezi, Mangosuthu Gatsha, 10, 145, 146, 148–150, 152, 159, 174, 177, 181, 183–189, 199
  and Tienie Groenewald, 169, 170, 172, 187, 188

Cameroon, 275, 276
Cannibalism, 23, 37, 38
Carter administration, 75, 80, 83, 94, 184, 213, 237
  Carter Doctrine, 81
Casey, William, 76, 98, 213
Castro, Fidel, 116
Cattle herders, 208, 216
CDR. *See* Rwanda, Coalition for the Defense of the Republic
Central Intelligence Agency (CIA), 70, 77, 82, 98, 109, 110, 112, 116, 117, 172, 180, 213, 225, 250
Chad, 48
Checkpoints/roadblocks, 54, 106, 130, 206, 212, 227, 246, 277
Chege, Michael, 13, 19, 90
Chiefs, 228. *See also* South Africa; Sudan
Children/teenagers, 22–23, 23–24, 38, 49, 50, 53, 179, 203, 221, 224, 227, 230, 233, 242, 255, 267, 268. *See also* Infant mortality; Students; Zaire, JUFERI youth brigade
Cholera, 49, 85, 268
Christians, 196, 219, 229, 231
Churchill, Winston, 227
CIA. *See* Central Intelligence Agency
Clark, William P., 76
Clarke, Wilfred, 131, 131(n)
Clarridge, Duane ("Dewey"), 98
Clinton, Bill, 237, 250

Clinton administration, 17, 88, 224, 225, 226, 238–239, 240, 249
Cobalt, 110, 113, 117, 126
Coetzee, Dirk, 173, 174(n), 174, 193, 219
Cohen, Herman, 82–83, 91, 112
Cold War, 17, 30, 39, 63, 69, 75, 78, 79, 81, 82, 91, 99, 116, 167, 211, 222, 249
   post–Cold War era, 14, 15, 16, 24, 79, 113, 120, 260
Colombia, 192, 262
Color-against-color principle, 14. See also South Africa, black-on-black violence
"The Coming Anarchy" (Kaplan), 9
Communism, 159, 168, 172, 174, 180, 249
Congo, 9, 11, 18, 109–111, 115, 116–117, 238, 239, 240, 266. See also Democratic Republic of the Congo; Zaire
Conrad, Joseph, 8, 115
Constructive engagement, 64, 69, 71, 89, 92, 93, 94, 96, 97, 99
CONTRALESA. See South Africa, Congress of Traditional Leaders of South Africa
Copper, 112, 116, 117, 126, 140
Corleone, Vito, 15
Corruption, 29–30, 33, 34, 47(n), 75, 78, 85, 127, 132
Coups, 25, 32, 41, 43, 48, 65, 75, 83, 86, 91, 111, 198, 211, 212, 214, 220, 229, 230. See also Liberia, November 12 business
Croats, 263
Crime, 13, 53, 84, 107, 128, 148, 152, 154, 156, 160, 184, 190, 191, 192, 261, 262
   and ethnic conflict, 15, 24, 125, 140, 196, 260
Crimes against humanity, 248, 283
Crocker, Chester A., 63–75, 81, 86–87, 88, 89–90, 91–92, 96, 100–101, 172, 213, 239–240
   biographical background, 70–72

Crocker, Chester A. (continued)
   and Congress, 64–65, 64–66, 67–68
   and Mobutu, 80
   on Ronald Reagan, 98
   See also Constructive engagement; Doe, Samuel K., Crocker on
Cronyism, 132
Cuba, 80, 95, 96, 98, 110, 116, 135, 180
Culture of obedience. See under Rwanda
Currencies, 34, 113, 127, 201, 231
Czechoslovakia, 80

Dahn, Sammy, 130
Daily Observer, 79
Danané, Ivory Coast, 36
Deaths, 225
   in Angola, 96, 147, 167
   in Colombia, 262
   in Congo/Zaire, 9, 17, 115, 118, 119, 120, 123, 128, 132, 140, 238, 240
   from criminal vs. political murders, 156
   from famine/disease, 18, 105, 147, 215, 217, 221, 242
   of journalists/photographers, 129(n)
   in Liberia, 18, 22, 24, 27, 30, 31, 33, 35, 37, 44, 47, 49, 51, 55, 61, 73, 86
   in Mozambique, 96, 147, 167
   in Rwanda, 1, 2, 15, 17, 18, 245, 247, 253, 254, 256, 258, 259, 260, 261, 263–264, 267, 269–270, 276–277, 278
   in South Africa, 14, 18, 144, 152, 153, 159, 162, 173, 174, 182, 185, 190, 191
   in Sudan, 6, 18, 196, 214, 215, 217, 221, 224
   in Uganda, 8, 226, 230, 232, 230, 233
   See also Executions; Genocide; Massacres
Death squads, 144, 151, 159, 164, 172, 173, 175, 177, 181, 182, 183, 187.

Death squads (*continued*)
  See also Hutus; Krahn ethnic
  group
Decolonization, 79
De Klerk, F. W., 165, 174(n), 175,
  190
De Kock, Eugene, 175, 177
Dellaire, Romeo, 250–251
Dellums, Ron, 90
Democracy, 6, 74, 89, 91, 120, 123,
  125, 128, 133, 144, 192, 214, 222.
  See also Uganda, and
  multipartyism
Democratic Republic of the Congo
  (DRC), 139, 140. *See also* Congo;
  Zaire
Denton, Jeremiah, 180
Dependency theory, 90
Des Forges, Alison, 271
Destabilization, 125, 128, 147, 167,
  168, 170, 174, 175, 177, 210
De Temmerman, Luc, 276
Devlin, Larry, 109
De Vos, Peter, 82
Diamonds, 52, 53, 55, 113, 127, 140
Didcott, John, 155
Dinka ethnic group, 216, 217, 220,
  223
Disease, 18, 40, 50, 105, 118, 140,
  203–204, 242, 256. *See also* AIDS;
  Cholera
Dissidents, 198, 230
Divide and rule, 94, 96, 117, 125, 144,
  148, 149, 173, 209, 216, 218, 223,
  228
Doe, Jackson, 56, 60, 130, 131(n)
Doe, Samuel K., 21, 24, 26, 27, 30, 31,
  32, 36, 41, 42, 46, 48, 50, 55, 56,
  63, 69, 75–76, 84, 91, 92, 93
  Crocker on, 65–67, 72, 73
  death of, 51, 86
  Decrees 2A and 88A of, 33–34, 65
  Executive Mansion Guard of, 33,
  44, 48, 86
  and Thomas Quiwonkpa, 35, 222
  and William Casey, 76
Dokie, Lewis, 41, 57

Dokie, Sammy, 41, 47, 48, 57–58
  death of, 58, 59
  See also Taylor, Charles McArthur
Dollars, 34
DRC. *See* Democratic Republic of the
  Congo
Drugs, 23, 50, 191, 192, 203. *See also*
  Marijuana
Duarte, José Napoléon, 76
Dulles, Allen, 110

Eastern Europe, 117
East Germany, 249
ECOMOG peacekeeping force, 53,
  54, 59, 84, 86
Economist, 242–243
Education, 11, 34, 114, 115, 119, 126,
  149, 155, 159, 228, 230, 258,
  272
Egypt, 211, 213, 217, 224
Eisenhower administration, 79, 110,
  116
Ekeh, Peter, 12
Elections, 78, 91, 97, 198, 214. *See also*
  Liberia, election of 1985; *See also*
  Uganda
Elites, 25. *See also* Liberia, Americo-
  Liberians
Ellis, Stephen, 37, 192–193
El Salvador, 76
*The Ends of the Earth: A Journey at the
  Dawn of the New Century*
  (Kaplan), 9
Eritrea, 18, 224, 237, 238
Ethiopia, 18, 81, 213, 215, 222, 223,
  224, 237, 238
Ethnicity, 15, 31, 148, 158, 222, 223,
  231, 235, 249
  ethnic cleansing, 105, 117, 140, 149,
  150, 227
  ethnic consciousness, 12–13
  ethnic mobilization, 13, 15, 23, 35,
  48, 69, 79, 119, 123, 139, 150,
  216, 232, 257
  harmonious ethnic relations, 36,
  229, 263
  and multipartyism, 227, 228

Ethnicity *(continued)*
  and privilege/resentment, 120, 123,
    228, 257, 258
  See also Crime, and ethnic conflict
Evil, 7, 10, 11, 16, 19, 23, 109, 175,
  225, 246
Executions, 32, 41, 42, 59, 113, 234,
  273

Fahnbullah, Boima, 55
Failed states, 15, 260
Famine, 6, 18, 147, 196, 198, 221
  famine relief, 195, 201, 215, 216, 243
Federalism, 184
Felgate, Walter, 166
Films, 28
Firearms. *See* Weapons
Firestone company, 17, 29, 82
Floggings, 32, 41, 43, 57, 85
Focus on Africa (BBC news program),
  39
Folgers company, 17
Food as weapon, 216
Food distribution, 27. *See also* Famine,
  famine relief
Forced labor, 29
Ford administration, 80
Foreign Affairs, 71, 88, 94
Foreign exchange, 52, 126, 127, 261
Fossey, Dian, 261
France, 53, 54, 83, 100, 120, 229, 250,
  261
Fundamentalism, 14

Garang, John, 195, 199, 215, 218, 220,
  221–222, 222–223, 223–224,
  225–226, 241, 242, 243, 266
Gates, Robert, 84
Gatreak, Peter, 243
Gaye, Nixon, 59
Gécamines mining company, 105, 106,
  112, 117, 123, 126–128, 132
Gemayal, Amin, 76
Genocide, 2, 6, 9, 15–16, 17, 23, 36,
  88, 140, 150, 219, 227, 237, 245,
  246, 250, 255, 258, 260, 261, 262,
  264, 268, 273, 274, 276, 283, 284

Genocide *(continued)*
  trials concerning, 16, 272. *See also*
    United Nations, International
    Criminal Tribunal for Rwanda
Georgetown University, Center for
  Strategic and International
  Studies, 70
Germany, 257, 272
Ghana, 26
Gio ethnic group, 23, 35, 37, 38, 39,
  41, 43–44, 47, 48, 55, 56, 58, 60,
  130, 131(n)
Gola ethnic group, 56
Gold, 52, 199
Goldstone, Richard, 155, 174, 263
Gongloe, Tiawan, 44–45
Gorbachev, Mikhail, 97
Gorillas, 261
Grebo ethnic group, 43–44
Green Berets, 31, 75
Grenada, 99
Groenewald, Pieter Hendrik "Tienie,"
  10, 145, 146, 147, 165, 169–173,
  183, 187, 188, 192, 199
  biographical background, 170–171
  and Buthelezi, 169, 170, 172, 187,
    188
Guatemala, 69
Gwala, Harry, 154, 161, 164, 186, 274

Habyarimana, Agathe, 276
Habyarimana, Juvenal, 140, 250, 258,
  259, 261, 271, 275, 276
Haglund, William, 277
Hague. *See* The Hague
Haig, Alexander M., Jr., 70
Haiti, 31, 90
Hamitic hypothesis, 258
Heart of Darkness (Conrad), 9, 115
Hierarchies, 260, 261
*High Noon in Southern Africa: Making
  Peace in a Rough Neighborhood*
  (Crocker), 70, 72, 87, 88–89, 91,
  97
Hit squads. *See* Death squads
Hochschild, Adam, 115
Holbrooke, Richard, 240–241

Hospitals, 219–220, 230
Hostages, 18
Hugo, Jan, 143, 181, 182
Human rights, 45–46, 78, 85, 86, 172, 182, 222, 235, 251
Human Rights Watch, 104, 123, 135, 222, 252, 253, 271
Hussein, Saddam, 84
Hutus, 17, 140, 141, 245, 248, 251, 252, 253, 255, 257, 258, 259–260, 261, 262, 263–264, 265, 268, 270, 271, 283
    death squads, 1–2. See also Militias, Interahamwe militia

Identity cards, 212, 246, 258. See also Pass systems
Idols of the Tribe (Isaacs), 200
IFP. See South Africa, Inkatha Freedom Party
Illiteracy, 34, 272
IMF. See International Monetary Fund
Immunity, 174(n), 176, 188
Incomes, 29, 115, 128
Indirect rule, 119, 148, 149, 157, 188, 209, 228, 229, 257–258
Infant mortality, 34, 116, 204
Inflation, 34, 231
    hyperinflation, 113, 114, 121, 128
Informers, 155, 175, 178, 197, 212
Intellectuals, 10, 212, 258
Intelligence operations/agents, 30, 77, 116, 166, 172, 173, 180, 182, 185, 192, 225. See also Informers
International Criminal Court, 249, 274
International Monetary Fund (IMF), 100, 113, 231
Interrogations, 103–109, 129, 135, 139, 176, 179
Iran, 81, 199
Iran-contra scandal, 76, 98
Ireland, 18
Iron ore, 52
Isaacs, Harold, 200
Islam, 6, 74, 196, 197, 198, 199, 200, 208, 210, 213, 214, 221, 224, 229, 243

Israel, 18, 30, 76, 211, 224, 264
ITU. See South Africa, Investigative Task Unit
Ivory, 115, 192
Ivory Coast, 22, 36, 50, 52, 53

Jackson, Robert, 249
Jails, 49, 136. See also Liberia, detention; Rwanda, prisons; South Africa, prison detention
Jews, 198, 264–265
Jihad, 208, 213, 243
Johnson administration, 80
Johnson, Prince Y., 51, 86
Johnson, Roosevelt, 5
Journalists, 39, 129(n), 131, 199
Judiciary, 198, 232, 234, 236
    international, 249, 274
    in Rwanda, 273
Julu, Charles, 21, 40–41, 48, 57, 83
    in U.S., 85, 86
Justice, 13, 15, 16, 17, 18, 44, 61, 87, 234, 249, 253, 260, 272, 274, 284
    and political parties, 154

Kabila, Laurent, 18, 100–101, 140, 238, 239, 241, 251
Kaburame, Joas, 256
Kadjat, Tshibang, 123
Kagame, Paul, 237, 238, 239, 240, 251, 264, 265, 266
Kakwa ethnic group, 228, 229, 230
Kama, Laity, 248, 273, 280, 283
Kambanda, Jean, 245, 252
Kamuhanda, Emmanuel, 269–270
Kangura (newspaper), 252
Kanyama Mbayabu, 105–106, 112, 124, 125, 128, 136–137, 138–140
Kaplan, Robert D., 9
Karangwa, Ephraim, 254–255, 261, 283
Kasaian ethnic group, 105, 118, 119, 120–124, 125, 126–127, 132, 133, 217
Kassebaum, Nancy, 64
Katangese ethnic group, 105, 118, 119, 122, 124, 132, 139, 217

Kawaya, Mbaka, 132, 133–134
Kayishema, Clement, 268, 276
Kennan, George F., 88
Kennedy administration, 80, 110
Kenya, 12, 81, 224, 225, 227
    Nairobi, 274–275
Kerry, John, 64
Khrushchev, Nikita, 79
Khumalo, M. Z., 146, 187
Kimonyo, Isaac, 1
King Leopold's Ghost (Hochschild), 115
Kinship systems, 12–13, 30, 31
Kissinger, Henry, 70, 80
Kohl, Helmut, 184
Kony, Joseph, 232
Krahn ethnic group, 22, 23, 28–29, 35,
    36–37, 41, 43, 56, 57, 85, 86
    death squads, 48–49
    reprisals against, 42, 44, 48, 49, 50
Kubwimana, Silas, 277, 278, 279–282
Kulah, Alfred, 43
Kuwait, 85
Kyungu wa Kumwanza, Gabriel, 105,
    121–123, 127, 133, 134–135
KZP. *See* South Africa, KwaZulu
    Police

Lake, Anthony, 239–240, 240(n)
Lamb, David, 8–9
LAMCO. *See* Liberian-American
    Swedish Minerals Company
Langi ethnic group, 228, 230, 231
Law of unintended consequences, 225,
    226, 241, 265
Laws. *See* Rule of law
Lawyers Committee for Human
    Rights, 86
Leaders, 10, 14, 15, 16, 28, 29, 32, 33,
    35, 36, 37, 45, 55, 56, 60, 78, 88,
    90, 100, 120, 133, 161, 165, 174,
    190, 195, 201, 218, 221, 225, 226,
    229, 231, 236, 237, 238, 239, 240,
    249, 252, 255, 260, 266. *See also*
    South Africa, chiefs; Sudan,
    chiefs
Lebanon, 76
Leopold II (king of Belgium), 9, 115

Leyden, Pete, 207
Liberia, 10, 11, 17, 18, 20(map),
    21–61, 63–86, 130–131, 222, 237,
    240, 266
    American influence, 28
    Americo-Liberians, 25, 28, 29, 30,
        31, 32, 36, 37, 56, 75, 83, 93
    Armed Forces of Liberia (AFL), 31,
        36
    border with Ivory Coast, 36
    Buchanan, 21, 24, 52
    civil war, 9, 27, 36, 47, 57, 82. *See
        also* Taylor, Charles
    detention, 40, 107
    election of 1985, 33, 56, 66, 68, 74,
        77, 83
    Gbarnga, 54, 55, 59
    General Services Agency, 25
    Grand Gedeh region, 36, 43, 49
    historical details, 28–32
    indigenous people, 29, 30, 36, 93
    Justice Ministry, 45
    Monrovia, 22, 27, 30, 31, 33, 34, 45,
        48–49, 50, 51, 55, 84, 85
    National Patriotic Front of
        Liberia (NPFL), 22, 49, 50, 52,
        58, 59
    Nimba County, 35, 37, 38, 40, 47,
        52, 56
    November 12 business, 35–38, 44,
        45, 48, 64, 66, 67, 92
    People's Redemption Council
        (PRC), 25, 31, 33
    population, 24
    Special Security Unit (SSS), 59, 60
    True Whig party, 29
    United Liberation Movement of
        Liberia for Democracy
        (ULIMO), 86
    University of Liberia, 33, 45
    U.S. investments/aid, 65, 75, 76, 77.
        See also United States, and
        Liberia
    Zle Town, 44–45
Liberian-American Swedish Minerals
    Company (LAMCO), 41
Libya, 48–49, 65, 74, 76, 210, 215

Life and Times of Michael K. (Coetzee),
193
Life expectancy, 34, 204, 273
Looting, 54, 85, 113, 121, 215, 262
of Gécamines mining installation,
127–128
Los Angeles, 262
Los Angeles Times, 147
LRA. *See* Uganda, Lord's Resistance
Army
Lukudu, Paolino (Archbishop), 219
Lumumba, Patrice, 110–111, 117
Luthuli, Albert, 156
Luthuli, Philbert and John, 157

McCuen, J. J., 168
Machar, Riek, 195, 199, 220–222, 223,
243
McNally, Tim, 144, 182
Mafayela, Senzo, 155
Mafia, 15, 55, 112, 199, 222, 229
Mahdi, 200, 208, 214
Major, John, 184
Majority rule, 83, 174, 190
Malan, Magnus, 144, 145–146, 166,
168, 187, 192. *See also* South
Africa, Magnus Malan trial
Malaria, 40, 118
Mandela, Nelson, 144, 149, 165, 182,
184, 190
Mann, Jannean, 131
Mano ethnic group, 35, 37, 38, 43–44,
47, 48, 55, 57
Maphumulo, Mhlabunzima Joseph,
159
Marcos, Ferdinand, 76, 85
Marijuana, 50, 191, 202, 261. *See also*
Drugs
Martial law, 31, 33
Massacres, 8, 9, 10, 18, 50, 122, 147,
162, 174, 221, 222, 239, 251, 253,
263, 276
at KwaMakhutha, 144, 145, 181. *See
also* South Africa, Magnus Malan
trial
See also Deaths

Mazmuku family, 152
Mbeki, Thabo, 163(n)
Mchunu, Albert, 157
Mdluli, Thomas, 158
Médecins Sans Frontières, 118, 220
Mengistu Haile Miriam, 222, 223, 237
Mexico, 192
Meyer, Karl, 79
Middle class, 229, 231
Middle East, 225, 264
Militias, 11, 14, 27, 38, 53–54, 59, 145,
152, 160, 191, 199, 201, 216, 218,
223, 243, 250
Interahamwe militia, 1–2, 3, 254,
262, 268, 269, 276, 277, 279, 282
Krahn-dominated, 22, 35, 55
Liberation Peace Council militia, 55
Ulimo-Johnson militia, 55
Milosovic, Slobodan, 150
Mitchell, Brian, 174
Mitterrand, François, 250
Mitterrand, Jean-Christophe, 53
MK. *See* South Africa, Umkhonto we
Sizwe
Mlaba, Msinga and Zibuse, 159
Mobutu Sese Seko, 7, 18, 34, 69, 76,
79, 80, 90, 100, 109–115, 117,
119, 121, 125, 126, 134, 137, 139,
199–200, 217, 227, 238, 241, 251,
261
biographical background, 109, 110,
116
and campaign against Kasai, 120,
124
death of, 140
and U.S. presidents, 116–117. *See
also* Reagan, Ronald, and Mobutu
wealth of, 111–112, 114, 140
See also Zaire
Moi, Daniel arap, 81, 275
Moji a Kapasu, P. Anschaire, 105,
134–135
Mondari ethnic group, 216–217
Money-laundering, 33–34, 55, 113
Moose, Richard, 48, 75
More, John, 169

Mozambique, 95, 96, 98, 118, 177
    Resistercia Nacional Moçambicana
        (RENAMO), 95, 147, 167, 168,
        173, 182
MPLA. *See* Angola, Movimento
    Popular de Libertação de Angola
MPR. *See* Zaire, Mouvement
    Populaire de la Révolution
Mthiyana, Sipho and Lucky, 152–154
Mubarak, Hosni, 224
Mucchielli, Roger, 271
Mujahideen, 225
Munyakazi, Isadore, 266–267,
    271–273
Museveni, Yoweri, 197, 226, 227–228,
    230–237, 238, 239, 240–242, 266
Music, 28, 111
Muslim Brothers, 212
Muyembe wa Banze, 120

Nahimana, Ferdinand, 252, 258
Namibia, 81, 91, 96, 144, 169, 175,
    177
Nanking, Rape of, 9
Nasser, Gamal Abdel, 80
Nationalism, 14, 149, 166, 231
Necklacing, 155
Nelson, Blamo, 27
New Republic, 7, 147
New Yorker, 147
New York Times, 65, 68, 100, 119, 147,
    240
Ngema, Xolani, 151–152
Ngeze, Hassan, 252
Nguza Karl-I-Bond, Jean, 112, 121,
    122, 123
Nicaragua, 99
NIF. *See* Sudan, National Islamic
    Front
Nigeria, 48, 53, 54, 60, 90, 192
Nimeiry, Jaafar, 69, 79, 81, 200,
    211–214
Nixon, Richard, 80
Niyibizi, Bonaventure, 266–267,
    271–273
North, Oliver, 76

NPFL. *See* Liberia, National Patriotic
    Front of Liberia
NRA. *See* Uganda, National
    Resistance Army
NRM. *See* Uganda, National
    Resistance Movement
Ntebela, Jacky, 150
Ntombela, David, 162–163, 174
Nubians, 228, 230
Nuer ethnic group, 206, 207, 220,
    223, 224, 243
Nuremberg trials, 249, 275
Nypen, Wleh, 49
Nzongola-Ntalaja, George, 128

Obote, Milton, 8, 129, 197, 226, 228,
    229, 230, 231, 232, 241
Oder, Arthur, 236
Okadimiri, Billy, 236
Onassis, Jackie, 115
Operation Lifeline Sudan, 195, 215,
    220, 243
Operation Marion, 169, 170, 173, 188
Operation Octopus, 27, 51
Opperman, J. P., 168, 169, 187
Ottomans, 208
*Out of Africa: A Black Man Confronts
    Africa* (Richburg), 9

Pakistan, 76, 91, 225
Palestinians, 18
Pass systems, 209. *See also* Identity
    cards
Patronage, 30, 31, 149, 160, 199, 212
Perkins, Edward, 92–93
Persian Gulf, 81
Personality cults, 34, 111
Philippines, 69, 76, 85
PIDE. *See* Portugal, Policia
    Internacional e de Defesa do
    Estado
Pillay, Navenethem, 252–253,
    273–274, 281, 282–283
Poindexter, John M., 76
Police, 13, 28, 41, 108, 127, 149, 151,
    154, 191, 202, 204, 206, 212, 234,

Police *(continued)*, 274. *See also* Secret
    police; South Africa, KwaZulu
    Police; South Africa, South
    African Police
Political correctness, 90–91
Political parties, 154, 231. *See also*
    Uganda, multipartyism
The Politics of Africa's Economic
    Stagnation (Sandbrook), 13
Portugal, 80, 118
    Policia Internacional e de Defesa do
    Estado (PIDE), 167
Powell, Philip, 171, 183
PRC. *See* Liberia, People's
    Redemption Council
Press, 88, 120, 198, 230, 274
Primitivism, 9, 10, 15, 208, 209,
    272
Prisons. *See* Jails; Liberia, detention;
    South Africa, prison detention;
    See also Rwanda
Propaganda, 258, 270–271
Prosper, Pierre-Richard, 247–248,
    262, 278, 281
Prunier, Gérard, 258, 265–266
Psychologie de la publicité et de la
    propagande (Mucchielli), 271

Qaddafi, Muammar, 48, 76, 210, 211,
    213
Quiwonkpa, Thomas, 25, 44, 46, 51,
    222
    death of, 37, 38
    See also Liberia, November 12
    business

Racism, 87, 89, 90, 91, 93, 154, 208,
    209
    racist states, 218–219
    See also Bigotry
Radio broadcasting, 2, 28, 39, 48, 68,
    111, 122, 133, 243, 264, 270–271,
    272
Railroads. *See* Sudan, trains
Rape, 24, 33, 45, 54, 61, 73, 85, 222,
    227, 233, 246, 252–253, 259
    defined as act of genocide, 283

Reagan, Ronald, 209, 210–211, 213
    and Mobutu, 80, 109, 116
    See also Reagan administration
Reagan administration, 22, 63, 65, 67,
    70, 76, 77, 85, 212, 213
    Reagan Doctrine, 76, 81, 99, 117
    and South Africa, 93–94, 96, 97, 98,
    184
    See also Crocker, Chester A.;
    Reagan, Ronald
Realpolitik, 70
Reforms, 30, 238
Refugees, 27, 36, 47, 50, 85, 97, 117,
    118, 126, 127, 160, 230, 231, 243,
    251, 262
    refugee camps, 197, 202, 216, 218,
    219, 260
Religion, 196, 200, 209, 229. *See also*
    Christians; Islam
Remo, Santino, 219–220
RENAMO. *See* Mozambique,
    Resistercia Nacional
    Moçambicana
Reno, William, 53
Revenge, 43, 44, 48, 49, 55, 57, 86,
    154, 191, 192, 216
Rhodesia, 81, 167, 176–177
Rice riots, 30
Richburg, Keith B., 9
Ritual violence, 37–38
Roadblocks. *See*
    Checkpoints/roadblocks
Roberts Field, 30, 77–78, 82
Robinson, Randall, 89
Roosevelt, Franklin D., 79
The Roots of Evil: The Origins of
    Genocide and Other Group Violence
    (Staub), 261
RPF. *See* Rwanda, Rwandan Patriotic
    Front
Rubber, 17, 29, 52, 115
Rule of law, 17, 30, 38, 44, 74, 125,
    135, 152, 229, 234, 239, 240, 261,
    266, 272–273, 284
Russell, Bertrand, 263
Russia, 192. *See also* Soviet Union
Rutaganda, Georges, 276–277

Ruzindana, Obed, 276
Rwanda, 1–3, 11, 14, 15, 17, 18, 23,
    53, 88, 119, 140, 227, 237, 238,
    244(map), 245–284
  Coalition for the Defense of the
    Republic (CDR), 271
  culture of obedience, 254, 255, 256,
    261
  génocidaires, 16, 140, 255, 272, 273
  judiciary, 273
  Kibungo Prefecture, 1, 16, 255, 269
  Kigali, 266, 277
  prisons, 255–256, 273, 283
  Radio Rwanda, 271
  Radio-Télévision Libre des Mille
    Collines, 2, 270
  Rwandan Patriotic Front (RPF),
    241, 258, 259, 264, 265, 270, 271
  structural order, 260
  See also United Nations,
    International Criminal Tribunal
    for Rwanda
Rwanda Crisis, The (Prunier), 265–266

Sacrifices, 38
SADF. *See* South Africa, South African
    Defense Forces
Sadiq al-Mahdi, 211, 214–215, 218,
    219, 242
SAMI. *See* South Africa, South African
    Military Intelligence
Sandbrook, Richard, 13
Sankoh, Foday, 18
SAP. *See* South Africa, South African
    Police
Saudi Arabia, 201
Savimbi, Jonas, 77, 80, 95, 97, 98, 116,
    117, 167
Scheffer, David J., 249
Scott, Jenkins Z. B., 45–47, 47(n), 61,
    66, 73, 172
Secret police, 13, 30, 47, 57, 104, 167,
    197, 212, 225, 230, 239
Secret societies, 38
Security, 13, 131, 132, 167
SELF organization, 27
Serbs, 263

Seyon, Patrick, 32
Sharia, 200, 213, 217
Shaw, Emmanuel, 47(n)
Shepstone, Theophilus, 148, 157
Shortages, 190, 203
Siad Barre, Mohammed, 69, 79, 81
Sibomana, François-Xavier, 1, 2, 3, 15,
    16, 253–254, 269
Sierra Leone, 17–18, 26, 55, 129(n)
Slavery, 6, 12, 21, 28, 29, 54, 56, 208,
    209, 216, 219
Smuggling, 13, 55, 113, 192, 261
Smuts, Jan, 157
SNIP. *See* Zaire, Service Nationale
    d'Intelligence et de Protection
Sollac company, 53
Somalia, 64, 69, 79, 81, 129(n), 250
South Africa, 12, 14, 18, 71, 76, 125,
    129(n), 142(map), 143–193, 208,
    274
  African National Congress (ANC),
    96, 98, 144, 149, 150, 152, 153,
    154, 155, 158, 161, 163, 164, 165,
    166, 170, 172, 173, 174, 180, 187,
    189
  Afrikaners, 14, 172
  apartheid, 5, 10, 11, 64, 69, 71, 89,
    91, 98, 144, 150, 153, 155,
    156–157, 158, 161, 163, 166, 171,
    180, 185, 186, 189, 191, 192
  black-on-black violence, 14, 93, 98,
    99, 147, 148, 153, 154, 157, 166,
    173, 182
  Bureau of State Security (BOSS),
    166
  Caprivi trainees, 144, 169, 183, 187
  chiefs, 157–158, 159, 160
  Communist Party, 158
  Congress of Traditional Leaders of
    South Africa (CONTRALESA),
    159
  Directorate of Special Tasks and
    Joint Management Centers, 166,
    1769
  Durban, 143, 151, 155, 160
  Eshowe, 151
  Freedom Alliance, 170

South Africa (*continued*)
  Government of National Unity, 189
  homeland (bantustan) system, 148,
    150, 157, 158
  hostels, 163, 165
  Influx Control, 160
  Inkatha Freedom Party (IFP),
    144–145, 148–150, 151, 152, 153,
    155, 156, 159, 160, 161, 162, 163,
    166, 168, 169, 171, 174, 177, 181,
    182, 185, 186, 189
  Investigative Task Unit (ITU), 165,
    182
  Johannesburg, 192
  KwaZulu-Natal province, 18–19,
    97, 99, 143, 148, 149, 151, 153,
    155, 157–158, 160, 161, 162, 172,
    173, 174, 177, 181, 190, 274
  KwaZulu Police (KZP), 145, 149,
    151–152, 171, 174, 175, 177, 189
  Magnus Malan trial, 144–147, 166,
    168–169, 171, 175, 181–183, 186,
    187
  murder rate, 156, 191. *See also*
    Deaths, in South Africa
  and Namibia, 97
  National Party, 182, 189
  parliament, 94
  Port Shepstone, 148, 159
  prison detentions, 179, 274
  sanctions against, 77, 93, 94, 96,
    149
  Seven Days War, 162
  shantytowns, 156, 160
  South African Defense Forces
    (SADF), 144, 164, 167, 170, 171,
    173
  South African Military Intelligence
    (SAMI), 95, 98, 145, 156, 165,
    167, 170, 192
  South African Police (SAP), 151,
    153, 155, 159, 162, 171, 173, 174
  Special Branch, 175, 176
  State Security Council, 165, 167,
    170
  Third Force, 144–145, 165, 172,
    173, 174, 189

South Africa (*continued*)
  township uprising in (1980s), 153,
    155
  Transkei and Ciskei, 150, 158, 163
  Trust Feed town, 162, 174
  Truth and Reconciliation
    Commission, 174(n), 177, 182,
    189
  Umkhonto we Sizwe (MK), 161,
    164, 176, 187
  United Democratic Front (UDF),
    150, 151, 159, 161, 162–163, 185
  Vlakplaas police unit, 173, 175,
    177–178
  Wesselton Township, 156
  See also Zulus
"South Africa: A Strategy for Change"
    (Crocker), 72, 94
South West African People's
    Organization (SWAPO), 175
Soviet Union, 9, 13, 16–17, 65, 76, 79,
    80–81, 95, 97, 110, 167, 173, 180,
    211, 213, 222, 225. *See also* Cold
    War
SPLA. *See* Sudan, Sudanese People's
    Liberation Army
SSS. *See* Liberia, Special Security Unit
States, neocolonial, 12–13
  criminal control of, 15
  failed, 15, 260
Staub, Ervin, 261
Students, 44, 120, 122, 133, 185, 212
Sudan, 48, 64, 69, 76, 79, 81, 193,
    194(map), 195–226, 227, 236,
    241, 266
  Akobo village, 220
  Anyanya guerrilla movement, 217
  Arab domination of, 11, 14
  chiefs, 195, 210, 223
  civil war, 6, 18, 195, 196, 199, 202,
    207, 209, 211, 212, 214, 215, 218,
    243
  colonial rule, 200, 208–209, 217
  electric power, 203, 204
  Equatoria province, 217
  Juba, 204, 216, 217, 218
  Juba hospital, 219–220

Sudan (continued)
  Khartoum, 197, 203, 208, 212, 225
  Kosti, 209–210
  logistics, 204–206
  Lokichokio, 195
  National Islamic Front (NIF), 197,
    198, 199, 201, 214, 222
  northern/southern areas of, 197,
    207, 215, 217
  Omdurman, 214
  Popular Defense Forces, 201
  poverty, 203
  roads, 209–210
  South Sudan Independence
    Movement, 220
  Sudanese Communist Party, 211
  Sudanese People's Liberation Army
    (SPLA), 215, 216, 217–218, 222,
    223, 224, 243
  Sudanese Socialist Party, 211
  trains, 202–203, 206
  and Uganda, 232–233
Superstition, 9, 10
Supuwood, Laveli, 58
SWAPO. See South West African
  People's Organization
Switzerland, 52

Taft, William Howard, 30
Talisman Energy Corporation, 243
Tanzania, 225, 246, 262, 273
Tate, Joe, 59
Taxation, 29, 31, 55, 128, 150, 159,
  160
Taylor, Charles McArthur, 10, 18, 23,
    27, 34, 35, 37, 44, 47–48, 50–51,
    55–57, 73, 140, 199, 266
  bank accounts of, 53
  biographical background, 25–26
  characterized, 26–27
  on Edward Perkins, 93
  elected president, 58
  and Sammy Dokie, 58, 60
  and Small Boys Unit, 22, 24
Taylor, Nelson, 54
Television, 26, 88, 243
Tempelsman, Maurice, 115

Tente wa Tente, 107, 137
Terrorism, 198, 225, 252, 271
Thatcher, Margaret, 184
The Hague, 249, 275
Theocracy, 199, 200
Third World, 69, 79, 97, 117, 148
Timber, 52, 53, 54
Tolbert, William, 25, 30, 31, 32, 75
Torture, 22, 54, 73, 85, 86, 96, 122,
    136, 143, 172, 179, 189, 198, 233,
    274
Trade unions, 174, 198
TransAfrica, 89
Tribalism, 8, 10, 12, 13, 14, 15, 35, 57,
    88, 98, 123, 147, 248
Truman administration, 79
Tshisekedi, étienne, 121, 123
Tshombe, Moise, 110, 126
Tubman, William V. S., 29–30
Turabi, Hassan al-, 196, 197–200, 201,
    209, 212, 214, 219, 221, 222, 223,
    224, 232–233, 234, 242–243
Tutsis, 2, 3, 17, 119, 140, 237, 238,
    241, 245, 246, 247, 248, 252, 254,
    255, 257, 258, 259, 260, 261, 262,
    263–264, 265, 266, 268, 270, 271,
    276, 277, 278, 279
Tutu, Desmond, 94–95
Tyranny, 11, 13–14, 17, 18, 69, 90, 97,
    118, 135, 140, 214, 241, 242, 248,
    252
  and anarchy, 14, 22, 24, 39, 44, 47,
    49, 55, 60, 61, 119, 140, 146, 147,
    151, 154, 190, 216, 229, 260
  white tyranny, 19, 144, 149, 150,
    167, 186, 217

UDF. See South Africa, United
  Democratic Front
UFERI. See Zaire, Union des
  Fédéralistes et des Répulicains
  Indépendents
Uganda, 8, 12, 18, 122, 129, 140, 197,
    224, 226–243, 258, 266
  amnesty declared, 235
  Asians, 229, 230, 231
  borders of, 228

Uganda *(continued)*
  elections, 228, 236
  Human Rights Commission, 235
  Kampala, 228
  Lord's Resistance Army (LRA),
    232–233
  Luwero Triangle, 8
  and multipartyism, 227–228, 231,
    232, 233
  National Resistance Army (NRA),
    230, 232, 233–234
  National Resistance Movement
    (NRM), 235
  Popular National Congress, 242
  Uganda National Liberation Army
    (UNLA), 8, 232
  Uganda People's Congress (UPC),
    231, 233
ULIMO. *See* Liberia, United
  Liberation Movement of Liberia
  for Democracy
Unemployment, 128, 155, 161, 190,
  201
UNITA. *See* Angola, National Union
  for the Total Independence of
  Angola
United Nations, 30, 53, 71, 88, 94,
    140, 195, 201, 215, 275
  International Criminal Tribunal for
    Rwanda (Arusha tribunal),
    246–248, 249, 251, 252–253, 259,
    263, 274–284
  peacekeeping forces, 18, 23, 27, 49,
    112, 250, 251, 257. *See also*
    ECOMOG peacekeeping force
United States, 16–17, 53, 78
  and Afghanistan, 225
  African policy, 87, 237
  civil rights movement, 91
  Comprehensive Anti-Apartheid Act
    of 1986, 89
  Congressional Black Caucus, 89
  Congressional Committees on
    Foreign Relations, 63, 67, 77
  First Amendment, 39
  infant mortality, 204

United States *(continued)*
  and Liberia, 22–23, 31, 39, 47(n),
    48, 68, 73, 77, 83, 85–86, 91, 97.
    See also Liberia, U.S.
    investment/aid
  and Mobutu/Zaire, 80, 91, 97, 98,
    100, 116, 120, 237, 239
  murder rate, 191
  National Security Council, 88
  Navy, 22–23, 83
  Rapid Deployment Force, 76, 213
  and Rwanda, 249, 250, 273
  security assistance programs, 7
  Senate Subcommittee on Terrorism,
    180
  and South Africa, 95, 168
  and Sudan, 211, 212, 213, 215,
    224–225, 233
  and UNITA, 95
  and Zaire. *See* United States, and
    Mobutu/Zaire
  See also Cold War; *individual
    administrations*
UNLA. *See* Uganda, Uganda National
  Liberation Army
UPC. *See* Uganda, Uganda People's
  Congress

Vance, Cyrus, 81
Van der Westhuizen, Pieter, 95, 98
Van Neikirk, Cornelius, 169
Van Tonder, Cornelius, 169
Varney, Howard, 165, 166, 182
Veil (Woodward), 76
Verwoerd, Hendrik, 148, 157
Vigilantism, 44, 122, 154, 161, 191,
  219
Voice of America, 30, 65, 68, 82

War crimes/criminals, 51, 57, 68, 100,
  275, 283. *See also* United Nations,
  International Criminal Tribunal
  for Rwanda
Warlords, 6, 7, 14, 18, 54, 80, 100,
  150, 151, 160, 162, 163, 174, 186,
  195, 196, 223

Washington Post, 147, 237
Water, 34, 136, 207, 220
Weapons, 12, 21, 53, 55, 80, 123, 128,
    147, 149, 156, 159, 178, 183, 187,
    191, 196, 207, 213, 215, 216, 221,
    223, 224, 225, 227, 238, 250, 257,
    261
  antipersonnel mines, 218, 219
Wesseh, Commany, 32–33
White man's *juju*, 106, 129–132
Williams, Gabriel, 21–22
Witness protection, 276
Woewiyu, Tom, 58
Wolpe, Howard, 77–78
Women, 24, 54, 179, 201, 206, 210,
    222, 255
  Tutsi, 252, 279
  See also Rape
Woodward, Bob, 76
World Bank, 100, 112

Xhosa ethnic group, 150, 153, 158,
    163

Yeaten, Benjamin, 59, 60
Yugoslavia, 150, 155, 248, 272, 277

Zaire, 7, 11, 34, 53, 64, 69, 76, 77, 79,
    80, 102(map), 103–141, 192, 227,
    241
  central bank, 113–114, 121, 127
  Garde Civile, 103, 106, 129,
    135–136, 137, 138
  infrastructure, 116
  JUFERI youth brigade, 122–123,
    124, 126, 132, 134, 139
  Katanga province, 117. *See also*
    Zaire, Shaba province

Zaire *(continued)*
  Kinshasa, 113, 117
  Kolwezi, 117, 118, 124, 132, 139
  Likasi, 118–119
  Mouvement Populaire de la
    Révolution (MPR), 103, 121,
    123
  pillage of September of 1991, 121,
    127
  Service Nationale d'Intelligence et
    de Protection (SNIP), 104, 105,
    129, 134, 135, 138
  Shaba province, 105, 113, 116–117,
    120, 123, 140, 141
  spending for human services, 114
  Union des Fédéralistes et des
    Répulicains Indépendents
    (UFERI), 122
  Union Sacrée de l'Opposition, 121,
    122
  University of Lumumbashi, 120
  U.S. consulate, 108, 137
  See also Congo; Democratic
    Republic of the Congo; Mobutu
    Sese Seko; United States, and
    Mobutu/Zaire
Zaires (currency), 113, 128
Zenawi, Meles, 237
Zia, Mohammed, 76
Zimbabwe, 208
Zionism, 198, 200
Zulu, Gideon, 151
Zulus, 144, 145, 148, 149–151, 163,
    165, 186, 217
  ANC supporters, 153–154, 156
  indunas and *amabutho*, 152, 159,
    160, 162, 164
Zuma, Jacob, 163, 163(n)